The Public Domain

It has been pretended by some (and in England especially) that inventors have a natural and exclusive right to their inventions; & not merely for their own lives, but inheritable to their heirs. but while it is a moot question whether the origin of any kind of property is derived from nature at all, it would be singular to admit a natural, and even an hereditary right to inventions. it is agreed by those who have seriously considered the subject, that no individual has, of natural right, a separate property in an acre of land, for instance. by an universal law indeed, whatever, whether fixed or moveable, belongs to all men equally and in common, is the property, for the moment, of him who occupies it; but when he relinquishes the occupation the property goes with it. stable ownership is the gift of social law, and is given late in the progress of society. it would be curious then if an idea, the fugitive fermentation of an individual brain, could, of natural right, be claimed in exclusive and stable property. if nature has made any one thing less susceptible, than all others, of exclusive property, it is the action of the thinking power called an Idea; which an individual may exclusively possess as long as he keeps it to himself; but the moment it is divulged, it forces itself into the possession of every one, and the receiver cannot dispossess himself of it. it's peculiar character too is that no one possesses the less, because every other possesses the whole of it. he who receives an idea from me, receives instruction himself, without lessening mine; as he who lights his taper at mine, receives light without darkening me. that ideas should freely spread from one to another over the globe, for the moral and mutual instruction of man, and improvement of his condition, seems to have been peculiarly and benevolently designed by nature, when she made them, like fire, expansible over all space, without lessening their density in any point; and like the air in which we breathe, move, and have our physical being, incapable of confinement, or exclusive appropriation. inventions then cannot in

Thomas Jefferson to Isaac McPherson, August 13, 1813, p. 6.

James Boyle

The
Public
Domain

Enclosing the Commons of the Mind

Yale University Press

New Haven & London

A Caravan book. For more information, visit www.caravanbooks.org.

Printed in the United States of America.

ISBN: 978-0-300-13740-8
Library of Congress Control Number: 2008932282

A catalogue record for this book is available from the British Library.

This paper meets the requirements of ANSI/NISO Z39.48–1992 (Permanence of
Paper). It contains 30 percent postconsumer waste (PCW) and is certified by the
Forest Stewardship Council (FSC)

Contents

v

Acknowledgments

The ideas for this book come from the theoretical and practical work I have been doing for the last ten years. None of that work has been done alone. As a result, the list of people to whom I am indebted makes Oscar night acknowledgments look haiku-terse by comparison. Here I can mention only a few. I beg pardon for the inevitable omissions.

First and foremost, my family has tolerated my eccentricities and fixations and moderated them with gentle and deserved mockery. "Want that insignia torn off your car, Dad? Then it would be in the public domain, right?"

My colleagues at Duke are one of the main influences on my work. I am lucky enough to work in the only "Center for the Study of the Public Domain" in the academic world. I owe the biggest debt of gratitude to my colleague Jennifer Jenkins, who directs the Center and who has influenced every chapter in this book. David Lange brought me to Duke. His work on the public domain has always been an inspiration to mine. Arti Rai's remarkable theoretical and empirical studies have helped me to understand everything from software patents to synthetic biology. Jerry Reichman has supplied energy, insight, and a spirited and cosmopolitan focus on the multiple ways in which property can be protected. Jed Purdy and Neil Siegel commented on drafts and provided crucial insights on the construction of my argument. Catherine Fisk, Jim Salzman, Stuart Benjamin, Jonathan Wiener, Mitu Gulati, Jeff Powell, Chris Schroeder, and many, many others helped out—sometimes without knowing it, but often at the cost of the scarcest of all resources: time. Amidst a brilliant group of research assistants, Jordi Weinstock and David Silverstein stood out. Jordi showed a dogged ability to track down obscure 1950s songs that was almost scary. Additional thanks go to Jennifer Ma, Tolu Adewale, Paulina Orchard, and Emily Sauter. Balfour Smith, the coordinator of our Center, shepherded the manuscript through its many drafts with skill and erudition.

Duke is the most interdisciplinary university I have ever encountered and so the obligations flow beyond the law school. Professor Anthony Kelley, a brilliant composer, not only educated me in composition and the history of musical borrowing but co-taught a class on musical borrowing that dramatically influenced Chapter 6. Colleagues in the business school—particularly Jim Anton, a great economic modeler and greater volleyball partner, and Wes Cohen, a leading empiricist—all left their marks. Dr. Robert Cook-Deegan, leader of Duke's Center for Public Genomics, and my wife Lauren Dame, associate director of the Genome Ethics, Law and Policy Center, provided crucial support to my work with the sciences in general and synthetic biology in particular. I was also inspired and informed by colleagues and students in computer science, English, history, and political science.

But the work I am describing here is—as the last chapter suggests—something that goes far beyond the boundaries of one institution. A large group of intellectual property scholars have influenced my ideas. Most importantly, Larry Lessig and Yochai Benkler have each given far more than they received from me in the "sharing economy" of scholarship. If the ideas I describe here have a future, it is because of the astounding leadership Larry has provided and the insights into "the wealth of networks" that Yochai brings. Jessica Litman, Pam Samuelson, Michael Carroll, Julie Cohen, Peggy Radin, Carol Rose, Rebecca Eisenberg, Mark Lemley, Terry Fisher, Justin Hughes, Neil Netanel, Wendy Gordon, David Nimmer, Tyler Ochoa, Tim Wu, and many others have all taught me things I needed to know. Jessica in particular caught and corrected (some of) my many errors, while Pam encouraged me to think about the definition of the public domain in ways that have been vital to this book. Michael suggested valuable edits—though I did not always listen. Historical work by Carla Hesse, Martha Woodmansee, and Mark Rose has been central to my analysis, which also could not have existed but for work on the governance of the commons by Elinor Ostrom, Charlotte Hess, and Carol Rose. Kembrew McLeod and Siva Vaidhyanathan inspired my work on music and sampling. Peter Jaszi was named in my last book as the person who most influenced it. That influence remains.

Beyond the academy, my main debt is to the board members and staff of Creative Commons, Science Commons, and ccLearn. Creative Commons, on whose board I am proud to have served, is the brainchild of Larry Lessig and Hal Abelson; Science Commons and ccLearn are divisions of Creative Commons that I helped to set up which concentrate on the sciences and on education, respectively. The practical experience of building a "creative commons" with private tools—of allowing creative collaboration with people you have never met—has shaped this book far beyond the chapter devoted to it. Hal Abelson, Michael Carroll, and Eric Saltzman were on the midwife team for the birth of those organizations and became close friends in the process. Since the entire Creative Commons staff has made it routine to do seven impossible things before breakfast, it is hard to single out any one individual—but without Glenn Brown at Creative Commons and John Wilbanks at Science Commons, neither organization would exist today. Jimmy Wales, founder of Wikipedia and another Creative Commons board member, also provided key insights. Finally, but for the leadership of Laurie Racine neither Creative Commons nor our Center at Duke would be where they are today, and thus many of the experiments I describe in this book would not have happened.

The intellectual property bar is a fascinating, brilliant, and engagingly eccentric group of lawyers. I owe debts to many of its members. Whitney Broussard told me the dirty secrets of the music industry. Daphne Keller—a former student and later a colleague—helped in more ways than I can count.

A number of scientists and computer scientists made me see things I otherwise would not have—Drew Endy and Randy Ruttenberg in synthetic biology, Nobel laureates Sir John Sulston and Harold Varmus in genomics and biology more generally, Paul Ginsparg in astrophysics, and Harlan Onsrud in geospatial data. Paul Uhlir's work at the National Academy of Sciences introduced me to many of these issues. The work of Richard Stallman, the creator of the free software movement, remains an inspiration even though he profoundly disagrees with my nomenclature here—and with much else besides.

Activists, civil rights lawyers, bloggers, and librarians have actually done much of the hard work of building the movement I describe at the end of this book. Jamie Love has touched, sparked, or masterminded almost every benign development I write about here, and novelist Cory Doctorow has either blogged it or influenced it. I have worked particularly closely with Manon Ress, Fred von Lohmann, Cindy Cohn, Jason Schultz, and Gigi Sohn. John Howkins and Gilberto Gil have provided considerable leadership internationally. But there are many, many others. The entire community of librarians deserves our thanks for standing up for free public access to knowledge for over two hundred years. Librarians are my heroes. They should be yours, too.

Some of the work contained here has been published in other forms elsewhere. Portions of Chapters 2 and 3 appeared as "The Second Enclosure Movement and the Construction of the Public Domain";[1] Chapter 7 shares little textually but much in terms of inspiration with an article I co-wrote for *PLoS Biology* with Arti Rai, "Synthetic Biology: Caught between Property Rights, the Public Domain, and the Commons."[2] For several years now I have been a columnist for the *Financial Times*'s "New Economy Policy Forum." Portions of Chapter 5 and Chapter 9 had their origins in columns written for that forum. Chapter 10 has its roots both in my article "A Politics of Intellectual Property: Environmentalism for the Net?"[3] and in the symposium, *Cultural Environmentalism @ 10,*[4] that Larry Lessig kindly organized for the tenth anniversary of that article.

Finally, I need to thank the institutions who have supported this study. The Rockefeller Center in Bellagio provided an inspiring beginning. The Ford, Rockefeller, MacArthur, and Hewlett Foundations have generously supported my work, as have Duke Law School's research grants and Bost Fellowships. My work on synthetic biology and the human genome was supported in part by a CEER grant from the National Human Genome Research Institute and the Department of Energy (P50 HG003391-02). In addition, my thanks go out to the anonymous donor whose generous donation allowed us to found the Center for the Study of the Public Domain, and to Bob Young and Laurie Racine, whose work made the Center possible. Yale University Press were supportive and critical in all the right places. I would like to thank them for agreeing to release this work under a Creative Commons license. What could be more appropriate to the book's theme?

I could go on and on. But I will not. This flurry of names and areas of knowledge signifies more than just the deep thanks of a dilettante. It signifies the emergence of an area of concern, the coming together of very different groups around a shared problem—an imbalance in the rules that define property in the information age. It is that problem, its history, philosophy, and politics that I try to sketch out in the pages ahead.

Preface: Comprised of at Least Jelly?

Each person has a different breaking point. For one of my students it was United States Patent number 6,004,596 for a "Sealed Crustless Sandwich." In the curiously mangled form of English that patent law produces, it was described this way:

> A sealed crustless sandwich for providing a convenient sandwich without an outer crust which can be stored for long periods of time without a central filling from leaking outwardly. The sandwich includes a lower bread portion, an upper bread portion, an upper filling and a lower filling between the lower and upper bread portions, a center filling sealed between the upper and lower fillings, and a crimped edge along an outer perimeter of the bread portions for sealing the fillings there between. The upper and lower fillings are preferably comprised of peanut butter and the center filling is comprised of at least jelly. The center filling is prevented from radiating outwardly into and through the bread portions from the surrounding peanut butter.[1]

"But why does this upset you?" I asked; "you've seen much worse than this." And he had. There are patents on human genes, on auctions, on algorithms.[2] The U.S. Olympic Committee has an expansive right akin to a trademark over the word "Olympic" and will not permit gay activists to hold a "Gay Olympic Games." The Supreme Court sees no First Amendment problem with this.[3] Margaret Mitchell's estate famously tried to use copyright to prevent *Gone With the Wind* from being told from a slave's point of view.[4] The copyright over the words you are now reading will not expire until seventy years after my death; the men die young in my family, but still you will allow me to hope that this might put it close to the year 2100. Congress periodically considers legislative proposals that would allow the ownership of facts.[5] The Digital Millennium Copyright Act gives content providers a whole array of legally protected digital fences to enclose their work.[6] In some cases it effectively removes the privilege of fair use. Each day brings some new Internet horror story about the excesses of intellectual property. Some of them are even true. The list goes on and on. (By the end of this book, I hope to have convinced you that this matters.) With all of this going on, this enclosure movement of the mind, this locking up of symbols and themes and facts and genes and ideas (and eventually people), why get excited about the patenting of a peanut butter and jelly sandwich? "I just thought that there were limits," he said; "some things should be sacred."

This book is an attempt to tell the story of the battles over intellectual property, the range wars of the information age. I want to convince you that intellectual property is important, that it is something that any informed citizen needs to know a little about, in the same way that any informed citizen needs to know at least something about the environment, or civil rights, or the way the economy works. I will try my best to be fair, to explain the issues and give both sides of the argument. Still, you should know that this is more than mere description. In the pages that follow, I try to show that current intellectual property policy is overwhelmingly and tragically *bad* in ways that everyone, and not just lawyers or economists, should care about. We are making bad decisions that will have a negative effect on our culture, our kids' schools, and our communications networks; on free speech, medicine, and scientific research. We are wasting some of the promise of the Internet, running the risk of ruining an amazing system of scientific innovation, carving out an intellectual property exemption to the First Amendment. I do not write this as an enemy of intellectual property, a dot-communist ready to end all property rights; in fact, I am a fan. It is precisely *because* I am a fan that I am so alarmed about the direction we are taking.

Still, the message of this book is neither doom nor gloom. None of these decisions is irrevocable. The worst ones can still be avoided altogether, and there are powerful counterweights in both law and culture to the negative trends I describe here. There are lots of reasons for optimism. I will get to most of these later, but one bears mentioning now. Contrary to what everyone has told you, the subject of intellectual property is both accessible and interesting; what people can understand, they can change—or pressure their legislators to change.

I stress this point because I want to challenge a kind of willed ignorance. Every news story refers to intellectual property as "arcane," "technical," or "abstruse" in the same way as they referred to former attorney general Alberto Gonzales as "controversial." It is a verbal tic and it serves to reinforce the idea that this is something about which popular debate is impossible. But it is also wrong. The central issues of intellectual property are not technical, abstruse, or arcane. To be sure, the *rules* of intellectual property law can be as complex as a tax code (though they should not be). But at the heart of intellectual property law are a set of ideas that a ten-year-old can understand perfectly well. (While writing this book, I checked this on a ten-year-old I then happened to have around the house.) You do not need to be a scientist or an economist or a lawyer to understand it. The stuff is also a lot of fun to think about. I live in constant wonder that they pay me to do so.

Should you be able to tell the story of *Gone With the Wind* from a slave's point of view even if the author does not want you to? Should the Dallas Cowboys be able to stop the release of *Debbie Does Dallas*, a cheesy porno flick, in which the title character brings great dishonor to a uniform similar to that worn by the Dallas Cowboys Cheerleaders? (After all, the audience might end up associating the Dallas Cowboys Cheerleaders with . . . well, commodified sexuality.)[7]

Should the U.S. Commerce Department be able to patent the genes of a Guyami Indian woman who shows an unusual resistance to leukemia?[8] What would it mean to patent someone's genes, anyway? Forbidding scientific research on the gene without the patent holder's consent? Forbidding human reproduction? Can religions secure copyrights over their scriptures? Even the ones they claim to have been dictated by gods or aliens? Even if American copyright law requires "an author," presumably a human one?[9] Can they use those copyrights to discipline heretics or critics who insist on quoting the scripture in full?

Should anyone own the protocols—the agreed-upon common technical standards—that make the Internet possible? Does reading a Web page count as "copying" it?[10] Should that question depend on technical "facts" (for example, how long the page stays in your browser's cache) or should it depend on some choice that we want to make about the extent of the copyright holder's rights?

These questions may be hard, because the underlying moral and political and economic issues need to be thought through. They may be weird; alien scriptural dictation might qualify there. They surely aren't uninteresting, although I admit to a certain prejudice on that point. And some of them, like the design of our telecommunications networks, or the patenting of human genes, or the relationship between copyright and free speech, are not merely interesting, they are important. It seems like a bad idea to leave them to a few lawyers and lobbyists simply because you are told they are "technical."

So the first goal of the book is to introduce you to intellectual property, to explain why it matters, why it is the legal form of the information age. The second goal is to persuade you that our intellectual property policy is going the wrong way; two roads are diverging and we are on the one that doesn't lead to Rome.

The third goal is harder to explain. We have a simple word for, and an intuitive understanding of, the complex reality of "property." Admittedly, lawyers think about property differently from the way lay-people do; this is only one of the strange mental changes that law school brings. But everyone in our society has a richly textured understanding of "mine" and "thine," of rights of exclusion, of division of rights over the same property (for example, between tenant and landlord), of transfer of rights in part or in whole (for example, rental or sale). But what about the opposite of property—property's antonym, property's outside? What is it? Is it just stuff that is not worth owning—abandoned junk? Stuff that is not yet owned—such as a seashell on a public beach, about to be taken home? Or stuff that cannot be owned— a human being, for example? Or stuff that is collectively owned—would that be the radio spectrum or a public park? Or stuff that is owned by no one, such as the deep seabed or the moon? Property's outside, whether it is "the public domain" or "the commons," turns out to be harder to grasp than its inside. To the extent that we think about property's outside, it tends to have a negative connotation; we want to get stuff out of the lost-and-found office and back into circulation as property. We talk of "the tragedy of the commons,"[11] meaning that unowned or collectively owned resources will be managed poorly; the common pasture will be overgrazed by the villagers' sheep because no one has an incentive to hold back.

When the subject is intellectual property, this gap in our knowledge turns out to be important because our intellectual property system depends on a balance between what is property and what is not. For a set of reasons that I will explain later, "the opposite of property" is a concept that is much more important when we come to the world of ideas, information, expression, and invention. We want a lot of material to be in the public domain, material that can be spread without property rights. "The general rule of law is, that the noblest of human productions—knowledge, truths ascertained, conceptions, and ideas—become, after voluntary communication to others, free as the air to common use."[12] Our art, our culture, our science depend on this public domain every bit as much as they depend on intellectual property. The third goal of this book is to explore property's outside, property's various antonyms, and to show how we are undervaluing the public domain and the information commons at the very moment in history when we need them most. Academic articles and clever legal briefs cannot solve this problem alone.

Instead, I argue that precisely because we are in the information age, we need a movement—akin to the environmental movement—to preserve the public domain. The explosion of industrial technologies that threatened the environment also taught us to recognize its value. The explosion of information technologies has precipitated an intellectual land grab; it must also teach us about both the existence and the value of the public domain. This enlightenment does not happen by itself. The environmentalists helped us to see the world differently, to see that there was such a thing as "the environment" rather than just my pond, your forest, his canal. We need to do the same thing in the information environment.

We have to "invent" the public domain before we can save it.

A word about style. I am trying to write about complicated issues, some of which have been neglected by academic scholarship, while others have been catalogued in detail. I want to advance the field, to piece together the story of the second enclosure movement, to tell you something new about the balance between property and its opposite. But I want to do so in a way that is readable. For those in my profession, being readable is a dangerous goal. You have never heard true condescension until you have heard academics pronounce the word "popularizer." They say it as Isadora Duncan might have said "dowdy." To be honest, I share their concern. All too often, clarity is achieved by leaving out the key qualification necessary to the argument, the subtlety of meaning, the inconvenient empirical evidence.

My solution is not a terribly satisfactory one. A lot of material has been exiled to endnotes. The endnotes for each chapter also include a short guide to further reading. I have used citations sparingly, but more widely than an author of a popular book normally does, so that the scholarly audience can trace out my reasoning. But the core of the argument is in the text.

The second balance I have struggled to hit is that between breadth and depth. The central thesis of the book is that the line between intellectual property and the public domain is important in every area of culture, science, and technology. As a result, it ranges widely in subject matter. Yet readers come with different backgrounds, interests, and bodies of knowledge. As a result, the structure of the book is designed to facilitate self-selection based on interest. The first three chapters and the conclusion provide the theoretical basis. Each chapter builds on those themes, but is also designed to be largely free-standing. The readers who thrill to the idea that there might be constitutional challenges to the regulation of digital speech by copyright law may wallow in those arguments to their hearts' content. Others may quickly grasp the gist and head on for the story of how Ray Charles's voice ended up in a mashup attacking President Bush, or the discussion of genetically engineered bacteria that take photographs and are themselves the subject of intellectual property rights. To those readers who nevertheless conclude that I have failed to balance correctly between precision and clarity, or breadth and depth, I offer my apologies. I fear you may be right. It was not for want of trying.

I

Why Intellectual Property?

Imagine yourself starting a society from scratch. Perhaps you fought a revolution, or perhaps you led a party of adventurers into some empty land, conveniently free of indigenous peoples. Now your task is to make the society work. You have a preference for democracy and liberty and you want a vibrant culture: a culture with a little chunk of everything, one that offers hundreds of ways to live and thousands of ideals of beauty. You don't want everything to be high culture; you want beer and skittles and trashy delights as well as brilliant news reporting, avant-garde theater, and shocking sculpture. You can see a role for highbrow, state-supported media or publicly financed artworks, but your initial working assumption is that the final arbiter of culture should be the people who watch, read, and listen to it, and who remake it every day. And even if you are dubious about the way popular choice gets formed, you prefer it to some government funding body or coterie of art mavens.

At the same time as you are developing your culture, you want a flourishing economy—and not just in literature or film. You want innovation and invention. You want drugs that cure terrible diseases, and designs for more fuel-efficient stoves, and useful little doodads, like mousetraps, or Post-it notes, or solar-powered backscratchers. To be exact, you want lots of innovation but you do not know exactly what innovation or even what types of innovation you want.

Given scarce time and resources, should we try to improve typewriters or render them obsolete with word processors, or develop functional voice recognition software, or just concentrate on making solar-powered backscratchers? Who knew that they needed Post-it notes or surgical stents or specialized rice planters until those things were actually developed? How do you make priorities when the priorities include things you cannot rationally value because you do not have them yet? How do you decide what to fund and when to fund it, what desires to trade off against each other?

The society you have founded normally relies on market signals to allocate resources. If a lot of people want petunias for their gardens, and are willing to pay handsomely for them, then some farmer who was formerly growing soybeans or gourds will devote a field to petunias instead. He will compete with the other petunia sellers to sell them to you. *Voila!* We do not need a state planner to consult the vegetable five-year plan and decree "Petunias for the People!" Instead, the decision about how to deploy society's productive resources is being made "automatically," cybernetically even, by rational individuals responding to price signals. And in a competitive market, you will get your petunias at very close to the cost of growing them and bringing them to market. Consumer desires are satisfied and productive resources are allocated efficiently. It's a *tour de force*.

Of course, there are problems. The market measures the value of a good by whether people have the ability and willingness to pay for it, so the whims of the rich may be more "valuable" than the needs of the destitute. We may spend more on pet psychiatry for the traumatized poodles on East 71st Street than on developing a cure for sleeping sickness, because the emotional well-being of the pets of the wealthy is "worth more" than the lives of the tropical world's poor. But for a lot of products, in a lot of areas, the market works—and that is a fact not to be taken for granted.

Why not use this mechanism to meet your cultural and innovation needs? If people need *Madame Bovary* or *The New York Times* or a new kind of antibiotic, surely the market will provide it? Apparently not. You have brought economists with you into your brave new world—perhaps out of nostalgia, or because a lot of packing got done at the last minute. The economists shake their heads.[1] The petunia farmer is selling something that is "a rivalrous good." If I have the petunia, you can't have it. What's more, petunias are "excludable." The farmer only gives you petunias when you pay for them. It is these factors that make the petunia market work. What about *Madame Bovary,* or the antibiotic, or *The New York Times?* Well, it depends. If books have to be copied out by hand, then *Madame Bovary* is just like the petunia. But if thousands of copies of *Madame Bovary* can be printed on a printing press, or photocopied, or downloaded from www.flaubertsparrot.com, then the book becomes something that is nonrival; once *Madame Bovary* is written, it can satisfy many readers with little additional effort or cost. Indeed, depending on the technologies of reproduction, it may be very hard to exclude people from *Madame Bovary.*

Imagine a Napster for French literature; everyone could have *Madame Bovary* and only the first purchaser would have to pay for it. Because of these "nonrival" and "nonexcludable" characteristics, Flaubert's publisher would have a more difficult time coming up with a business plan than the petunia farmer. The same is true for the drug company that invests millions in screening and testing various drug candidates and ends up with a new antibiotic that is both safe and effective, but which can be copied for pennies. Who will invest the money, knowing that any product can be undercut by copies that don't have to pay the research costs? How are authors and publishers and drug manufacturers to make money? And if they can't make money, how are we to induce people to be authors or to be the investors who put money into the publishing or pharmaceutical business?

It is important to pause at this point and inquire how closely reality hews to the economic story of "nonexcludable" and "nonrival" public goods. It turns out that the reality is much more complex. First, there may be motivations for creation that do not depend on the market mechanism. People sometimes create because they seek fame, or out of altruism, or because an inherent creative force will not let them do otherwise. Where those motivations operate, we may not need a financial incentive to create. Thus the "problem" of cheap copying in fact becomes a virtue. Second, the same technologies that make copying cheaper may also lower the costs of advertising and distribution, cutting down on the need to finance expensive distribution chains. Third, even in situations that do require incentives for creativity and for distribution, it may be that being "first to market" with an innovation provides the innovator with enough of a head start on the competition to support the innovation.[2] Fourth, while some aspects of the innovation may truly be nonrival, other aspects may not. Software is nonrival and hard to exclude people from, but it is easy to exclude your customers from the help line or technical support. The CD may be copied cheaply; the concert is easy to police. The innovator may even be advantaged by being able to trade on the likely effects of her innovation. If I know I have developed the digital camera, I may sell the conventional film company's shares short. Guarantees of authenticity, quality, and ease of use may attract purchasers even if unauthorized copying is theoretically cheaper.

In other words, the economic model of pure public goods will track our reality well in some areas and poorly in others—and the argument for state intervention to fix the problems of public goods will therefore wax and wane correspondingly. In the case of drug patents, for example, it is very strong. For lots of low-level business innovation, however, we believe that adequate incentives are provided by being first to market, and so we see no need to give monopoly power to the first business to come up with a new business plan— at least we did not until some disastrous patent law decisions discussed later in this book. Nor does a lowering of copying costs hurt every industry equally. Digital copies of music were a threat to the traditional music business, but digital copies of books? I am skeptical. This book will be freely and legally available online to all who wish to copy it. Both the publisher and I believe that this will increase rather than decrease sales.

Ignore these inconvenient complicating factors for a moment. Assume that wherever things are cheap to copy and hard to exclude others from, we have a potential collapse of the market. That book, that drug, that film will simply not be produced in the first place—unless the state steps in somehow to change the equation. This is the standard argument for intellectual property rights. And a very good argument it is. In order to solve the potentially "market-breaking" problem of goods that are expensive to make and cheap to copy, we will use what my colleague Jerry Reichman calls the "market-making" device of intellectual property. The state will create a right to exclude others from the invention or the expression and confer it on the inventor or the author. The most familiar rights of this kind are copyrights and patents. (Trademarks present some special issues, which I will address a little later.) Having been given the ability to forbid people to copy your invention or your novel, you can make them pay for the privilege of getting access. You have been put back in the position of the petunia farmer.

Pause for a moment and think of what a brilliant social innovation this is— at least potentially. Focus not on the incentives alone, but on the decentralization of information processing and decision making that a market offers.

Instead of having ministries of art that define the appropriate culture to be produced this year, or turning the entire path of national innovation policy over to the government, intellectual property decentralizes the choices about what creative and innovative paths to pursue while retaining the possibility that people will actually get paid for their innovation and creative expression.

The promise of copyright is this: if you are a radical environmentalist who wants to alert the world to the danger posed by climate change, or a passionate advocate of homeschooling, or a cartoonist with a uniquely twisted view of life, or a musician who can make a slack key guitar do very strange things, or a person who likes to take amazingly saccharine pictures of puppies and put them on greeting cards—maybe you can quit your day job and actually make a living from your expressive powers. If the market works, if the middlemen and distributors are smart enough, competitive enough, and willing to take a chance on expression that competes with their in-house talent, if you can make it somehow into the public consciousness, then you can be paid for allowing the world to copy, distribute, and perform your stuff. You risk your time and your effort and your passion and, if the market likes it, you will be rewarded. (At the very least, the giant producers of culture will be able to assemble vast teams of animators and musicians and software gurus and meld their labors into a videotape that will successfully anesthetize your children for two hours; no small accomplishment, let me tell you, and one for which people will certainly pay.)

More importantly, if the system works, the choices about the content of our culture—the mix of earnest essays and saccharine greeting cards and scantily clad singers and poetic renditions of Norse myths—will be decentralized to the people who actually read, or listen to, or watch the stuff. This is our cultural policy and it is driven, in part, by copyright.

The promise of patent is this: we have a multitude of human needs and a multitude of individuals and firms who might be able to satisfy those needs through innovation. Patent law offers us a decentralized system that, in principle, will allow individuals and firms to pick the problem that they wish to solve. Inventors and entrepreneurs can risk their time and their capital and, if they produce a solution that finds favor in the marketplace, will be able to reap the return provided by the legal right to exclude—by the legal monopoly over the resulting invention. The market hints at some unmet need—for drugs that might reduce obesity or cure multiple sclerosis, or for Post-it notes or windshield wipers that come on intermittently in light rain—and the innovator and her investors make a bet that they can meet that need. (Not all of these technologies will be patentable—only those that are novel and "nonobvious," something that goes beyond what any skilled person in the relevant field would have done.)

In return for the legal monopoly, patent holders must describe the technology well enough to allow anyone to replicate it once the patent term ends. Thus patent law allows us to avert two dangers: the danger that the innovation will languish because the inventor has no way to recover her investment of time and capital, and the danger that the inventor will turn to secrecy instead, hiding the details of her innovation behind black box technologies and restrictive contracts, so that society never gets the knowledge embedded in it. (This is a real danger. The medieval guilds often relied on secrecy to maintain the commercial advantage conveyed by their special skills, thus slowing progress down and sometimes simply stopping it. We still don't know how they made Stradivarius violins sound so good. Patents, by contrast, keep the knowledge public, at least in theory;[3] you must describe it to own it.) And again, decisions about the direction of innovation have been largely, though not entirely, decentralized to the people who actually might use the products and services that result. This is our innovation policy and it is increasingly driven by patent.

What about the legal protection of trademarks, the little words or symbols or product shapes that identify products for us? Why do we have trademark law, this "homestead law for the English language"?[4] Why not simply allow anyone to use any name or attractive symbol that they want on their products, even if someone else used it first? A trademark gives me a limited right to exclude other people from using my mark, or brand name, or product shape, just as copyright and patent law give me a limited right to exclude other people from my original expression or my novel invention. Why create such a right and back it with the force of law?

According to the economists, the answer is that trademark law does two things. It saves consumers time. We have good reason to believe that a soap that says "Ivory" or a tub of ice cream that says "Häagen-Dazs" will be made by the same manufacturer that made the last batch of Ivory soap or Häagen-Dazs ice cream. If we liked the good before and we see the symbol again, we know what we are getting. I can work out what kind of soap, ice cream, or car I like, and then just look for the appropriate sign rather than investigating the product all over again each time I buy. That would be wasteful and economists hate waste. At the same time, trademarks fulfill a second function: they are supposed to give manufacturers an incentive to make good products—or at least to make products of consistent quality or price—to build up a good brand name and invest in consistency of its key features, knowing that no other firm can take their name or symbol. (Why produce a high-quality product, or a reliable cheap product, and build a big market share if a free rider could wait until people liked the product and then just produce an imitation with the same name but of lower quality?) The promise of trademark is that quality and commercial information flow regulate themselves, with rational consumers judging among goods of consistent quality produced by manufacturers with an interest in building up long-term reputation.

So there we have the idealized vision of intellectual property. It is not merely supposed to produce incentives for innovation by rewarding creators, though that is vital. Intellectual property is also supposed to create a feedback mechanism that dictates the contours of information and innovation production. It is not an overstatement to say that intellectual property rights are designed to shape our information marketplace. Copyright law is supposed to give us a self-regulating cultural policy in which the right to exclude others from one's original expression fuels a vibrant public sphere indirectly driven by popular demand. At its best, it is supposed to allow a decentralized and iconoclastic cultural ferment in which independent artists, musicians, and writers can take their unique visions, histories, poems, or songs to the world—and make a living doing so if their work finds favor. Patent law is supposed to give us a self-regulating innovation policy in which the right to exclude others from novel and useful inventions creates a cybernetic and responsive innovation marketplace. The allocation of social resources to particular types of innovation is driven by guesses about what the market wants. Trademark law is supposed to give us a self-regulating commercial information policy in which the right to exclude others from one's trade name, symbol, or slogan produces a market for consumer information in which firms have incentives to establish quality brand names and consumers can rely on the meaning and the stability of the logos that surround them. Ivory soap will always mean Ivory soap and Coke will mean Coke, at least until the owners of those marks decide to change the nature of their products.

Some readers will find my use of the term "intellectual property" mistaken and offensive. They will argue, and I agree, that the use of the term "property" can cause people mistakenly to conflate these rights with those to physical property. (I outline that process and its negative consequences in the next chapter.) They will argue, and again I agree, that there are big differences between the three fields I have described. Should we not just list the specific rights about which we are speaking—copyright, patent, or trademark? Both of these concerns are real and well-founded, but I respectfully disagree with the conclusion that we should give up the term "intellectual property."

First, as I have tried to show above, while there are considerable differences between the three fields I discussed, there is also a core similarity—the attempt to use a legally created privilege to solve a potential "public goods problem." That similarity can enlighten as well as confuse. Yes, copyright looks very different from patent, just as a whale looks very different from a mouse. But we do not condemn the scientist who notes that they are both "mammals"—a socially constructed category—so long as he has a reason for focusing on that commonality. Second, the language of intellectual property exists. It has political reality in the world. Sometimes the language confuses and misleads. There are two possible reactions to such a reality. One can reject it and insist on a different and "purified" nomenclature, or one can attempt to point out the misperceptions and confusions using the very language in which they are embedded. I do not reject the first tactic. It can be useful. Here, though, I have embraced the second.

I have provided the idealized story of intellectual property. But is it true? Did the law really develop that way? Does it work that way now? Does this story still apply in the world of the Internet and the Human Genome Project? If you believed the idealized story, would you know what kind of intellectual property laws to write? The answer to all of these questions is "not exactly."

Like most social institutions, intellectual property has an altogether messier and more interesting history than this sanitized version of its functioning would suggest. The precursors of copyright law served to force the identification of the author, so that he could be punished if he proved to be a heretic or a revolutionary. The Statute of Anne—the first true copyright statute—was produced partly because of publishers' fights with booksellers; the authorial right grew as an afterthought.[5] The history of patents includes a wealth of attempts to reward friends of the government and restrict or control dangerous technologies. Trademark law has shuttled uneasily between being a free-floating way to police competition so as to prohibit actions that courts thought were "unfair" and an absolute property right over an individual word or symbol.

But does intellectual property work this way now, promoting the ideal of progress, a transparent marketplace, easy and cheap access to information, decentralized and iconoclastic cultural production, self-correcting innovation policy? Often it does, but distressingly often it does the reverse. The rights that were supposed to be limited in time and scope to the minimum monopoly necessary to ensure production become instead a kind of perpetual corporate welfare—restraining the next generation of creators instead of encouraging them. The system that was supposed to harness the genius of both the market and democracy sometimes subverts both. Worse, it does so inefficiently, locking up vast swaths of culture in order to confer a benefit on a tiny minority of works. But this is too abstract. A single instance from copyright law will serve as a concrete example of what is at stake here. Later in the book I will give other examples.

YOU'LL GET MY LIBRARY OF CONGRESS WHEN . . .

Go to the Library of Congress catalogue. It is online at http://catalog.loc.gov/. This is an astounding repository of material—not just books and periodicals, but pictures, films, and music. The vast majority of this material, perhaps as much as 95 percent in the case of books, is commercially unavailable.[6] The process happens comparatively quickly. Estimates suggest that a mere twenty-eight years after publication 85 percent of the works are no longer being commercially produced. (We know that when U.S. copyright required renewal after twenty-eight years, about 85 percent of all copyright holders did not bother to renew. This is a reasonable, if rough, guide to commercial viability.)[7]

Yet because the copyright term is now so long, in many cases extending well over a century, most of twentieth-century culture is still under copyright—copyrighted but unavailable. Much of this, in other words, is lost culture. No one is reprinting the books, screening the films, or playing the songs. No one is allowed to. In fact, we may not even know who holds the copyright. Companies have gone out of business. Records are incomplete or absent. In some cases, it is even more complicated. A film, for example, might have one copyright over the sound track, another over the movie footage, and another over the script. You get the idea. These works—which are commercially unavailable and also have no identifiable copyright holder—are called "orphan works." They make up a huge percentage of our great libraries' holdings. For example, scholars estimate that the majority of our film holdings are orphan works.[8] For books, the estimates are similar. Not only are these works unavailable commercially, there is simply no way to find and contact the person who could agree to give permission to digitize the work or make it available in a new form.

Take a conservative set of numbers. Subtract from our totals the works that are clearly in the public domain. In the United States, that is generally work produced before 1923. That material, at least, we can use freely. Subtract, too, the works that are still available from the copyright holder. There we can gain access if we are willing to pay. Yet this still leaves a huge proportion of twentieth and twenty first century culture commercially unavailable but under copyright. In the case of books, the number is over 95 percent, as I said before; with films and music, it is harder to tell, but the percentages are still tragically high. A substantial proportion of that total is made up of orphan works. They cannot be reprinted or digitized even if we were willing to pay the owner to do so. And then comes the Internet. Right now, you can search for those books or films or songs and have the location of the work instantly displayed, as well as a few details about it. And if you live in Washington, D.C., or near some other great library, you can go to a reading room, and if the work can be found and has not been checked out, and has not deteriorated, you can read the books (though you probably will not be able to arrange to see the movies unless you are an accredited film scholar).

I was searching the Library of Congress catalogue online one night, tracking down a seventy-year-old book about politics and markets, when my son came in to watch me. He was about eight years old at the time but already a child of the Internet age. He asked what I was doing and I explained that I was printing out the details of the book so that I could try to find it in my own university library. "Why don't you read it online?" he said, reaching over my shoulder and double-clicking on the title, frowning when that merely led to another information page: "How do you get to read the actual book?" I smiled at the assumption that all the works of literature were not merely in the Library of Congress, but actually on the Net: available to anyone with an Internet connection anywhere in the world—so that you could not merely search for, but also read or print, some large slice of the Library's holdings. Imagine what that would be like. Imagine the little underlined blue hyperlink from each title—to my son it made perfect sense. The book's title was in the catalogue. When you clicked the link, surely you would get to read it. That is what happened in his experience when one clicked a link. Why not here? It was an old book, after all, no longer in print. Imagine being able to read the books, hear the music, or watch the films—or at least the ones that the Library of Congress thought it worthwhile to digitize. Of course, that is ridiculous.

I tried to explain this to my son. I showed him that there were some works that could be seen online. I took him to the online photograph library, meaning to show him the wealth of amazing historical photographs. Instead, I found myself brooding over the lengthy listing of legal restrictions on the images and the explanation that reproduction of protected items may require the written permission of the copyright owners and that, in many cases, only indistinct and tiny thumbnail images are displayed to those searching from outside the Library of Congress "because of potential rights considerations." The same was true of the scratchy folk songs from the twenties or the early film holdings. The material was in the Library, of course—remarkable collections in some cases, carefully preserved, and sometimes even digitized at public expense. Yet only a tiny fraction of it is available online. (There is a fascinating set of Edison's early films, for example.)

Most of the material available online comes from so long ago that the copyright could not possibly still be in force. But since copyright lasts for seventy years after the death of the author (or ninety-five years if it was a corporate "work for hire"), that could be a very, very long time indeed. Long enough, in fact, to keep off limits almost the whole history of moving pictures and the entire history of recorded music. Long enough to lock up almost all of twentieth-century culture.

But is that not what copyright is supposed to do? To grant the right to restrict access, so as to allow authors to charge for the privilege of obtaining it? Yes, indeed. And this is a very good idea. But as I argue in this book, the goal of the system ought to be to give the monopoly only for as long as necessary to provide an incentive. After that, we should let the work fall into the public domain where all of us can use it, transform it, adapt it, build on it, republish it as we wish. For most works, the owners expect to make all the money they are going to recoup from the work with five or ten years of exclusive rights. The rest of the copyright term is of little use to them except as a kind of lottery ticket in case the work proves to be a one-in-a-million perennial favorite. The one-in-a-million lottery winner will benefit, of course, if his ticket comes up. And if the ticket is "free," who would not take it? But the ticket is not free to the public. They pay higher prices for the works still being commercially exploited and, frequently, the price of complete unavailability for the works that are not.

Think of a one-in-a-million perennial favorite—Harry Potter, say. Long after J. K. Rowling is dust, we will all be forbidden from making derivative works, or publishing cheap editions or large-type versions, or simply reproducing it for pleasure. I am a great admirer of Ms. Rowling's work, but my guess is that little extra incentive was provided by the thought that her copyright will endure seventy rather than merely fifty years after her death. Some large costs are being imposed here, for a small benefit. And the costs fall even more heavily on all the other works, which are available nowhere but in some moldering library stacks. To put it another way, if copyright owners had to purchase each additional five years of term separately, the same way we buy warranties on our appliances, the economically rational ones would mainly settle for a fairly short period.

Of course, there are some works that are still being exploited commercially long after their publication date. Obviously the owners of these works would not want them freely available online. This seems reasonable enough, though even with those works the copyright should expire eventually. But remember, in the Library of Congress's vast, wonderful pudding of songs and pictures and films and books and magazines and newspapers, there is perhaps a handful of raisins' worth of works that anyone is making any money from, and the vast majority of those come from the last ten years. If one goes back twenty years, perhaps a raisin. Fifty years? A slight raisiny aroma. We restrict access to the whole pudding in order to give the owners of the raisin slivers their due. But this pudding is almost all of twentieth-century culture, and we are restricting access to it when almost of all of it could be available.

If you do not know much about copyright, you might think that I am exaggerating. After all, if no one has any financial interest in the works or we do not even know who owns the copyright, surely a library would be free to put those works online? Doesn't "no harm, no foul" apply in the world of copyright? In a word, no. Copyright is what lawyers call a "strict liability" system. This means that it is generally not a legal excuse to say that you did not believe you were violating copyright, or that you did so by accident, or in the belief that no one would care, and that your actions benefited the public. Innocence and mistake do not absolve you, though they might reduce the penalties imposed. Since it is so difficult to know exactly who owns the copyright (or copyrights) on a work, many libraries simply will not reproduce the material or make it available online until they can be sure the copyright has expired—which may mean waiting for over a century. They cannot afford to take the risk.

What is wrong with this picture? Copyright has done its job and encouraged the creation of the work. But now it acts as a fence, keeping us out and restricting access to the work to those who have the time and resources to trudge through the stacks of the nation's archives. In some cases, as with film, it may simply make the work completely unavailable.

So far I have been talking as though copyright were the only reason the material is not freely available online. But of course, this is not true. Digitizing costs money (though less every year) and there is a lot of rubbish out there, stuff no one would ever want to make available digitally (though it must be noted that one man's rubbish is another man's delight). But that still leaves vast amounts of material that we would want, and be willing to pay, to have digitized. Remember also that if the material were legally free, anyone could get in on the act of digitizing it and putting it up. Google's much-heralded effort to scan the books in major libraries is just the kind of thing I mean. But Google is being sued for violating copyright—even though it allows any author to "opt out" of its system, and even though under the Google system you cannot click to get the book if it is still under copyright, merely a snippet a few sentences long from the book.

If you are shaking your head as you read this, saying that no one would bother digitizing most of the material in the archives, look at the Internet and ask yourself where the information came from the last time you did a search. Was it an official and prestigious institution? A university or a museum or a government? Sometimes those are our sources of information, of course. But do you not find the majority of the information you need by wandering off into a strange click-trail of sites, amateur and professional, commercial and not, hobbyist and entrepreneur, all self-organized by internal referrals and search engine algorithms? Even if Google did not undertake the task of digitization, there would be hundreds, thousands, maybe millions of others who would—not with Google's resources, to be sure. In the process, they would create something quite remarkable.

The most satisfying proofs are existence proofs. A platypus is an existence proof that mammals can lay eggs. The Internet is an existence proof of the remarkable information processing power of a decentralized network of hobbyists, amateurs, universities, businesses, volunteer groups, professionals, and retired experts and who knows what else. It is a network that produces useful information and services. Frequently, it does so at no cost to the user and without anyone guiding it. Imagine that energy, that decentralized and idiosyncratically dispersed pattern of interests, turned loose on the cultural artifacts of the twentieth century. Then imagine it coupled to the efforts of the great state archives and private museums who themselves would be free to do the same thing. Think of the people who would work on Buster Keaton, or the literary classics of the 1930s, or the films of the Second World War, or footage on the daily lives of African-Americans during segregation, or the music of the Great Depression, or theremin recordings, or the best of vaudeville. Imagine your Google search in such a world. Imagine *that* Library of Congress. One science fiction writer has taken a stab. His character utters the immortal line, "Man, you'll get my Library of Congress *when you pry my cold dead fingers off it!*"[9]

Familiar with the effect of this kind of train of thought on his father, my son had long since wandered off in search of a basketball game to watch. But I have to admit his question was something of an epiphany for me: Where *do* you click to get the actual book?

The response I get from a lot of people is that this vision of the Library of Congress is communism, pure and simple. Such people view Google's attempt to digitize books as simple theft. Surely it will destroy the incentives necessary to produce the next beach novel, the next academic monograph, the next teen band CD, the next hundred-million-dollar movie? But this mistakes my suggestion. Imagine a very conservative system. First, let us make people demonstrate that they want a copyright, by the arduous step of actually writing the word copyright or the little © on the work. (At the moment, everyone gets a copyright as soon as the work is written down or otherwise fixed, whether they want one or not.) But how long a copyright? We know that the majority of works are only valuable for five or ten years. Let us give copyright owners more than double that, say twenty-eight years of exclusive rights. If prior experience is any guide, 85 percent of works will be allowed to enter the public domain after that period. If that isn't generous enough, let us say that the small proportion of owners who still find value in their copyright at the end of twenty-eight years can extend their copyright for another twenty-eight years. Works that are not renewed fall immediately into the public domain. If you check the register after twenty-eight years and the work has not been renewed, it is in the public domain. Works that are renewed get the extra time.

Now this is a conservative suggestion, too conservative in my view, though still better than what we have now. Is it feasible? It would be hard to argue that it is not. This pretty much *was* the law in the United States until 1978. (My system is a little simpler, but the broad strokes are the same.) Since that point, in two broad stages, we have moved away from this system at the very moment in history when the Internet made it a particularly stupid idea to do so.

How have we changed the system? We have given copyrights to the creator of any original work as soon as it is fixed, so that you, reader, are the author of thousands of copyrighted works. Almost everything up on the Internet is copyrighted, even if its creators do not know that and would prefer it to be in the public domain. Imagine that you want to make a documentary and use a film clip that a student filmmaker has put up on his home page. Perhaps you want to adapt the nifty graphics that a high school teacher in Hawaii created to teach her calculus class, thinking that, with a few changes, you could use the material for your state's K-12 physics program. Perhaps you are a collage artist who wishes to incorporate images that amateur artists have put online. None of the works are marked by a copyright symbol. Certainly they are up on the Internet, but does that mean that they are available for reprinting, adaptation, or incorporation in a new work?

In each of these cases, you simply do not know whether what you are doing is legal or not. Of course, you can take the risk, though that becomes less advisable if you want to share your work with others. Each broadening of the circle of sharing increases the value to society but also the legal danger to you. What if you want to put the course materials on the Net, or publish the anthology, or display the movie? Perhaps you can try to persuade your publisher or employer or distributor to take the risk. Perhaps you can track down the authors of every piece you wish to use and puzzle through the way to get a legal release from them stating that they give you permission to use the work they did not even know they had copyright over. Or you can give up. Whatever happens, you waste time and effort in trying to figure out a way of getting around a system that is designed around neither your needs nor the needs of many of the people whose work you want to use.

Apart from doing away with the need to indicate that you *want* your works to be copyrighted, we have lengthened the copyright term. We did this without any credible evidence that it was necessary to encourage innovation. We have extended the terms of living and even of dead authors over works that have already been created. (It is hard to argue that this was a necessary incentive, what with the works already existing and the authors often being dead.) We have done away with the need to renew the right. Everyone gets the term of life plus seventy years, or ninety-five years for corporate "works for hire." All protected by a "strict liability" system with scary penalties. And, as I said before, we have made all those choices just when the Internet makes their costs particularly tragic.

In sum, we have forgone the Library of Congress I described without even apparently realizing we were doing so. We have locked up most of twentieth-century culture and done it in a particularly inefficient and senseless way, creating vast costs in order to convey proportionally tiny benefits. (And all without much complaint from those who normally object to inefficient government subsidy programs.) Worst of all, we have turned the system on its head. Copyright, intended to be the servant of creativity, a means of promoting access to information, is becoming an obstacle to both.

That, then, is one example of the stakes of the debate over intellectual property policy. Unfortunately, the problem of copyright terms is just one example, one instance of a larger pattern. As I will try to show, this pattern is repeated again and again in patents, in trademarks, and elsewhere in copyright law. This is not an isolated "glitch." It is a complicated but relentless tendency that has led to a hypertrophy of intellectual property rights and an assault on the public domain. In fact, in many cases, the reality is even worse: there appears to be a complete ignorance about the value of the public domain. Property's opposite, its outside, is getting short shrift.

To paraphrase a song from my youth, "how did we get here?" Where should we turn to understand the role of intellectual property in the era of the Internet and the decoding of the human genome? We could turn to the cutting edge of technology or to economics or information theory. But none of those would be as useful a starting place as a letter that was written about two hundred years ago, using a high-tech quill pen, about a subject far from the digital world.

2

Thomas Jefferson Writes a Letter

On August 13, 1813, Thomas Jefferson took up his pen to write to Isaac McPherson.[1] It was a quiet week in Jefferson's correspondence. He wrote a letter to Madison about the appointment of a tax assessor, attempted to procure a government position for an acquaintance, produced a fascinating and lengthy series of comments on a new "Rudiments of English Grammar," discussed the orthography of nouns ending in "y," accepted the necessary delay in the publication of a study on the anatomy of mammoth bones, completed a brief biography of Governor Lewis, and, in general, confined himself narrowly in subject matter.[2] But on the 13th of August, Jefferson's mind was on intellectual property, and most specifically, patents.

Jefferson's writing is, as usual, apparently effortless. Some find his penmanship a little hard to decipher. To me, used to plowing through the frenzied chicken tracks that law students produce during exams, it seems perfectly clear. If handwriting truly showed the architecture of the soul, then Jefferson's would conjure up Monticello or the University of Virginia. There are a few revisions and interlineations, a couple of words squeezed in with a caret at the bottom of the line, but for the most part the lines of handwriting simply roll on and on—"the fugitive fermentation of an individual brain,"[3] to quote a phrase from the letter, caught in vellum and ink, though that brain has been dust for more than a century and a half.

I love libraries. I love the mushroom smell of gently rotting paper, the flaky crackle of manuscripts, and the surprise of matching style of handwriting with style of thought. Today, though, I am viewing his letter over the Internet on a computer screen. (You can too. The details are at the back of the book.)

I think Jefferson would have been fascinated by the Internet. After all, this was the man whose library became the Library of Congress,[4] who exemplifies the notion of the brilliant dabbler in a hundred fields, whose own book collection was clearly a vital and much consulted part of his daily existence, and whose vision of politics celebrates the power of an informed citizenry. Admittedly, the massive conflicts between Jefferson's announced principles and his actions on the issue of slavery have led some, though not me, to doubt that there is *any* sincerity or moral instruction to be found in his words.[5] But even those who find him a sham can hardly fail to see the continual and obvious joy he felt about knowledge and its spread.

In the letter to Isaac McPherson, a letter that has become very famous in the world of the digerati,[6] this joy becomes manifest. The initial subject of the correspondence seems far from the online world. McPherson wrote to Jefferson about "elevators, conveyers and Hopper-boys." Specifically, he wanted to know Jefferson's opinion of a patent that had been issued to Mr. Oliver Evans. Jefferson devotes a paragraph to a recent retrospective extension of patent rights (he disapproves) and then turns to Evans's elevators.

Patents then, as now, were only supposed to be given for inventions that were novel, nonobvious, and useful. Jefferson had considerable doubt whether Evans's device, essentially a revolving string of buckets used to move grain, actually counted as "an invention." "The question then whether such a string of buckets was invented first by Oliver Evans, is a mere question of fact in mathematical history. Now, turning to such books only as I happen to possess, I find abundant proof that this simple machinery has been in use from time immemorial." Jefferson cites from his library example after example of references to the "Persian wheel"—a string of buckets to move water. The display of scholarship is effortless and without artifice. If the device existed to move water, he declares, Mr. Evans can hardly patent it to move grain. "If one person invents a knife convenient for pointing our pens, another cannot have a patent right for the same knife to point our pencils. A compass was invented for navigating the sea; another could not have a patent right for using it to survey land."[7]

So far as we can tell, this was the only part of the letter that interested McPherson. Later correspondence indicates that he had a pamphlet printed questioning the patent.[8] But while it is impressive to see Jefferson's easy command of historical evidence or his grasp of the importance of limiting the subject matter, scope, and duration of patents, these qualities alone would not have given the letter the fame it now has. It is when Jefferson turns to the idea of intellectual property itself that the letter becomes more than a historical curiosity. In a couple of pages, quickly jotted down on a humid August day in 1813, he frames the issue as well as anyone has since.

He starts by dismissing the idea "that inventors have a natural and exclusive right to their inventions, and not merely for their own lives, but inheritable to their heirs." In lines that will sound strange to those who assume that the framers of the Constitution were property absolutists, Jefferson argues that "stable ownership" of even tangible property is "a gift of social law." Intellectual property, then, has still less of a claim to some permanent, absolute, and natural status.

> [W]hile it is a moot question whether the origin of any kind of property is derived from nature at all, it would be singular to admit a natural and even an hereditary right to inventors. It is agreed by those who have seriously considered the subject, that no individual has, of natural right, a separate property in an acre of land, for instance. By an universal law, indeed, whatever, whether fixed or movable, belongs to all men equally and in common, is the property for the moment of him who occupies it, but when he relinquishes the occupation, the property goes with it. Stable ownership is the gift of social law, and is given late in the progress of society. It would be curious then, if an idea, the fugitive fermentation of an individual brain, could, of natural right, be claimed in exclusive and stable property.[9]

Jefferson's point here may seem obscure to us. We are not used to starting every argument from first principles. But it is in fact quite simple. It is society that creates property rights that go beyond mere occupancy. It does so for several reasons—reasons of both practicality and natural justice. (Elsewhere in his writings, Jefferson expands on this point at greater length.) One of those reasons has to do with the difficulty, perhaps even the impossibility, of two different people having full and unfettered ownership of the same piece of property simultaneously. Another linked reason comes from the practicality of excluding others from our property, so that we can exploit it secure from the plunder or sloth of others. The economists you encountered in Chapter 1 have, with their usual linguistic felicity, coined the terms "rivalrous" and "excludable" to describe these characteristics.

With rivalrous property, one person's use precludes another's. If I drink the milk, you cannot. Excludable property is, logically enough, property from which others can easily be excluded or kept out. But ideas seem to have neither of these characteristics.

> If nature has made any one thing less susceptible than all others of exclusive property, it is the action of the thinking power called an idea, which an individual may exclusively possess as he keeps it to himself; but the moment it is divulged, it forces itself into the possession of every one, and the receiver cannot dispossess himself of it. Its peculiar character, too, is that no one possess the less, because every other possess the whole of it. He who receives an idea from me, receives instruction himself without lessening mine; as he who lights his taper at mine, receives light without darkening me. That ideas should freely spread from one to another over the globe, for the moral and mutual instruction of man, and improvement of his condition, seems to have been peculiarly and benevolently designed by nature, when she made them, like fire, expansible over all space, without lessening their density in any point, and like the air in which we breathe, move, and have our physical being, incapable of confinement or exclusive appropriation. Inventions then cannot, in nature, be a subject of property.[10]

Those who quote the passage sometimes stop here, which is a shame, because it leaves the impression that Jefferson was unequivocally against intellectual property rights. But that would be a considerable overstatement. When he says that inventions can never be the subject of property, he means a permanent and exclusive property right which, as a matter of natural right, no just government could abridge. However, inventions *could* be covered by temporary state-created monopolies instituted for the common good. In the lines immediately following the popularly quoted excerpt, Jefferson goes on:

> Society may give an exclusive right to the profits arising from [inventions], as an encouragement to men to pursue ideas which may produce utility, but this may or may not be done, according to the will and convenience of the society, without claim or complaint from any body. Accordingly, it is a fact, as far as I am informed, that England was, until we copied her, the only country on earth which ever, by a general law, gave a legal right to the exclusive use of an idea. In some other countries it is sometimes done, in a great case, and by a special and personal act, but, generally speaking, other nations have thought that these monopolies produce more embarrassment than advantage to society; and it may be observed that the nations which refuse monopolies of invention, are as fruitful as England in new and useful devices.[11]

Jefferson's message was a skeptical recognition that intellectual property rights *might* be necessary, a careful explanation that they should not be treated as natural rights, and a warning of the monopolistic dangers that they pose.

He immediately goes on to say something else, something that is, if anything, more true in the world of patents on Internet business methods and gene sequences than it was in the world of "conveyers and Hopper-boys."

> Considering the exclusive right to invention as given not of natural right, but for the benefit of society, I know well the difficulty of drawing a line between the things which are worth to the public the embarrassment of an exclusive patent, and those which are not.[12]

So Jefferson gives us a classic set of cautions, cautions that we should be required to repeat, as police officers repeat the Miranda Warning to a suspect. In this case, they should be repeated before we rush off into the world of intellectual property policy rather than before we talk to the police without our lawyers present.

THE JEFFERSON WARNING

Like the Miranda Warning, the Jefferson Warning has a number of important parts.

- First, the stuff we cover with intellectual property rights has certain vital differences from the stuff we cover with tangible property rights. Partly because of those differences, Jefferson, like most of his successors in the United States, does not see intellectual property as a claim of natural right based on expended labor. Instead it is a temporary state-created monopoly given to encourage further innovation.
- Second, there is no "entitlement" to have an intellectual property right. Such rights may or may not be given as a matter of social "will and convenience" without "claim or complaint from any body."
- Third, intellectual property rights are not and should not be permanent; in fact they should be tightly limited in time and should not last a day longer than necessary to encourage the innovation in the first place.
- Fourth, a linked point, they have considerable monopolistic dangers—they may well produce more "embarrassment than advantage." In fact, since intellectual property rights potentially restrain the benevolent tendency of "ideas . . . [to] freely spread from one to another over the globe, for the moral and mutual instruction of man," they may in some cases actually hinder rather than encourage innovation.
- Fifth, deciding whether to have an intellectual property system is only the first choice in a long series.[13] Even if one believes that intellectual property *is*

a good idea, which I firmly do, one will still have the hard job of saying which types of innovation or information are "worth to the public the embarrassment" of an exclusive right, and of drawing the limits of that right. This line-drawing task turns out to be very difficult. Without the cautions that Jefferson gave us it is impossible to do it well.

Jefferson's message was famously echoed and amplified thirty years later in Britain by Thomas Babington Macaulay.[14] Macaulay's speeches to the House of Commons in 1841 on the subject of copyright term extension still express better than anything else the position that intellectual property rights are necessary evils which must be carefully circumscribed by law. In order for the supply of valuable books to be maintained, authors "must be remunerated for their literary labour. And there are only two ways in which they can be remunerated. One of those ways is patronage; the other is copyright." Patronage is rejected out of hand. "I can conceive no system more fatal to the integrity and independence of literary men than one under which they should be taught to look for their daily bread to the favour of ministers and nobles."[15]

> We have, then, only one resource left. We must betake ourselves to copyright, be the inconveniences of copyright what they may. Those inconveniences, in truth, are neither few nor small. Copyright is monopoly, and produces all the effects which the general voice of mankind attributes to monopoly. . . . I believe, Sir, that I may safely take it for granted that the effect of monopoly generally is to make articles scarce, to make them dear, and to make them bad. And I may with equal safety challenge my honorable friend to find out any distinction between copyright and other privileges of the same kind; any reason why a monopoly of books should produce an effect directly the reverse of that which was produced by the East India Company's monopoly of tea, or by Lord Essex's monopoly of sweet wines. Thus, then, stands the case. It is good that authors should be remunerated; and the least exceptionable way of remunerating them is by a monopoly. Yet monopoly is an evil. For the sake of the good we must submit to the evil; but the evil ought not to last a day longer than is necessary for the purpose of securing the good.[16]

Notice that it is the *monopolistic* quality of intellectual property that really disturbs Macaulay. His was a generation of thinkers for whom the negative effect of monopolies of any kind (and state-granted monopolies in particular) was axiomatic. He becomes almost contemptuous when one of the supporters of copyright extension declared that it was merely "a theory" that monopoly makes things expensive. Macaulay agrees, tongue in cheek. "It is a theory in the same sense in which it is a theory, that day and night follow each other, that lead is heavier than water, that bread nourishes, that arsenic poisons, that alcohol intoxicates."[17]

These words from Jefferson and Macaulay encapsulate an eighteenth- and nineteenth-century free-trade skepticism about intellectual property, a skepticism that is widely, but not universally, believed to have played an important role in shaping the history of intellectual property in both the United States and the United Kingdom. Certainly the U.S. Supreme Court has offered support for that position,[18] and, with one significant recent exception,[19] historians of intellectual property have agreed.[20] Jefferson himself had believed that the Constitution should have definite limits on both the term and the scope of intellectual property rights.[21] James Madison stressed the costs of any intellectual property right and the need to limit its term and to allow the government to end the monopoly by compulsory purchase if necessary.[22] Adam Smith expressed similar views. Monopolies that carry on long after they were needed to encourage some socially beneficial activity, he said, tax every other citizen "very absurdly in two different ways: first, by the high price of goods, which, in the case of a free trade, they could buy much cheaper; and, secondly, by their total exclusion from a branch of business which it might be both convenient and profitable for many of them to carry on."[23]

It is important to note, though, that the eighteenth- and nineteenth-century writers I have quoted were not against intellectual property. All of them—Jefferson, Madison, Smith, and Macaulay—could see good reason why intellectual property rights should be granted. They simply insisted on weighing the costs and benefits of a new right, each expansion of scope, each lengthening of the copyright term. Here is Macaulay again, waxing eloquently sarcastic about the costs and benefits of extending the copyright term so that it would last many years after the author's death:

> I will take an example. Dr. Johnson died fifty-six years ago. If the law were what my honourable and learned friend wishes to make it, somebody would now have the monopoly of Dr. Johnson's works. Who that somebody would be it is impossible to say; but we may venture to guess. I guess, then, that it would have been some bookseller, who was the assign of another bookseller, who was the grandson of a third bookseller, who had bought the copyright from Black Frank, the Doctor's servant and residuary legatee, in 1785 or 1786. Now, would the knowledge that this copyright would exist in 1841 have been a source of gratification to Johnson? Would it have stimulated his exertions? Would it have once drawn him out of his bed before noon? Would it have once cheered him under a fit of the spleen? Would it have induced him to give us one

more allegory, one more life of a poet, one more imitation of Juvenal? I firmly believe not. I firmly believe that a hundred years ago, when he was writing our debates for the Gentleman's Magazine, he would very much rather have had twopence to buy a plate of shin of beef at a cook's shop underground.[24]

Again, I am struck by how seamlessly Macaulay coupled beautiful, evocative writing and careful, analytic argument. Admittedly, he was remarkable even in his own time, but it is hard to imagine a contemporary speechwriter, let alone a politician, coming up with Dr. Johnson "cheered . . . under a fit of the spleen" or buying a "plate of shin of beef at a cook's shop underground." Almost as hard as it is to imagine any of them engaging in Jefferson's correspondence about mammoth bones, orthography, and the practicalities of the nautical torpedo. But I digress.

Macaulay is not against using a lengthened copyright term to give an extra reward to writers, even if this would dramatically raise the price of books. What he objects to is dramatically raising the price of books written by long-dead authors in a way that benefits the authors hardly at all.

> Considered as a reward to him, the difference between a twenty years' and a sixty years' term of posthumous copyright would have been nothing or next to nothing. But is the difference nothing to us? I can buy *Rasselas* for sixpence; I might have had to give five shillings for it. I can buy the *Dictionary*, the entire genuine *Dictionary*, for two guineas, perhaps for less; I might have had to give five or six guineas for it. Do I grudge this to a man like Dr. Johnson? Not at all. Show me that the prospect of this boon roused him to any vigorous effort, or sustained his spirits under depressing circumstances, and I am quite willing to pay the price of such an object, heavy as that price is. But what I do complain of is that my circumstances are to be worse, and Johnson's none the better; that I am to give five pounds for what to him was not worth a farthing.[25]

Though Macaulay won the debate over copyright term extension, it is worth noting here that his opponents triumphed in the end. As I pointed out in the last chapter, the copyright term in most of Europe and in the United States now lasts for the life of the author and an additional seventy years afterward, ten years more than the proposal which made Macaulay so indignant. In the United States, corporate owners of "works-for-hire" get ninety-five years.[26] The Supreme Court recently heard a constitutional challenge to the law which expanded the term of copyrights by twenty years to reach this remarkable length.[27] (Full disclosure: I helped prepare an amicus brief in that case.)[28] This law, the Sonny Bono Copyright Term Extension Act, also extended existing copyrights over works which had already been created.[29] As I observed earlier, this is particularly remarkable if the idea is to give an incentive to create. Obviously the authors of existing works *were* given sufficient incentive to create; we know that because they did. Why do we need to give the people who now hold their copyrights *another* twenty years of monopoly? This is all cost and no benefit. Macaulay would have been furious.

When the Supreme Court heard the case, it was presented with a remarkable friend-of-the-court brief from seventeen economists, several of them Nobel laureates.[30] The economists made exactly Macaulay's argument, though in less graceful language. They pointed out that copyright extension imposed enormous costs on the public and yet conveyed tiny advantages, if any, to the creator. Such an extension, particularly over works that had already been written, hardly fit the limits of Congress's power under the Constitution "to promote the Progress of Science and useful Arts, by securing for limited Times to Authors and Inventors the exclusive Right to their respective Writings and Discoveries."[31] Macaulay doubted that these enormously long terms would encourage the living. Surely they would do little to encourage the dead, while imposing considerable costs of access on the living? Thus they could hardly be said to "promote the progress" of knowledge as the Constitution requires. The Court was unmoved by this and other arguments. It upheld the law. I will return to its decision at the end of the book.

The intellectual property skeptics had other concerns. Macaulay was particularly worried about the power that went with a transferable and inheritable monopoly. It is not only that the effect of monopoly is "to make articles scarce, to make them dear, and to make them bad." Macaulay also pointed out that those who controlled the monopoly, particularly after the death of the original author, might be given too great a control over our collective culture. Censorious heirs or purchasers of the copyright might prevent the reprinting of a great work because they disagreed with its morals.[32] We might lose the works of Fielding or Gibbon, because a legatee found them distasteful and used the power of the copyright to suppress them. This is no mere fantasy, Macaulay tells us. After praising the novels of Samuel Richardson in terms that, to modern eyes, seem a little fervid ("No writings, those of Shakespeare excepted, show more profound knowledge of the human heart"), Macaulay recounts the story of Richardson's grandson, "a clergyman in the city of London." Though a "most upright and excellent man," the grandson "had conceived a strong prejudice against works of fiction," "thought all novel-reading not only frivolous but sinful," and "had never thought it right to read one of his grandfather's books."[33] Extended copyright terms might hand over the copyright to such a man. The public would lose, not because they had to pay exorbitant prices that denied some access to the work, but because the work would be altogether suppressed. Richardson's novels—*Pamela, Clarissa Harlowe*, and so on—are now the preserve of the classroom rather than the drawing room, so this might not seem like much of a loss. But Macaulay's next example is not so easy to dismiss.

> One of the most instructive, interesting, and delightful books in our language is Boswell's *Life of Johnson*. Now it is well known that Boswell's eldest son considered this book, considered the whole relation of Boswell to Johnson, as a blot in the escutcheon of the family. He thought, not perhaps altogether without reason, that his father had exhibited himself in a ludicrous and degrading light. And thus he became so sore and irritable that at last he could not bear to hear the *Life of Johnson* mentioned. Suppose that the law had been what my honourable and learned friend wishes to make it. Suppose that the copyright of Boswell's *Life of Johnson* had belonged, as it well might, during sixty years, to Boswell's eldest son. What would have been the consequence? An unadulterated copy of the finest biographical work in the world would have been as scarce as the first edition of Camden's *Britannia*.[34]

From more recent examples we can see that outright suppression is not the only thing to fear. The authors' heirs, or the corporations which have purchased their rights, may keep policing the boundaries of the work long after the original author is dead. In 2001, Alice Randall published *The Wind Done Gone*. As its title might indicate, *The Wind Done Gone* was a 220-page "critique of and reaction to" the world of *Gone With the Wind* by Margaret Mitchell.[35] Most crucially, perhaps, it was a version of *Gone With the Wind* told from the slaves' point of view. Suddenly the actions of Rhett ("R"), Scarlett ("Other"), and an obviously gay Ashley ("Dreamy Gentleman") come into new perspective through the eyes of Scarlett's "mulatto" half-sister. Mitchell's estate wanted to prevent publication of the book. At first they were successful.[36] As Yochai Benkler puts it,

> Alice Randall, an African American woman, was ordered by a government official not to publish her criticism of the romanticization of the Old South, at least not in the words she wanted to use. The official was not one of the many in Congress and the Administration who share the romantic view of the Confederacy. It was a federal judge in Atlanta who told Randall that she could not write her critique in the words she wanted to use—a judge enforcing copyright law.[37]

"They killed Miss Scarlett!" the astonished trial judge said after reading Randall's book. My colleague Jennifer Jenkins, one of the lawyers in the case, recounts that the judge saw the case in relentlessly physical terms, seeing the parody as a "bulldozer" and *Gone With the Wind* as a walled country estate into which the bulldozer had violently trespassed. He was consequently unimpressed with the claim that this "bulldozer" was protected by the First Amendment. Eventually, the court of appeals overturned the district court's judgment.[38] Fifty-two years after Margaret Mitchell's death, it was a hotly debated point how much leeway copyright gave to others to comment upon, critique, embellish upon, and parody the cultural icon she had conjured up.

A NATURAL RIGHT?

To some people, my argument so far—and Jefferson's and Macaulay's—will seem to miss the point. They see intellectual property rights not as an incentive, a method of encouraging the production and distribution of innovation, but as a natural or moral right. My book is mine because I wrote it, not because society or the law gives me some period of exclusivity over allowing the copying of its contents. My invention is mine because it came from my brain, not because the law declares a twenty-year monopoly over its production or distribution. My logo is mine because I worked hard on it, not because the state grants me a trademark in order to lower search costs and prevent consumer confusion. One answer is simply to say "In the United States, the framers of the Constitution, the legislature, and the courts have chosen to arrange things otherwise. In copyright, patent, and trademark law—despite occasional deviations—they have embraced the utilitarian view instead."

Broadly speaking, that answer is correct.[39] It also holds, to a lesser extent, in Britain. Even in the *droits d'auteur* countries, which have a markedly different copyright law regime, it largely holds for their patent and trademark law systems, and utilitarian strands suffuse even "the sacred rights of authors." So, on a national level, we have rejected or dramatically limited the natural rights view, and on an international level, we have rejected it in "industrial property"—patent and trademark—and modified it in copyright.

I think this answer is correct and important, but we have an obligation to go further. Partly that is because intuitions about ownership coming naturally with labor or discovery continue to influence the law. Partly it is because those moral intuitions are important and appealing. Partly it is because we might wish to modify or criticize our current system. Using the views of the framers, or current law, to preempt discussion is unsatisfactory—even though those views are of particular importance for the legal policy decisions we face in the short run, the issues on which much of my argument is concentrated.

There are varying stated grounds for natural or moral rights in intellectual creations. Some people may think the book is mine because I worked on it— a Lockean conception where I mix my sweat with these words and receive a property right in the process.

For all its attractions, there are considerable difficulties with such a view. Even within the world of tangible property, Locke's theory is more complicated than a simple equation of labor with property right. Jefferson's account of property is actually closer to Locke's than many would realize. When Jefferson points out the difficulty in justifying a natural right even in an acre of land, let alone a book, his premises are not radically different from Locke's. The same is true when Jefferson says that "[s]table ownership is the gift of social law, and is given late in the progress of society." Even if natural right does create the ground for the property claim, it is "social law" that shapes its contours and guarantees its stability. Jefferson, of course, thought that was particularly true for intellectual property rights. In that context, he felt the natural rights argument was much weaker and the need for socially defined purposive contours and limitations stronger.

Locke's own views on what we would think of as copyright are hard to determine. We do know that he had a strong antipathy to monopolies—particularly those affecting expression. He believed, for example, that giving publishers monopolies over great public domain books caused a disastrous fall in quality. Instead, he argued, such books should be open for all to compete to produce the best edition. Of course, he was writing in the context of monopolistic printing privileges—to which he was strongly opposed—rather than of individual authorial rights. Yet he went further and suggested that even for contemporary works, after a particular time in print—say fifty years—books could be printed by anyone.

> I demand whether, if another act for printing should be made, it be not reasonable that nobody should have any peculiar right in any book which has been in print fifty years, but any one as well as another might have liberty to print it: for by such titles as these, which lie dormant, and hinder others, many good books come quite to be lost.[40]

This sounds like a strongly utilitarian argument, rather than one based on labor and natural right. Of course, we are not bound by what Locke or Jefferson thought. Still it is striking to see the turn to a utilitarian conception from both of them.

The Lockean tradition is not the only one, of course. Others believe that the property right stems from the unique personality of each individual—the configurations of your individual genius made manifest in the lines of your sonnet. (Some limit the natural right to literary and expressive work; can a mousetrap or a drug molecule express the riddle and wonder of the human spirit?) Whatever their moral basis or their ambit, the common ground between these positions is the belief in a rationale for intellectual property rights beyond the utilitarian concerns of Jefferson or Macaulay.

The norms embodied in the moral rights or natural rights tradition are deeply attractive—at least to me. Many of us feel a special connection to our expressive creations—even the humble ones such as a term paper or a birthday poem. It is one of the reasons that the central moral rights in the French *droits d'auteur*, or author's rights, tradition resonate so strongly with us. The entitlement of an author to be correctly attributed, to have some control over the integrity of his work, seems important regardless of its utilitarian functions.

Yet even as we find this claim attractive, we become aware of the need to find limiting principles to it. It gives us pause to think that Margaret Mitchell or her heirs could forbid someone parodying her work. Are there no free-speech limitations? When other forms of authorship, such as computer programs, are brought into copyright's domain, does the power of the moral right decrease, while the need to limit its scope intensifies?

Then there is the question of length. How long is a natural right in expression or invention supposed to last? It seems absurd to imagine that Shakespeare's or Mozart's heirs, or those who had bought their copyrights, would still be controlling the performance, reproduction, and interpretation of their works hundreds of years after their death. If the rights are truly formed for a nonutilitarian purpose, after all, why should they expire? The person who first acquires property rights in land by work or conquest passes those rights down to heirs and buyers with the chain of transmission reaching to the present day. Should copyright follow suit? Even in France, the home of the strongest form of the *droits d'auteur* and of the "moral rights" tradition, the answer to this question was in the negative.

We owe a large part of the literary moral rights tradition to the immediate aftermath of the French Revolution. In France before the Revolution, as in England before the Statute of Anne, the first true copyright legislation, the regulation of publishing was through a set of "privileges" given to printers, not rights given to authors. Publishers would have a guild-enforced monopoly over certain titles. Their right was against competing publishers printing the list of titles over which they had the privilege. The Revolution abolished these privileges and, at first, put nothing in their place. On the other hand, as Carla Hesse's fascinating work reveals, there was intermittent interference by the Prefecture of Police with those who copied most flagrantly. One such publisher was sternly instructed by the police in these terms:

> [A]ccording to the Declaration of the Rights of Man, liberty means only the freedom to do what does not harm others; and that it harms others to appropriate the work of an author, because it is an infringement of the sacred right of property; and that such an enterprise, if it were to remain unpunished, would deprive citizens of the instruction they await from celebrated authors like M. Bernardin de St. Pierre, because no author would want to consecrate his labors to the instruction of his age if piracy were ever authorized.[41]

Note the interesting mixture of the language of the "sacred rights of property" and the strong utilitarian justification which cites effects on future literary production and the "instruction" of citizens.

More expansive conceptions of the rights of authors and, particularly, of publishers were also offered. Even before the Revolution, publishers had been making the arguments that their privileges were a form of property rights and had the very good sense to hire the young Diderot to make those arguments. Hesse quotes his words:

> What form of wealth could belong to a man, if not a work of the mind, . . . if not his own thoughts, . . . the most precious part of himself, that will never perish, that will immortalize him? What comparison could there be between a man, the very substance of man, his soul, and a field, a tree, a vine, that nature has offered in the beginning equally to all, and that an individual has only appropriated through cultivating it?[42]

Diderot's theme is that authors' rights should actually be stronger than other property rights for two reasons. First, they relate to the very essence of the person, the most "precious part of himself." Second, they are the only property rights over something that has been added to the existing store of wealth rather than taken from it. Authorial property, unlike property in land, adds to the common store rather than detracting from it. Locke believed that a just assertion of property rights must leave "enough and as good" for others in the society. What could better satisfy this condition than a property right over a novel that did not exist before I wrote it? One hundred years later Victor Hugo echoed the same thoughts in a speech to the Conseil d'Etat and pointed out at the same time that literary property rights could potentially "reconcile" troublesome authors to society and state.

> You feel the importance and necessity of defending property today. Well, begin by recognising the first and most sacred of all properties, the one which is neither a transmission nor an acquisition but a creation, namely literary property . . . reconcile the artists with society by means of property.[43]

Diderot wanted perpetual copyrights for authors and, agreeably to his employers, a correspondingly perpetual printing privilege. If the author's heirs could not be traced, the copyright would devolve to the current publisher.

But as Hesse points out, there was another view of literary property—a much more skeptical one put forward best by Condorcet. This view is also an influential part of the heritage of the *droits d'auteur*, even if it is downplayed in its contemporary rhetoric. Condorcet began by framing the question of literary property as one of political liberty. "Does a man have the right to forbid another man to write the same words that he himself wrote first? That is the question to resolve."[44] Like Jefferson, Condorcet is utterly unconvinced that property rights in a book can be compared to those in a field or a piece of furniture which can be occupied or used by only one man. The type of property is "based on the nature of the thing." He concluded, again in language strikingly similar to Jefferson's and Macaulay's, that literary property was not a real property right but a privilege, and one which must be assessed on a utilitarian basis in terms of its contribution to enlightenment.[45]

> Any privilege therefore imposes a hindrance on freedom, placing a restriction on the rights of other citizens; As such it is not only harmful to the rights of others who want to copy, but the rights of all those who want copies, and that which increases the price is an injustice. Does the public interest require that men make this sacrifice? That is the question that must be considered; In other words, are [literary] privileges needed and useful or harmful to the progress of enlightenment?[46]

Condorcet's conclusion was that they were not necessary and that they could be harmful. "The books that most furthered the progress of enlightenment, the *Encyclopédie*, the works of Montesquieu, Voltaire, Rousseau, have not enjoyed the benefits of a privilege." Instead he seemed to favor a combination of "subscriptions" to authors with a trademark-like protection which allowed an author to identify a particular edition of his work as the genuine one, but which also allowed competing editions to circulate freely. In such a market, he believed that the price of the competing editions would fall to "natural" levels—today we would call it marginal cost—but the original author would still be able to charge a modest premium for the edition he authorized or certified because readers would prefer it as both more accurate and more authentic. One possible analogy is to the history of the fashion industry in the United States. It operates largely without design protection but relies heavily on the trademarks accorded to favored designers and brands. There are "knockoffs" of Armani or Balenciaga, but the wealthy still pay an enormous premium for the real thing.

Condorcet also insisted that whatever protection was accorded to literary works must not extend to the ideas within them. It is the truths within books that make them "useful"—a word that does not have the same luminance and importance for us today as it did for the philosophers of the Enlightenment or the French Revolution. He argued that any privilege given the author could not extend to "preventing another man from exhibiting the same truths, in perfectly the same order, from the same evidence" or from extending those arguments and developing their consequences. In a line that Hesse rightly highlights, he declares that any privileges do not extend over facts or ideas. "Ce n'est pas pour les choses, les idées; c'est pour les mots, pour le nom de l'auteur."

In sum, Condorcet favors a limited privilege, circumscribed by an inquiry into its effects in promoting progress and enlightenment. The privilege only applies to expression and to "the author's name," rather than to facts and ideas. This is very much within the tradition of Jefferson and Macaulay.

Hesse argues, correctly I think, that two warring ideas shaped—or are at least useful ways of understanding—the development of the *droits d'auteur* tradition. On one side were Diderot and the publishers promoting an expansive and perpetual natural authorial right, which nevertheless was supposed to vest suspiciously easily in publishers. On the other was Condorcet, looking skeptically at authorial privileges as merely one type of state interference with free markets and the free circulation of books and ideas. In place of Diderot's perpetual natural right, Condorcet sketched out a regime that encourages production and distribution by granting the minimum rights necessary for progress.

Different as they are, these two sides share a common ground. They both focus, though for different reasons, on "expression"—the imprimatur of the author's unique human spirit on the ideas and facts that he or she transmits. It is this "original expression" that modern copyright and the modern *droits d'auteur* actually cover. In today's copyright law, the facts and ideas in an author's work proceed immediately into the public domain. In other work, I have argued that by confining the property right tightly to the "original expression" stemming from the unique personality of an individual author the law seems to accomplish a number of things simultaneously. It provides

a *conceptual basis* for partial, limited property rights, without completely collaps-
ing the notion of property into the idea of a temporary, limited, utilitarian state
grant, revocable at will. [At the same time it offers] a *moral and philosophical justification* for fencing in the commons, giving the author property in something
built from the resources of the public domain—language, culture, genre, scientific community, or what have you. If one makes originality of spirit the assumed
feature of authorship and the touchstone for property rights, one can see the
author as creating something entirely *new*—not recombining the resources of the
commons.[47]

That is an account of the romantic theory of authorship in the context of
contemporary Anglo-American copyright law. But when one looks at the history of the French *droits d'auteur* tradition, it is striking how well those words
describe that system as well. When the French legislature finally produced a
law of authors' rights it turned out, in Hesse's words, to reflect "an epistemo-
logically impure and unstable legal synthesis that combined an instrumentalist
notion of the public good with a theory of authorship based on natural rights."

Although it drew on a Diderotist rhetoric of the sanctity of individual creativity as
an inviolable right, it did not rigorously respect the conclusions Diderot drew from
this position. In contrast to the *privilège d'auteur* of 1777, the law did not recognize
the author's claim beyond his lifetime but consecrated the notion, advanced first by
Pierre Manuel to defend his edition of Mirabeau, that the only true heir to an
author's work was the nation as a whole. This notion of a public domain, of democratic access to a common cultural inheritance on which no particular claim could
be made, bore the traces not of Diderot, but of Condorcet's faith that truths were
given in nature and, although mediated through individual minds, belonged ultimately to all. Progress in human understanding depended not on private knowledge claims, but on free and equal access to enlightenment. An author's property
rights were conceived as recompense for his service as an agent of enlightenment
through publication of his ideas. The law of 1793 accomplished this task of synthesis through political negotiation rather than philosophical reasoning—that is, by
refashioning the political identity of the author in the first few years of the Revolution from a privileged creature of the absolutist police state into a servant of public
enlightenment.[48]

Hesse argues that this instability would continue through the revolutionary
period. I agree; indeed I would argue that it does so to the present day. Why?
The answer is simple. The moral rights view simply proved too much. Without
a limiting principle—of time, or scope, or effect—it seemed to presage a perpetual and expansive control of expressive creations, and perhaps of inventions.

Our intuition that this is a bad idea comes from our intuitive understanding that "Poetry can only be made out of other poems; novels out of other novels. All of this was much clearer before the assimilation of literature to private enterprise."[49]

This is the flip side of the arguments that Diderot and later Hugo put forward. Perhaps the romantic author does not create out of thin air. Perhaps he or she is deeply embedded in a literary, musical, cultural, or scientific tradition that would not flourish if treated as a set of permanently walled private plots. Even within the *droits d'auteur* tradition, we see a recognition that the continuing progress of enlightenment and the sacred genius of authors might both require a certain level of freedom in knowledge inputs and a certain level of control over knowledge outputs. We see also the recognition that these two requirements are in fundamental tension. When it comes to reconciling that tension we must turn in part to utilitarian effects. In short, we should pay attention to Jefferson and Macaulay and Condorcet, not just because their thoughts shaped the legal and philosophical traditions in which we now work—though that is particularly true in the case of the United States—but because they were right, or at least more right than the alternative.

Of course, we could build a culture around a notion of natural, absolute, and permanent rights to invention and expression. It is not a world many of us would want to live in. There are exceptions of course. In a recent *New York Times* op-ed, Mark Helprin—author of *Winter's Tale*—argued that intellectual property should become perpetual.[50] After all, rights in real estate or personal property do not expire—though their owners might. Why is it that copyrights should "only" last for a lifetime plus seventy additional years, or patents for a mere twenty? Mr. Helprin expresses respect for the genius of the framers, but is unmoved by their firm command that rights be granted only for "limited times." He concludes that it was a misunderstanding. Jefferson did not realize that while ideas cannot be owned, their expression can. What's more, the framers were misled by their rustic times. "No one except perhaps Hamilton or Franklin might have imagined that services and intellectual property would become primary fields of endeavor and the chief engines of the economy. Now they are, and it is no more rational to deny them equal status than it would have been to confiscate farms, ropewalks and other forms of property in the 18th century." Poor Jefferson. How lucky we are to have Mr. Helprin to remedy the consequences of his lack of vision.

Or perhaps not. Think of the way that Jefferson traced the origins of the mechanical arts used in the elevators and hopper-boys all the way back to ancient Persia. (In Mr. Helprin's utopia, presumably, a royalty stream would run to Cyrus the Great's engineers.) Jefferson's point was that for the process of invention to work, we need to confine narrowly the time and scope of the state-provided monopoly, otherwise further inventions would become impossible. Each process or part of a new invention would risk infringing a myriad of prior patents on its subcomponents. Innovation would strangle in a thicket of conflicting monopolies with their roots vanishing back in time. Presumably the title of Mr. Helprin's excellent novel would require clearance from Shakespeare's heirs.

Of course, one could construct a more modest Lockean idea of intellectual property[51]—building on the notion of "enough and as good" left over for others and drawing the limits tightly enough to avoid the worst of Mr. Helprin's excesses. But as one attempts to do this systematically, the power of the Jeffersonian vision becomes all the more apparent—at least as a starting place.

The Jefferson Warning will play an important role in this book. But my arguments here have implications far beyond Jefferson's time, country, or constitutional tradition. In the last analysis, I hope to convince you of the importance of the Jefferson Warning or the views of Macaulay not because they are famous authorities and revered thinkers or because they framed constitutions or debated legislation. I wish to convince you that their views are important because they encapsulate neatly an important series of truths about intellectual property. We should listen to the Jefferson Warning not because it is prestigious but because of its insight. As the Diderot-Condorcet debates point out, the questions on which Jefferson and Macaulay focused do not disappear merely because one embraces a philosophy of moral rights—if anything, they become more pressing, particularly when one comes to define the limits of intellectual property in scope and time. I ask that those readers who remain leery of the Jeffersonian focus concentrate on that last issue. In an era when we have been expanding intellectual property rights relentlessly, it is a crucial one. If the Jefferson Warning produces in my unconvinced reader even a slight queasiness about the likely effects of such a process of expansion, it will have done its job—though in fact the tradition it represented was much richer than a simple utilitarian series of cautions.

A TRADITION OF SKEPTICAL MINIMALISM

Eighteenth- and nineteenth-century intellectual property debates went beyond Macaulay's antimonopolist focus on price, access, quality, and control of the nation's literary heritage. While Macaulay is the best-remembered English skeptic from the 1840s, there were other, more radical skeptics who saw copyright primarily as a "tax on literacy" or a "tax on knowledge," identical in its effects to the newspaper stamp taxes.[52] This was a time when mass literacy and mass education were the hotly debated corollaries to the enlargement of the franchise. The radical reformers looked with hostility on anything that seemed likely to raise the cost of reading and thus continue to restrict political and social debate to the wealthier classes. Macaulay worried about a world in which "a copy of *Clarissa* would . . . [be] as rare as an Aldus or a Caxton."[53] His more radical colleagues saw copyright—to use our ugly jargon rather than theirs—as one of the many ways in which state communications policy is set and the communicative landscape tilted to favor the rich and powerful.[54] Macaulay worried about the effects of monopoly on literature and culture. All of them worried about the effects of copyright on democracy, on speech, on education. In the world of the Internet, these skeptics too have their contemporary equivalents.

Patent law also attracted its share of attacks in the mid-nineteenth century. A fusillade of criticism, often delivered by economists and cast in the language of free trade, portrayed the patent system as actively harmful.

> At the annual meeting of the Kongress deutscher Volkswirthe held in Dresden, September 1863, the following resolution was adopted "by an overwhelming majority": "Considering that patents hinder rather than further the progress of invention; that they hamper the prompt general utilization of useful inventions; that on balance they cause more harm than benefit to the inventors themselves and, thus, are a highly deceptive form of compensation; the Congress of German Economists resolves: that patents of invention are injurious to common welfare."[55]

In the Netherlands, the patent system was actually abolished in 1869 as a result of such criticisms. Observers in a number of other countries, including Britain, concluded that their national patent systems were doomed. Various proposals were made to replace patents, with state-provided prizes or bounties to particularly useful inventions being the most popular.[56]

These snippets are hardly sufficient to constitute any kind of survey of critical reactions to intellectual property systems, but I believe that nevertheless they give us some sense of typical debates. What do these debates tell us?

From the early days of intellectual property as we know it now, the main objections raised against it were framed in the language of free trade and "anti-monopoly." In the United States, the founding generation of intellectuals had been nurtured on the philosophy of the Scottish Enlightenment and the history of the struggle against royal monopolies. They saw the arguments in favor of intellectual property but warned again and again of the need to circumscribe both its term and its scope. This is the point at the heart of Jefferson's letter. This is why he insisted that we understand the policy implications of the differences between tangible property and ideas, which "like fire" are "expansible over all space, without lessening their density in any point."

What were the concerns of these early critics? They worried about intellectual property producing artificial scarcity, high prices, and low quality. They insisted that the benefits of each incremental expansion of intellectual property be weighed against its costs. Think of Macaulay discussing Johnson's preference for a shin of beef rather than another slice of postmortem copyright protection. They worried about its justice; given that we all learn from and build on the past, do we have a right to carve out our own incremental innovations and protect them by intellectual property rights?[57] Price aside, they also worried that intellectual property (especially with a lengthy term) might give too much control to a single individual or corporation over some vital aspect of science and culture. In more muted fashion, they discussed the possible effects that intellectual property might have on future innovation. The most radical among them worried about intellectual property's effects on political debate, education, and even control of the communications infrastructure, though they did not use that particular phrase. But the overwhelming theme was the promotion of free trade and a corresponding opposition to monopolies.

Now if we were to stop here and simply require that today's policy makers, legislators, and judges recite the Jefferson Warning before they rush off to make new intellectual property rules for the Internet and the genome, we would have accomplished a great deal. National and international policy makers are keen to set the "rules of the road for the digital age." If they would momentarily pause their excited millenarian burbling and read the points scratched out with a quill pen in 1813, or delivered (without PowerPoint support) on the floor of the House of Commons in the 1840s, we would be better off. Everyone is beginning to understand that in the world of the twenty-first century the rules of intellectual property are both vital and contentious. How good it would be then if our debate on intellectual property policy were as vigorous and as informed as the debates of the nineteenth century. (Though we might hope it would also be more democratic.)

And yet . . . there is much that is missing from the skepticism of the eighteenth and nineteenth centuries and much that remains unclear. Look at the structure of these comments; they are framed as criticisms of intellectual property rather than defenses of the public domain or the commons, terms that simply do not appear in the debates. There is no real discussion of the world of intellectual property's outside, its opposite. Most of these critics take as their goal the prevention or limitation of an "artificial" monopoly; without this monopoly our goal is to have a world of—what? The assumption is that we will return to a norm of freedom, but of what kind? Free trade in expression and innovation, as opposed to monopoly? Free access to expression and innovation, as opposed to access for pay? Or free access to innovation and expression in the sense of not being subject to the right of another person to pick and choose who is given access, even if all have to pay some flat fee? Or is it common ownership and control that we seek, including the communal right to forbid certain kinds of uses of the shared resource? The eighteenth- and nineteenth-century critics brushed over these points; but to be fair, we continue to do so today. The opposite of property, or perhaps we should say the *opposites* of property, are much more obscure to us than property itself.

For the most part, the antimonopolist view of intellectual property makes a simple case. Monopolies are bad. Have as few as possible and make them as narrow and as short as possible. This is a fine principle, but it falls short of an affirmative explanation and defense of the role of the public domain or the commons in enabling creativity, culture, and science. That is a shame because just as intellectual property is different from tangible property, so too is its opposite, its outside.

What are those opposites? The two major terms in use are "the public domain" and "the commons." Both are used in multiple ways—probably a good thing. The public domain is material that is not covered by intellectual property rights. Material might be in the public domain because it was never capable of being owned. Examples would be the English language or the formulae of Newtonian physics. Alternatively, something might be in the public domain because rights have expired. The works of Shakespeare or the patents over powered flight are examples.

Some definitions of the public domain are more granular. They focus not only on complete works but on the reserved spaces of freedom inside intellectual property. The public domain would include the privilege to excerpt short quotations in a review. This vision is messier, but more instructive. If one uses a spatial metaphor, the absolutist vision is a tessellated map. Areas of private property are neatly delineated from areas of the public domain. Mozart's plot sits next to that of Britney Spears; one public, the other private. In the granular view, the map is more complex. Ms. Spears' plot is cut through with rights to make fair use, as well as with limitations on ownership of standard themes. Instead of the simple tiled map, the granular vision has private plots with public roads running through them.

In popular discussion, we tend to use the absolutist view of both property and the public domain. Lawyers prefer the more complex view of property and are coming slowly to have a similarly complex view of the public domain. That is the definition I will be using.

The term "commons" is generally used to denote a resource over which some group has access and use rights—albeit perhaps under certain conditions. It is used in even more ways than the term "public domain." The first axis along which definitions of the term "commons" vary is the size of the group that has access rights. Some would say it is a commons only if the whole society has access. That is the view I will take here.

The other difference between public domain and commons is the extent of restrictions on use. Material in the public domain is free of property rights. You may do with it what you wish. A commons can be restrictive. For example, some open source software makes your freedom to modify the software contingent on the condition that your contributions, too, will be freely open to others. I will discuss this type of commons in Chapter 8.

So these are working definitions of public domain and commons. But why should we *care*? Because the public domain is the basis for our art, our science, and our self-understanding. It is the raw material from which we make new inventions and create new cultural works. Why is it so important? Let us start with the dry reasons.

Information and innovation are largely nonrival and nonexcludable goods. This is Jefferson's point, though expressed in less graceful language. It has some interesting corollaries. Information is hard to value until you have it, but once you have it, how can you dispossess yourself of it? The apple can be taken back by the merchant if you decide not to buy. The facts or the formulae cannot. The moment when you might have decided to pay or not to pay is already over. The great economist Kenneth Arrow formalized this insight about information economics,[58] and it profoundly shapes intellectual property policy. (To a large extent, for example, the requirement of "patent disclosure" attempts to solve this problem. I can read all about your mousetrap but I am still forbidden from using it. I can decide whether or not to license your design at that point.) But for all the material in the public domain, where no intellectual property right is necessary, this point is solved elegantly by having the information be "free as the air to common use." All of us can use the same store of information, innovation, and free culture. It will be available at its cost of reproduction—close to zero—and we can all build upon it without interfering with each other. Think of the English language, basic business methods, tables of logarithms, the Pythagorean theorem, Shakespeare's insights about human nature, the periodic table, Ohm's law, the sonnet form, the musical scale.

Would you have paid to purchase access to each of these? I might tell you that English was a superior communication tool—a really good command language for your cognitive operating system. There could be levels of access with corresponding prices. Would you pay to get access to "English Professional Edition"? We can certainly imagine such a way of organizing languages. (To some extent, scribal conventions operated this way. The languages of the professions still do. One paid for access to "law French" in the common law courts of England. One pays for an interpreter of contemporary legal jargon in today's legal system. But even there the language is free to the autodidact.) We can imagine language, scientific knowledge, basic algebra, the tonic scale, or the classics of four-hundred-year-old literature all being available only as property. Those who had the highest "value for use" would purchase them. Those who did not value them highly—whether because they could not know what could be built with them until they had done so or because they did not have the money—would not. What would this world, this culture, this science, this market look like?

It would probably be very inefficient, the economists tell us. Perfect information is a defining feature of the perfect market. The more commodified and restricted our access to information, the less efficient the operation of the market, the more poorly it allocates resources in our society. (The permanent and in some sense insoluble tension between the need to provide incentives to generate information, thus raising its cost, and the need to have access to perfect information for efficiency is the central feature of our intellectual property policy.)[59] When we commodify too much we actually undermine creativity, since we are raising the price of the inputs for future creations—which might themselves be covered by intellectual property rights. But "inefficient" is too bloodless a way to describe this world. It would be awful.

Our markets, our democracy, our science, our traditions of free speech, and our art all depend more heavily on a public domain of freely available material than they do on the informational material that is covered by property rights. The public domain is not some gummy residue left behind when all the good stuff has been covered by property law. The public domain is the place we quarry the building blocks of our culture. It is, in fact, the *majority* of our culture. Or at least it has been.

I deliberately gave easy examples. It is obvious how unnecessary but also how harmful it would be to extend property rights to language, to facts, to business methods and scientific algorithms, to the basic structures of music, to art whose creators are long dead. It is obvious that this would not produce more innovation, more debate, more art, more democracy. But what about the places where the value of the public domain is not obvious?

What if we were actually moving to extend patents to business methods, or intellectual property rights to unoriginal compilations of facts? What if we had locked up most of twentieth-century culture without getting a net benefit in return? What if the basic building blocks of new scientific fields were being patented long before anything concrete or useful could be built from them? What if we were littering our electronic communication space with digital barbed wire and regulating the tiniest fragments of music as if they were stock certificates? What if we were doing all this in the blithe belief that more property rights mean more innovation? The story of this book is that we are.

The Jefferson Warning is important. It is, however, just a warning. While it would be excellent to print it on pocket cards and hand it to our elected representatives, that alone will not solve the most pressing problems we face. In the chapters that follow, I shall try to go further. In Chapter 3, I set the process of expansion we are engaged in—our "second enclosure movement"—in perspective by comparing it to the original enclosures of the grassy commons of old England. In Chapter 4, I jump from the world of the fifteenth or nineteenth century to the world of the twenty-first, from elevators and grain hoppers to video recorders, the Internet, and file-sharing services. I use the story of several key legal disputes to illustrate a broader history—the history of intellectual property's struggle with communications technologies that allow people to copy more cheaply. Strangely enough, the Jefferson Warning will be crucial in understanding the debate over copyright online and, in particular, in understanding the fear that drives our current policy making, a fear I refer to as the Internet Threat.

3
The Second Enclosure Movement

The law locks up the man or woman
Who steals the goose from off the common
But leaves the greater villain loose
Who steals the common from off the goose.

The law demands that we atone
When we take things we do not own
But leaves the lords and ladies fine
Who take things that are yours and mine.

The poor and wretched don't escape
If they conspire the law to break;
This must be so but they endure
Those who conspire to make the law.

The law locks up the man or woman
Who steals the goose from off the common
And geese will still a common lack
Till they go and steal it back.

[Anon.][1]

In fits and starts from the fifteenth to the nineteenth century, the English "commons" was "enclosed."[2] Enclosure did not necessarily mean physical fencing, though that could happen. More likely, the previously common land was simply converted into private property, generally controlled by a single landholder.

The poem that begins this chapter is the pithiest condemnation of the process. It manages in a few lines to criticize double standards, expose the controversial nature of property rights, and take a slap at the legitimacy of state power. And it does this all with humor, without jargon, and in rhyming couplets. Academics should take note. Like most criticisms of the enclosure movement, the poem depicts a world of rapacious, state-aided "privatization," a conversion into private property of something that had formerly been common property or perhaps had been outside the property system altogether. One kind of "stealing" is legal, says the poet, because the state changes the law of property to give the "lords and ladies" a right over an area formerly open to all. But let a commoner steal something and he is locked up.

The anonymous author was not alone in feeling indignant. Thomas More (one of only two saints to write really good political theory) made similar points, though he used sheep rather than geese in his argument. Writing in the sixteenth century, he had argued that enclosure was not merely unjust in itself but harmful in its consequences: a cause of economic inequality, crime, and social dislocation. In a wonderfully bizarre passage he argues that sheep are a principal cause of theft. Sheep? Why, yes.

> [Y]our sheep that were wont to be so meek and tame, and so small eaters, now, as I hear say, be become so great devourers and so wild, that they eat up, and swallow down the very men themselves. They consume, destroy, and devour whole fields, houses, and cities.

Who were these sheep? Bizarre Dolly-like clones? Transgenic killer rams? No. More meant only that under the economic lure of the wool trade, the "noblemen and gentlemen" were attempting their own enclosure movement.

> [They] leave no ground for tillage, they enclose all into pastures; they throw down houses; they pluck down towns, and leave nothing standing, but only the church to be made a sheep-house. . . . Therefore that one covetous and insatiable cormorant and very plague of his native country may compass about and enclose many thousand acres of ground together within one pale or hedge, the husbandmen be thrust out of their own.[3]

The sheep devour all. The dispossessed "husbandmen" now find themselves without land or money and turn instead to theft. In More's vision, it is all very simple. Greed leads to enclosure. Enclosure disrupts the life of the poor farmer. Disruption leads to crime and violence.

Writing 400 years later, Karl Polanyi echoes More precisely. He calls the enclosure movement "a revolution of the rich against the poor" and goes on to paint it in the most unflattering light. "The lords and nobles were upsetting the social order, breaking down ancient law and custom, sometimes by means of violence, often by pressure and intimidation. They were literally robbing the poor of their share in the common. . . ."[4] And turning them to "beggars and thieves." The critics of enclosure saw other harms too, though they are harder to classify. They bemoaned the relentless power of market logic to migrate to new areas, disrupting traditional social relationships and perhaps even views of the self, or the relationship of human beings to the environment. Fundamentally, they mourned the loss of a form of life.

So much for the bad side of the enclosure movement. For many economic historians, everything I have said up to now is the worst kind of sentimental bunk, romanticizing a form of life that was neither comfortable nor noble, and certainly not very egalitarian. The big point about the enclosure movement is that it worked; this innovation in property systems allowed an unparalleled expansion of productive possibilities.[5] By transferring inefficiently managed common land into the hands of a single owner, enclosure escaped the aptly named "tragedy of the commons." It gave incentives for large-scale investment, allowed control over exploitation, and in general ensured that resources could be put to their most efficient use. Before the enclosure movement, the feudal lord would not invest in drainage systems, sheep purchases, or crop rotation that might increase yields from the common—he knew all too well that the fruits of his labor could be appropriated by others. The strong private property rights and single-entity control that were introduced in the enclosure movement avoid the tragedies of overuse and underinvestment: more grain will be grown, more sheep raised, consumers will benefit, and fewer people will starve in the long run.[6]

If the price of this social gain is a greater concentration of economic power, the introduction of market forces into areas where they previously had not been so obvious, or the disruption of a modus vivendi with the environment—then, enclosure's defenders say, so be it! In their view, the agricultural surplus produced by enclosure helped to save a society devastated by the mass deaths of the sixteenth century. Those who weep over the terrible effects of private property should realize that it literally saves lives.

Now it is worth noting that while this view was once unchallenged,[7] recent scholarship has thrown some doubts on the effects of enclosure on agricultural production.[8] Some scholars argue that the commons was actually better run than the defenders of enclosure admit.[9] Thus, while enclosure did produce the changes in the distribution of wealth that so incensed an earlier generation of critical historians, they argue that there are significant questions about whether it led to greater efficiency or innovation. The pie was carved up differently, but did it get bigger? The debate about these issues is little known, however, outside the world of economic historians. "Everyone" knows that a commons is by definition tragic and that the logic of enclosure is as true today as it was in the fifteenth century. I will not get involved in this debate. Assume for the sake of argument that enclosure did indeed produce a surge in agriculture. Assume, in other words, that converting the commons into private property saved lives. This is the logic of enclosure. It is a powerful argument, but it is not always right.

This is all very well, but what does it have to do with intellectual property? I hope the answer is obvious. The argument of this book is that we are in the middle of a second enclosure movement. While it sounds grandiloquent to call it "the enclosure of the intangible commons of the mind," in a very real sense that is just what it is.[10] True, the new state-created property rights may be "intellectual" rather than "real," but once again things that were formerly thought of as common property, or as "uncommodifiable," or outside the market altogether, are being covered with new, or newly extended, property rights.

Take the human genome as an example. Again, the supporters of enclosure have argued that the state was right to step in and extend the reach of property rights; that only thus could we guarantee the kind of investment of time, ingenuity, and capital necessary to produce new drugs and gene therapies.[11] To the question, "Should there be patents over human genes?" the supporters of enclosure would answer that private property saves lives.[12] The opponents of enclosure have claimed that the human genome belongs to everyone, that it is literally the common heritage of humankind, that it should not and perhaps in some sense *cannot* be owned, and that the consequences of turning over the human genome to private property rights will be dreadful, as market logic invades areas which should be the farthest from the market. In stories about stem cell and gene sequence patents, critics have mused darkly about the way in which the state is handing over monopoly power to a few individuals and corporations, potentially introducing bottlenecks and coordination costs that slow down innovation.[13]

Alongside these accounts of the beneficiaries of the new property scheme run news stories about those who were not so fortunate, the commoners of the genetic enclosure. Law students across America read *Moore v. Regents of University of California,* a California Supreme Court case deciding that Mr. Moore had no property interest in the cells derived from his spleen.[14] The court tells us that giving private property rights to "sources" would slow the freewheeling practice researchers have of sharing their cell lines with all and sundry.[15] The doctors whose inventive genius created a billion-dollar cell line from Mr. Moore's "naturally occurring raw material," by contrast, are granted a patent. Private property rights here, by contrast, are a necessary incentive to research.[16] Economists on both sides of the enclosure debate concentrate on the efficient allocation of rights. Popular discussion, on the other hand, doubtless demonstrating a reprehensible lack of rigor, returns again and again to more naturalistic assumptions such as the essentially "common" quality of the property involved or the idea that one owns one's own body.[17]

The genome is not the only area to be partially "enclosed" during this second enclosure movement. The expansion of intellectual property rights has been remarkable—from business method patents, to the Digital Millennium Copyright Act, to trademark "anti-dilution" rulings, to the European Database Protection Directive.[18] The old limits to intellectual property rights—the antierosion walls around the public domain—are also under attack. The annual process of updating my syllabus for a basic intellectual property course provides a nice snapshot of what is going on. I can wax nostalgic looking back to a five-year-old text, with its confident list of subject matter that intellectual property rights could not cover, the privileges that circumscribed the rights that did exist, and the length of time before a work falls into the public domain. In each case, the limits have been eaten away.

HOW MUCH OF THE INTANGIBLE
COMMONS SHOULD WE ENCLOSE?

So far I have argued that there are profound similarities between the first enclosure movement and our contemporary expansion of intellectual property, which I call the second enclosure movement. Once again, the critics and proponents of enclosure are locked in battle, hurling at each other incommensurable claims about innovation, efficiency, traditional values, the boundaries of the market, the saving of lives, the loss of familiar liberties. Once again, opposition to enclosure is portrayed as economically illiterate: the beneficiaries of enclosure telling us that an expansion of property rights is needed in order to fuel progress. Indeed, the post-Cold War "Washington consensus" is invoked to claim that the lesson of history itself is that the only way to get growth and efficiency is through markets; property rights, surely, are the sine qua non of markets.[19]

This faith in enclosure is rooted in a correspondingly deep pessimism about the possibility of managing resources that are either commonly owned or owned by no one. If all have the right to graze their herds on common land, what incentive does anyone have to hold back? My attempt to safeguard the future of the pasture will simply be undercut by others anxious to get theirs while the getting is good. Soon the pasture will be overgrazed and all our flocks will go hungry. In a 1968 article, Garrett Hardin came up with the phrase that would become shorthand for the idea that there were inherent problems with collectively managed resources: "the tragedy of the commons."[20] The phrase, more so than the actual arguments in his article, has come to exercise considerable power over our policies today. Private property—enclosure—is portrayed as the happy ending for the tragedy of the commons: when policy makers see a resource that is unowned, they tend to reach reflexively for "the solving idea of property." According to this view, enclosure is not a "revolution of the rich against the poor," it is a revolution to save the waste of socially vital resources. To say that some social resource is *not* owned by an individual, that it is free as the air to common use, is automatically to conjure up the idea that it is being wasted.

But if there are similarities between our two enclosures, there are also profound dissimilarities; the networked commons of the mind has many different characteristics from the grassy commons of Old England.[21] I want to concentrate here on two key differences between the intellectual commons and the commons of the first enclosure movement, differences that should lead us to question whether this commons is truly tragic and to ask whether stronger intellectual property rights really are the solution to our problems. These differences are well known, indeed they are the starting point for most intellectual property law, a starting point that Jefferson and Macaulay have already laid out for us. Nevertheless, reflection on them might help to explain both the problems and the stakes in the current wave of expansion.

Unlike the earthy commons, the commons of the mind is generally "nonrival." Many uses of land are mutually exclusive: if I am using the field for grazing, it may interfere with your plans to use it for growing crops. By contrast, a gene sequence, an MP3 file, or an image may be used by multiple parties; my use does not interfere with yours. To simplify a complicated analysis, this means that the threat of overuse of fields and fisheries is generally not a problem with the informational or innovational commons.[22] Thus, one type of tragedy of the commons is avoided.

The concerns in the informational commons have to do with a different kind of collective action problem: the problem of incentives to create the resource in the first place. The difficulty comes from the assumption that information goods are not only nonrival (uses do not interfere with each other), but also nonexcludable (it is impossible, or at least hard, to stop one unit of the good from satisfying an infinite number of users at zero marginal cost). Pirates will copy the song, the mousetrap, the drug formula, the brand. The rest of the argument is well known. Lacking an ability to exclude, creators will be unable to charge for their creations; there will be inadequate incentives to create. Thus, the law must step in and create a limited monopoly called an intellectual property right.

How about the argument that the increasing importance of information-intensive products to the world economy means that protection must increase? Must the information commons be enclosed because it is now a more important sector of economic activity?[23] This was certainly one of the arguments for the first enclosure movement. For example, during the Napoleonic Wars enclosure was defended as a necessary method of increasing the efficiency of agricultural production, now a vital sector of a wartime economy.

Here we come to another big difference between the commons of the mind and the earthy commons. As has frequently been pointed out, information products are often made up of fragments of other information products; your information output is someone else's information input.[24] These inputs may be snippets of code, discoveries, prior research, images, genres of work, cultural references, or databases of single nucleotide polymorphisms—each is raw material for future innovation. Every increase in protection raises the cost of, or reduces access to, the raw material from which you might have built those future products. The balance is a delicate one; one Nobel Prize–winning economist has claimed that it is actually impossible to strike that balance so as to produce an informationally efficient market.[25]

Whether or not it is impossible in theory, it is surely a difficult problem in practice. In other words, even if enclosure of the arable commons always produced gains (itself a subject of debate), enclosure of the information commons clearly has the potential to harm innovation as well as to support it.[26] More property rights, even though they supposedly offer greater incentives, do not necessarily make for more and better production and innovation—sometimes just the opposite is true. It may be that intellectual property rights *slow down* innovation, by putting multiple roadblocks in the way of subsequent innovation.[27] Using a nice inversion of the idea of the tragedy of the commons, Heller and Eisenberg referred to these effects—the transaction costs caused by myriad property rights over the necessary components of some subsequent innovation—as "the tragedy of the anticommons."[28]

In short, even if the enclosure movement was a complete success, there are important reasons to believe that the intangible world is less clearly a candidate for enclosure, that we should pause, study the balance between the world of the owned and the world of the free, gather evidence. After all, even in physical space, "common" property such as roads increases the value of the surrounding private tracts. If there are limits to the virtues of enclosure even there, how much more so in a world of intangible and nonrival goods, which develop by drawing on prior creations? Yet the second enclosure movement proceeds confidently nevertheless—with little argument and less evidence.

To be sure, there is a danger of overstatement. The very fact that the changes have been so one-sided makes it hard to resist exaggerating their impact. In 1918, Justice Brandeis confidently claimed that "[t]he general rule of law is, that the noblest of human productions—knowledge, truths ascertained, conceptions, and ideas—become, after voluntary communication to others, free as the air to common use."[29] That baseline—intellectual property rights are the exception rather than the norm; ideas and facts must always remain in the public domain—is still supposed to be our starting point.[30] It is, however, under attack.

Both overtly and covertly, the commons of facts and ideas is being enclosed. Patents are increasingly stretched to cover "ideas" that twenty years ago all scholars would have agreed were unpatentable.[31] Most troubling of all are the attempts to introduce intellectual property rights over mere compilations of facts.[32] If U.S. intellectual property law had an article of faith, it was that unoriginal compilations of facts would remain in the public domain, that this availability of the raw material of science and speech was as important to the next generation of innovation as the intellectual property rights themselves.[33] The system would hand out monopolies in inventions and in original expression, while the facts below (and ideas above) would remain free for all to build upon. But this premise is being undermined. Some of the challenges are subtle: in patent law, stretched interpretations of novelty and nonobviousness allow intellectual property rights to move closer and closer to the underlying data layer; gene sequence patents come very close to being rights over a particular discovered arrangement of data—C's, G's, A's, and T's.[34] Other challenges are overt: the European Database Protection Directive did (and various proposed bills in the United States would) create proprietary rights over compilations of facts, often without even the carefully framed exceptions of the copyright scheme, such as the usefully protean category of fair use.

The older strategy of intellectual property law was a "braided" one: thread a thin layer of intellectual property rights around a commons of material from which future creators would draw.[35] Even that thin layer of intellectual property rights was limited so as to allow access to the material when that was necessary to further the goals of the system. Fair use allows for parody, commentary, and criticism, and also for "decompilation" of computer programs so that Microsoft's competitors can reverse engineer Word's features in order to make sure their program can convert Word files. It may sound paradoxical, but in a very real sense protection of the commons was one of the fundamental goals of intellectual property law.

In the new vision of intellectual property, however, property should be extended everywhere; more is better. Expanding patentable and copyrightable subject matter, lengthening the copyright term, giving legal protection to "digital barbed wire," even if it is used to prevent fair use: each of these can be understood as a vote of no confidence in the productive powers of the commons. We seem to be shifting from Brandeis's assumption that the "noblest of human productions are free as the air to common use" to the assumption that any commons is inefficient, if not tragic.

The expansion is more than a formal one. It used to be relatively hard to violate an intellectual property right. The technologies of reproduction or the activities necessary to infringe were largely, though not entirely, industrial. Imagine someone walking up to you in 1950, handing you a book or a record or a movie reel, and saying "Quick! Do something the law of intellectual property might forbid." (This, I admit, is a scenario only likely to come to the mind of a person in my line of work.) You would have been hard-pressed to do so. Perhaps you could find a balky mimeograph machine, or press a reel-to-reel tape recorder into use. You might manage a single unauthorized showing of the movie—though to how many people? But triggering the law of intellectual property would be genuinely difficult. Like an antitank mine, it would not be triggered by the footsteps of individuals. It was reserved for bigger game.

This was no accident. The law of intellectual property placed its triggers at the point where commercial activity by competitors could undercut the exploitation of markets by the rights holder. Copying, performance, distribution—these were things done by other industrial entities who were in competition with the owner of the rights: other publishers, movie theaters, distributors, manufacturers. In practice, if not theory, the law was predominantly a form of horizontal industry regulation of unfair competition—made by the people in the affected industries for the people in the affected industries. The latter point is worth stressing. Congress would, and still does, literally hand over the lawmaking process to the industries involved, telling them to draft their intra-industry contract in the form of a law, and then to return to Congress to have it enacted. The public was not at the table, needless to say, and the assumption was that to the extent there was a public interest involved in intellectual property law, it was in making sure that the industries involved got their act together, so that the flow of new books and drugs and movies would continue. Members of the public, in other words, were generally thought of as passive consumers of finished products produced under a form of intra-industry regulation that rarely implicated any act that an ordinary person would want, or be able, to engage in.

In the world of the 1950s, these assumptions make some sense—though we might still disagree with the definition of the public interest. It was assumed by many that copyright need not and probably should not regulate private, noncommercial acts. The person who lends a book to a friend or takes a chapter into class is very different from the company with a printing press that chooses to reproduce ten thousand copies and sell them. The photocopier and the VCR make that distinction fuzzier, and the networked computer threatens to erase it altogether.

So how are things different today? If you are a person who routinely uses computers, the Internet, or digital media, imagine a day when you do not create—intentionally and unintentionally—hundreds of temporary, evanescent copies. (If you doubt this, look in the cache of your browser.) Is there a day when you do not "distribute" or retransmit fragments of articles you have read, when you do not seek to share with friends some image or tune? Is there a day when you do not rework for your job, for your class work, or simply for pastiche or fun, some of the digital material around you? In a networked society, copying is not only easy, it is a necessary part of transmission, storage, caching, and, some would claim, even reading.[36]

As bioinformatics blurs the line between computer modeling and biological research, digital production techniques blur the lines between listening, editing, and remaking. "Rip, mix, and burn," says the Apple advertisement. It marks a world in which the old regime of intellectual property, operating upstream as a form of industrial competition policy, has been replaced. Intellectual property is now in and on the desktop and is implicated in routine creative, communicative, and just plain consumptive acts that each of us performs every day. Suddenly, the triggers of copyright—reproduction, distribution—can be activated by individual footsteps.

Of course, we would hope that in your daily actions you scrupulously observed the rights—all the rights—of the companies that have interests in the texts, tunes, images of celebrities, trademarks, business method patents, and fragments of computer code you dealt with. Did you? Can you be sure? I teach intellectual property, but I admit to some uncertainty.

I would not have imagined that a temporary image of a Web page captured in the cache of my browser counted as a "copy" for the purposes of copyright law.[37] I would have thought that it was fair use for a company to photocopy articles in journals it subscribed to, and paid for, in order to circulate them to its researchers.[38] If a conservative Web site reposted news articles from liberal newspapers with critical commentary, that, too, would have seemed like fair use.[39] I would have thought that it was beneficial competition, and not a trespass, for an electronic "aggregator" to gather together auction prices or airline fares, so as to give consumers more choice.[40] I would not have thought that a search engine that catalogued and displayed in framed format the digital graphics found on the Internet would be sued for infringing the copyrights of the owners of those images.[41] I would not have thought that I might be sued for violating *intellectual property law* if I tried to compete with a printer company by making toner cartridges that were compatible with its printers.[42]

The examples go on. I know that the "research exemption" in U.S. patent law is very tightly limited, but I would have laughed if you had told me that even a research university was forbidden from doing research unless that research had no conceivable practical or academic worth—in other words that even in academia, in a project with no commercial goal, the research exemption only covered research that was completely pointless.[43] Why have an exemption at all, in that case? I would have told an academic cryptography researcher that he need not fear legal threats from copyright owners simply for researching and publishing work on the vulnerabilities of copy protection schemes.[44] I would not have thought that one could patent the idea of having an electronic Dutch auction on the Internet, working out the daily prices of a bundle of mutual funds through simple arithmetic, or buying something online with one click.[45] I would have assumed that celebrities' rights to control their images should end with their deaths, and that courts would agree that those rights were tightly limited by the First Amendment. Yet, in each of these cases, I would have been wrong, or at least I *might* be wrong—enough that a sane person would worry. Not all of the expansive claims eventually triumphed, of course, but some did. Guessing which would and which would not was hard even for me, though, as I said, I teach intellectual property law. You, probably, do not.

In 1950 none of this would have mattered. Unless you were in some related business—as a publisher, broadcaster, film distributor, or what have you—it would have been hard for you to trigger the rules of intellectual property law. If you were in such a business, you were probably very familiar with the rules that governed your activities and well represented by corporate counsel who knew them even better. What's more, the rules were neither as complex nor as counterintuitive as they are now. They also did not reach as far. The reach of the rights has been expanded, and their content made more difficult to understand, at the exact moment that their practical effect has been transformed. It is not merely that the triggers of intellectual property law can easily be set off by individual footsteps. There are now many more triggers and their trip wires are harder to see.

From the point of view of the content industries, of course, all this is foolishness. It is not some undesirable accident that intellectual property has come to regulate personal, noncommercial activity. It is absolutely necessary. Think of Napster. When individuals engaging in noncommercial activity have the ability to threaten the music or film industry's business plan by engaging in the very acts that copyright law always regulated—namely reproduction and distribution—of course it is appropriate for them, and the networks they "share" on, to be subject to liability. What's more, to the extent that copying becomes cheaper and easier, it is necessary for us to strengthen intellectual property rights. We must meet the greater danger of copying with more expansive rights, harsher penalties, and expanded protections, some of which may indeed have the practical effect of reducing rights that citizens thought they had, such as fair use, low-level noncommercial sharing among personal friends, resale, and so on. Without an increase in private property rights, in other words, cheaper copying will eat the heart out of our creative and cultural industries. I call this claim the Internet Threat.

4

The Internet Threat

The conventional wisdom is that governments respond slowly to technological change. In the case of the Internet, nothing could be further from the truth. In 1994 and 1995, "dot-com" was still a mystical term for many. Most stories about the Internet dealt with sexual predation rather than possibilities of extreme wealth. Internet commerce itself was barely an idea, and some of the most exciting sites on the Web had pictures of coffeepots in university departments far away. ("See," one would proudly say to a technological neophyte friend when introducing him to the wonders of the Net, "the pot is *empty* and we can see that live from here! This changes *everything*!") It was an innocent time. Yet the U.S. government was already turning the wheels of intellectual property policy to respond to the threat (and promise) of the Internet. More precisely, they were trying to shape the future of the cumbersomely named "National Information Infrastructure," the official name for the "information superhighway" that it was presumed would replace the "immature" technology of the Net. The government was wrong about that, and about a lot else.

The blueprint for new intellectual property policy online came from the Patent and Trademark Office. That office promulgated first a Green Paper and then, after further hearings, a White Paper, on "Intellectual Property and the National Information Infrastructure."[1] As policy and legal documents these are in one sense long out of date. Some of their legal arguments were successfully challenged. Some of their most important proposals were rejected, while many others have become law. But as a starting point from which to trace the frame of mind that has come to dominate intellectual property policy online, they are hard to equal.

These documents contained proposals that nowadays would be seen as fairly controversial. Internet service providers were said to be "strictly liable" for copyright violations committed by their subscribers; that is to say, they were legally responsible whether or not they knew about the violation or were at fault in any way. Loading a document into your browser's transient cache memory while reading it was said to be making a "copy." There was more: the beginnings of what later became the Digital Millennium Copyright Act,[2] making it illegal to cut through the digital fences which content providers put around their products. The attitude toward fair use was particularly revealing. At one point in the White Paper it was hinted that fair use might be a relic of the inconveniences of the analog age, to be discarded now that we could have automated fractional payments for even the most insignificant use.[3] (It was noted, however, that some disagreed with this conclusion.) At another point, fair use was described as a "tax" on rights holders and a "subsidy" to those who benefited from it, such as educational institutions.[4] The White Paper also suggested that while any potential loss to rights holders caused by the new technology needed to be countered with new rights and new protections, any potential gain to them through the new technology was simply theirs. Potential gain did not offset the need to compensate for potential loss.

So what views of intellectual property were we carrying forward into the Internet age? Intellectual property is just like other property. Rights are presumptively absolute. Any limitations on them, such as fair use, are *taxes* on property owners, *subsidies* to the society at large. It sounds like a perfect time to administer the Jefferson Warning I sketched out in Chapter 2. After all, Jefferson was specifically warning against each of these errors two hundred years ago. To find them in a student paper would be disappointing—irritating, even. But this document was the blueprint for the intellectual property regime of cyberspace.

But do these mistakes matter? How important is it that we get the rules of intellectual property right? To me, a number of my colleagues, some librarians, and a few software gurus, the White Paper was more than just a bit of bad policy in a technical field—like a poorly drafted statute about the witnessing of wills, say. When you set up the property rules in some new space, you determine much about the history that follows. Property rules have a huge effect on power relationships and bargaining positions. Think of rules setting out water rights or the right to drive cattle over homesteaders' land in the American West. But they also are part of a larger way of seeing the world; think of the early-twentieth-century rules treating unions as "conspiracies in restraint of trade" or the Supreme Court decisions that dispossessed the American Indians on the theory that they did not comprehend the concept of property and thus did not "own" the land being taken from them.[5] We were at a comparable point in the history of cyberspace. What was being set up here was a vision of economy and culture, a frame of mind about how the world of cultural exchange operates, and eventually a blueprint for our systems of communication. At this stage, the range of possibilities is extremely wide. A lot of different choices could be made, but subsequent changes would be harder and harder as people and companies built their activities around the rules that had been laid down. This was, in short, a tipping point where it was particularly important that we make the right decisions.

Conventional political science told us there were a lot of reasons to fear that we would not make the right decisions. The political process was going to be particularly vulnerable to problems of capture by established industries, many of whom would (rightly) see the Internet as a potential threat to their role as intermediaries between artists and creators on the one hand and the public on the other.

Intellectual property legislation had always been a cozy world in which the content, publishing, and distribution industries were literally asked to draft the rules by which they would live. The law was treated as a kind of contract between the affected industries. Rationally enough, those industries would wish to use the law not merely to protect their legitimate existing property rights, but to make challenges to their basic business plans illegal. (Imagine what would have happened if we had given the lamp-oil sellers the right to define the rules under which the newfangled electric light companies would operate.) There would be no easy counterweight to these pressures, as Jessica Litman points out in a wonderful set of reflections on copyright lawmaking, because the potential competitors to existing titans were just being born and could thus be strangled safely in their cradles.[6] Certainly the public would have little grasp as yet of what was at stake.

In any event, when had the public played a role in intellectual property legislation? That kind of law affected businesses with printing presses or TV towers, not normal citizens. It did not help that the legislators were largely both ignorant and distrustful of the technology of the Internet—which was, at the time, thought to be dominated by foreign hackers, suicidal cults, pirates, and sleazy pornographers. (Terrorists and Nigerian spammers would be added to the mix later.)

Given an area of law that legislators were happy to hand over to the affected industries and a technology that was both unfamiliar and threatening, the prospects for legislative insight were poor. Lawmakers were assured by lobbyists

a) that this was business as usual, that no dramatic changes were being made by the Green or White papers; or
b) that the technology presented a terrible menace to the American cultural industries, but that prompt and statesmanlike action would save the day; or
c) that layers of new property rights, new private enforcers of those rights, and technological control and surveillance measures were all needed in order to benefit consumers, who would now be able to "purchase culture by the sip rather than by the glass" in a pervasively monitored digital environment.

In practice, somewhat confusingly, these three arguments would often be combined. Legislators' statements seemed to suggest that this was a *routine* Armageddon in which firm, decisive statesmanship was needed to *preserve* the digital status quo in a profoundly *transformative* and proconsumer way. Reading the congressional debates was likely to give one conceptual whiplash.

To make things worse, the press was—in 1995, at least—clueless about these issues. It was not that the newspapers were ignoring the Internet. They were paying attention—obsessive attention in some cases. But as far as the mainstream press was concerned, the story line on the Internet was sex: pornography, online predation, more pornography. The lowbrow press stopped there. To be fair, the highbrow press was also interested in Internet legal issues (the regulation of pornography, the regulation of online predation) and constitutional questions (the First Amendment protection of Internet pornography). Reporters were also asking questions about the social effect of the network (including, among other things, the threats posed by pornography and online predators).

There were certainly important issues within the areas the press was willing to focus on, and I do not mean to trivialize them. I worked with a couple of civil liberties groups in opposing the hapless Communications Decency Act, one of the most poorly drafted pieces of speech regulation ever to come out of Congress.[7] It was a palpably unconstitutional statute, eventually struck down by a unanimous Supreme Court.[8] Its proposals would have burdened the speech of adults while failing to protect the interests of minors. Reporters loved the topic of the Communications Decency Act. It was about sex, technology, and the First Amendment. It foreshadowed the future of online speech regulation. One could write about it while feeling simultaneously prurient, principled, and prescient: the journalistic trifecta. For law professors who worked on digital issues, the Communications Decency Act was an easy topic to get the public to focus on; we had the reporters and editors calling *us*, pleading for a quote or an opinion piece.

Intellectual property was something quite different. It was occasionally covered in the business pages with the same enthusiasm devoted to changes in derivatives rules. Presented with the proposals in the Green and White Papers, the reporters went looking for opinions from the Software Publishers Association, the Recording Industry Association of America, or the Motion Picture Association of America. This was not bias or laziness—to whom else would they go? Who was on the "other side" of these issues? Remember, all of this occurred before Napster was a gleam in Sean Fanning's eye. Sean Fanning was in middle school. Amazon.com was a new company and "Google" was not yet a verb.

In this environment, convincing the legislature or the press that fundamental public choices were implicated in the design of intellectual property rights for the digital world was about as easy as convincing them that fundamental public choices were implicated in the rules of tiddlywinks. My own experience is probably representative. I remember trying to pitch an article on the subject to a charming but uncomprehending opinion page editor at the *Washington Post*. I tried to explain that decisions about property rules would shape the way we thought about the technology. Would the relatively anonymous and decentralized characteristics of the Internet that made it such a powerful tool for global speech and debate come to be seen as a bug rather than a feature, something to be "fixed" to make the Net safe for protected content? The rules would also shape the economic interests that drove future policy. Would we try to build the system around the model of proprietary content dispensed in tightly controlled chunks? Would fair use be made technologically obsolescent? Would we undercut the various nontraditional methods of innovation, such as free software, before they ever managed to establish themselves? What would become of libraries in the digital world, of the ideal that access to books had important differences from access to Twinkies? After I concluded this lengthy and slightly incoherent *cri de coeur*, there was a long pause; then the editor said politely, "Are you sure you couldn't make some of these points about a free speech issue, like the Communications Decency Act, maybe?"

I finally placed the piece in the *Washington Times*,[9] which was best known at the time as the only metropolitan newspaper owned by the Unification Church, familiarly referred to as the Moonies. This hardly counted as a direct line to the popular imagination (though the article's mild criticisms elicited an extraordinary reaction from the Clinton administration's lead official on intellectual property policy—throwing me for several weeks into a surreal world of secondhand threats, third-party leaks, and a hilarious back-and-forth in the letters page).[10]

Things were not completely one-sided. An unlikely group of critics had formed: librarians, a few software developers, law professors, some Internet libertarians. Of particular note was the Digital Future Coalition, which grew to represent a broad range of interested groups and industries thanks in part to the prescient analysis and remarkable energy of one of my colleagues, Peter Jaszi.[11] Together with Pamela Samuelson, Jessica Litman, and a number of other distinguished legal scholars, Peter turned his considerable intellectual talents to explaining why writers, telecom companies, scientists, manufacturers of consumer electronics, and a host of other groups should be interested in the rules being debated. There had been a series of official hearings in which complaints were carefully collected and just as carefully ignored. This became harder to do as the critics became more numerous and better organized. Nevertheless, the currents were clearly running against them. It would be nice to say that this was merely because of the clubby history of intellectual property legislation, or the difficulty in getting press attention, or the various issues of industry capture and collective action problems. Yet this would be to miss a vital element of the situation.

Conventional political science showed that there were structural reasons why the legislative process was likely to succumb to industry capture.[12] The reality turned out to be much worse. The real problem was not a political process dominated by cynical power politics, nor an initial absence of critical newspaper coverage, though both of those factors contributed. The real problem was that most of the proponents of the White Paper's policies believed their own arguments so deeply and sincerely that they saw any criticism of those positions as either godless communism or hippy digital anarchism. (Frequently, in fact, they clung to their arguments even when there was fairly strong evidence that they would actually be harming themselves by putting these policies into effect. I will expand on this point later.) More importantly, they succeeded in getting their story about the threats and promises of the digital future accepted as the basis for all discussion of intellectual property policy. It became the organizing set of principles, the master narrative—call it what you will.

The heart of the story is beguilingly simple. The Internet makes copying cheaper and does so on an unparalleled global scale. Therefore we must meet the greater danger of illicit copying with more expansive rights, harsher penalties, and expanded protections. True, as I pointed out before, some of these expansions may indeed have the practical effect of reducing rights that citizens *thought* they had, such as fair use, low-level noncommercial sharing among personal friends, resale, and so on. But without an increase in private property rights, cheaper copying will eat the heart out of our creative and cultural industries. I call this story the Internet Threat. It is a powerful argument and it deserves some explanation.

Think back for a moment to the first chapter and the difference between *Madame Bovary* and the petunia. If the reason for intellectual property rights is the "nonrival" and "nonexcludable" nature of the goods they protect, then surely the lowering of copying and transmission costs implies a corresponding need to increase the strength of intellectual property rights. Imagine a line. At one end sits a monk painstakingly transcribing Aristotle's *Poetics*. In the middle lies the Gutenberg printing press. Three-quarters of the way along the line is a photocopying machine. At the far end lies the Internet and the online version of the human genome. At each stage, copying costs are lowered and goods become both less rival and less excludable. My MP3 files are available to anyone in the world running Napster. Songs can be found and copied with ease. The symbolic end of rivalry comes when I am playing the song in Chapel Hill, North Carolina, at the very moment that you are both downloading and listening to it in Kazakhstan—now *that* is nonrival.

THE LOGIC OF PERFECT CONTROL

My point is that there is a teleology—a theory about how intellectual property law must develop historically—hidden inside the argument I call the Internet Threat. The argument, which is touted endlessly by the content industries—and not without reason—can be reduced to this: The strength of intellectual property rights must vary inversely with the cost of copying. With high copying costs, one needs weak intellectual property rights if any at all. To deal with the monk-copyist, we need no copyright because physical control of the manuscript is enough. What does it matter if I say I will copy your manuscript, if I must do it by hand? How will this present a threat to you? There is no need to create a legal right to exclude others from copying, no need for a "copy right." As copying costs fall, however, the need to exclude increases. To deal with the Gutenberg press, we need the Statute of Anne—the first copyright statute—and the long evolution of copyright it ushered in.

But then comes the Internet. To deal with the Internet, we need the Digital Millennium Copyright Act,[13] the No Electronic Theft Act,[14] the Sonny Bono Copyright Term Extension Act,[15] and perhaps even the Collections of Information Antipiracy Act.[16] As copying costs approach zero, intellectual property rights must approach perfect control. We must strengthen the rights, lengthen the term of the rights, increase the penalties, and make noncommercial illicit copying a crime. We must move outside the traditional realm of copyright altogether to regulate the technology around the copyrighted material. Companies are surrounding their digital materials with digital fences. We must make it a violation of the law to cut those digital fences, even if you do so to make a "fair use" of the material on the other side. We must prohibit the making of things that can be used as fence-cutters—a prospect that worries researchers on encryption. In the long run, we must get rid of the troublesome anonymity of the Internet, requiring each computer to have an individual ID. We must make click-wrap contracts enforceable, even on third parties, even when you cannot read them before clicking—so that you never actually *buy* the software, music, movies, and e-books you download, merely "license" them for a narrowly defined range of uses. We must create interlocking software and hardware systems that monitor and control the material played on those systems—so that songs can be licensed to particular computers at particular times. Uses that the owners wish to forbid will actually be impossible, whether they are legal or not.

In other words, we must make this technology of the Internet, which was hailed as the great "technology of freedom," into a technology of control and surveillance. The possibility of individuals circulating costless perfect digital copies requires it. It would be facile (if tempting) to say we must remake the Internet to make it safe for Britney Spears. The "Internet Threat" argument is that we must remake the Net if we want digital creativity—whether in music or software or movies or e-texts. And since the strength of the property rights varies inversely with the cost of copying, costless copying means that the remade

Net must approach perfect control, both in its legal regime and its technical architecture.

Like any attractive but misleading argument, the Internet Threat has a lot of truth. Ask the software company producing expensive, specialized computer-assisted design programs costing thousands of dollars what happens when the program is made available on a "warez" site or a peer-to-peer file-sharing network. The upstart computer game company pinning its hopes and its capital on a single new game would tell you the same thing. The easy availability of perfect, costless copies *is* a danger to all kinds of valuable cultural and economic production. The story of the Internet Threat is not *wrong*, it is simply dramatically incomplete in lots of ways. Here are two of them.

Costless Copying Brings Both Costs and Benefits

The Internet does lower the cost of copying and thus the cost of illicit copying. Of course, it also lowers the costs of production, distribution, and advertising, and dramatically increases the size of the potential market. Is the net result a loss to rights holders such that we need to increase protection and control in order to maintain a constant level of incentives? A large, leaky market may actually provide more revenue than a small one over which one's control is much stronger. What's more, the same technologies that allow for cheap copying also allow for swift and encyclopedic search engines—the best devices ever invented for detecting illicit copying. What the Net takes away with one hand, it often gives back with the other. Cheaper copying does not merely mean loss, it also means opportunity. Before strengthening intellectual property rights, we would need to know whether the loss was greater than the gain and whether revised business models and new distribution mechanisms could avoid the losses while capturing more of the gains.

But wait, surely theft is theft? If the new technologies enable more theft of intellectual property, must we not strengthen the laws in order to deal with the problem? If some new technology led to a rash of car thefts, we might increase police resources and prison sentences, perhaps pass new legislation creating new crimes related to car theft. We would do all of this even if the technology in question gave car owners significant benefits elsewhere. Theft is theft, is it not?

The answer in a word is no. Saying "theft is theft" is exactly the error that the Jefferson Warning is supposed to guard against. We should not assume that intellectual property and material property are the same in all regards. The goal of creating the limited monopoly called an intellectual property right is to provide the minimum necessary incentive to encourage the desired level of innovation. Anything extra is deadweight loss. When someone takes your car, they have the car and you do not. When, because of some new technology, someone is able to get access to the MP3 file of your new song, they have the file and so do you. You did not lose the song. What you may have lost is the opportunity to sell the song to that person or to the people with whom they "share" the file. We should not be indifferent to this kind of loss; it is a serious concern. But the fact that a new technology brings economic benefits as well as economic harm to the creation, distribution, and sale of intellectual property products means that we should pause before increasing the level of rights, changing the architecture of our communications networks, creating new crimes, and so on.

Remember, many of the things that the content industries were concerned about on the Internet were already illegal, already subject to suit and prosecution. The question is not whether the Internet should be an intellectual property-free zone; it should not be, is not, and never was. The question is whether, when the content industries come asking for *additional* or *new* rights, for *new* penalties, for the criminalization of certain types of technology, we should take into account the gains that the Internet has brought them, as well as the costs, before we accede to their requests. The answer, of course, is that we should. Sadly, we did not. This does not mean that all of the content industries' attempts to strengthen the law are wrong and unnecessary. It means that we do not know whether they are or not.

There is a fairly solid tradition in intellectual property policy of what I call "20/20 downside" vision. All of the threats posed by any new technology—the player piano, the jukebox, the photocopier, the VCR, the Internet—are seen with extraordinary clarity. The opportunities, however, particularly those which involve changing a business model or restructuring a market, are dismissed as phantoms. The downside dominates the field, the upside is invisible. The story of video recorders is the best-known example. When video recorders—another technology promising cheaper copying—first appeared, the reaction of movie studios was one of horror. Their business plans relied upon showing movies in theaters and then licensing them to television stations. VCRs and Betamaxes fit nowhere in this plan; they were seen merely as copyright violation devices. Hollywood tried to have them taxed to pay for the losses that would be caused. Their assumption? Cheaper copying demands stronger rights.

Having lost that battle, the movie studios tried to have the manufacturers of the recording devices found liable for contributory copyright infringement;

liable, in other words, for assisting the copyright violations that *could* be carried out by the owners of Sony Betamaxes. This, of course, was exactly the same legal claim that would be made in the *Napster* case. In the *Sony* case, however, the movie companies lost. The Supreme Court said that recording of TV programs to "time-shift" them to a more convenient hour was a fair use.[17] The movie studios' claims were rejected.

Freed from the threat of liability, the price of video recorders continued to fall. They flooded consumers' houses at a speed unparalleled until the arrival of the World Wide Web. All these boxes sitting by TVs now cried out for content, content that was provided by an emerging video rental market. Until the triumph of DVDs, the videocassette rental market made up more than 50 percent of the movie industry's revenues.[18] Were losses caused by video recorders? To be sure. Some people who might have gone to see a movie in a theater because the TV schedule was inconvenient could instead record the show and watch it later. Videos could even be shared with friends and families—tattered copies of Disney movies recorded from some cable show could be passed on to siblings whose kids have reached the appropriate age. VCRs were also used for copying that was clearly illicit—large-scale duplication and sale of movies by someone other than the rights holder. A cheaper copying technology definitely caused losses. But it also provided substantial gains, gains that far outweighed the losses. Ironically, had the movie companies "won" in the *Sony* case, they might now be worse off.

The *Sony* story provides us with some useful lessons—first, this 20/20 downside vision is a poor guide to copyright policy. Under its sway, some companies will invariably equate greater control with profit and cheaper copying with loss. They will conclude, sometimes rightly, that their very existence is threatened, and, sometimes wrongly, that the threat is to innovation and culture itself rather than to their particular way of delivering it. They will turn to the legislature and the courts for guarantees that they can go on doing business in the old familiar ways. Normally, the marketplace is supposed to provide correctives to this kind of myopia. Upstart companies, not bound by the habits of the last generation, are supposed to move nimbly to harvest the benefits from the new technology and to outcompete the lumbering dinosaurs. In certain situations, though, competition will not work:

- if the dinosaurs are a cartel strong enough to squelch competition;
- if they have enlisted the state to make the threatening technology illegal, describing it as a predatory encroachment on the "rights" of the old guard rather than aggressive competition;

• if ingrained prejudices are simply so strong that the potential business benefits take years to become apparent; or
• if the market has "locked in" on a dominant standard—a technology or an operating system, say—to which new market entrants do not have legal access.

In those situations, markets cannot be counted on to self-correct. Unfortunately, and this is a key point, intellectual property policy frequently deals
with controversies in which all of these conditions hold true.

Let me repeat this point, because it is one of the most important ones in
this book. To a political scientist or market analyst, the conditions I have just
described sound like a rarely seen perfect storm of legislative and market dys-
function. *To an intellectual property scholar, they sound like business as usual.*

In the case of the VCR wars, none of these factors obtained. The state refused to step in to aid the movie companies by criminalizing the new technology. There were equally powerful companies on the other side of the issue
(the consumer electronics companies selling VCRs) who saw this new
market as a natural extension of a familiar existing market—audio recorders.
There was no dominant proprietary technological standard controlled by the
threatened industry that could be used to shut down any threats to their
business model. The market was allowed to develop and evolve without premature legal intervention or proprietary technological lockout. Thus we
know in this case that the movie companies were wrong, that their claims of
impending doom from cheap copies were completely mistaken. The public
and, ironically, the industry itself benefited as a result. But the *Sony* case
is the exception rather than the rule. That is why it is so important. If competition and change can be forbidden, we will get relatively few cases that
disprove the logic that cheaper copying must always mean stronger rights.
The "natural experiments" will never be allowed to happen. They will be
squelched by those who see only threat in the technologies that allow cheaper
copies and who can persuade legislators or judges to see the world their way.
The story line I describe here, the Internet Threat, will become the conventional wisdom. In the process, it will make it much less likely that we will
have the evidence needed to refute it.

The Holes Matter as Much as the Cheese

The *Sony* case is important in another way. The Supreme Court's decision
turned on the judgment that it was a "fair use" under U.S. copyright law for
consumers to record television programs for time-shifting purposes. Since fair

use comes up numerous times in this book, it is worth pausing for a moment to explain what it is.

The content industries like to portray fair use as a narrow and grudging defense against an otherwise valid case for copyright infringement—as if the claim were, "Yes, I trespassed on your land, which was wrong, I admit. But I was starving and looking for food. Please give me a break." This is simply inaccurate. True, fair use is asserted as "an affirmative defense"; that is the way it is brought up in a copyright case. But in U.S. law, fair uses are stated quite clearly to be limitations on the exclusive rights of the copyright holder—uses that were never within the copyright holder's power to prohibit. The defense is not "I trespassed on your land, but I was starving." It is "I did *not* trespass on your land. I walked on the public road that runs through it, a road you never owned in the first place." When society hands out the right to the copyright holder, it carves out certain areas of use and refuses to hand over control of them. Again, remember the Jefferson Warning. This is not a presumptively absolute property right. It is a conditional grant of a limited and temporary monopoly. One cannot start from the presumption that the rights holder has absolute rights over all possible uses and therefore that any time a citizen makes use of the work in any way, the rights holder is entitled to get paid or to claim "piracy" if he does not get paid. Under the sway of the story line I called the Internet Threat, legislators have lost sight of this point.

So what is "fair use"? When I am asked this question by nonlawyers, I offer to show them the actual provision in the copyright act. They recoil, clearly imagining they are about to be shown something the size and complexity of the tax code. Here is the statutory fair use provision in its entirety:

Sec. 107. - Limitations on exclusive rights: Fair use

Notwithstanding the provisions of sections 106 and 106A, the fair use of a copyrighted work, including such use by reproduction in copies or phonorecords or by any other means specified by that section, for purposes such as criticism, comment, news reporting, teaching (including multiple copies for classroom use), scholarship, or research, is not an infringement of copyright. In determining whether the use made of a work in any particular case is a fair use the factors to be considered shall include—

(1) the purpose and character of the use, including whether such use is of a commercial nature or is for nonprofit educational purposes;

(2) the nature of the copyrighted work;

(3) the amount and substantiality of the portion used in relation to the copyrighted work as a whole; and

(4) the effect of the use upon the potential market for or value of the copyrighted work.

The fact that a work is unpublished shall not itself bar a finding of fair use if such finding is made upon consideration of all the above factors.

"But this seems quite sensible," people often say, as though they had expected both Byzantine complexity and manifest irrationality. (Perhaps they have had some experience with legal matters after all.) The ones who think about it a little longer realize that these factors cannot be mechanically applied. Look at factor 3, for example. Someone who is making a parody frequently needs to take large chunks of the parodied work. That is the nature of a parody, after all. They might then sell the parody, thus also getting into trouble with factor 1. And what about factor 4? Someone might quote big chunks of my book in a devastating review that ruined any chance the book had of selling well. Come to think of it, even a parody might have a negative effect on the "potential market" for the parodied work. But surely those uses would still be "fair"? (In both instances, the Supreme Court agrees that they are fair uses.)

In coming up with these hypothetical problem cases, the copyright novice is probably closer to having a good understanding of the purpose of fair use than many people who have studied it for years. In fact, the novice's questions shed light on *all* of the exceptions, limitations, and defenses to proprietary rights—the holes in the cheese of intellectual property. The scholar's urge is to find one theory that explains all the possible applications of the fair use doctrine, to arrange all of the cases like targets and shoot a single arrow through all of them. Perhaps fair use is designed to reduce the difficulty of clearing rights when it would be uneconomical or impossibly complex to do so: to reduce the paperwork, hassle, delay, ignorance, and aggravation that economists refer to under the sanguine name of "transaction costs."[19] (Though the idea that fair use is about transaction costs hardly explains some of the types of fair use we care most about—the rights to parody, to criticize, to reverse engineer.) Or perhaps fair use allows the rights of a transformative author to be trumped only by a second transformative author, who is building on the first—the parodist, reviewer, collage artist, or what have you.[20] (Then again, photocopying for classroom use does not sound very "transformative.") Could fair use be dictated by the Constitution or by international free speech guarantees? In this view, fair use provides a safety valve that allows copyright to coexist with the First Amendment, property rights over speech to coexist with freedom of expression.[21] After all, it is not entirely obvious how it could be constitutional to forbid me, in the name of a federal law, from translating *Mein Kampf* in order to warn of the dangers of fascism or parodying some piece of art to subversive effect.

Each of these ideas about fair use has much to recommend it, as do the many other grand theories that have been offered to explain the puzzle. And therein lies the problem.

Intellectual property is a brilliant social invention which presents us with great benefits but also with a multitude of dangers:

1. the danger that the monopoly is unnecessary to produce the innovation, or that it is broader or lasts for longer than is necessary to encourage future production;
2. that overly broad rights will chill speech, criticism, or scientific progress;
3. that it will restrict access in ways that discourage "follow-on" innovation;
4. that it will lead to industry concentration in a way that hurts consumers or citizens while being less subject to antitrust regulation precisely because the monopoly or oligopoly rests on intellectual property rights;
5. that it will establish strong "network effects" which cause the market to tip over to some inefficient technology; and
6. that it will give the rights holder control over some technology outside the range of the monopoly but closely linked to it.

The list of dangers goes on and on, and so does the list of exceptions, limitations, and restraints designed to prevent them. We restrict the *length* of intellectual property rights. (At least, we used to. The framers thought it so important to do so that they put the need to have a limited term in the Constitution itself; nevertheless both Congress and the Supreme Court seem to have given up on that one.) We restrict the *scope* of intellectual property rights, so that they cannot cover raw facts or general ideas, only the range of innovation and expression in between. (At least, we used to. Developments in database protection, gene patents, and business method patents are clearly eroding those walls.) As with fair use, we impose limitations on the rights when we hand them out in the first place. The exclusive right conferred by copyright does not include the right to prevent criticism, parody, classroom copying, decompilation of computer programs, and so on. (Though as the next chapter shows, a number of recent legal changes mean that the practical ability to exercise fair use rights is seriously threatened.)

These limitations on intellectual property do not fit a single theory, unless that theory is "avoiding the multiple and evolving dangers of intellectual property itself." Even a single limitation such as fair use clearly responds to many different concerns about the dangers of intellectual property rights. Indeed it will evolve to fit new circumstances. When computer programs were first clearly covered by copyright law, software engineers wondered if this would cripple the industry. Why? Anyone who wishes to compete with a dominant program needs to "decompile" it in order to make their program "interoperable," or simply better. For example, a new word processing program, no matter how good, would be dead on arrival unless it could read all the files people had created with the old, dominant word processing software. But to do this, the engineers at the upstart company would have to take apart their competitor's program. In the process they would have to create temporary copies of the old program, even though the final product—the hot new software—would be completely different from the old. Would this be a violation of copyright law?

In a series of remarkable and far-seeing cases involving such issues, the courts said no.[22] "Decompilation" was fair use. The law of fair use had evolved in the context of expressive, nonfunctional, stand-alone works such as books, poems, songs. Now it was being applied to a functional product whose economics depended strongly on "network effects"—many types of programs are useful only if they are widely used. Without interoperability, we could never take our existing documents or spreadsheets or datasets and move to a new program, even if it was better. One program would not be able to read the files created by another. It would be as if language itself had been copyrighted. To have said that the incidental copies created in the process of decompiling software were actually infringements of copyright would have turned the law on its head because of a technological accident (you needed temporarily to "copy" the programs in order to understand how they worked and make yours work with them) and a legal accident (copyright was now being used to regulate functional articles of commerce: "machines" made of binary code). The difference between copying and reading, or copying and understanding, had changed because of the technology. The context had changed because the law was being stretched to cover new types of products, whose economics were very different from those of novels. Rather than let the dominant software companies use copyright to stop others from making interoperable software, the courts used an escape hatch—fair use—to prevent that danger and to uphold the basic goal of copyright: encouraging progress in science and the useful arts.

This long story is told to make a simple point. The variegated and evolving limitations on intellectual property are as important as the rights they constrain, curtail, and define. The holes matter as much as the cheese.

What does this have to do with the *Sony* case? In that case, remember, the Supreme Court had said that copying TV shows in order to time-shift was fair use. The Court could simply have stopped there. It could have said, "since most of what consumers do is legal, there can be no claim of contributory or vicarious infringement. Sony is not contributing to infringement since consumers are not infringing copyright by copying shows in the first place." Interestingly, though this is the heart of the ruling, the court went further. It quoted some seemingly unrelated patent law doctrine on contributory infringement: "A finding of contributory infringement does not, of course, remove the article from the market altogether; it does, however, give the patentee effective control over the sale of that item. Indeed, a finding of contributory infringement is normally the functional equivalent of holding that the disputed article is within the monopoly granted to the patentee." Clearly, the Justices were concerned that, by using copyright law, the movie studios could actually get control of a new technology.

The fact that the Court expressed this concern through an analogy to patent law was, at first sight, fairly surprising. Courts do not normally look at copyrights in quite the same way as they look at patents. For one thing, patent rights are stronger, though they are harder to obtain and last for a shorter period of time. For another, while courts often express concern about the dangers of a patent-driven monopoly over a particular technology, it is strange to see that concern in the context of copyright law. An unnecessary monopoly over a plow or a grain elevator may, as Jefferson pointed out, slow technological development. But a monopoly over *Snow White* or "Ode on a Grecian Urn"? We do not normally think of rights over *expression* (the realm of copyright) threatening to sweep within their ambit an entire new technological *invention* (the realm of patent).

But in the *Sony* case, the Supreme Court quite clearly saw that, in a world where technological developments made copying easier, the idea of contributory infringement in copyright could be used to suppress or control entire technologies that seemed, in the logic of 20/20 downside vision, to pose a threat to the copyright holder. Indeed, in some sense, the logic behind the Internet Threat—"cheaper copying requires greater control"—demands this result, though the *Sony* case antedates the World Wide Web by a considerable time. If it is cheap copying itself that poses the threat, then the content owners will increasingly move to gain control over the technologies of cheap copying, using copyright as their stalking horse. That is why the *Sony* Court went beyond the simple ruling on fair use to explain the consequences of the movie companies' claim. In a footnote (the place where judges often bury their most trenchant asides) the Court was almost snide:

> It seems extraordinary to suggest that the Copyright Act confers upon all copyright owners collectively, much less the two respondents in this case, the exclusive right to distribute VTR's [Video Tape Recorders] simply because they may be used to infringe copyrights. That, however, is the logical implication of their claim. The request for an injunction below indicates that respondents seek, in effect, to declare VTR's contraband. Their suggestion in this Court that a continuing royalty pursuant to a judicially created compulsory license would be an acceptable remedy merely indicates that respondents, for their part, would be willing to license their claimed monopoly interest in VTR's to Sony in return for a royalty.[23]

The real heart of the *Sony* case is not that "time-shifting" of TV programs is fair use. It is an altogether deeper principle with implications for all of the holes in the intellectual property cheese. The *Sony* Court declared that because video recorders were capable of substantial noninfringing uses, the manufacturers of those devices were not guilty of contributory infringement. If the rights of copyright holders were absolute, if they had the authority to prohibit any activity that appeared to pose a threat to their current business model, then it is quite possible that video recorders *would* have been guilty of contributory infringement. It is because we have, and need, multiple exceptions and limitations on intellectual property that the Supreme Court was able to resist the claim that copyright itself forbids technologies of cheaper copying. To put it another way, without a robust set of exceptions and limitations on copyright, the idea that cheaper copying requires greater control will inexorably drive us toward the position that the technologies of cheaper reproduction must be put under the governance of copyright holders.

Thus we have a corollary to the Jefferson Warning—call it the Sony Axiom: cheaper copying makes the limitations on copyright *more* rather than less important. Without those limitations, copyright law will bloat and metastasize into a claim of monopoly, or at least control, over the very architectures of our communications technology. And that is exactly where the logic of the Internet Threat is taking us today.

FROM NAPSTER TO GROKSTER

Seventeen years after the *Sony* decision, another court had to deal with a suit by outraged copyright holders against the creators of a technology that allowed individuals to copy material cheaply and easily. The suit was called

A&M Records v. Napster.[24] Napster was a "peer-to-peer" file sharing system.
The files were not kept on some huge central server. Instead, there was a central directory—think of a telephone directory—which contained a constantly
updated list of the addresses of individual computers and the files they contained. Anyone who had the software could query the central registry to find
a file's location and then establish a direct computer-to-computer connection—
anywhere in the world—with the person who had the file they desired. This
decentralized design meant the system was extremely "robust," very fast, and
of nearly infinite capacity. Using this technology, tens of millions of people
around the world were "sharing" music, an activity which record companies
quite understandably viewed as simple theft. In fact, it would be hard to think
of a situation that illustrated the Internet Threat better. The case ended up in
front of the U.S. Court of Appeals for the Ninth Circuit, which hears cases in
an area that includes California and thus has decided a lot of copyright cases
over the years.

There was an irony here. When the Supreme Court decided the *Sony* case,
it was on appeal from the Ninth Circuit Court of Appeals. *Sony*, with its rule
about reproductive technologies with substantial noninfringing uses, reversed
the appeals court decision. The Supreme Court was, in effect, telling the
Ninth Circuit that it was wrong, that its ruling would have required the "extraordinary" (legal shorthand for "stupid") conclusion that copyright law gave
copyright holders a veto on new technology. In the process, the Supreme
Court told the Ninth Circuit that it also did not understand the law of fair
use, or the freedom that should be given to individuals to make "noncommercial" private copies. The identities of the judges had changed, but now,
seventeen years later, the same Circuit Court had another high-profile case on
exactly the same issues. In case any of the judges might have missed this irony,
it took David Boies, the lawyer for Napster, about ninety seconds to remind
them in his oral argument. "This court," he said, adding as if in afterthought,
"in the decision that the Supreme Court ultimately reversed in *Sony*. . . ."[25] To
the laypeople in the audience it probably just seemed like another piece of legal
droning. But to the lawyers in the room the message was quite clear. "The last
time you got a case about a major new technology of consumer reproduction,
you *really* screwed it up. Hope you can do better this time." The judges'
mouths quirked—not entirely in pleasure. The point had been registered.

Think for a moment of the dilemma in which the court had been placed.
On the one hand, you had tens of millions of people "sharing" music files and
Napster was the service that allowed them to do it. If this was not contributory

copyright infringement, what was? On the other hand, Napster seemed to fit very nicely under the rule announced in the *Sony* case.

The argument went like this. Like the VCR, the Napster service had substantial noninfringing uses. It allowed bands to expose their music to the world through the "New Artists" program. It made it easy to share music which was no longer under copyright. These uses clearly do not infringe copyright. There were also the claims that it permitted "space-shifting" by consumers who already owned the music or "sampling" of music by listeners as they decided whether or not to buy. One could argue that space-shifting and sampling were fair use (though in the end the court disagreed). But since we have two clear noninfringing uses, the technology obviously does have substantial uses that do not violate copyright. Thus, Napster cannot be liable as a contributory infringer, just as Sony could not be liable for the Betamax. Supreme Court precedent covers this case. The Ninth Circuit is bound by that precedent. All the judges can do, goes the argument, is to apply the words of the rule laid down in *Sony*, say that Napster wins, and move on to the next case. If Congress wants to make services like Napster illegal, it is going to have to pass a new law. The boundaries of the *Sony* rule are clear and Napster fits within them. (Of course, the last point is subject to argument, but the argument for Napster on this issue was a good one. Not overwhelming—there were *more* noninfringing uses in the *Sony* case because the normal way consumers used the technology in question was found to be a fair use—but certainly powerful.)

A more daring strategy was to suggest that all the copying done over Napster was fair use, or at least *presumptively* fair. In *Sony*, the Supreme Court had said that the law presumes that noncommercial private copying—such as taping a show at home for future viewing—is a fair use. This presumption shifts the burden to the copyright holder to prove that the practice caused harm to them. Copying on Napster was done by private individuals. No money was exchanged. Does this mean we must presume it was fair use and require the music companies and songwriters to show clear evidence of "market harm" if they want to convince us otherwise?

It sounds as though proving market harm would be pretty easy. How could millions of people exchanging hundreds of millions of songs not be causing harm? But it is more complicated. Remember the Jefferson Warning. We are not talking about swiping shoes from a shoe store. There one merely has to show the theft to prove the loss. By contrast, music files are copied without being "taken" from their owner. The record companies would have to show harm to their market—the people downloading who do not purchase music because it is available for free. Those who download, but would not have purchased, do not count. And we have to balance those who are deterred from purchasing against those who purchase a whole CD because they are exposed to new music through Napster. One very interesting empirical study on the subject indicates that the result is a wash, with hardly any measurable effect on sales; the overall drop in CD purchases results from larger macroeconomic issues.[26] This study, however, has been subject to detailed methodological criticism.[27] Another study shows a weak effect on sales, though rather woundingly it seems to suggest that the result is economically efficient—fewer people end up with music they do not like.[28] Other studies, by contrast, support the record company position—suggesting that illicit file sharing does indeed undercut sales of both CDs and authorized digital downloads.[29] Given the complexities of the issue, the record companies did not want to engage in a war of dueling empirical studies.

So, if Napster's users were not infringing copyright law in the first place—at least until the record companies came up with convincing evidence of market harm—because their copying was noncommercial, then Napster could hardly be guilty of contributory infringement, could it? There would be no infringement at all!

You could see Mr. Boies's arguments as simple equations between the cases.

- Noninfringing uses such as recording public domain films and "time-shifting" programs are equivalent to noninfringing uses such as the New Artists program or sharing public domain music (and maybe "space-shifting" one's own music?); or
- Private noncommercial videotaping is equivalent to private noncommercial file sharing. Both are presumptively fair uses.
- Either way, Sony = Napster and Napster wins.

Napster did not win, of course, though when the judges handed down their decision it was clear they had been paying attention to Mr. Boies, at least enough to make them very wary of tampering with *Sony*. They claimed that they were upholding that case, but that Napster could be liable anyway. How? Because there was enough evidence here to show that the controllers of Napster had "actual knowledge that specific infringing material is available using its system, that it could block access to the system by suppliers of the infringing material, and that it failed to remove the material." There was indeed evidence that Napster knew how its system was being used—an embarrassing amount of it, including early memos saying that users will want anonymity because they are trading in "pirated music." Then there were nasty circumstantial details, like the thousands of infringing songs on the hard drive of one particular Napster employee—the compliance officer tasked with enforcing the Digital Millennium Copyright Act! (The recording company lawyers waxed wonderfully sarcastic about that.)

But despite the ludicrously dirty hands of Napster as a company, lawyers could see that the appeals court was making a lot of new law as it struggled to find a way to uphold *Sony* while still making Napster liable. The court's ruling sounded reasonable and clear, something that would only strike at bad actors while paying heed to the Sony Axiom and the assurance of safety that the rule in *Sony* had provided to technology developers for the previous twenty years. But hard cases make bad law. In order to accomplish this piece of legal legerdemain, the court had to alter or reinterpret the law in ways that are disturbing.

The first thing the court did was to reject the argument that the "sharing" was private and noncommercial. As to the idea that it is not private, fair enough. Sharing one's music with fifty-four million people does not sound that private, even if it is done for private ends, in private spaces. What about noncommercial? Embracing some earlier rulings on the subject, the court said a use was "commercial" if you got for nothing something for which you would otherwise have to pay. On the surface this sounds both clever and reasonable—a way to differentiate home taping from global file sharing—but the argument quickly begins to unravel. True, the Betamax owners could get TV shows for free just by watching at the regular time. But they could not get a copy of the show for free at the moment they wanted to watch it. That was why they taped. One could even argue that Napster users would have access to most songs over the radio for free. But lawyers' quibbling about which way the rule cuts in this case is not the point. Instead, we need to focus on the change in the definition of "commercial," because it illustrates a wider shift.

Remember, a finding that a use is "noncommercial" makes it more likely that a court will find it to be legal—to be a fair use. The old test focused mainly on whether the motive for the copying was to make money. (A different stage of the inquiry concerned whether there was harm to the copyright holder's market.) The *Napster* court's test concentrates on whether the person *consuming* the copy got something for free. Instead of focusing on the fact that the person making the copy is not making money out of it—think of a professor making electronic copies of articles for his students to download—it focuses on the presumptively dirty hands of those who are "getting something for nothing." But lots of copyright law is about "getting something for nothing."

To put it differently, one central goal of copyright is to limit the monopoly given to the copyright owner so that he or she cannot force citizens to pay for every single type of use. The design of the law itself is supposed to facilitate that. When "getting something for free" comes to equal "commercial" in the analysis of fair use, things are dangerously out of balance. Think back to Jefferson's analogy. If I light my candle at yours, am I getting fire for free, when otherwise I would have had to pay for matches? Does that make it a "commercial" act?

Having dismissed the claim that this was noncommercial sharing, the court then reinterpreted the *Sony* decision to allow liability when there was "actual knowledge" of specific copyright violations, an ability to block access by infringers, and a failure to do so. Neither side was entirely happy with this ruling, but the record companies believed—rightly—that it would allow them effectively to shut Napster down. Yet the *Napster* ruling only postponed the issue. The next set of file sharing services to be sued after Napster were even more decentralized peer-to-peer systems; the *Napster* court's reinterpretation of *Sony* would not be able to reach them.

The peer-to-peer file sharing service called Grokster is a relatively typical example. Unlike Napster, Grokster had no central registry. The system was entirely run by the individual "peer" computers. Because the system was designed this way, the people who made and distributed the software had no knowledge of specific infringing files. The users were doing the searching, indexing, and storing, and Grokster had no ability to control their behavior. For those reasons, a court of appeals held that Grokster was not liable. As in *Sony*, the system had substantial noninfringing uses. Lots of interesting content was traded on Grokster with the copyright holder's consent. Other material was in the public domain. Grokster made money by streaming advertisements to the users of its software. The movie companies and record companies saw this as a flagrant, for-profit piracy ring. Grokster's response was that like the makers of the VCR, it was simply providing a technology. Its financial interest was in people using that technology, not in using it for illicit purposes— though, like the VCR manufacturer, it would profit either way. The court of appeals agreed. True, the majority of the material traded on Grokster was illicitly copied, but the court felt that it could not give the recording or movie companies control over a technology simply because it allowed for easier copying, even if most of that copying was illegal. As I tried to point out in the section on the Sony Axiom, that line of thought leads to copyright holders having a veto over technological development.

It was at this point that the Supreme Court stepped in. In the case of *MGM v. Grokster*,[30] the Supreme Court followed the line of the *Napster* court, but went even further. The Court created a new type of contributory copyright infringement—while apparently denying it was doing so. Grokster and its fellow services were liable because of three different kinds of evidence that they had "intended" to induce copyright violation. First, they were trying "to satisfy a known demand for copyright infringement." This could be shown by the way that they advertised themselves as alternatives to the "notorious file-sharing service, Napster." Second, the file sharing services did not try to develop filtering software to identify and eliminate copyrighted content—though this alone would not have been enough to make them liable. Finally, their advertising-supported system clearly profited by high-intensity use, which they knew was driven in the most part by illicit copying. This too would not have been enough by itself, the Court added, but had to be seen in the context of the whole record of the case.

Let me be clear. I wept no tears for Napster, Grokster, and their ilk. I see no high-minded principle vindicated by middle-class kids getting access to music they do not want to pay for. It is difficult to take seriously the sanctimonious preening of those who cast each junior downloader of corporate rock as a Ché Guevara, fighting heroically to bring about a new creative landscape in music. (It is almost as hard to take seriously the record industry executives who moralistically denounce the downloading in the name of the poor, suffering artists, when they preside over a system of contracts with those same artists that makes feudal indenture look benign.) The file sharing companies themselves were also pretty unappealing. Many of the services were bloated with adware and spyware. True, some of their software engineers started with a dewy-eyed belief that this was a revolutionary technology that would break the record companies and usher in a new era of musical creativity. Whether one agrees or disagrees with them, it is hard—for me at least—to doubt their sincerity. But even this quality did not last long. For most of the people involved, the words "stock options" worked their normal, morally debilitating magic. In internal company correspondence, attacks on the hypocrisy of the music companies and defenses of a democratic communications structure imperceptibly gave way to discussions of "customer base," "user experience," and "saleable demographics." I care little that Napster and Grokster—as individual companies—lost their specific legal battles. There are few heroes in this story. But if we had to rely on heroes, nothing would ever get done.

I do care about the technology behind Napster and Grokster—about the kind of decentralized system it represents. I also care about the principle I identified as the Sony Axiom—a principle that goes far beyond music, peer-to-peer systems, or the Internet as a whole. The Supreme Court's decision in *Grokster* could have been much worse. But it still offers a modest threat both to that technology and to that axiom.

What is so great about peer-to-peer systems? We talk about "cheap speech" on the Internet, but bandwidth is actually expensive. If one is talking about music or video files, and one wishes to speak to many people in a short period of time, one vital way to have cheap speech is over peer-to-peer networks. If many of your viewers or listeners are willing to become broadcasting stations as they watch, you can cheaply reach a million people in a short period of time with your video of abuse in Abu Ghraib or your parody of political leaders. You do not need to rely on a broadcasting station, or even on the continued existence of entities such as YouTube, which face their own legal worries. By making your listeners your distributors, you can quickly reach the same number of ears that the payola-soaked radio waves allow the record companies to reach.

One need not cheer Grokster. Much of what went on there was indeed illicit. But there are two key things to understand about peer-to-peer networks. The first is that they are hard to police. They have multiple nodes. That is why they work. It means they will have both infringing and noninfringing uses, and the noninfringing uses will be centrally connected to our deepest values of free speech and cultural decentralization.

The second feature of peer-to-peer networks is even more basic. They are networks and thus subject to the laws of network economics. In short, they only work well if many people use them. A person who uses a peer-to-peer system that no one else uses is in the position of the person who owns the only fax machine in the world. Peer-to-peer networks provide cheap and unregulable audiovisual or data-heavy "speech" to a mass audience. And if the past is any guide, those networks will also carry large amounts of illicit material, just as photocopying machines (and VCRs) are widely used to violate copyright. The *Grokster* case makes it harder, but not impossible, to have successful, widely used peer-to-peer systems that are not themselves illicit. If they are widely used, there will be infringing content. If you try to police them and filter them, you will know more about that infringing content and thus might be liable—that was the point of the *Napster* case. If you do not, you will be failing to take precautions. That was the point of the *Grokster* case. What is a poor peer-to-peer network to do? Apart from making sure that the last four letters of your service's name are not "-ster," I am hard-pressed to advise you.

A decision does not need to make an activity illegal in order to impede it. It only needs to make it uncertain. Already, for example, the free—and so far as I could tell, entirely well-meaning—service "bonpoo," which allowed you to send large file attachments to many people at once, has shut down all of its capabilities except photo transfer. That is simply one trivial instance of a larger harm. Lots of new communications technologies will remain undeveloped because of the uncertainties left by this ruling.

My colleague Jennifer Jenkins gave one useful hyperbolic illustration, drawing on earlier work by the Electronic Frontier Foundation: if one were launching the iPod today, it is not clear how it would fare under *Grokster*'s standard. Of course, there is no danger that the iPod will be challenged. It has become respectable and the music companies ended up sanctioning it. But how does it fare if we simply apply the tests laid down in the *Grokster* case? There is Apple's "tainted" advertising campaign, urging users to "Rip, Mix, and Burn." Does this not suggest complicity, or even intent? There is the fact that the iPod does not restrict itself solely to proprietary formats protected by digital rights management. It also allows uncontrolled MP3 files despite the fact that this format is "notoriously" used to transfer files against the wishes of the copyright owner. This, surely, is a "failure to police." And finally, there is the fact that it would cost about $10,000 to fill an iPod with songs downloaded from iTunes. Clearly Apple must be aware that much of the music that fills iPods is illicitly copied. They are profiting from that fact to drive demand for the product, just as Grokster was profiting from the attractions of illicit traffic to drive people to use their service!

No one is going to sue Apple now, of course. In fact, established players in the marketplace are probably fairly safe (and have better lawyers). But what if a product as good as the iPod were being developed now by some upstart company? What if it were no more and no less likely to be used for infringing purposes? Would the business plan ever see the light of day? Or would it be quietly smothered due to legal uncertainty? I have little sympathy for Grokster the company, but the decision that doomed it is a bad piece of technology policy.

There is a second reason to dislike the *Grokster* decision. Despite some of the angst-ridden announcements made when the decision was handed down, the Supreme Court has not killed peer-to-peer systems. The concept is far too well entrenched. But the decision will mean that there are fewer of them that are widely used, easy to operate, and made by responsible and reputable people you can trust. This will probably lessen, but not end, illicit copying online. But that effect comes with a price—it makes our communications architecture a little bit more tightly controlled, reducing but not removing the availability of methods of mass distribution that are entirely outside central-ized public or private control. It is another—relatively small—step toward an Internet that is more like cable TV or iTunes, a one-way flow of approved content. One might decide that such a price was well worth paying. But where is the limiting principle or end point of the logic that led to it?

There is *no* provision in U.S. statutory copyright law that imposes liabil-ity for contributory or vicarious infringement. None. The patent statute has such a provision; not the Copyright Act. The courts have simply made the scheme up themselves. Then they made up limitations—such as *Sony*—in order to rein it in. In *Grokster*, the Supreme Court went further. It made up a new type of "inducement" liability. Fine. As I have tried to indicate here, the decision is not as dreadful as it is reputed to be. But so long as there is any un-regulated space in our communications network, some portion of it will have illicitly copied content on it. The more the system is free of central control, the more it is open to use by any citizen, the cheaper it gets—all very desirable characteristics—the more illicit content there will be. That is the premise of the Internet Threat—the belief that control must rise as copying costs fall. I have tried here to suggest an alternative interpretation, the Sony Axiom: with-out a strong internal set of limitations over copyright, cheaper copying and the logic of the Internet Threat will *always* drive us toward giving control over our communications architecture to the content industries.

There was one particularly striking moment in the *Napster* oral argument. The lawyer for the recording companies was arguing that Napster was illegal. The judges interrupted, as they often do, and there was a back-and-forth de-bate about the likely reach of any ruling that would shut down Napster. "I am not trying to say the Internet is illegal," said the lawyer. There was a pause as everyone weighed those words carefully.

My response would be "Really? Why not?" The logic of the Internet Threat leads to the position that a network is either controlled or illegal. The better and cheaper the network, the tighter the control needed. The Internet itself could have been designed differently. There could have been more centralized control, filtering of content, a design based on one-way transmission, closed protocols that allow users only a limited number of options. Indeed there were such systems—the national French Minitel system is an example. The

Internet represents the opposite set of choices—freedom from centralized control, absence of intervention. In a famous article, Saltzer, Reed, and Clark provided the argument that an "end-to-end" network that is "dumb" and leaves processing to the "ends"—the smart terminals at either end of the wires—will be stable and robust.[31] But it will also be remarkably uncontrolled and it will lower global copying costs close to zero for digital content. It is that principle that has made it successful. To put it tersely: the logic of the Internet Threat runs in exactly the opposite direction to the Internet itself. The logic of control is not the logic of the Net.

Here is one last thought experiment. Apply the same test I suggested for the iPod to the Internet itself.[32] Imagine you knew nothing of the Net. (Those of you who are over twenty-five may actually be able to remember when you knew nothing of the Net.) Imagine that you are sitting in a room somewhere discussing—perhaps with a group of government bureaucrats or some policy analysts from the Commerce Department—whether to develop this particular network. The scientists are enthusiastic. They talk of robustness and dumb networks with smart terminals. They talk of TCP/IP and HTML and decentralized systems that run on open protocols, so that anyone can connect to this network and use it any way they want to. You, of course, know nothing about the truly astounding outburst of creativity and communication that would actually flower on such a system, that would flower precisely because it is so open and no one country or company controls it or the protocols that run it. You do not know that millions of people worldwide will assemble the greatest factual reference work the world has ever seen on this network—often providing their information for free out of some bizarre love of sharing. You do not know about Amazon.com or Hotornot.com or the newspapers of the world online, or search engines, automatic page translation, plug-ins, or browsers. You cannot imagine free or open-source software being assembled by thousands of programmers worldwide. E-mail is only a dimly understood phenomenon to you. Teenagers in your world have never heard of instant messaging—a nostalgic thought.

As the scientists talk, it becomes clear that they are describing a system without centralized direction or policing. Imagine that your decision is framed by the logic of control I have described in this chapter, by the fears that the content industry has had for at least the last thirty years—by the logic of the suit they brought in *Sony*. Imagine, in other words, that we make the up-or-down decision to develop the Internet based on the values and fears that our copyright policy now exhibits, and that the content industries have exhibited for thirty years. There is no way, no way at all, that a network like it would ever be developed. It would be strangled at birth. You would be told by the lawyers and policy wonks that it would be a haven for piracy and illegality. (And it would be, of course—though it would also be much, much more.) You would be told that the system needed to be designed to be safe for commerce or it would never attract investment, that it would need to be controlled and centralized for it to be reliable, that it would need to be monitored to stop it being a hotbed of crime. With the copyright lawyers in the room, you would end up designing something that looked like cable TV or Minitel. The Internet would never get off the ground.

The Internet is safe now, of course, because it developed so fast that it was a reality before people had time to be afraid of it. But it should give us pause that if we had our current guiding set of policy goals in place, our assumption that cheaper copying means we need greater regulation, we would never have allowed it to flourish. As Jessica Litman points out, we are increasingly making our decisions about technology and communications policy inside copyright law. We are doing so according to the logic of control that I have sketched out in this chapter. But the logic of control is a partial logic. It blinds us to certain possibilities, ones that have huge and proven potential—look at the Internet.

The law has not been entirely one-sided, however. The *Sony* case drew a line in the sand which promised to halt the inevitable drift toward greater and greater control over communications technology by content owners. It turned out the heavens did not fall. Indeed, the content companies thrived. Perhaps that line was drawn in the wrong place; reasonable people can disagree about that. But *Grokster* smudges the line without drawing a clear new one. If that new line is drawn according to the logic of control, what technologies will we never see? Could they be technologies that would transform our lives as unimaginably as the Internet has since 1995?

I have described the story line—the cluster of metaphors and images and concerns—that pervades our copyright policy. I labeled it "the Internet Threat." In the next chapter, I discuss an alternative story line, a different way of understanding our current policies. The subject of that story line is the best-known example of contemporary attempts to control the digital world, the Digital Millennium Copyright Act or DMCA.

5

The Farmers' Tale:
An Allegory

Imagine that a bustling group of colonists has just moved into a new area, a huge, unexplored plain. (Again, assume the native inhabitants have conveniently disappeared.) Some of the colonists want to farm just as they always did in the old country. "Good fences make good neighbors" is their motto. Others, inspired by the wide-open spaces around them, declare that this new land needs new ways. They want to let their cattle roam as they will; their slogan is "Protect the open range." In practice, the eventual result is a mixture of the two regimes. Fields under cultivation can be walled off but there is a right of passage through the farmers' lands for all who want it, so long as no damage is done. This means travelers do not need to make costly and ineffi-cient detours around each farm. In the long run, these "public roads" actually increase the value of the private property through which they pass. They also let the ranchers move their cattle around from one area of pasture to another. The ranchers become strong propo-nents of "public, open highways" (though some people muse darkly that they do very well out of that rule). Still, most people want open highways; the system seems to work pretty well, in fact.

Two new technologies are introduced. First, the automobile is developed. Now thieves can drive through the farmers' fields, stop quickly to grab some corn or a lettuce, and be back on the highway before they can be caught. Of course, the farmers' costs have also fallen dramatically; now they have tractors to work their fields and trucks to take their products to distant markets. The farmers do not dwell on the benefits of the new technology, however. Understandably, they focus more on the profits they could reap if they could get all the advantages of the technology and none of its costs. They demand new legal protections aimed at producing that result. "What's good for agriculture is good for the nation," they say. But now comes the second technological shock—the development of barbed wire. The cost of erecting impassable barriers falls dramatically. The farmers begin to see the possibility of enclosing *all* of their land, roads and fields alike. This will help them protect their crops from pilfering, but it will also allow them to charge people for opening the gates in their fences—even the gates on public roads. That is a nice extra revenue stream which will, the farmers say, "help encourage agriculture." After all, more fences mean more money for farmers, and more money for farmers means they can invest in new methods of farming, which will mean everyone is better off, right?

What is to be done? Assume that each side presents its case to the legislature. There are three obvious possibilities:

First, the legislature can simply tell each side to work it out amongst themselves. The law will continue to forbid trespass, but we are neither going to make it a crime to put up a barbed wire fence if it blocks legitimate public rights of way nor to make it a crime to cut a barbed wire fence, unless the fence cutter is also a trespasser. The farmers can attempt to enclose land by putting barbed wire around it. Ranchers and drivers can legally cut those fences when they are blocking public rights of way. Trespass remains trespass, nothing more.

Second, the legislature could heed the ranchers' fears that barbed wire will permit the farmers not only to protect their own land, but to rob the public of its existing rights of way, turning open highways into toll roads. (The ranchers, of course, are more concerned with the rights of cattle than people, but most drivers agree with them.) As a result, the state could forbid the erection of a barbed wire fence where it might block a public right of way—classing it as a kind of theft, perhaps.

Third, the legislature could take the farmers' side. Theorizing that this new automobile technology presents "a terrible threat to agriculture, because of rampant crop piracy," the state could go beyond the existing law of trespass and make it a crime to cut barbed wire fences wherever you find them (even if the fences are enclosing public lands as well as private, or blocking public roads). To back up its command, it could get into the technology regulation business—making the manufacture or possession of wire cutters illegal.

The state picks option three. Wire cutting becomes a crime, wire cutters are classed with lock picks and other "criminals' tools," and the people who make wire cutters are told their business is illegal. A storm of protest arises in the rural driving community. The wire cutter manufacturers claim that their products have lots of legitimate uses. All to no avail: the farmers press on. They have two new demands. Cars should be fitted with mandatory radio beacons and highways put under constant state surveillance in order to deter crop theft. In addition, car trunks should be redesigned so they can hold less—just in case the owner plans to load them up with purloined produce. Civil libertarians unite with car manufacturers to attack the plan. The farmers declare that the car manufacturers are only interested in making money from potential thieves and that the civil libertarians are Nervous Nellies: no one has anything to fear except the criminals. "What's good for agriculture is good for the nation," they announce again. As the barbed wire gates swing shut across the highways of the region, the legislature heads back into session.

BETWEEN PARANOIA
AND REALITY: THE DMCA

I have argued that confusing intellectual property with physical property is dangerous. I stand by that argument. Yet analogies to physical property are powerful. It is inevitable that we attempt to explain new phenomena by comparing them to material with which we are more familiar. While the content companies' tales of "theft" and "piracy" are the most prevalent, they are by no means the only such analogy one can make. In this chapter I try to prove that point.

The Farmers' Tale is my allegorical attempt to explain the struggle over the single most controversial piece of intellectual property legislation in recent years, the Digital Millennium Copyright Act, or DMCA.[1] The DMCA did many things, but for our purposes its crucial provisions are those forbidding the "circumvention of copyright protection systems," the technological measures that copyright holders can use to deny access to their works or control our behavior once we get access. These measures include encryption, controls on how many times a file can be copied, password protection, and so on. Copyright protection systems are, in other words, the digital equivalent of barbed wire, used to add an additional layer of "physical" protection to the property owner's existing legal protection. But, unlike barbed wire, they can also control what we do once we get access to the property.

The rules that forbid circumvention of these systems are logically, if not elegantly, referred to as the anticircumvention provisions. They are to be found in Section 1201 of the Copyright Act, an ungainly and lumpily written portion of the law that was inserted in 1998 as part of the complex set of amendments collectively referred to as the DMCA. I will explain the significance of these rules in a moment. My hope is that the analogy to the Farmers' Tale will make them a little easier to understand—at least for those of you for whom talk of digital rights management, anticircumvention provisions, and network effects is not second nature.

Notice the differences between this allegory and the "Internet Threat" story line I described in the last chapter. There are two sets of bad guys in the Farmers' Tale. The greedy thieves (who are still thieves in this story—not heroes) and the greedy farmers who use a genuine if indefinite "threat" posed by a new technology to mask a power grab. The Internet Threat is the story of an industry devastated by piracy, in desperate need of help from the state to protect its legitimate property interests. By contrast, the Farmers' Tale is the story of a self-interested attempt not only to protect property but to cut off recognized rights of public access in a way that will actually make the whole society worse off. The legitimate role of the state in protecting private property has been stretched into an attempt to regulate technology so as to pick winners in the marketplace, enriching the farmers at the expense of consumers and other businesses. In the long run this will not be good for business as a whole. A patchwork of private toll roads is an economic nightmare.

That is not the most worrying part of the story: the farmers' proposals are moving in the direction of regulating still more technology—the mandatory radio beacons and constantly monitored roads conjure up a police state—and all to protect a bunch of hysterical vegetable growers whose political clout far outweighs their actual economic importance.

Both the Internet Threat and the Farmers' Tale are, of course, ways to understand what is currently going on in the intellectual property wars. In the digital realm, the part of the farmers is played by the content companies, the recording industry associations, the movie and software trade groups. Pointing to the threat of digital piracy, they demanded and received extra legal protection for their copyrighted content. Unlike earlier expansions—longer copyright terms, more stringent penalties, the shrinking of exceptions and limitations, expansions in copyrightable subject matter—this was not a protection of the work itself; it was a protection of the digital fences wrapped around it, and a regulation of the technology that might threaten those fences.

What is the significance of this? The digital revolution makes it easier to copy copyrighted content. It also makes it easier to protect that content, and to do so in a more granular and precisely calibrated way. Imagine being able to sell a paperback book that could only be read by the original purchaser or a song that could only be listened to by a particular person in a particular room. Digital rights management technology makes it a lot easier to do these things. Suddenly the copyright owners have considerable physical control over their songs, e-books, and software, even after they have sold them. It is as if the recording industry or the publishers had a representative in your living room. They can use that control not merely to prevent illicit copying but to control and limit usage in ways that go far beyond their exclusive rights under copyright. All of this happens without the law or the state doing anything. Like barbed wire, this is a technological protection measure.

Like the farmers, the content companies were not content with their barbed wire alone. They wanted *legally protected* barbed wire in addition to their existing legal rights under copyright. Under the Digital Millennium Copyright Act, it became illegal to circumvent a technical protection measure such as encryption—the digital barbed wire behind which content companies secrete their work—even if what you did with the content when you got past the barbed wire was a fair use; excerpting a fragment of a film for a school presentation, for example, or making a copy of an encrypted audio file for personal use in another device. In other words, by using digital barbed wire, the content companies could prevent citizens from making the "fair uses" the copyright law allowed. This undermines some of the limitations on their exclusive rights that the Copyright Act explicitly carves out in Section 107, and thus shifts the balance of power that the Copyright Act establishes. Cutting barbed wire became a civil wrong, and perhaps a crime, even if the wire blocked a public road. Under most circumstances, making wire cutters was also now against the law.

The ranchers—whose digital equivalents are communications companies and hardware manufacturers—chafed under these new rules. The most powerful groups managed to get special dispensations. Internet service providers, for example, got a qualified immunity from copyright infringement that occurs over their networks. But ordinary citizens, librarians, and civil libertarians also complained, and they were not as well represented in the legislature. It is true that the new rules may help to prevent illicit copying, but they also strike a blow against the exercise of fair use rights—rights that are important both to free speech and competition. Even if the content companies were absolutely right about the threats from digital piracy, this consequence should make us pause. But critics of the DMCA say that there is little evidence that the content companies are right. They quote some of the empirical studies I mentioned in the last chapter, particularly the ones that show no net negative effect from unauthorized music downloading on CD sales. They claim—and they are on strong ground here—that even if there are some losses from the new copying technologies, there are also benefits. Like the farmers, the critics would argue, the content companies take the benefits of the new technology for granted, but wish the law to step in to ameliorate the harms it also creates. And like the farmers, they are not yet satisfied. Their new proposals go even further—scarily further. Thus runs the critics' argument.

The critics of the DMCA conjure up a world in which it will be illegal to lend each other books or songs, where it will be impossible for us to copy even small fragments of digital work for criticism or parody, where encryption research will be severely "chilled," and where large quantities of the public domain will be enclosed together with the copyrighted content that the DMCA is supposed to protect. (The Electronic Frontier Foundation's "Unintended Consequences" studies give concrete examples.)[2] They think the DMCA undoes the balance at the heart of copyright law, that it can be used to entrench existing businesses and their business methods, that it threatens speech, competition, privacy, and innovation itself. In short, they think the DMCA is the worst intellectual property law Congress has ever passed and view the adoption of similar laws around the world with a reaction little short of horror.

Those who supported the DMCA disagree, of course, and do so honestly. They see rampant piracy as a reality and the threat to fair use as some kind of academic hypothetical rarely encountered in reality. What's more, many of them do not think fair use is that important economically or culturally. If markets work well, users could be made to pay for the rights that fair use gives—but only if they wanted them. One could buy expensive digital books which one was allowed to share, quote, or copy for classroom use, and cheaper ones which one had to keep to oneself. Remember that for many of the people who supported the DMCA, fair use is something of a "loophole"; certainly not an affirmative right of the public or a reserved limitation on the original property grant from the state. (Remember the Sony Axiom from Chapter 4?) They find the analogy of fair use to a public road ludicrous. This film, or book, or song, is *mine*; anything you do with it, or to it, you do at my sufferance. (Remember the Jefferson Warning from Chapter 2?)

How has the DMCA worked in reality? Which group's attitudes were vindicated? Two case studies may help us to answer these question.

Infectious Speech: The DMCA and Freedom of Expression

Jon Johansen, a 16-year-old Norwegian, was the unwitting catalyst for one of the most important cases interpreting the DMCA. He and two anonymous helpers wrote a program called DeCSS. Depending on whom you listen to, DeCSS is described either as a way of allowing people who use Linux or other open source operating systems to play DVDs on their computers, or as a tool for piracy that threatened the entire movie industry and violated the DMCA.

A little background is in order. When you play a commercial DVD, your actions are partly controlled by a simple encryption scheme called CSS, or the Content Scramble System. The DVD Copy Control Association licenses the keys to this encryption system to the manufacturers of DVD players. Without a key, most DVDs could not be played. The manufacturer then embeds this key in its hardware design in such a way that it is easy for your player to decode and play the movie but hard, at least for a person of average technical competence, to copy the decoded "stream."

Because the DVD Copy Control Association will only license keys to manufacturers whose DVD players conform exactly to their specifications, the CSS scheme can also be used to control viewers in other ways. For example, DVD players are required to have one of six "region codes," depending on where in the world they are sold. Region 1 is the United States and Canada. Region 2 is Japan, Europe, South Africa, the Middle East, and—bizarrely—Greenland. Region 3 is South Korea, Taiwan, and Hong Kong; and so on. The CSS scheme can be used to restrict a movie to a player with the appropriate region code. If you try to play a movie coded for region 6 (China) in a DVD player from region 1, it will not play. This allows filmmakers to distribute different versions of films to different regions at different times based on sequential release in cinemas, or simply to distribute DVDs with different prices to different regions without worrying about whether the cheaper DVDs will "leak" into the more lucrative markets. CSS and the hardware scheme that unlocks it can also be used to prevent you from fast-forwarding through the commercials at the beginning of the movie if the copyright owner does not want you to, or from skipping the FBI notice. The machine will not do it. In fact, it is deliberately built so that it *cannot* do it.

What we have here is a digital fence that is partly used to prevent copying. Movie studios are understandably worried about the worldwide circulation of perfect digital copies of their movies. CSS was supposed to help to prevent that, or at least make it much harder. But because almost all movies are encrypted with CSS and access to the keys comes with conditions, CSS also allows a more fine-grained control over consumers. Manufacturers are not *allowed* to make players which can view movies from all region codes or skip portions of the DVD that the owners do not want you to skip. The licensing body puts it this way on its Web site: "Q. Under the terms of the CSS licensing agreement, is it legal for a licensed manufacturer to produce and sell a product which allows a user to disable any CSS protections? A. No. Such products are not allowed under the terms of the CSS license. They are illegal."[3] A technology introduced to protect intellectual property rights allows control in ways that those rights alone do not.

Before the DMCA, the movie companies could have done exactly this. They could have wrapped their movies in a digital fence. The consumer electronics companies that wanted to could license a key and be allowed to use a trademark that indicated that they were approved by the DVD Copy Control Association. But what if a manufacturer of DVD players felt that American consumers wanted to be able to play their Japanese anime movies without buying another DVD player to do so? Or what if they thought people were antsy and did not want to watch the FBI notice before every film? The manufacturer could have tried to "reverse engineer" the CSS system, to figure out how it worked. If they succeeded, they could make a player that was free of the restrictions that the CSS licensing authority imposed.

Of course there were some legal limitations even before the DMCA. Our hypothetical manufacturer could not break into the safe where the CSS code was being held or bribe an employee to provide it. (That would be a trespass or a violation of trade secret law.) It could not violate copyright laws over the various types of software that controlled DVD players. It could not use the trademarks of any of the entities involved, including any seal of approval granted by the DVD Copy Control Association. But it could—at least in the United States—try to reverse engineer the product so as to make a competing product with features that the customers liked more. It would be no more illegal than a company making a cheaper generic razor cartridge that fits my expensive Gillette Mach 3 razor, a generic printer cartridge to replace the expensive one in my Lexmark printer, or, for that matter, a generic remote control for my garage door opener. In each case, of course, the original manufacturer would prefer that I use their products rather than the unlicensed ones. They can design their product to make it hard to use a generic replacement or even tell me that my warranty will be void if I use one. But they cannot say that the unlicensed product is *illegal*. We are back in option one of the Farmers' Tale, before the legislature acted. The farmers can put up their wire, and even use it to block passage that would be otherwise legal, but it is not a crime to figure out a way through the fence unless the fence cutter is also a trespasser. The DMCA, however, might have changed all of that.

Let us return to Mr. Johansen, the 16-year-old Norwegian. He and his two anonymous collaborators claimed that they were affected by another limitation imposed by the CSS licensing body. At that time, there was no way to play DVDs on a computer running Linux, or any other free or open source operating system. (I will talk more about free and open source software later.) Let's say you buy a laptop. A Sony Vaio running Windows, for example. It has a slot in the side for DVDs to slide in and software that comes along with it which allows the DVD reader to decode and play the disk. The people who wrote the software have been licensed by the DVD Copy Control Association and provided with a CSS key. But at the time Mr. Johansen set out to create DeCSS, the licensing body had not licensed keys to any free or open source software developers. Say Mr. Johansen buys the Sony Vaio, but with the Linux operating system on it instead of Windows. The computer is the same. The little slot is still there. Writing an open source program to control the DVD player is trivial. But without the CSS key, there is no way for the player to decode and play the movie. (The licensing authority later did license an open source player, perhaps because they realized its unavailability gave Mr. Johansen a strong defense, perhaps because they feared an antitrust suit, or perhaps because they just got around to it.)

Mr. Johansen and his supporters claimed strenuously that DeCSS was not in fact an aid to illicit copying. In fact, they argued that CSS was not really designed to protect DVDs against illicit copying. Commercial DVD "pirates" do not need to crack the CSS encryption. Quite the contrary: they produce exact copies of the DVD, CSS encryption and all, and the buyer's player dutifully decodes it and plays it. Mr. Johansen claimed that his goals were very different from those of the pirates.

The motivation was being able to play DVDs the way we want to. I don't like being forced to use a specific operating system or a specific player to watch movies (or listen to music). Nor do I like being forced to watch commercials. When your DVD player tells you "This operation is not allowed" when you try to skip commercials, it becomes pretty clear that DRM really stands for Digital Restrictions Management.[4]

In Mr. Johansen's view, CSS was simply an attempt to control consumers, an attempt which should be a valid target for legal reverse engineering. He has a point. There were indeed other ways to copy DVDs which did not require DeCSS and which gave you files of more manageable size. CSS was indeed more than a simple anticopying device. The entire scheme—the keys, the licenses, the hardware requirements—was designed to give movie studios greater control over their movies in a number of ways, some of them unrelated to copying. On the other hand, he overstated the point. One function of CSS was indeed to make it harder for the average person playing a DVD on a computer to copy the file from the DVD to her hard disk and give it to a friend. It is very easy for the average 14-year-old to take a commercial music CD, change the songs into smaller files in the MP3 format, and share them with a friend. It is not as easy to do the same thing to a DVD—not impossible, just harder—and CSS is one of the reasons why.

Mr. Johansen's program, DeCSS, was quickly made available worldwide. Mirror sites provided copies of the program and lists of such locations were easy to find using standard search tools. One such list was provided by the online site run by a magazine called *2600: The Hacker Quarterly*. The magazine features everything from pictures of pay phones from around the world to tips on how to hack into computer or telephone systems. Its publisher is one Eric Corley, who goes by the name Emmanuel Goldstein—the resistance leader in George Orwell's *1984*.

In 1999, Universal City Studios brought suit against a number of individuals for distributing DeCSS. The case was called *Universal City Studios v. Reimerdes et al.* Corley was among the defendants. The suit prominently included a claim that the defendants were violating the DMCA. It was in this case that the DMCA received its first major legal challenge.

Depending on the characterization of the facts, the case seems to be about very different things. It could seem a classic First Amendment fight. ("Plucky magazine publisher told copyright law forbids him from linking to other sites on the Internet!") Or it could seem the very essence of illegal activity. ("Shadowy site which unashamedly caters to computer 'hackers' tries to spread access to the burglar's tools of cyberspace!")

Of course, most lawsuits involve conflicts over facts. Much of what lawyers do is put the same facts into different conceptual boxes. But here, merely describing what Corley does, what hackers are, or what *2600* magazine is all about involves one in a profound culture clash. The best way to capture the clash may be to quote from an early entry about Corley in Wikipedia, the remarkable online encyclopedia.

The encyclopedia first quotes the description of *2600* magazine from Judge Lewis A. Kaplan, the federal district court judge who decided the *Reimerdes* case.

> "2600: The Hacker Quarterly has included articles on such topics as how to steal an Internet domain name, how to write more secure ASP code, access other people's e-mail, secure your Linux box, intercept cellular phone calls, how to put Linux on an Xbox, how to remove spyware, and break into the computer systems at Costco stores and Federal Express. One issue contains a guide to the federal criminal justice system for readers charged with computer hacking. In addition, 2600 operates a web site located at 2600.com (http://www.2600.com), which is managed primarily by Mr. Corley and has been in existence since 1995."

The Wikipedia article then continues as follows:

> While the judge's tone is clearly disapproving, others would point out that bookstores, movies and television channels are filled with material on how to commit murder . . . and that without the efforts of the hacker community, however ill-intentioned, computer insecurity would be even more of a problem than it already is.[5]

In fact, Judge Kaplan was *not* entirely disapproving. He mentions articles in *2600* that cover laudable or innocuous tasks, as well as others about tasks that most readers would find objectionable and rightly think to be illegal. But the anonymous volunteer who wrote this version of Corley's Wikipedia entry clearly saw the issue differently. Wikipedia does not portray the hacker community as universally benevolent ("however ill-intentioned"), but that community is also seen as providing a useful service rather than merely a set of how-to guides for would-be digital burglars.

To most people, pointing out vulnerabilities in computer security systems seemed, at least in 1999, like telling the world that your neighbor has forgotten to lock his door and all his possessions are there for the taking. But to the online community, it is by no means so clear. From the perspective of those who are knowledgeable in the field, there is a moral continuum. There is clearly legitimate computer security and cryptography research, which includes attempts to break into computer systems to test their defenses—that is how one finds out they are secure, after all. Then there are "hackers." This term could be used to describe those who merely like to program. Richard Stallman, for example, the originator of the free software movement, describes himself thus. But the term could also be used for those who are interested in security or interoperability—making two systems work together. That was Mr. Johansen's declared goal, after all. But some self-described hackers go further. They believe that exploring and disclosing the weaknesses of supposedly secure systems is intellectually fulfilling, practically important, and protected by the First Amendment. They disclaim both moral and legal responsibility for the consequences of their disclosures. (Or at least the negative consequences; they frequently take credit for the positive consequences, such as improved security.) Finally, there are "crackers," whose interest in gaining entry to computer systems is malicious or for financial gain. At what point on this continuum does the activity become legally, or morally, unacceptable? As the *Reimerdes* trial went on, it became clear that the answer the DMCA gave might not be the same as the one given even by undeniably legitimate computer scientists.

A large number of legal arguments were involved in the *Reimerdes* case, but for our purposes here the most important ones dealt with the relationship between copyright and the First Amendment. What is that relationship?

In one obvious sense copyright actually aids free speech. By providing an incentive to create works, copyright "add[s] the fuel of interest to the fire of genius,"[6] and thus helps to create the system of decentralized creative production and distribution I described in Chapter 1. But copyright also restrains speech. At its base, it allows an individual to call upon the state to prevent someone from speaking or expressing themselves in a particular way. This may involve a simple refusal to let the speaker use some text, picture, verse, or story in their message, or it may involve a refusal to let them transform it in some way.

Neither copyright law nor the American Constitution is blind to these dangers. Copyright has a number of built-in safeguards. The most important of these is that copyright only covers "original expression"—both the ideas and facts in this book can be used by anyone without my permission. Thus, goes the theory, the speaker's freedom of expression is never truly restrained. The only thing I am barred from is using your words, your exact plot, your photograph, your music—not your facts, your ideas, your genre, the events you describe.

That is not always enough, of course. Sometimes the problem is that the speaker *cannot* paraphrase around the restraints posed by copyright. He needs to use the particular text or image in question to convey his message. The ideas, the facts, or a mere paraphrase of the expression would not be enough. In cases like that copyright's answer is "fair use." A politician could not prevent journalists who disagree with him from quoting his autobiography in discussing his life. If an African-American author wishes to tell the story of *Gone With the Wind* from the slaves' perspective, she may do so in the face of the copyright holders' attempts to stop her. Even fair use, though, may not cover every concern about free expression. Before World War II, Alan Cranston— later a U.S. Senator—wanted to convince American readers that the version of Hitler's *Mein Kampf* published in the United States was distorted. He believed it to be slanted toward American sensibilities, downplaying both anti-Semitism and German expansionism. His solution? To publish his own English translation, taken direct and uncut from the German edition. He wanted to prove, with Hitler's own words, that the United States had a dangerously distorted version of the German leader. But this is the kind of thing copyright law forbids and it is not clear that fair use allows. (In the end he did it anyway.)[7]

For the moment though, it is enough to realize that copyright law is not immune from the First Amendment or from free speech concerns more generally. If we do not notice that most of the time, it is because the internal limitations of copyright—fair use, the idea-expression distinction, and so on—generally take care of the First Amendment issue, not because the issue was never there.

So what First Amendment issues did the DMCA present? Most obviously, the DMCA gave a new right to copyright owners. By using a few simple technological measures, they could distribute a work in a particular format and yet, because of their new intellectual property right, they could make illegal an otherwise lawful process of gaining access for the purposes of making fair use. Of course, the First Amendment allows me to make fair use *factually impossible.* I can do that without raising any constitutional issues by hiding my manuscript and never letting you see it or just by using unbreakable encryption on my digital products. It allows me to use existing conventional property rights to make fair use *illegal.* If I own the only copy of the book and it is inside my house, it would be trespass for you to enter. No First Amendment problem there. But in passing the DMCA, Congress had created a new intellectual property right inside copyright law itself, a law aimed directly at expression, that made it illegal to get access for the purpose of making fair use *even when you legally bought the physical book, or the physical DVD, and now wish to quote it or parody it.* Even that is not the problem. It is that Congress cannot grant the exclusive rights of copyright without simultaneously accompanying them by the limitations of fair use.[8] Regardless of what physical constraints and tangible property rights might do to limit my ability to make fair uses, *Congress* had now, by law, allowed a copyright owner to distribute a particular work *with* the exclusive rights but *without* some of those limitations.

Imagine that Congress had passed the following law instead of the DMCA: "Any copyright owner can make it illegal to make a fair use of a copyrighted work by putting a red dot on their books, records, and films before selling them. It shall be a crime to circumvent the red dot even if, but for the dot, the use would have been fair." That would be clearly unconstitutional. It gives copyright owners a new intellectual property right to "turn off fair use" in copyrighted works distributed to the mass market. Is the DMCA not the same thing?

This was the issue in *Reimerdes.* True, if I cut through the digital fence on a DVD in order to excerpt a small portion in a critical documentary, I would not be violating your copyright, but I would be violating the anticircumvention provisions. And DeCSS seemed to be a tool for doing what the DMCA forbids. By providing links to it, Mr. Corley and *2600* were "trafficking" in a technology that allows others to circumvent a technological protection measure. DeCSS could, of course, be used for purposes that did not violate copyright— to make the DVD play on a computer running Linux, for example. It enabled various noninfringing fair uses. It could also be used to aid illicit copying. But the alleged violation of the DMCA had nothing to do with that. The alleged violation of the DMCA was making the digital wire cutters available in the first place. So one First Amendment problem with the DMCA can be stated quite simply. It appeared *to make it illegal to exercise at least some of the limitations and exceptions copyright law needs in order to pass First Amendment scrutiny.* Or did it just make it very, very difficult to exercise those rights legally? I could, after all, make a videotape of the DVD playing on my television, and use that grainy, blurry image in my documentary criticizing the filmmaker. The DMCA would not be violated, though my movie might be painful to watch.

The other possible First Amendment problem with the DMCA was that in regulating programs such as DeCSS, the DMCA was actually regulating "speech." The first challenge to the DMCA was that, by making tools like DeCSS illegal, the DMCA took away a constitutionally necessary escape hatch to copyright, thus making copyright law *as a whole* violate the First

Amendment's guarantee of freedom of speech. The second challenge was different. The problem was that the program itself was speech and the DMCA was regulating it illicitly.

The reasoning went like this. A computer program is a form of expression and communication. The source code can even be read by human beings. True, it is an abstract form of communication—like musical notation and mathematical algorithms. But those are clearly protected by the First Amendment. Congress could not make Schoenberg's twelve-tone scale illegal or punish mathematicians for physics equations that seemed to support a theory of the universe's origin other than the creationism that is currently so popular. True, the source code is a description of a method of doing something, and the code can, if run on a computer, produce a result—but one could argue that those attributes do not affect the First Amendment's protection. Neither a recipe for hash brownies nor a player piano roll for the Nazi "Horst Wessel" song could constitutionally be prohibited, even though actually to make the hash brownies would be illegal, and even though the piano roll is functional (it "makes" the player piano play the tune). True, most people cannot read computer code, but speech does not need to be common or accessible to be protected. In fact, the courts have even held that the choice to communicate in a particular language is constitutionally protected in some settings.

On the other hand, software code is undeniably functional. Lots of functional articles can be said to have some expressive content—a gun, an airbag, a crash helmet, a set of burglar's tools, a computer virus. And many actions have expressive content: a terrorist bombing, for example. Surely these could be regulated by Congress? To the defendants, DeCSS looked like a physics equation, a musical score, or a recipe. To the movie studios, DeCSS had all the First Amendment significance of a crowbar, lock pick, or, for that matter, a car bombing. The same argument was repeated over the hyperlinks that Corley and others provided to sites which carried the DeCSS program. Speech or function? To the defendants, forbidding *2600* to link to these sites was like preventing the *Washington Post* from describing the availability of drugs on certain blocks of 16th Street. To the movie companies, the hyperlinks were the equivalent of loading potential buyers into a van, taking them down there, and giving them enough money to make the purchase.

Which of the two First Amendment arguments is more convincing? That the DMCA is a congressionally created off-switch for fair use? Or that software code is speech and the DMCA restricts it? Like a lot of scholars, before

Reimerdes went to trial, I thought that the first argument was by far the more powerful. I still do. I thought the odds of the court buying the "code is speech" argument were low. About that I was wrong, though it turned out not to matter.

A number of the reports noted that after some initial skepticism, Judge Kaplan had been impressed by the defendants' expert witnesses, particularly those who had testified that code was speech. When the ruling came out, this impression was confirmed. Judge Kaplan agreed that code was a form of speech or expression. But celebration was premature. Having done so, he disagreed with the defendants' claim that it could not be regulated.

> Computer code is expressive. To that extent, it is a matter of First Amendment concern. But computer code is not purely expressive any more than the assassination of a political figure is purely a political statement. Code causes computers to perform desired functions. Its expressive element no more immunizes its functional aspects from regulation than the expressive motives of an assassin immunize the assassin's action. In an era in which the transmission of computer viruses— which, like DeCSS, are simply computer code and thus to some degree expressive— can disable systems upon which the nation depends and in which other computer code also is capable of inflicting other harm, society must be able to regulate the use and dissemination of code in appropriate circumstances. The Constitution, after all, is a framework for building a just and democratic society. It is not a suicide pact.[9]

Judge Kaplan is right in saying that there cannot be a bright-line rule immunizing computer code from regulation merely because it has expressive elements. The First Amendment does not protect computer viruses. But the defendants were not arguing that computer code was constitutionally inviolable, only that any law that regulated it had to be subject to First Amendment scrutiny. After all, the government makes the description of how to make a nuclear weapon classified information. That is clearly "speech," but its regulation is also constitutional. The First Amendment is not, and never was, an absolute guarantee of freedom of speech. Instead, the question is whether the law is within the realm of "the freedom of speech" guarantee, which in turn depends on what kind of a law it is. Where does it fit in the "levels of scrutiny" that courts have constructed to discriminate between types of legislation affecting speech? Is the DMCA a "content-based" regulation, such as a law forbidding labor picketing but allowing other kinds of demonstrations? Content-based regulations are given the highest and most demanding level of scrutiny. Alternatively, is it a "content-neutral" regulation, such as a law that forbids talking—about any subject—in a library? To Judge Kaplan, the answer was clear, and grounds for sarcasm.

> The reason that Congress enacted the anti-trafficking provision of the DMCA had nothing to do with suppressing particular ideas of computer programmers and everything to do with functionality—with preventing people from circumventing technological access control measures—just as laws prohibiting the possession of burglar tools have nothing to do with preventing people from expressing themselves by accumulating what to them may be attractive assortments of implements and everything to do with preventing burglaries.

I agree, though it is worth noting that the burglar tool analogy is a disputed one. Johansen claimed DeCSS was more like a screwdriver—something with both licit and illicit uses.

So the DMCA was content-neutral regulation. That means it still has to pass a fairly daunting legal threshold. It will only be upheld if "it furthers an important or substantial governmental interest; if the governmental interest is unrelated to the suppression of free expression; and if the incidental restriction on alleged First Amendment freedoms is no greater than is essential to the furtherance of that interest."[10] Judge Kaplan felt that the DMCA satisfied that standard. I am not so sure. Yes, the governmental interest in protecting copyright holders' rights is important. And yes, I must disagree with some of my friends in the civil liberties world and say that the government's interest is unrelated to the suppression of free expression. But is "the incidental restriction of First Amendment freedoms *no greater than is essential* to the furtherance of that interest"? In other words, could the DMCA have achieved its goals without imposing as great a limitation on the expression of people like Mr. Johansen and Mr. Corley?

Congress could have passed many laws less restrictive than the DMCA. It could have only penalized the use of programs such as DeCSS for an illicit purpose. If it wished to reach those who create the tools as well as use them, it could have required proof that the creator intended them to be used for illegal purposes. Just as we look at the government's intention in creating the law, we could make the intent of the software writer critical for the purposes of assessing whether or not his actions are illegal. If I write a novel detailing a clever way to kill someone and you use it to carry out a real murder, the First Amendment does not allow the state to punish me. If I write a manual on how to be a hit man and sell it to you, it may. First Amendment law is generally skeptical of statutes that impose "strict liability" without a requirement of intent. But Judge Kaplan believed that the DMCA made the motives of Mr. Johansen irrelevant, except insofar as they were relevant to the narrowly tailored exceptions of the DMCA, such as encryption research. In other words, even if Mr. Johansen made DeCSS so that he and his friends could watch DVDs they purchased legally on computers running Linux, they could still be liable for breaking the DMCA.

The DMCA's breadth goes further than its treatment of intent. The statute could have only made it illegal to provide a program yourself. But Judge Kaplan interpreted it to prohibit even linking to a site where the program is to be found. No requirement of intent. No requirement that you actually supply the infringing program. That is a pretty broad interpretation and one which he admits restricts expression. How could he conclude that restrictions this broad were "no greater than essential"? From his rhetoric, the answer is clear. Judge Kaplan believes the story of the Internet Threat I discussed in Chapter 4. He sees DeCSS as a poison. In fact, he thinks it is worse than a poison because it may spread to infect others. It is a disease, a virus. The DMCA is the stern and harsh quarantine required to control it—a digital public health measure. His reasoning is worth quoting at length.

> There was a time when copyright infringement could be dealt with quite adequately by focusing on the infringing act. . . . The copyright holder . . . usually was able to trace the copies up the chain of distribution, find and prosecute the infringer, and shut off the infringement at the source. In principle, the digital world is very different. Once a decryption program like DeCSS is written, it quickly can be sent all over the world. Every recipient is capable not only of decrypting and perfectly copying plaintiffs' copyrighted DVDs, but also of retransmitting perfect copies of DeCSS and thus enabling every recipient to do the same. . . . The process potentially is exponential rather than linear. Indeed, the difference is illustrated by comparison of two epidemiological models describing the spread of different kinds of disease. In a common source epidemic, as where members of a population contract a non-contagious disease from a poisoned well, the disease spreads only by exposure to the common source. If one eliminates the source, or closes the contaminated well, the epidemic is stopped. In a propagated outbreak epidemic, on the other hand, the disease spreads from person to person. Hence, finding the initial source of infection accomplishes little, as the disease continues to spread even if the initial source is eliminated.[11]

This is a very good point, and one that the critics of the DMCA sometimes gloss over too quickly. The structure of digital replication is indeed different from the old centralized model of copying and distribution. Instead of tracing all illicit copies back to a single infringing printing press, we face the fear that the machinery of piracy can be copied just as fast as the copies it allows us to make.

It is here that the defendants lose the battle of the metaphors. Yes, code is speech, it conveys information. But viruses are codes and they convey information too. Judge Kaplan explicitly invokes this comparison several times. Biological viruses are tools for the replication of genetic information. They subvert their hosts' cellular programming to make copies of themselves, just as a computer virus hijacks an infected computer and causes it to send out more copies of the virus. True, DeCSS requires human intervention to download the program and use it. Yet from Judge Kaplan's language it is evident that he sees the program not as an act of expression but as a virus spreading like wildfire. Seen this way, the individual "choices" to download or redistribute are simply the program's method of spreading itself, like the irritation produced by the cold virus that encourages sneezes and coughs, thereby transmitting the illness to others. Just as in an epidemic, the harshest measures are called for. There is no poisoned well here, no pirate with a printing press we can shut down. Anyone is potentially an infringer. Individuals cannot be presumed to be healthy. We cannot give their immune systems, or their motives, the benefit of the doubt. Instead we must see them as potential carriers. The healthy must be quarantined as well as the sick. Facing such a danger, Judge Kaplan agrees that Congress needed to be draconian. We cannot wait for illegal copying. We must strike preemptively at the technology that might enable it. There is no place for inquiries into "intent" here; no way that we can restrict liability to those who actually provide the program. Thus, though "code is speech" and the DMCA does incidentally restrict expression, Judge Kaplan concludes that its restraints are no greater than is necessary.

There are three questions here. The first is whether Congress was right. The second is whether, in the context of the movie industry, we can see evidence of the evil it needed to combat. The third question is very different: whether the DMCA is constitutional. In my opinion, the answer to questions one and two is no, for the reasons outlined in Chapter 4's analysis of the Internet Threat. Yes, cheaper copying can increase the rate of illicit copying, but it also lowers advertising costs and offers new business models—Netflix, downloads on demand, viral distribution of trailers, and so on. The technology helps as well as hurts. It does not help the movie industry as much as it might help the music industry, which can more easily distribute its products over the Internet. But the Internet also does not pose as much danger to movies as it does to music.

The movie industry's doomsaying aside, there is no exact movie equivalent of Napster and there is unlikely to be one in the near future.[12]

This is not just because movies are longer and harder to download than songs. It is because most people only watch a film once. Most people do not *want* a library of two thousand films to play again and again. Music is a repeated experience good in a way that movies simply are not, and that social fact profoundly affects the likelihood of downloading as opposed to rental. The transient song on a radio or an Internet stream is not an adequate substitute for possessing the song permanently—something which costs a lot more. Apart from kids' movies, which can be used to induce catatonia in one's progeny time and again, and a few classic favorites, most people do not want to own movies. Watching the film on television or renting it for a night is perfectly satisfactory. Both of these involve little hassle or cost. The content industries are fond of saying "you cannot compete with free." But this is simply not true. Cheap and easily acquired goods of certified quality compete very well with free goods of uncertain quality whose acquisition involves some difficulty. This is one of the main reasons the movie companies were wrong in the *Sony* case.

Thus while Judge Kaplan's discussion of the looming digital Black Death is nicely apocalyptic, it does not seem very accurate. How many of your friends download movies illicitly over the Internet, let alone movies that were ripped from DVDs? Yes, it can be done. But the actual descriptions of the process in the *Reimerdes* case smack more of bathos than terror.

Although the process is computationally intensive, plaintiffs' expert decrypted a store-bought copy of *Sleepless in Seattle* in 20 to 45 minutes. . . . The decryption of a CSS-protected DVD is only the beginning of the tale, as the decrypted file is very large. . . . One solution to this problem, however, is DivX, a compression utility available on the Internet that is promoted as a means of compressing decrypted motion picture files to manageable size. . . . While the compressed sound and graphic files then must be synchronized, a tedious process that took plaintiffs' expert between 10 and 20 hours, the task is entirely feasible. . . . At trial, defendants repeated, as if it were a mantra, the refrain that plaintiffs, as they stipulated, have no direct evidence of a specific occasion on which any person decrypted a copyrighted motion picture with DeCSS and transmitted it over the Internet. But that is unpersuasive. Plaintiffs' expert expended very little effort to find someone in an IRC chat room who exchanged a compressed, decrypted copy of *The Matrix*, one of plaintiffs' copyrighted motion pictures, for a copy of *Sleepless in Seattle*. While the simultaneous electronic exchange of the two movies took approximately six hours, the computers required little operator attention during the interim.

So the epidemic threat that hangs over the movie industry consists of the danger that someone will spend fifteen minutes decrypting and ten to twenty hours tediously synchronizing a movie that is then available for a speedy six-hour download?

Admittedly, someone only needs to do the synchronizing once. There are newer tools that make the task easier. And we could improve the download time. But even so, would you bother? Faced with the colossal expense and hassle of renting the same movie at Blockbuster for $3, some consumers *might* prefer this process, I suppose. But I would not sell my shares in movie studios quite yet. In fact, the real threat to movie studios is the large-scale criminal distribution of illicitly copied DVDs—copied bit for bit from the original. The distributors of those do not *need* to use programs like DeCSS. A more distant threat comes from legal recordings from television made on TiVo's and ReplayTVs—where consumers' actions are legal and CSS is not an issue. So far as we can tell, there is no measurable effect of illicit digital downloads on sales or rentals of DVDs. We could go through the process Judge Kaplan describes, I suppose, just as when the VCR was invented we could have taped movies from television and swapped them with our friends. But as the movie studios discovered after the *Sony* case, most of us would rather just rent the movie. Because something is possible does not mean it will happen.

So in my view, Congress generally overestimated the threat posed by the digital world and underestimated the benefits. In addition, the movie industry is a weak place to make the case for the necessity of the DMCA. Fine, but that is not the legal issue here. The constitutionality of the DMCA does not turn on whether the DMCA was a good idea. That is not the court's decision to make. The question is not even whether the particular industry involved is, in reality, facing much of a threat from digital downloading. The law, after all, exists for all digital works, not just the ones at issue here. The question is whether the restriction on speech imposed by the DMCA was "no greater than is essential." And that is a harder question.

I still disagree with Judge Kaplan. A more narrowly tailored statute could have accomplished the DMCA's legitimate goals without impinging as greatly on expression. I think that the rhetoric of the Internet Threat blinded Judge Kaplan to some important issues and led him to overestimate the danger and thus the severity of the measures necessary to combat it. Thus, even under the "code is speech" part of the analysis, I think the DMCA fails First Amendment scrutiny. But if we are confining ourselves to the expression inherent in the software itself, I acknowledge that it is a close call.

Sadly, Judge Kaplan spent much less time on the other First Amendment argument against the DMCA—that it is unconstitutional because it gives copyright holders a new intellectual property entitlement, created by Congress under the Copyright Clause, a legal power to deprive users of a constitutionally required limitation on copyright's exclusive rights. In my view, he also framed the argument wrongly when he did discuss it. To be fair, these problems can partly be traced to the fact that the defendants spent most of their energy on the argument that code was expression, paying less attention to everything else. As Judge Kaplan explained it, the claim was that the DMCA might have the effect of restricting an alleged fair use right of access to copyrighted material. Predictably enough, he responded that there was no such right of access. Copyright holders could always lock up the book or restrict entrance to the gallery. In any event, while fair use of DVDs might be curtailed, he argued that most movies are also available on videotape. Even if the film were only available on DVD, the prospective fair user could write down the words and quote them, or record the sound from the screen. Finally, Judge Kaplan pointed out that even if the DMCA might allow a significant erosion of fair use to develop over time, such a problem was not present here. Those making First Amendment claims are sometimes allowed by courts to show that, even if the law as it applied to them were constitutional, it would restrict the First Amendment rights of others. Judge Kaplan declined to apply that doctrine here. In effect, he said "come back when there is a problem."

On appeal, the case was decided by a panel led by Judge Jon Newman. Here the fair use argument received more attention but the result was the same: "Come back when there is a problem." Significantly, both courts pointed out another concern. The DMCA could effectively make copyright perpetual because even though the copyright term would expire, the legally protected encryption would continue, and tools such as DeCSS, which would have allowed access to the public domain work, would be illegal.[13] This is a major issue because it appears to violate both the First Amendment and the Copyright Clause's requirement of a limited time. The defendants did not spend adequate time on this argument, however, and the courts again left it for later consideration.

The court of appeals saw the defendants' argument in just the same way as Judge Kaplan had seen it: a claim that there was a fair use right of actual access to the finest version of every work in every medium, on which the DMCA put a practical limitation. Such a claim was easy to dismiss. There was no such right of guaranteed practical access. Copyright owners could restrict the practical ability to exercise fair use in many ways without the Constitution being involved. In addition, in a world where copyrighted content is frequently available in both analog and digital form, the actual effects of the DMCA might be trivial and were, in any event, constitutionally acceptable. Judge Newman repeated Judge Kaplan's point that one could always make fair use of the work in a way the DMCA did not reach, such as by videotaping a picture of the screen.

> The fact that the resulting copy will not be as perfect or as manipulable as a digital copy obtained by having direct access to the DVD movie in its digital form, provides no basis for a claim of unconstitutional limitation of fair use. A film critic making fair use of a movie by quoting selected lines of dialogue has no constitutionally valid claim that the review (in print or on television) would be technologically superior if the reviewer had not been prevented from using a movie camera in the theater, nor has an art student a valid constitutional claim to fair use of a painting by photographing it in a museum. Fair use has never been held to be a guarantee of access to copyrighted material in order to copy it by the fair user's preferred technique or in the format of the original.

Once the issue is framed this way, the case has been lost. I would argue that there are three baseline errors here: a focus on "affirmative rights of access" as opposed to limits on Congress's power in handing out exclusive rights over expression without their constitutionally necessary limitations, a focus on practical effects of the provisions rather than on formal constitutional limitations on the copyright system over all classes of works, and a confusion between intellectual property rights and physical property rights that goes to the heart of the Jefferson Warning discussed in Chapter 2. The question is not whether users have a constitutionally protected right of practical access to a preferred version of a work. The question is whether it violates the First Amendment for *Congress* to give to copyright holders an intellectual property right to exempt their copyrighted works in some formats from fair use and other provisions that are necessary for copyright law in general to be constitutional.

Remember my earlier example. What if Congress amended Section 1201 to say "Any copyright owner can make it illegal to make a fair use of a copyrighted work by putting a red dot on their books, records, and films before selling them. It shall be a crime to circumvent the red dot even if, but for the dot, the use would have been fair"? This statute, I think, is clearly unconstitutional. It would be no answer to say that some owners will not use the red dot, and even for those that do, there will be older, dotless versions still available. It is irrelevant that I might be able to copy down the crucial lines of the book over your shoulder while you read it and thus claim that I, personally, had not circumvented the dot. The unconstitutionality of the statute does not turn on whether the dots might fall off because of bad adhesive, or whether there are many secondhand bookstores in the area, in which undotted volumes can be found. Even if the red dot rule were only to be applied to hardback books, or graphic novels, or cassette tapes, it would still be unconstitutional. Nor do we have to wait until the entire marketplace is dominated by red-dotted products before considering the issue. It is no answer to say that even before the red dot rule, copyright holders could always have hidden their works, or locked them in safes, or even negotiated individual contracts with the purchasers that have the effect of limiting fair use. That way of framing it just misunderstands the issue on a fundamental level. The claim is not about the happenstance of practical access or the way that a copyright holder can use physical control of an object or existing tangible property rights to undercut fair use.

The point is that Congress violates the First Amendment when, with respect to any work, it gives me an intellectual property right to prohibit copying and distribution of an expressive work sold in the marketplace and an additional legal power to opt out of the limitations contained in Section 107 over that work. The bundle of rights conveyed by the DMCA does exactly that. It is not the DMCA alone that we must analyze. The question is *whether Congress can give the exclusive rights contained in Section 106 of the Copyright Act over a particular class of works (say digital works), if it also gives a new right to prohibit citizens from gaining access to those works for the purposes of making a fair use.* If Judge Kaplan and Judge Newman are correct, then the DMCA gives an entirely new intellectual property right (technically, a legal power) to the copyright holders to do exactly that. To put it the other way around, the DMCA subtracts from the citizen's bundle of entitlements under federal copyright law, the right (technically, lawyers would call it a privilege) to gain access to a work legally in his possession for the purpose of making a fair use. It is *that* rule change that is unconstitutional, I would argue, and the way Judge Kaplan and Judge Newman frame that issue makes them miss the point.

Framing is important. The confusions that I have talked about in this book all make an appearance. It starts with the whole controversy being framed by the Internet Threat story line from Chapter 4. Because Judge Kaplan is convinced that every citizen is now a potential infringer, a potentially infectious virus carrier, he is ill disposed to listen to claims about fair use. Civil liberties claims do not do very well in epidemics. It is only right for him to defer to Congress's perception of the problem and the solution, of course. But he buys so deeply into the magnitude of the threat, the extent of the potential piracy pandemic, that it is very hard for him to take seriously the idea that even here there is a legitimate constitutional fair use claim.

The Sony Axiom from Chapter 4 is also ignored, or at least undervalued. As I pointed out there, without a robust set of exceptions and limitations on copyright, the idea that cheaper copying requires greater control will inexorably drive us toward the position that the technologies of cheaper reproduction must be put under the governance of copyright holders. The DMCA continues that logic; its drafters concluded that the right to get access to digital works for purposes of making a fair use must be taken from the bundle of rights possessed by citizens, while the right to enjoin both access and the technologies of access is added to those of copyright holders. Never mind the correctness of such a conclusion as a matter of policy. Are there *constitutional* limitations on Congress taking such an action? Kaplan and Newman in effect tell us, "not yet."

More important than the perception of the threat is the understanding of what intellectual property is all about. In Chapter 2, Jefferson warned us that intellectual property rights are not like physical property rights. In analyzing the DMCA, where do we turn for analogies? To physical property, violence, and theft. The cases analyzing the DMCA are full of analogies to trespass, to breaking and entering, to burglars' tools, and to safecrackers. Private property carries a lot of baggage with it, but we know it well—it is the place we naturally turn for insight. Even I, in order to point out some of the difficulties with those analogies, had to turn to farmers and barbed wire and public rights-of-way along highways. There is nothing wrong with analogies. They help us understand things that are new by comparing them to things we think we understand better. Analogies are only bad when they ignore the key difference between the two things being analyzed. That is what happens here.

Jefferson reminded us that intellectual property rights are clearly artifacts of state creation, monopolies whose internal limitations in scope, duration, and so on are just as important as the rights themselves. Jefferson doubts whether even property rights over land can be understood as natural and absolute—copyrights and patents, which cover subject matter that can be infinitely reproduced without diminishing its substance, clearly cannot. They frequently involve a claim to control purchasers' behavior with respect to some aspect of an artifact after it has been sold to them in the marketplace, making simpleminded analogies to "breaking and entering" inappropriate—the extent of the property in question is precisely the issue in dispute. (When Johansen was tried in Norway under the national computer crime law, the court laconically observed that he had bought the DVDs, and one cannot break into one's own property—effectively turning the analogy on its head.) Jefferson starts from the baseline that monopoly is the exception and freedom is the rule—any limitations on that freedom have to be justified. That is why he always discusses the right and the limitations on the right as an inseparable pair. One cannot discuss them in isolation.

Kaplan and Newman are fine, thoughtful judges. They do not altogether ignore those points. But look how the analysis is set up. At several points in the discussion, there seems to be the assumption that copyright owners have entitlements to total control as of right and that fair use is a mere lucky loophole which, because it can be negated by the happenstance of whether one can get physical access, can hardly have major First Amendment status. They keep pointing out that physical control and tangible property rights frequently allow copyright holders to make fair use impracticable. "And so what?" Jefferson might have responded. This is a classic non sequitur. The question is whether the Congress has the power to add a *new* right of access-denial to the intellectual property monopoly it is constructing, undermining—as to some works and some fair uses—the balance that the law sets up. The citizen is not pleading for a new right of access, trumping all physical restraint and tangible property rights. The citizen is claiming that Congress has no power to give exclusive rights to restrain copying of digital content while simultaneously taking away the citizen's existing right to get access to that content for the purposes of fair use—at least in those cases where access is physically possible and violates no other property right, real or intellectual.

The Constitution does not require the United States to break into President Nixon's desk to get me his tapes, buy me a tape recorder, or give me a right to 18.5 minutes on the broadcast airwaves to play them. But if I can get access to the tapes legally, it does forbid the government from giving President Nixon the power to put a red dot on those tapes and thus claim an intellectual property right to stop me playing them on TV or digitizing them to make the sounds clearer. The restraints imposed by physical happenstance and tangible property rights are different from those imposed by copyright—a congressionally created monopoly over *expression*. We cannot assume because one is constitutionally acceptable that the others are too. Jefferson understood that, and his analysis can help us even in a constitutional conflict over a technology he could hardly have dreamt of. (Though perhaps with Jefferson, this is a bad bet.)

The same point comes up in a different way when the court disconnects the fair use discussion from the exclusive rights discussion. The question is not "Do I have a constitutionally protected right of physical access to a preferred version of a movie, so as to make my task easy?" That gets the court caught up in questions of when a majority of movies will only be available on DVD, or how poor a substitute the analog version would be, or how many fair uses will require actually cutting a digital fence. But all of these inquiries miss the point. The question is "Can Congress hand out the exclusive rights of copyright over digital works if it does not accompany those rights with the suite of limitations that the court has repeatedly said "saves" copyright from violating the First Amendment?" The proportion of digital works to the total number of works produced in other formats is irrelevant. As to *these* works, the rule is unconstitutional. But what about the number or proportion of types of fair uses affected? That is more relevant but still not dispositive in the way Kaplan and Newman imagined. True, not every trivial statutory modification of fair use makes copyright unconstitutional. But this is not a trivial modification: over an entire class of works, copyright owners are given a legal power to deprive users of their privilege to gain otherwise lawful access for the purposes of fair use. If you give the digital filmmaker the exclusive rights of copyright but forbid the film professor from going through the otherwise lawful process of parodying or quoting, *that* rule is unconstitutional, no matter how many other fair uses are unaffected. If the copyright law were amended to forbid journalists playing, on a Friday, excerpts of legally acquired red-dotted tapes made by presidents whose last name begins with *N*, it would still be unconstitutional.

The legal implementation of this conclusion would be simple. It would be unconstitutional to punish an individual for gaining access in order to make a fair use. However, if they cut down the digital fence to make illicit copies, both the cutting and the copying would be illegal. But what about the prohibition of trafficking in digital wire cutters, technologies such as DeCSS? There the constitutional question is harder. I would argue that the First Amendment requires an interpretation of the antitrafficking provisions that comes closer to the ruling in the *Sony* case. If Mr. Johansen did indeed make DeCSS to play DVDs on his Linux computer, and if that were indeed a substantial noninfringing use, then it cannot be illegal for him to develop the technology. But I accept that this is a harder line to draw constitutionally. About my first conclusion, though, I think the argument is both strong and clear.

Ironically, there is some support for my claim and it comes from an even higher, if not uniformly more thoughtful, set of judges than Newman and Kaplan. In the depressing case of *Eldred v. Ashcroft*, the Supreme Court upheld retrospective copyright term extensions against a variety of constitutional challenges. (Full disclosure: I assisted in the preparation of an amicus curiae brief in the case.) One of those challenges was based on the First Amendment. The fairly reasonable claim was that Congress could not retroactively lock up an entire twenty-year swathe of culture that had already been produced. Such a law would be all restraint of expression, performance, republication, adaption, and so on, *with no incentive benefits*. The Court was unconvinced. But it did say:

> To the extent such assertions raise First Amendment concerns, copyright's built-in free speech safeguards are generally adequate to address them. We recognize that the D.C. Circuit spoke too broadly when it declared copyrights "categorically immune from challenges under the First Amendment." . . . But when, as in this case, *Congress has not altered the traditional contours of copyright protection*, further First Amendment scrutiny is unnecessary.[14]

The DMCA, of course, does exactly this. As to digital works it alters the "traditional contours of copyright protection" in a way that affects "copyright's built-in free speech safeguards." That is what the Farmers' Tale was all about. Perhaps one day, in a case not involving a Norwegian teenager, a hacker magazine run by a long-haired editor with an Orwellian nom de plume, and an obscure technology that is accused of posing apocalyptic threats to the American film industry, that point will come out more clearly.

But the issue of speech regulation is only half of the story. Intellectual property rights over digital technologies affect not only speech, but the framework of competition and markets as well, as the next example makes clear.

The Apple of Forbidden Knowledge:
The DMCA and Competition

You could tell it was a bizarre feud by the statement Apple issued, one strangely at odds with the Californian Zen-chic the company normally projects. "We are stunned that RealNetworks has adopted the tactics and ethics of a hacker to break into the iPod, and we are investigating the implications of their actions under the DMCA and other laws."[15]

What vile thing had RealNetworks done? They had developed a program called Harmony that would allow iPod owners to buy songs from Real's Music

Store and play them on their own iPods. That's it. So why all the outrage? It turns out that like the story of DeCSS, this little controversy has a lot to teach us about the landscape of intellectual property disputes, about the mental topography of the high-tech economy. But where the DeCSS case was a war of metaphors around the boundaries of freedom of expression, the iPod story is about ways in which intellectual property marks the limits of competition.

Apple iPods can be used to store all kinds of material, from word processing documents to MP3 files. If you want to use these popular digital music players to download copy-protected music, though, you have only one source: Apple's iTunes service, which offers songs at 99 cents a pop in the United States, 79 pence in the United Kingdom. If you try to download copy-protected material from any other service, the iPod will refuse to play it. Or at least, that had been the case until Real managed to make their Harmony service compatible.

Real's actions meant that consumers had two sources of copy-protected music for their iPods. Presumably all the virtues of competition, including improved variety and lowered prices, would follow. The iPod owners would be happy. But Apple was not. The first lesson of the story is how strangely people use the metaphors of tangible property in new-economy disputes. How exactly had Real "broken into" the iPod? It had not broken into my iPod, which is after all *my* iPod. If I want to use Real's service to download music to my own device, where's the breaking and entering?

What Real had done was make the iPod "interoperable" with another format. If Boyle's word processing program can convert Microsoft Word files into Boyle's format, allowing Word users to switch programs, am I "breaking into Word"? Well, Microsoft might think so, but most of us do not. So leaving aside the legal claim for a moment, where is the ethical foul?

Apple was saying (and apparently believed) that Real had broken into something different from my iPod or your iPod. They had broken into the *idea* of an iPod. (I imagine a small, platonic white rectangle, presumably imbued with the spirit of Steve Jobs.) Their true sin was trying to understand the iPod so that they could make it do things that Apple did not want it to do. As an ethical matter, does figuring out how things work, in order to compete with the original manufacturer, count as breaking and entering? In the strange netherworld between hardware and software, device and product, the answer is often a morally heartfelt "yes!" I would stress "morally heartfelt." It is true manufacturers want to make lots of money and would rather not have competitors. Bob Young of Red Hat claims "every business person wakes up in the morning and says 'how can I become a monopolist?'" Beyond that, though, innovators actually come to believe that they have the moral right to control the uses of their goods after they are sold. This isn't your iPod, it's *Apple's* iPod.

Yet even if they believe this, we don't have to agree. In the material world, when a razor manufacturer claims that a generic razor blade maker is "stealing my customers" by making compatible blades, we simply laugh. The "hacking" there consists of looking at the razor and manufacturing a blade that will fit. To say this is somehow immoral seems laughable. Is the conclusion changed when the information about compatibility is inscribed in binary code and silicon circuits, rather than the molded plastic of a razor cartridge? What if ensuring the "fit" between the two products is not a matter of making sure the new blades snugly connect to the razor but of making sure the software embedded in my generic product sends the right code to the original product in order to be recognized? Our moral intuitions are a little less confident here. All kinds of bad policy can flourish in that area of moral uncertainty.

This leads us to the law. Surely Apple's suggestion that the DMCA might prohibit what Real had done is as baseless as their moral argument? In the United States, the answer is "probably," at least if the courts continue in the direction they are currently taking, but it is a closer call than you would think. Internationally, the answer is even less certain. That is where the iPod war provides its second new-economy lesson. Think for a moment about the way that the law shapes the business choices in this dispute.

In a competitive market, Apple would choose whether to make the iPod an open platform, able to work with everyone's music service, or to try to keep it closed, hoping to extract more money by using consumers' loyalty to the hardware to drive them to the tied music service. If they attempted to keep it closed, competitors would try to make compatible products, acting like the manufacturers of generic razor blades or printer cartridges.

The war would be fought out on the hardware (and software) level, with the manufacturer of the platform constantly seeking to make the competing products incompatible, to bad-mouth their quality, and to use fear, uncertainty, and doubt to stop consumers from switching. (Apple's actual words were: "When we update our iPod software from time to time, it is highly likely that Real's Harmony technology will cease to work with current and future iPods.") Meanwhile the competitors would race to untangle the knots as fast as the platform manufacturer could tie them. If the consumers got irritated enough they could give up their sunk costs and switch to another product altogether.

All of this seems fine, even if it represents the kind of socially wasteful arms race that led critics of capitalism to prophesy its inevitable doom. Competition is good and competition will often require interoperability. But what do we mean by competition? Is it competition if I assassinate your employees or poison the food in your restaurant? If I trespass on your land in order to sell a competing product? If I break into your safe to steal your trade secrets, use my monopoly position in the market to impose resale price agreements, or violate your patent? It is the law that draws the line between competition and theft, between virtuous competitive imitation and illicit "piracy."

Sometimes we need to give innovators property rights that allow them to prevent second-comers from free riding on their efforts. We have to do so because it is necessary to encourage future innovation. On the other hand, sometimes we not only allow the second-comer to free ride, we positively encourage it, believing that this is an integral part of competition and that there are adequate incentives to encourage innovation without the state stepping in. Intellectual property policy, indeed a large part of the policy behind all property rights, is about drawing the line between the two situations. Too far in one direction and innovation suffers because potential investors realize good ideas will immediately be copied. Too far in the other direction and monopolies hurt both competition and future innovation.

Imagine you are the first person to invest in getting the public to eat burritos for breakfast, or to place a petrol station at a certain crossroads, or to clip papers together with a folded bit of wire. In each case we give you some property rights. The fast-food vendor may own a trademarked phrase or jingle that the public learns to associate with his product. Since the patent office issued a patent for the sealed and crimped "peanut butter and jelly" sandwich I described at the beginning of the book, even a patent is not out of the question if your disgusting concoction is sufficiently novel and nonobvious. But we should not allow you to have a patent over all burritos, or burritos for breakfast, still less over the idea of fast food. As for the paper clip maker, there might be a trademark over the particular paper clip, but the idea of folding wire to secure paper stays in the public domain. The owner of the petrol station gets physical ownership of the land, but cannot stop a second-comer from setting up shop across the road, even if the first-comer's labor, capital, and effort proved that the location is a good one. We positively encourage follow-on imitation in those cases.

Now how about the case in point? What does Apple get in the way of property rights? Think back to my description of the intellectual property system in Chapter 1. They can get patents over those aspects of the iPod—both hardware and software—that are sufficiently innovative. Patents are what we use to protect inventions. They also get a copyright over the various pieces of software involved. That protects them only against someone who copies their code, not someone who writes new software to do the same thing. Copyrights are what we use to protect original expression. They get rights under trademark law over the name and perhaps parts of the design of the product—maybe the distinctive look of the iPod—though that is a bit more complex. All of these rights, plus being the first to break into the market in a big way, the brilliance of the design, and the tight integration between the hardware and the service, produce a formidable competitive advantage. The iPod is a very good product.

Now if a competitor infringes any of Apple's rights, for example by making a literal copy of the code, using their trademark in a way the law does not allow, or infringing on one of their patents, then Apple can shut them down and extract hefty damages. Quite right, too. But should they be able to prevent someone from making an interoperable product, provided they do not violate any of these existing rights in the process? Laws like the DMCA make that question more complicated.

Nowadays, there is software in many, many more products than you would imagine. Your watch, your phone, your printer, your thermostat, your garage door opener, your refrigerator, your microwave, your television—the odds are that if you bought them in the last ten years, they have some software component. In the 1970s the courts and Congress had concluded that software could be copyrighted as original expression, like a song or a novel, as well as being patented when it was novel, nonobvious, and useful. Frequently, different aspects of the same program will be covered by copyright and by patent. But software is a machine made of words, *the* machine of the digital age. That fact already causes some problems for our competition policy. Will the exceptions and limitations designed to deal with a copyright over a novel work adequately when they are applied to Microsoft Windows? That issue was already unclear. With the DMCA, we have added another crucial problem. Where there is copyrighted software there can be digital fences around it. If the copyright owner can forbid people to cut these fences to gain access to the software, then it can effectively enlarge its monopoly, capture tied services, and prohibit generic competition.

It was just this line of thought that led some other companies to do more than merely make threatening noises about the DMCA. Lexmark makes printers. But it also makes lots of money off the replacement ink or toner cartridges for those printers. In some cases, in fact, that is where printer companies make the majority of their profits. As a result, they are not exactly keen on generic replacements. Chamberlain makes garage door opener systems. But they also sell replacements for the controllers—the little devices that you use to trigger the door. Lawyers from both of those firms looked at the DMCA and saw a chance to do something most companies would love to do; to make generic competition illegal. Lexmark designed their printer program so that it would not accept a toner cartridge unless it received the correct "checksum" or validation number. So far, this looks no different from the razor manufacturer trying to make it difficult to manufacture a compatible replacement blade. Generic competitors now had to embed chips in their printer cartridges which would produce the correct code, otherwise they would not work in Lexmark printers.

Static Control Components is a North Carolina company that manufactures chips whose main function is to send the correct code to the printer program. With this chip implanted in them, generic cartridges would work in Lexmark printers. Lexmark's response could have been to change their program, rendering the chip obsolete, just as Apple could change the iTunes software to lock out Real Music's Rhapsody. Doing so would have been quite within their rights. Indeed it is a standard part of the interoperability wars. Instead, Lexmark sued Static Controls, claiming, among other things, a violation of the DMCA.[16] Like Apple in the press release I quoted earlier, Lexmark clearly saw this as a kind of digital breaking and entering. This was *their* printer, *their* printer program, *their* market for replacement cartridges. Static was just helping a bunch of cheats camouflage their generic cartridges as authentic Lexmark cartridges. Translated into the legal language of the DMCA the claim is a little different, but still recognizable. Static was "trafficking" in a device that allowed the "circumvention of a technical protection measure" used to prevent "access to a copyrighted work"—namely the computer program inside the printer. That is behavior that the DMCA forbids.

The garage door company, Chamberlain—who also claimed to be concerned about the security of their garage doors—made a similar argument. In order to get the garage door to open, the generic replacement opener had to provide the right code to the program in the actual motor system. That program is copyrighted. The code controls "access" to it. Suddenly, the manufacturers of generic printer cartridges and garage door openers start to look rather like Jon Johansen.

Surely the courts did not accept this argument? Bizarrely enough, some of them did—at least at first. But perhaps it was not so bizarre. The DMCA was indeed a radical new law. It did shift the boundaries of power between intellectual property owners and others. And intellectual property rights are *always* about restraining competition, defining what is legitimate and what is not—that is what they do. There was a respectable argument that these devices did in fact violate the DMCA. In fact, it was respectable enough to convince a federal judge. The district court judge in the *Lexmark* case concluded that Lexmark was likely to win on both the DMCA claim and on a more traditional copyright claim and issued an injunction against Static Control. In *Skylink*, the case involving garage door openers, by contrast, the district court held that the universal garage door opener did not violate the DMCA. Both cases were appealed and both appeals courts sided with the generic manufacturers, saying that the DMCA did not prohibit this kind of access—merely making a computer program work the way it was supposed to.

The U.S. Court of Appeals for the Federal Circuit (CAFC) heard the *Skylink* appeal. In a remarkably far-reaching decision, the court effectively took many of the positions that Mr. Corley's lawyers had argued for in the DeCSS case, but they did so not to protect speech, but to protect competition. In fact, they implied that taking Chamberlain's side in the case would silently overrule the antitrust statutes. They also interpreted the new right created by the DMCA so as to add an implicit limitation. In their construction, merely gaining access is not illegal; only gaining access for the purpose of violating the copyright holders' rights violates the statute. The *Reimerdes* court had been willing to accept that the new access right allows a copyright holder to prohibit "fair uses as well as foul." When Chamberlain made the same argument as to their garage door opener program, the CAFC was incredulous.

> Such an entitlement [as the one Chamberlain claims] would go far beyond the idea that the DMCA allows copyright owner to prohibit "fair uses . . . as well as foul." Reimerdes, 111 F. Supp. 2d at 304. Chamberlain's proposed construction would allow copyright owners to prohibit exclusively fair uses even in the absence of any feared foul use. It would, therefore, allow any copyright owner, through a combination of contractual terms and technological measures, to repeal the fair use doctrine with respect to an individual copyrighted work—or even selected copies of that copyrighted work.[17]

There are multiple ironies here. The CAFC rarely meets an intellectual property right it does not like. It has presided over a twenty-year expansion of

American patent law that many scholars find indefensible. But when (for dubious jurisdictional reasons) it sorties beyond its traditional ambit of patent
law, it is stunned by the potential expansiveness of the DMCA. Then there
is the comparison with the *Reimerdes* case. How interesting that the First
Amendment and concerns about free expression have comparatively little bite
when applied to the DMCA, but antitrust and concerns about competition
require that we curtail it. After all, the heart of Mr. Johansen's argument was
that he had to write the DeCSS program in order to play his own DVDs on
his own computer—to get access to his own DVDs, just as the purchaser of a
replacement garage door control is getting access to the program that operates
his own garage door. Indeed, Mr. Johansen's criticism of CSS was that it
allowed the movie companies, "through a combination of contractual terms
and technological measures, to repeal the fair use doctrine with respect to an
individual copyrighted work." Mr. Corley echoed those claims.

Of course, the situations are not identical. The key limitation in *Skylink*
is that the court saw no threat of "foul use." The *Reimerdes* court could see little
else. On the other hand, the rulings are not easily reconciled. The *Skylink*
court cannot imagine that Congress would want to give the copyright holder
a new "property" right to prevent access unconnected to any underlying copyright violation.

> As we have seen, Congress chose to create new causes of action for circumvention
> and for trafficking in circumvention devices. Congress did not choose to create new
> property rights. . . . Were we to interpret Congress's words in a way that eliminated
> all balance and granted copyright owners carte blanche authority to preclude all
> use, Congressional intent would remain unrealized.

Yet, arguably, that is exactly what the *Reimerdes* decision does, precisely
because it focuses on enabling access alone, not access for the purpose of violating one of the rights of the copyright holder. The *Reimerdes* court saw a violation of the law just in cutting the wire or making a wire cutter. The *Skylink*
court focused on whether the person cutting the wire was going to trespass
once the cutting was done. In effect, the two courts disagree on which of the
options offered to the legislature in the Farmers' Tale was actually enacted by
Congress. Which court is correct? The *Skylink* decision strikes me as sensible.
It also makes the statute constitutionally much more defensible—something
that the *Skylink* court does not consider. But in the process, it has to rewrite
the DMCA substantially. One should not presume that it will be this interpretation that will triumph.

SUMMING UP: EXAGGERATIONS,
HALF-TRUTHS, AND BIPOLAR DISORDERS
IN TECHNOLOGY POLICY

Let me return to the question with which I began the chapter. For many critics
of contemporary intellectual property law, the DMCA is the very embodi-
ment of all that is wrong. (I still cherish a friend's account of British protesters
outside the American Embassy in London singing "D-M-C-A" to the tune of
the Village People's "YMCA" and holding up signs calling for the law's repeal—
to the great confusion of the diplomatic personnel.) The critics conjure up
a digital apocalypse—a world of perfect control achieved through legally
backed digital fences, in which both speech and competition suffer, and where
citizens lose privacy, the privilege of fair use, and the right to criticize popular
culture rather than simply consume it. In their view, the legal disaster is only
exacerbated by bumbling judges who do not understand the technology and
who are easily fooled by the doom-laden rhetoric of the content companies.
The DMCA's supporters, on the other hand, think criticisms of the DMCA
are overblown, that the dark tales of digital control are either paranoid delu-
sions or tendentious exaggerations, and that far from being excessive, the
DMCA's provisions are not sufficient to control an epidemic of illicit copying. More draconian intervention is needed. As for fair use, as I pointed out
before, many of the DMCA's supporters do not think fair use is that important economically or culturally speaking. At best it is a "loophole" that
copyright owners should have the right to close; certainly not an affirmative
right of the public or a reserved limitation on the original property grant from
the state.

Who is right? Obviously, I disagree profoundly with the DMCA's supporters. I wrote this book partly to explain—using Jefferson and Macaulay and
the *Sony* case—what was wrong with their logic. It would be both convenient
and predictable for me to claim that the DMCA is the intellectual property
incarnation of the Antichrist. But it would not be true. In fact, I would not
even put the DMCA in the top three of bad intellectual property initiatives
worldwide. And many of the fears conjured up about it are indeed overblown.

Of course, the critics have a point. The DMCA is a very badly drafted law.
As I have tried to show here, its key provisions were probably unnecessary and
are, in my view, unconstitutional. If coupled with a number of other legal
"innovations" favored by the content industry, the DMCA could play a very
destructive role. In general, in fact, the Farmers' Tale is fairly accurate in de-

scribing both the origins of and the threats posed by the DMCA. Yet the single largest of those threats—the idea that the DMCA could be used to fence off large portions of the public domain and to make the fair use provisions of the Copyright Act essentially irrelevant—is still largely a threat rather than a reality. In some cases, fair use rights are curtailed. But for most citizens and for the majority of media, the DMCA has had relatively little effect. Digital rights management (DRM) certainly exists; indeed it is all around us. You can see that every time you try to play a DVD bought in another part of the world, open an Adobe eBook, or copy a song you have downloaded from iTunes. But so far, the world of legally backed digital rights management has not brought about the worst of the dystopian consequences that some people, including me, feared might result.

In many cases, citizens simply reject digital rights management. They will not buy products that use it. Attempts to introduce it into music CDs, for example, have been a resounding failure. In other cases, DRM has not been used in ways that the critics feared. There are genuine scandals, of course—cryptography research has been chilled, the DMCA has been turned to anti-competitive ends, and so on. It is also troubling to see federal judges issuing injunctions not only against banned material but also against those who *link* to the banned material. Somehow the blithe reassurance that this is consistent with the First Amendment fails to comfort one. But many of the evils prophesied for the DMCA remain as just that: prophecies.

There are also entries on the positive side of the ledger. The "safe harbors" that the DMCA gave Internet service providers and search services have been a vital and positive force in the development of the Internet. It may even be true that in some cases, such as iTunes, the DMCA did what its backers claimed it would—encourage new provision of digital content by reassuring the record companies that they could put their music online surrounded by legally backed digital rights management. (Notably, however, the trend is now going the other way. Companies are coming to realize that many consumers prefer, and will pay more for, unprotected MP3 files.)

Of course, depending on your view of the music industry, that might seem like a mixed blessing. One might also wonder if the same consumer benefits might have been produced with a much less restrictive law. But with the exception of a few important areas—such as cryptography research, where its effects are reported to be severe—I would have to say that the criticisms focus too much on the DMCA, to the exclusion of the rest of the intellectual property landscape. Yes, the DMCA offers enormous potential for abuse, particularly in conjunction with some other developments in intellectual property that I will discuss later, but much of the abuse has not yet happened. Yet even if it never did happen, the DMCA has important lessons to teach us.

In this section I have tried to show how legal rules—particularly intellectual property rules—define the boundaries of legitimate competition. We used to assume that this was principally the function of patent and trademark law, less so of copyright. Of course, copyright would affect competition in publishing and in the TV and movie industries, but it hardly seemed central to competition policy in general. But once courts and legislatures accepted that software is copyrightable, that assessment changed. The levers and cogs of the machines of the modern economy are forged out of ones and zeros instead of steel and brass. In that situation, copyright is central to the competition policy of a high-tech economy.

As the Apple case shows, our moral intuitions about competition are going to be cloudier in the world of digital content and cyberspace. The same is true of the law. Even in the material world it can be hard to draw the line between the legitimate and ruthless pursuit of commercial advantage and various forms of unfair competition, antitrust violations, and so on. But in the immaterial world, the boundaries are even harder to draw. Is this the digital equivalent of trespass or legitimate passage on a public road that runs through your property? As I pointed out earlier, the constant analogies to physical property are likely to conceal as much as they reveal. Is this virtuous competitive imitation or illicit copying? We have strong, and by no means coherent, moral and legal intuitions about the answers to such questions. And our legal structure often gives us the raw material to make a very good case for both sides of the argument.

Into this already troubled situation, with a set of rules designed for original expression in novels and poems being applied to machines made of computer code, we add the DMCA and its new rights of uncertain extent. Copyright had a well-developed set of exceptions to deal with anticompetitive behavior. Where the existing exceptions did not function, courts tended to turn to fair use as the universal method for patching the system up—the duct tape of the copyright system. Without an evolving idea of fair use, copyright would overshoot its bounds as it was applied to new technologies and new economic conditions. Indeed that was the point of the Sony Axiom. The DMCA threw this system into disarray, into a war of competing metaphors.

The *Skylink* court sees monopolists being handed carte blanche to abolish the restraints on their monopolies. Competition policy demands that we construe the DMCA narrowly. The *Reimerdes* court sees a virus masquerading as speech, a digital pandemic that must be stopped at all costs by a draconian program of electronic public health. Each proceeds to construe the statute around the reality they have created. It is by no means certain which metaphor will win the day, still less which resolution will triumph in other countries that have passed versions of the DMCA. International attitudes toward speech, competition, and the necessary exceptions in a copyright system vary widely. Yet backed by the story of the Internet Threat, the content companies are already saying that we need to go further both nationally and internationally—introducing more technology mandates, requiring computers to have hardware that will only play approved copyrighted versions, allowing content companies to hack into private computers in search of material they think is theirs, and so on. Remember the suggestion from the beginning of the chapter, that all cars be assumed to be getaway vehicles for the felonious filchers of vegetables, and thus that they should be fitted with radio beacons, have the size of their cargo space reduced, and so on? The Farmers' Tale continues to evolve.

6

I Got a Mashup

So far, I have talked about the root ideas of intellectual property. I have talked about its history, about the way it influences and is influenced by technology. I have talked about its effects on free speech and on competition. Until now, however, I have not described the way that it actually affects culture. This chapter aims to rectify the omission, looking at the way copyright law handles one specific form of cultural creation—music. It turns out that some of the problems identified in Chapters 4 and 5 are not simply the result of a mismatch between old law and new technology, or the difficulties posed in applying copyright to software, to machines made of words. The same issues appear at the heart of a much older cultural tradition.

This is the story of a song and of that song's history. But it is also a story about property and race and art, about the way copyright law has shaped, encouraged, and prohibited music over the last hundred years, about the lines it draws, the boundaries it sets, and the art it forbids.

Music is hard for copyright law to handle. If one had to represent the image of creativity around which copyright law and patent law, respectively, are built, patent law's model of creativity would be a pyramid and copyright law's a fountain, or even an explosion.

In patent law, the assumption is that technological development converges. Two engineers from two different countries tend to produce similar ways of catching mice or harnessing the power of steam. There are a limited number of good ways of accomplishing a technical task. In addition, technological progress is assumed to be incremental. Each development builds on the ones behind it. Based on this image, patent law makes a series of decisions about what gets covered by property rights, for how long, how to handle "subsequent improvements," and so on. Patent rights last for a short time, not only to lower costs to consumers, but because we want to build on the technology inventors have created as soon as possible, without getting their permission. Even during the patent term, subsequent "improvers" get their own rights and can bargain with the original patent holder to share the profits.

Copyright's assumptions are different. Copyright began with texts, with creative expression. Here the assumption is (generally) that there are infinite possibilities, that two writers will not converge on the same words, and that the next generation of storytellers does not need to take the actual "stuff" that copyright covers in order to make the next play or novel. (It may be because of this image that so few policy makers seem to worry that copyright now lasts for a *very* long time.) Subsequent "improvements" of copyrighted material are called derivative works, and without the rights holder's permission, they are illegal. Again, the assumption seems to be that you can just write your own book. Do not claim you need to build on mine.

Of course, each of these pictures is a caricature. The reality is more complex. Copyright can make this assumption more easily because it does not cover ideas or facts—just their expression. "Boy meets girl, falls in love, girl dies" is not supposed to be owned. The novel *Love Story* is. It is assumed that I do not need Erich Segal's copyrighted expression to write my own love story. Even if literary creativity does converge around standard genres, plots, and archetypes, it is assumed that those are in the public domain, leaving future creators free to build their own work without using material that is subject to copyright. We could debate the truth of that matter for literature: the expansion of copyright's ambit to cover plotlines and characters makes it more questionable. Certainly many recognized forms of creativity, such as the pastiche, the collage, the literary biography, and the parody need extensive access to prior copyrighted work. But regardless of how well we think the image of individual creativity fits literature, it fits very poorly in music where so much creativity is recognizably more collective and additive, and where much of the raw material used by subsequent creators is potentially covered by copyright.

So how does the accretive process of musical creativity fare in the modern law and culture of copyright? How would the great musical traditions of the twentieth century—jazz, soul, blues, rock—have developed under today's copyright regime? Would they have developed at all? How does the law apply to the new musicians, remixers, and samplers who offer their work on the Internet? Do the lines it draws fit with our ethics, our traditions of free speech and commentary, our aesthetic judgments? It would take a shelf of books to answer such questions definitively. In this chapter, all I can do is suggest some possibilities—using the history of a single song as my case study.

On August 29th, 2005, a hurricane made landfall in Louisiana. The forecasters called it "Hurricane Katrina," quickly shortened to "Katrina" as its story took over the news. The New Orleans levees failed. Soon the United States and then most of the world was watching pictures of a flooded New Orleans, seeing pleading citizens—mainly African-American—and a Keystone Cops response by the Federal Emergency Management Agency. The stories from New Orleans became more and more frightening. There were tales not only of natural disaster—drownings, elderly patients trapped in hospitals—but of a collapse of civilization: looting, murder and rape, stores being broken into with impunity, rescue helicopters fired upon, women and children sexually assaulted in the convention center where many of the refugees huddled. Later, it would turn out that many, perhaps most, of these reports were untrue, but one would not have guessed that from the news coverage.

The television played certain images over and over again. People—again, mainly African-Americans—were portrayed breaking into stores, pleading from rooftops, or later, when help still had not arrived, angrily gesturing and shouting obscenities at the camera.

As the disaster unfolded in slow motion, celebrities began appearing in televised appeals to raise money for those who had been affected by the storm. Kanye West, the hip hop musician, was one of them. Appearing on NBC on September 2, with the comedian Mike Myers, West started out seeming quietly upset. Finally, he exploded.

> I hate the way they portray us in the media. You see a black family, it says, "They're looting." You see a white family, it says, "They're looking for food." And, you know, it's been five days [waiting for federal help] because most of the people are black. . . . So anybody out there that wants to do anything that we can help—with

the way America is set up to help the poor, the black people, the less well-off, as slow as possible. I mean, the Red Cross is doing everything they can. We already realize a lot of people that could help are at war right now, fighting another way— and they've given them permission to go down and shoot us!

Myers, who, according to the *Washington Post*, "looked like a guy who stopped on the tarmac to tie his shoe and got hit in the back with the 8:30 to LaGuardia," filled in with some comments about the possible effect of the storm on the willingness of Louisiana citizens to live in the area in the future. Then he turned back to West, who uttered the line that came to epitomize Katrina for many people around the world, and to infuriate a large number of others. "George Bush doesn't care about black people!" Myers, the *Post* wrote, "now look[ed] like the 8:30 to LaGuardia turned around and caught him square between the eyes."[1] In truth, he did appear even more stunned than before, something I would not have thought possible.

In Houston, Micah Nickerson and Damien Randle were volunteering to help New Orleans evacuees at the Astrodome and Houston Convention Center during the weekend of September 3. They, too, were incensed both by the slowness of the federal response to the disaster and by the portrayal of the evacuees in the media. But Mr. Nickerson and Mr. Randle were not just volunteers, they were also a hip-hop duo called "The Legendary K.O." What better way to express their outrage than through their art? An article in the *New York Times* described their response.

> "When they got to Houston, people were just seeing for the first time how they were portrayed in the media," said Damien Randle, 31, a financial adviser and one half of the Legendary K.O. "It was so upsetting for them to be up on a roof for two days, with their kids in soiled diapers, and then see themselves portrayed as looters." In response, Mr. Randle and his partner, Micah Nickerson, wrote a rap based on the stories of the people they were helping. On Sept. 6, Mr. Nickerson sent Mr. Randle an instant message containing a music file and one verse, recorded on his home computer. Mr. Randle recorded an additional verse and sent it back, and 15 minutes later it was up on their Web site: www.k-otix.com.[2]

The song was called "George Bush Doesn't Care About Black People" (also referred to as "George Bush Doesn't Like Black People"). Appropriately, given that Mr. West was the one to come up with the phrase, the song was built around Mr. West's "Gold Digger." Much of the melody was sampled directly from the recording of that song. Yet the words were very different. Where "Gold Digger" is about a predatory, sensual, and materialist woman who "take[s] my money when I'm in need" and is a "triflin' friend indeed," The Legendary K.O.'s song is a lyrical and profane condemnation of the response to Katrina by both the government and the media. Here is a sample:

> Five days in this motherf__ attic
> Can't use the cellphone I keep getting static
> Dying 'cause they lying instead of telling us the truth
> Other day the helicopters got my neighbors off the roof
> Screwed 'cause they say they coming back for us too
> That was three days ago, I don't see no rescue
> See a man's gotta do what a man's gotta do
> Since God made the path that I'm trying to walk through
> Swam to the store, tryin' to look for food
> Corner store's kinda flooded so I broke my way through
> I got what I could but before I got through
> News say the police shot a black man trying to loot
> (Who!?) Don't like black people
> George Bush don't *like* black people
> George Bush don't *like* black people

This chapter is the story of that song. "George Bush Doesn't Care About Black People" is the end (for the moment) of a line of musical borrowing. That borrowing extends far beyond Kanye West's song "Gold Digger." "Gold Digger" is memorable largely because it in turn borrows from an even older song, a very famous one written half a century before and hailed by many as the birth of soul music. It is in the origins of *that* song that we will start the trail.

I GOT A WOMAN

In 1955, Ray Charles Robinson, better known as Ray Charles, released a song called "I Got a Woman." It was a defining moment in Charles's musical development. Early in his career he had unashamedly modeled himself on Nat King Cole.

> I knew back then that Nat Cole was bigger than ever. Whites could relate to him because he dealt with material they understood, and he did so with great feeling. Funny thing, but during all these years I was imitating Nat Cole, I never thought twice about it, never felt bad about copying the cat's licks. To me it was practically a science. I worked at it, I enjoyed it, I was proud of it, and I loved doing it. He was a guy everyone admired, and it just made sense to me, musical and commercial sense, to study his technique. It was something like when a young lawyer—just out of school—respects an older lawyer. He tries to get inside his mind, he studies to

see how he writes up all his cases, and he's going to sound a whole lot like the older man—at least till he figures out how to get his own shit together. Today I hear some singers who I think sound like me. Joe Cocker, for instance. Man, I know that cat must sleep with my records. But I don't mind. I'm flattered; I understand. After all, I did the same thing.[3]

In the early 50s Charles decided that he needed to move away from Cole's style and find his own sound, "sink, swim or die." But as with any musician, "his own sound" was the product of a number of musical traditions—blues and gospel particularly. It is out of those traditions that "I Got a Woman" emerged; indeed it is that combination that causes it to be identified as one of the birthplaces of soul music.

According to the overwhelming majority of sources, "I Got a Woman" stems from a fairly overt piece of musical borrowing—Charles reworded the hymn "Jesus Is All the World to Me"—sometimes referred to as "My Jesus Is All the World to Me."

> Musically, soul denotes styles performed by and for black audiences according to past musical practices reinterpreted and redefined. During its development, three performers played significant roles in shaping its sound, messages, and performance practice: Ray Charles, James Brown, and Aretha Franklin. If one can pinpoint a moment when gospel and blues began to merge into a secular version of gospel song, it was in 1954 when Ray Charles recorded "My Jesus Is All the World to Me," changing its text to "I Got A Woman."[4]

That story is repeated in the biography on Charles's Web site. "Charles reworded the gospel tune 'Jesus Is All the World to Me' adding deep church inflections to the secular rhythms of the nightclubs, and the world was never the same."[5] Michael Lydon, Charles's most impressive biographer, simply reports that "Jesus Is All the World to Me" is described as the song's origin in another published source,[6] and this origin is cited repeatedly elsewhere in books, newspaper articles, and online,[7] though the most detailed accounts also mention Renald Richard, Charles's trumpeter, who is credited with co-writing the song.[8]

To secular ears, "Jesus Is All the World to Me" is a plodding piece of music with a mechanical, up-and-down melodic structure. It conjures up a bored (and white) church audience, trudging through the verses, a semitone flat, while thinking about Sunday lunch rather than salvation. It is about as far removed as one could be from the syncopated beat and amorous subject matter of "I Got a Woman." The hymn was the product of Will Lamartine

Thompson—a severe-looking fellow with a faint resemblance to an elderly Doc Holliday—who died in 1909 and is buried in the same place he was born, East Liverpool, Ohio. But the words have an earnestness to them that gives life to the otherwise uninspired verse.

> Jesus is all the world to me, my life, my joy, my all;
> He is my strength from day to day, without Him I would fall.
> When I am sad, to Him I go, no other one can cheer me so;
> When I am sad, He makes me glad, He's my Friend.

Reading those words, one can understand the sincerity that made Mr. Thompson spurn commercial publishers for his devotional music, instead founding his own publishing house (also in East Liverpool) to make sure that his hymns reached the people. I can quote as much of the song as I want without worrying about legal consequences because the copyright on Mr. Thompson's lyrics has expired. So has the copyright over the music. The song was published in 1904. Copyright had only been extended to musical compositions in 1881. Like all copyrights back then, copyright over music lasted for only twenty-eight years, with a possible extension for another fourteen. If Ray Charles did indeed reword it fifty years later, he was doing nothing illegal. It had been in the public domain for at least eight years, and probably for twenty. Now maybe Charles's genius was to hear in this hymn, or in a syncopated gospel version of this hymn, the possibility of a fusion of traditions which would itself become a new tradition—soul. Or perhaps his genius was in knowing a good idea—Richard's—when he heard it, and turning that idea into the beginnings of its own musical genre.

Soul is a fusion of gospel on the one hand and rhythm and blues on the other. From gospel, soul takes the call-and-response pattern of preacher and congregation and the wailing vocals of someone "testifying" to their faith. From rhythm and blues it takes the choice of instruments, some of the upbeat tempo, and the distinctly worldly and secular attitude to the (inevitable) troubles of life. Musicologists delight in parsing the patterns of influence further; R&B itself had roots in "jump music" and the vocal style of the "blues shouters" who performed with the big bands. It also has links to jazz. Gospel reaches back to spirituals and so on.

As with all music, those musical traditions can be traced back or forward in time, the net of influence and borrowing widening as one goes in either direction. In each, one can point to distinctive musical motifs—the chords of the twelve-bar blues, or the flattened fifth in bebop. But musical traditions are also defined by performance styles and characteristic sounds: the warm guitar that came out of the valve amplifiers of early funk, the thrashing (and poorly miked) drums of '80s punk, or the tinny piano of honky-tonk. Finally, styles are often built around "standards"—classic songs of the genre to which an almost obligatory reference is made. My colleague, the talented composer Anthony Kelley, uses Henry Louis Gates's term "signifyin' " to describe the process of showing you are embedded in your musical tradition by referring back to its classics in your playing. In jazz, for example, one demonstrates one's rootedness in the tradition by quoting a standard, but also one's virtuosity in being able to trim it into a particular eight-bar solo, beginning and ending on the right note for the current moment in the chord progression. "I Got Rhythm" and "Round Midnight" are such songs for jazz. (The chord changes of "I Got Rhythm" are so standard, they are referred to as "the rhythm changes"—a standard basis for improvisation.) And to stretch the connections further, as Kelley points out, the haunting introduction to "Round Midnight" is itself remarkably similar to Sibelius's Fifth Symphony.

Through all these layers of musical borrowing and reference, at least in the twentieth century in the United States, runs the seam of race. When white musicians "borrowed" from soul to make "blue-eyed soul," when Elvis took songs and styles from rhythm and blues and turned them into rockabilly, a process of racial cleansing went on. Styles were adapted but were cleansed of those elements thought inappropriate for a larger white audience. Generally, this involved cutting some of the rawer sensuality, removing racially specific verbal and musical references, and, for much of the century, cutting the African-American artists out of the profits in the process.

There is another irony here. Styles formed by patterns of gleeful borrowing, formed as part of a musical commons—the blues of the Mississippi Delta, for example—were eventually commercialized and "frozen" into a particular form by white artists. Sometimes those styles were covered with intellectual property rights which denied the ability of the original community to "borrow back." In the last thirty or forty years of the century, African-American artists got into the picture too, understandably embracing with considerable zeal the commercial opportunities and property rights that had previously been denied to them. But aside from the issue of racial injustice, one has to consider the question of sustainability.

In other work, I have tried to show how a vision of intellectual property rights built around a notion of the romantic author can sometimes operate as a one-way valve vis-à-vis traditional and collective creative work.[8] There is a danger that copyright will treat collectively created musical traditions as unowned raw material, but will then prevent the commercialized versions of those traditions—now associated with an individual artist—from continuing to act as the basis for the next cycle of musical adaptation and development. One wonders whether jazz, blues, R&B, gospel, and soul would even have been possible as musical styles if, from their inception, they had been covered by the strong property rights we apply today. That is a question I want to return to at the end of this chapter.

Musical styles change over time and so do their techniques of appropriation. Sometimes musical generations find their successors are engaging in different *types* of borrowing than they themselves engaged in. They do not always find it congenial. It is striking how often musicians condemn a younger generation's practice of musical appropriation as theft, while viewing their own musical development and indebtedness as benign and organic. James Brown attacked the use of his guitar licks or the drum patterns from his songs by hip-hop samplers, for example, but celebrated the process of borrowing from gospel standards and from rhythm and blues that created the "Hardest Working Man in Show Business"—both the song and the musical persona. To be sure, there are differences between the two practices. Samplers take a three-second segment off the actual recording of "Funky Drummer," manipulate it, and turn it into a repeating rhythm loop for a hip-hop song. This is a different kind of borrowing than the adaptation of a chord pattern from a gospel standard to make an R&B hit. But which way does the difference cut as a matter of ethics, aesthetics, or law?

Charles himself came in for considerable criticism for his fusion of gospel intonations and melodic structures with the nightclub sound of rhythm and blues, but not because it was viewed as piracy. It was viewed as sacrilegious.

> Charles totally removed himself from the polite music he had made in the past. There was an unrestrained exuberance to the new Ray Charles, a fierce earthiness that, while it would not have been unfamiliar to any follower of gospel music, was almost revolutionary in the world of pop. Big Bill Broonzy was outraged: "He's crying, sanctified. He's mixing the blues with the spirituals. He should be singing in a church."[10]

Charles disagreed. "You can't run away from yourself. . . . What you are inside is what you are inside. I was raised in the church and was around blues and would hear all these musicians on the jukeboxes and then I would go to revival meetings on Sunday morning. So I would get both sides of music. A lot of people at the time thought it was sacrilegious but all I was doing was singing the way I felt."[11] Why the charge of sacrilege? Because beyond the breach of stylistic barriers, the relationships Charles described did not seem to belong in church.

"I Got a Woman" tells of a woman, "way over town," who is good to the singer—very good, in fact. She gives him money when he is in need, is a "kind of friend indeed," even saves her "early morning loving" just for him (and it is tender loving at that). In the third verse we learn she does not grumble, fuss, or run in the streets, "knows a woman's place is right there now in the home," and in general is a paragon of femininity. Gender roles aside, it is a fabulous song, from the elongated "We-e-ell . . ." in Charles's distinctive tones, to the momentary hesitation that heightens the tension, all the way through the driving beat of the main verses and the sense that a gospel choir would have fit right in on the choruses, testifying ecstatically to the virtues of Charles's lady friend. Charles liked women—a lot of women, according to his biographers—and a lot of women liked him right back. That feeling comes through very clearly from this song.

I would like to quote the song lyrics for you, just as I did the words of the hymn, but that requires a little more thought. Charles's song was released in 1955. By that time, the copyright term for a musical composition was twenty-eight years, renewable for another twenty-eight if the author wished. (Later, the twenty-eight-year second term would be increased to forty-seven years. Still later, the copyright term would be extended to life plus seventy years, or ninety-five years for a "work for hire." Sound recordings themselves would not be protected by federal law until the early 1970s.) Anyone who wrote or distributed a song under the "28 + 28" system was, in effect, saying "this is a long enough protection for me," enough incentive to create. Thus, we could have assumed that "I Got a Woman" would enter the public domain in either 1983 or, if renewed, 2011. Unfortunately for us, and for a latter-day Ray Charles, the copyright term has been extended several times since then, and each time it was also extended retrospectively. Artists, musicians, novelists, and filmmakers who had created their works on the understanding that they had twenty-eight or fifty-six or seventy-five years of protection now have considerably more. This was the point raised in Chapter 1. Most of the culture of the twentieth century, produced under a perfectly well-functioning system with much shorter copyright terms, is still locked up and will be for many years to come.

In the case of "I Got a Woman," it is now about fifty years since the song's release—the same length of time as between Thompson's hymn and Charles's alleged "rewording." If the words and music were properly copyrighted at the time of its publication, and renewed when appropriate, the copyright still has forty-five years to run. No one will be able to "reword" "I Got a Woman" and use it to found a new genre, or take substantial portions of its melody, until the year 2050. The freedoms Ray Charles says he used to create his song are denied to his successors until nearly a century after the song's release. (As we will see in a moment, this put certain constraints on Kanye West.)

Would it truly be a violation of copyright for me to quote the middle stanza in a nonfiction book on copyright policy? Not at all. It is a classic "fair use." In a moment I will do so. But it is something that the publisher may well fuss over, because copyright holders are extremely aggressive in asking for payments for the slightest little segment. Copyright holders in music and song lyrics are among the most aggressive of the lot. Year after year academics, critics, and historians pay fairly substantial fees (by our standards) to license tiny fragments of songs even though their incorporation is almost certainly fair use. Many of them do not know the law. Others do, but want to avoid the hassle, the threats, the nasty letters. It is simpler just to pay.

Unfortunately, these individual actions have a collective impact. One of the factors used to consider whether something is a fair use is whether or not there is a market for this particular use of a work. If there is, it is less likely to be a fair use to quote or incorporate such a fragment. As several courts have pointed out, there is a powerful element of circularity here. You claim you have a right to stop me from doing x—quoting two lines of your three-verse song in an academic book, say. I say you have no such right and it is a fair use. You say it is not a fair use because it interferes with your market—the market for selling licenses for two-sentence fragments. But when do you have such a market? When you have a right to stop me quoting the two-sentence fragment unless I pay you. Do you have such a right? But that is exactly what we are trying to decide! Is it a fair use or not? The existence of the market depends on it not being a fair use for me to quote it without permission. To say "I would have a market if I could stop you doing it, so it cannot be a fair use, so I *can* stop you" is perfectly circular.

How do we get out of the circle? Often the court will look to customs and patterns in the world outside. Do people accept this as a market? Do they traditionally pay such fees? Thus, if a lot of people choose to pay for quotes that actually should have been fair use, the "market" for short quotes will begin to emerge. That will, in turn, affect the boundaries of fair use for the worse. Slowly, fair use will constrict, will atrophy. The hypertrophied permissions culture starts as myth, but it can become reality.

In any event, Ray Charles had no need of fair use to make "I Got a Woman" because the hymn his biography claims it is based on was in the public domain. But is that the real source? I can hear little resemblance. As I researched the origins of "I Got a Woman," I found claims that there was a different source, a mysterious song by the Bailey Gospel Singers, or the Harold Bailey Gospel Singers, called "I've Got a Savior."[12] The Columbia Records gospel catalogue even provided a catalogue number.[13] There was such a song, or so it seemed. But there the research stalled. The exemplary librarians at Duke University Music Library could find no trace. Catalogues of published records showed nothing. Inquiries to various music librarian listservs also produced no answer. There was a man called Harold Bailey, who sang with a group of gospel singers, but though several Internet postings suggested he was connected to the song, his biography revealed he would have been only thirteen at the time. The Library of Congress did not have it. Eventually, Jordi Weinstock—a great research assistant who demonstrated willingness to pester anyone in the world who might conceivably have access to the recording—hit gold. The Rodgers and Hammerstein Archives of Recorded Sound at the New York Public Library for the Performing Arts had a copy—a 78 rpm vinyl record by the Bailey Gospel Singers with "Jesus Is the Searchlight" on the B-side. Our library was able to obtain a copy on interlibrary loan from the helpful curator, Don McCormick.

It sounds like the same song. Not the same words, of course: the introduction is different and the Bailey Gospel Singers lack the boom-chicky-boom backing of Charles's version, but the central melody is almost exactly the same. When the Bailey Gospel Singers sing "Keeps me up / Keeps me strong / Teach me right / When I doing wrong / Well, I've got a savior / Oh what a savior / yes I have," the melody, and even the intonation, parallel Charles singing the equivalent lines: "She gimme money / when I'm in need / Yeah she's a kind of / friend indeed / I've got a woman / way over town / who's good to me."

True, some of the lyrical and rhythmic patterns of "I've Got a Savior" are older still. They come from a spiritual called "Ain't That Good News," dating from 1940, which rehearses all the things the singer will have in the Kingdom of Heaven—a harp, a robe, slippers (!), and, finally, a savior. The author of "I've Got a Savior" was, like all the artists discussed here, taking a great deal from a prior musical tradition. Nevertheless, Charles's borrowing is particularly overt and direct. The term "rewording" is appropriate. So far as I can see, whether or not he also relied on a fifty-year-old hymn, Ray Charles appears to have taken both the melody and lyrical pattern of his most famous hit from a song that was made a mere three or four years earlier.

Like many 78 rpm records, this one was sold without liner notes. The center of the record provides the only details. It gives the name of the track and the band and a single word under the song title, "Ward"—presumably the composer. "Ward" might be Clara Ward of the Ward Singers, a talented gospel singer and songwriter who became Aretha Franklin's mentor and who had her own music publishing company.

There is a particular reason to think that she might have written the song: Ray Charles clearly liked to adapt her music to secular ends. We know that he "reworked" Ward's gospel classic "This Little Light of Mine" into "This Little Girl of Mine." Ward reportedly was irritated by the practice. So far as we know, the copying of the music did not annoy her because she viewed it as theft, but because she viewed it as an offense against gospel music.

> Charles is now starting to get criticism from some gospel music performers for secularizing gospel music and presenting it in usual R&B venues. Most adamant in her misgivings is Clara Ward who complains about "This Little Girl Of Mine" being a reworking of "This Little Light Of Mine" (which it is), as a slap against the gospel field.[14]

This stage of Charles's career is described, rightly, as the moment when his originality bursts forth, where he stops imitating the smooth sounds of Nat King Cole and instead produces the earthy and sensual style that becomes his trademark—his own sound. That is true enough; there had been nothing quite like this before. Yet it was hardly original creation out of nothing. Both Charles himself and the musicological literature point out that "his own sound," "his style," is in reality a fusion of two prior genres—rhythm and blues and gospel. But looking at the actual songs that created soul as a genre shows us that the fusion goes far beyond merely a stylistic one. Charles makes some of his most famous songs by taking existing gospel classics and reworking or simply rewording them. "I've Got a Savior" becomes "I Got a Woman." "This Little Light of Mine" becomes "This Little Girl of Mine."

The connection is striking: two very recent gospel songs, probably by the same author, from which Charles copies the melody, structure, pattern of verses, even most of the title—in each case substituting a beloved sensual woman for the beloved deity. Many others have noticed just how closely Charles based his songs on gospel tunes, although the prevalence of the story that "I Got a Woman" is derived from an early-twentieth-century hymn caused most to see only the second transposition, not the first.[15] Borrowing from a fifty-year-old hymn and changing it substantially in the process seems a little different from the repeated process of "search and replace" musical collage that Charles performed on the contemporary works of Clara Ward.

If I am right, Charles's "merger" of gospel and blues relied on a very direct process of transposition. The transposition was not just of themes: passion for woman substituted for passion for God. That is a familiar aspect of soul.[16] It is what allows it to draw so easily from gospel's fieriness and yet coat the religion with a distinctly more worldly passion. Sex, sin, and syncopation—what more could one ask? But Charles's genius was to take particular songs that had already proved themselves in the church and on the radio, and to grab large chunks of the melody and structure. He was not just copying themes, or merging genres, he was copying the melodies and words from recent songs.

Was this mere musical plagiarism, then? Should we think less of Ray Charles's genius because we find just how closely two of the canonical songs in the creation of soul were based on the work of his contemporaries? Hardly. "I Got a Woman" and "This Little Girl of Mine" are simply brilliant. Charles does in fact span the worlds of the nightclub at 3 A.M. on Sunday morning and the church later that day, of ecstatic testimony and good old-fashioned sexual infatuation. But the way he does so is a lot more like welding, or *bricolage,* than it is like designing out of nothing or creating anew while distantly tugged by mysterious musical forces called "themes" or "genres." Charles takes bits that have been proven to work and combines them to make something new. When I tell engineers or software engineers this story, they nod. Of course that is how creation works. One does not reinvent the wheel, or the method of debugging, so why should one reinvent the hook, the riff, or the melody? And yet Charles's creation does not have the degraded artistic quality that is associated with "mere" cut-and-paste or collage techniques. The combination is greater than the sum of its parts. If Charles's songs do not fit our model of innovative artistic creativity, perhaps we need to revise the model— at least for music—rather than devaluing his work.

When I began this study, it seemed to me that the greatest challenge to copyright law in dealing with music was preventing rights from "creeping," expanding from coverage of a single song or melody to cover essential elements of genre, style, and theme. In effect, we needed to apply the Jefferson Warning to music, to defeat the constant tendency to confuse intellectual property with real property, and to reject the attempts to make the right holder's control total. My assumption was that all we needed to do was to keep open the "common space" of genre and style, and let new artists create their new compositions out of the material in that commons and gain protection over them. In many ways, Charles's work lies at the very core of the stuff copyright wishes to promote. It is not merely innovative and expressive itself, it also helped form a whole new genre in which other artists could express themselves. But to create this work, Charles needed to make use of a lot more than just genres and styles created by others. He needed their actual songs. If the reactions of Clara Ward and Big Bill Broonzy are anything to go by, they would not have given him permission. To them, soul was a stylistic violation, a mingling of the sacred with the profane. If given a copyright veto over his work, and a culture that accepts its use, Ward might well have exercised it. Like the disapproving heirs that Macaulay talked about, she could have denied us a vital part of the cultural record. Control has a price.

Did Ray Charles commit copyright infringement? Perhaps. We would have to find if the songs are substantially similar, once we had excluded standard forms, public domain elements, and so on. I would say that they are substantially similar, but was the material used copyright-protected expression?

The Copyright Office database shows no entry for "I've Got a Savior." This is not conclusive, but it seems to indicate that no copyright was ever registered in the work. In fact, it is quite possible that the song was first written without a copyright notice. Nowadays that omission would be irrelevant. Works are copyrighted as soon as they are fixed in material form, regardless of whether any copyright notice is attached. In 1951, however, a notice was required when the work was published, and if one was not put on the work, it passed immediately into the public domain. However, later legislation decreed that the relevant publication was not of the record, but of the notation. If the record were pressed and sold without a copyright notice, the error could be corrected. If a lead sheet or a sheet music version of "I've Got a Savior" had been published without notice or registration, it would enter the public domain. It is possible that this happened. Intellectual property rights simply played a lesser role in the 1950s music business than they do today, both for better and for worse. Large areas of creativity operated as copyright-free zones. Even where copyrights were properly registered, permission fees were not demanded for tiny samples. While bootlegged recordings or direct note-for-note copies might well draw legal action, borrowing and transformation were apparently viewed as a normal part of the creative process. In some cases, artists simply did not use copyright. They made money from performances. Their records might receive some kind of protection from state law. These protections sufficed.

But the lack of protection also had a less attractive and more racially skewed side. African-American artists were less likely to have the resources and knowledge necessary to navigate the system of copyright. For both black and white artists, whatever rights there were moved quickly away from the actual creators toward the agents, record companies, and distributors. They still do. But African-American musicians got an even worse deal than their white counterparts. True, the copyright system was only an infinitesimal part of that process. A much larger part was the economic consequences of segregation and racial apartheid. But copyright was one of the many levers of power that were more easily pulled by white hands. This is an important point because the need to end that palpable racial injustice is sometimes used to justify every aspect of our current highly legalized musical culture. About that conclusion, I am less convinced.

In any event, it is possible that the musical composition for "I've Got a Savior" went immediately into the public domain. If that were the case, Ray Charles could draw on it, could change it, could refine it without permission or fee. Certainly there is no mention of seeking permission or paying fees in any of the histories of "I Got a Woman." Indeed, the only question of rectitude Charles was focused on was the stylistic one. Was it appropriate to mix gospel and R&B, devotional music and secular desire? Charles and Richard seemed to see the process of rewording and adapting as just a standard part of the musician's creative process. The only question was whether these two styles were aesthetically or morally suited, not whether the borrowing itself was illegal or unethical. So, whether they drew on a hymn that had fallen into the public domain after the expiration of its copyright term, or a gospel song for which copyright had never been sought, or whether they simply took a copyrighted song and did to it something that no one at the time thought was legally inappropriate, Renald Richard and Ray Charles were able to create "I Got a Woman" and play a significant role in founding a new musical genre—soul.

One thing is clear. Much of what Charles and Richard did in creating their song would be illegal today. Copyright terms are longer. Copyright protection itself is automatic. Copyright policing is much more aggressive. The musical culture has changed into one in which every fragment must be licensed and paid for. The combination is fatal to the particular pattern of borrowing that created these seminal songs of soul.

That should give us pause. I return to the ideas of the Jefferson Warning from Chapter 2 and the Sony Axiom from Chapter 4. Copyright is not an end in itself. It has a goal: to promote the progress of cultural and scientific creativity. That goal requires rights that are less than absolute. As Jessica Litman points out, building in the intellectual space is different from building in the physical space. We do not normally dismantle old houses to make new ones. This point is not confined to music. Earlier I quoted Northrop Frye: "Poetry can only be made out of other poems; novels out of other novels. All of this was much clearer before the assimilation of literature to private enterprise."[17] The question is, how big are the holes we need to leave in the private rights? How large a commons do we need to offer to future creators?

Ray Charles's creation of "I Got a Woman" is only one case. By itself, it proves nothing. Yet, if we find that the seminal, genre-creating artworks of yesteryear would be illegal under the law and culture of today, we have to ask ourselves "is this really what we want?" What will the music of the future look like if the Clara Wards and Will Lamartine Thompsons of today can simply refuse to license on aesthetic grounds or demand payment for every tiny fragment? Tracing the line further back, it is fascinating to wonder whether gospel, blues, and jazz would have developed if musical motifs had been jealously guarded as private property rather than developed as a kind of melodic and rhythmic commons. Like most counterfactuals, that one has no clear answer, but there is substantial cause for skepticism. If copyright is supposed to be promoting innovation and development in culture, is it doing its job?

AN INDUSTRY OF GOLD DIGGERS?

Fifty years after "I Got a Woman" was written, Kanye West released "Gold Digger" on the album *Late Registration*. Mr. West is an interesting figure in rap. At first he was shunned because his clean-cut looks and preppy clothing ran against the gangster image that often dominates the music. It is just hard imagining Mr. West delivering a line like Rakim's "I used to be a stick-up kid, so I think of all the devious things I did" with a straight face. (Still less "Stop smiling, ain't nothin' funny, nothing moves but the money.") Perhaps partly as a result, his lyrics are oddly bipolar in their views about exaggerated masculinity and the misogyny that sometimes accompanies it.

For the song, Mr. West recruited Jamie Foxx, who had played Ray Charles in the movie *Ray*. Showing an impressive expanse of oiled chest, Mr. Foxx imitates Charles's style and the melody of "I Got a Woman" to provide the lyrical chorus to "Gold Digger." "I Got a Woman" anchors West's song. It provides its melodic hook. It breaks up the rap with a burst of musical nostalgia. But Mr. West's gold digger is very different from Ray Charles's woman friend.

This woman does not *give* money when the singer is in need. She *takes* his money when he is in need and is a "triflin' friend indeed." Mr. Charles had a friend who gave him tender morning loving. Jamie Foxx sings of a mercenary gold digger who digs on him. When Mr. West adds the rap verses to the song, we get a perfect caricature of such a person, uninterested in any man who is broke, dragging around four kids and an entourage, insisting all of them be entertained at her boyfriend's expense, and wielding unfounded paternity suits like a proprietary business method. Mr. West's repeated disclaimer "I ain't sayin' she's a gold digger" is unconvincing, because both the words of the introduction and the implicit message of the rap tell us she is. We even get the absurd image of a man who is playing on the winning side in the Super Bowl but driving a Hyundai, so financially demanding is his girlfriend. At several points the song descends into ludicrous—and perhaps conscious—self-mockery, as it explores the concerns of the rich African-American celebrity male. My favorite line is "If you ain't no punk, holler 'We want prenup!!' " The audience obliges. It sounds like assertiveness training for show business millionaires.

It would be hard to get a feminist role model out of either "I Got a Woman" or "Gold Digger." One offers the feminine virtues of modesty and fidelity, but magically combines them with wantonness where the singer is concerned and an open checkbook. The other is a parody of the self-assertive economic actor, as rapacious as any multinational, who uses her sexuality for profit. Put them together and you have bookends—male fantasy and male nightmare. Was that Mr. West's point? Perhaps. The song itself takes several sly turns. The gold digger dogging Mr. West is used as part of a homily to black women on how to treat their (noncelebrity) black men. They should stick with their man because his ambition is going to take him from mopping floors to the fryers, from a Datsun to a Benz. It seems that Mr. West is getting a little preachy, while slamming the actual social mobility available to black men. Moving from floor cleaning to frying chicken is not actually going to provide a Mercedes. But he immediately undercuts that tone twice, once by acknowledging the boyfriend's likely infidelity and again by saying that even if the black woman follows his homily, "once you get on, he leave yo' ass for a white girl."

Mr. West has a tendency to make sudden turns like this in his lyrics—ironically upsetting the theme he has just set up. So it is not hard to imagine that he deliberately used a fragment of Charles's song, not just because it sounded good but to contrast the image of the fantasy woman from Charles's 1950s soul, who is faithful, sensual, and always willing to offer a loan, with an image from today's rap—sexually predatory and emasculating women who are uninterested in men except as a source of money. Even the retro cover of the single, with its 1950s-style pinup drawing of a white model, seems to draw the connection. Did he use Charles's song precisely because of these clashing cultural snapshots? Perhaps, or perhaps he just liked the tune. In any event, the contrast is striking. When it was released, Charles's song was seen as a sacrilegious depiction of sensuality and the woman was decried as a harlot. Compared to the woman in Mr. West's song, she sounds like a Girl Scout. It is also a little depressing. Ray Charles was neither an egalitarian metrosexual nor a Prince Charming where women were concerned—anything but. But as I said before, you do get a sense that he *liked* women—however unrealistic or two-dimensional their portrayal. It is hard to get that sense from "Gold Digger."

Was Mr. West legally required to ask permission—and pay, if necessary—to use a fragment of "I Got a Woman" for his chorus? The longest single piece of borrowing occurs in the introduction: twenty-six words and their accompanying music. "She takes my money, when I'm in need, oh she's a triflin' friend indeed. Oh she's a gold digger, way over town, who digs on me." As I pointed out, the lyrics from Charles's song present a very different story. "She gimme money / when I'm in need / Yeah she's a kind of / friend indeed / I've got a woman / way over town / who's good to me." But even if the message is the opposite, the musical borrowing is direct. It is also extensive. During Mr. West's rap, the entire background melody is a loop of Jamie Foxx singing the Ray Charles-inspired melody in the background. During the song, Mr. Foxx returns to words that are closer to Charles's original: "She gimme money, when I'm in need," a refrain that is conspicuously at odds with the woman being described by Mr. West. That eight-bar loop of a Ray Charles melody runs throughout Kanye West's song.

Mr. West is very successful, so the fragment of the song was "cleared"—payment was made to Charles's estate. It is fascinating to think of what might have happened if Charles's heirs had refused. After all, one could see West's song as a crude desecration of Charles's earlier work, rather than a good-humored homage. Since this is not a "cover version" of the song—one which does not change its nature and thus operates under the statutory licensing scheme—Charles's heirs would have the right to refuse a licensing request. Unlike Clara Ward, it is clear that Charles's heirs have the legal power to say no, to prevent reuse of which they disapprove.

Was West legally required to license? Would all this amount to a copyright violation? It is worth running through the analysis because it gives a beautiful snapshot of the rules with which current law surrounds musical creation.

Today, a song is generally covered by at least two copyrights. One covers the musical composition—the sheet music and the lyrics—and the other the particular sound recording of that composition. Just as there are two kinds of copyrights, so there are at least two kinds of borrowings that copyright might be concerned with. First, one musical composition might infringe another. Thus, for example, a court found that George Harrison "subconsciously" based his song "My Sweet Lord" on the melody of "He's So Fine" by the Chiffons.

How much does it take to infringe? That is a difficult question. The law's standard is "substantial similarity," but not every kind of similarity counts. Minimal or *de minimis* copying of tiny fragments is ignored. Certain styles or forms have become standards; for example, the basic chord structure of the twelve-bar blues or the habit of introducing instruments one at a time, from quietest to loudest. There are only so many notes—and so many ways to re-arrange them; inevitably any song will be similar to some other. Yet that can-not mean that all songs infringe copyright. Finally, even where there is substantial similarity of a kind that copyright is concerned with, the second artist may claim "fair use"—for parody or criticism, say. Copyright law, in other words, has tried to solve the problem with which I began the chapter. Because much of musical creativity is organic and collective and additive, be-cause it does use prior musical expression, some copyright decisions have tried to carve out a realm of freedom for that creativity, using doctrines with names such as *scènes à faire*, merger, and fair use. This is yet another example of judges trying to achieve the balance that this book is all about—between the realm of the protected and the public domain—recognizing that it is the bal-ance, not the property side alone, that allows for new creativity.

The second type of potential infringement comes when someone uses a fragment of the earlier recording as part of the later one, actually copying a portion of the recording itself and using it in a new song. One might imagine the same rules would be applied—*de minimis* copying irrelevant, certain stan-dard forms unprotected, and so on. And one would be wrong. In a case called *Bridgeport Music*, which I will discuss in a moment, the Court of Appeals ruled that taking even two notes of a musical recording counts as potentially ac-tionable copying. Where recordings are concerned, in other words, there is al-most no class of copying so minimal that the law would ignore it. This is a terrible decision, at least in my opinion, likely to be rejected by other Circuits and perhaps even eventually by the Supreme Court. But for the moment, it is a case that samplers have to deal with.

How does Kanye West fare under these rules? He may sample from the actual recording of Mr. Charles's song. It is hard to tell. He certainly copies portions of the melody. That means we have to look at the copyright in the musical composition—the words and the music of "I Got a Woman." For a copyright infringement, one needs a valid copyright and evidence of copying, the amount copied needs to be more than an insignificant fragment, substantial similarity is required, and the similarity has to be between the new work and the elements of the original that are actually protected by copyright. Elements taken from the public domain, standard introductions, musical clichés, and so forth, do not get included in the calculation of similarity. Finally, the copier can claim "fair use"—that his borrowing is legally privileged because it is commentary, criticism, parody, and so on.

Does Charles, or his record company, have a valid copyright in the musical composition? One huge problem in copyright law is that it is remarkably hard to find this out. Even with the best will in the world, it is hard for an artist, musician, or teacher to know what is covered by copyright and what is not. Nowadays, all works are copyrighted as soon as they are fixed, but at the time "I Got a Woman" was written one had to include a copyright notice or the song went immediately into the public domain. The Copyright Office database shows no copyright over the words and music of "I Got a Woman." There are copyrights over a variety of *recordings* of the song. If Mr. West is using a fragment of the recording, these would affect him. But the melody? It is possible that the underlying musical composition is in the public domain. Finding out whether it is or is not would probably cost one a lot of money.

Suppose that Mr. Charles has complied with all the formalities. The words and music were published with a copyright notice. A copyright registration was filed and renewed. Does Mr. West infringe this copyright? That is where the discovery of the Bailey Gospel Singers recording is potentially so important. Charles only gets a copyright in his original creation. Those elements taken from the public domain (if "I've Got a Savior" was indeed in the public domain) or from other copyrighted songs do not count. The irony here is that the elements that Kanye West borrows from Ray Charles are almost exactly the same ones Ray Charles borrows from the Bailey Gospel Singers. "I've got a savior, Oh what a savior" becomes "I got a woman, way over town" becomes "There's a Gold Digger, way over town." And of course, the music behind those words is even more similar. When The Legendary K.O. reached for Kanye West's song in order to criticize Mr. Bush, they found themselves sampling Jamie Foxx, who was copying Ray Charles, who was copying the Bailey

Gospel Singers, who themselves may have borrowed their theme from an older spiritual.

GEORGE BUSH DOESN'T CARE . . .

> Five damn days, five long days
> And at the end of the fifth he walking in like "Hey!"
> Chilling on his vacation, sitting patiently
> Them black folks gotta hope, gotta wait and see
> If FEMA really comes through in an emergency
> But nobody seem to have a sense of urgency
> Now the mayor's been reduced to crying
> I guess Bush said, "N———'s been used to dying!"
> He said, "I know it looks bad, just have to wait"
> Forgetting folks was too broke to evacuate
> N———'s starving and they dying of thirst
> I bet he had to go and check on them refineries first
> Making a killing off the price of gas
> He would have been up in Connecticut twice as fast . . .
> After all that we've been through nothing's changed
> You can call Red Cross but the fact remains that . . .
> George Bush ain't a gold digger,
> but he ain't f—ing with no broke n———s

"George Bush Doesn't Care About Black People," The Legendary K.O.

The song "George Bush Doesn't Care About Black People" was an immediate sensation. Hundreds of thousands of people downloaded it. Within days two different video versions had been made, one by Franklin Lopez and another by a filmmaker called "The Black Lantern." Both synchronized the lyrics of the song with news clips of the disaster and unsympathetic footage of President Bush apparently ignoring what was going on. The effect was both hilarious and tragic. The videos were even more popular than the song alone. The blogosphere was fascinated—entries were posted, e-mails circulated to friends with the usual "you have to see this!" taglines. In fact, the song was so popular that it received the ultimate recognition of an Internet fad: the *New York Times* wrote a story on it, setting the practice in historical context.

> In the 18th century, songwriters responded to current events by writing new lyrics to existing melodies. "Benjamin Franklin used to write broadside ballads every time a disaster struck," said Elijah Wald, a music historian, and sell the printed lyrics in

the street that afternoon. This tradition of responding culturally to terrible events had almost been forgotten, Mr. Wald said, but in the wake of Hurricane Katrina, it may be making a comeback, with the obvious difference that, where Franklin would have sold a few song sheets to his fellow Philadelphians, the Internet allows artists today to reach the whole world.[18]

Mr. Nickerson's and Mr. Randle's song started with Kanye West's words—taken from the fundraiser with Mike Myers. "George Bush doesn't care about black people." From there it launched into the song. The background melody comes almost entirely from a looped, or infinitely repeated, version of the hook that Kanye West and Jamie Foxx had in turn taken from Ray Charles: "She gimme money, when I'm in need. I gotta leave." Against that background, The Legendary K.O. provide their profane and angry commentary, part of which is excerpted above, with a chorus of "George Bush don't *like* black people," in case anyone had missed the point.

The videos differ in the issues they stress. Franklin Lopez's movie is, rather pointedly given its theme, just black and white. He uses ornate captions pages, reminiscent of silent film from the 1920s, to make political points against the background of the song and the news footage. As the captions read "Katrina Rapidly Approaches," we cut to a shot of the hurricane. "The President Ponders on What to Do." We have a shot of Mr. Bush playing golf. "I Think I'll Ride This One Out." Mr. Bush is shown relaxing on a golf cart, juxtaposed against pictures of African-Americans wading through the floods. The captions add, as an afterthought, "And Keep Dealing with the Brown People." (Pictures of soldiers shooting.) When FEMA's Michael Brown is shown—at the moment when Bush said "Brownie, you are doing a hell of a job"—the captions comment mockingly, "The Horse Judge to the Rescue."

Mr. Lopez's video obviously tries to use The Legendary K.O.'s song to make larger political arguments about the country. For example, it asserts that "in 2004 Bush diverted most of the funds for the levees to the war in Iraq." Scenes reminiscent of a Michael Moore documentary are shown. There are pictures of the Iraq war, Halliburton signs, and shots of the president with a member of the Saudi royal family. The captions accuse the president of showing insensitivity and disdain to racial minorities. One summarizes the general theme: "Since he was elected president, George Bush's policies have been less than kind toward Africans and Hispanics." Issues ranging from the response to the Darfur massacres, No Child Left Behind, and the attempted privatization of Social Security also make their appearance. The video concludes by giving the donation information for the Red Cross and saying that we are "onto" Bush. A picture of a Klansman removing his hood is shown, with the image manipulated so that the face revealed is Mr. Bush's.

The Black Lantern's video is just as angry, and it uses some of the same footage, but the themes it picks up are different. It starts with a logo that parodies the FBI copyright warning shown at the beginning of movies: "WARNING: Artist supports filesharing. Please distribute freely." That dissolves into a picture of Kanye West and Mike Myers. West is speaking, somewhat awkwardly as he goes "off script," and at first Mr. Myers is nodding, though he starts to look increasingly worried. West says, "I hate the way they portray us in the media. You see a black family it says they are looting. You see a white family, it says they are looking for food." Finally, West says "George Bush doesn't care about black people" and the camera catches Myers's mute, appalled reaction. Then the song begins. The film cuts repeatedly between a music video of Mr. Foxx as he sang the lines for "Gold Digger" and the news coverage of the debacle in New Orleans. At one point the music pauses and a news anchor says, "You simply get chills when you look at these people. They are so poor. And so black." The song resumes. Here the message is simpler. The media coverage is biased and governmental attention slowed because of negative racial stereotypes and lack of concern about black people.

Some readers will find that this song and these videos capture their own political perspectives perfectly. They will love the bitterly ironic and obscene outrage at the government's failure, the double standards of the press, and the disproportionate and callously disregarded impact on the poor and black. Others will find both song and films to be stupid, insulting, and reductionist—an attempt to find racial prejudice in a situation that, at worst, was an example of good old-fashioned governmental incompetence. Still others will find the language just too off-putting to even think about the message. Whatever your feelings about the content, I urge you to set them aside for a moment. For better or worse, Mr. Bush just happened to be president at the moment when the Internet was coming into its own as a method of distributing digitally remixed political commentary, which itself has recently become something that amateurs can do for pennies rather than an expensive activity reserved to professionals. The point is that whatever rules we apply to deal with "George Bush Doesn't Care About Black People" will also apply to the next video that alleges corruption in a Democratic administration or that attacks the sacred cows of the left rather than the right. How should we think about this kind of activity, this taking the songs and films and photos of others and remixing them to express political, satirical, parodic, or simply funny points of view?

SAMPLING

Let us begin with the music. Unlike the other songs I have discussed here, with the possible exception of Mr. West's, "George Bush Doesn't Care About Black People" makes use of digital samples of the work of others. In other words, this is not merely about copying the tune or the lyrics. The reason that Mr. Nickerson and Mr. Randle could make and distribute this song so fast (and so cheaply) is that they took fragments from the recording of "Gold Digger" and looped them to form the background to their own rap. That was also part of the reason for the positive public reaction. Kanye West (and Ray Charles and Clara Ward) are very talented musicians. West's song was already all over the airwaves. The Legendary K.O. capitalized on that, just as Benjamin Franklin capitalized on the familiarity of the songs he reworded. But where Franklin could only take the tune, The Legendary K.O. could take the actual ones and zeros of the digital sound file.

As I mentioned earlier, there are two types of copyright protection over music. There is the copyright over the musical composition and, a much more recent phenomenon, the copyright over the actual recording. This song potentially infringes both of them.

Readers who came of age in the 1980s might remember the music of Public Enemy and N.W.A.—a dense wall of sound on which rap lyrics were overlaid. That wall of sound was in fact made up of samples, sometimes hundreds of tiny samples in a single track. Rap and hip-hop musicians proceeded under the assumption that taking a fragment of someone else's recording was as acceptable legally (and aesthetically) as a jazz musician quoting a fragment of another tune during a solo. In both cases, the use of "quotation" is a defining part of the genre, a harmless or even complimentary homage. Or so they thought.

In a 1991 case called *Grand Upright*, that idea was squashed.[19] The rap artist Biz Markie had extensively sampled Gilbert O'Sullivan's song "Alone Again (Naturally)" for his own song "Alone Again." The court could have applied the rules described earlier in this chapter, decided whether or not this was a large enough usage to make the second song substantially similar to the original, discussed whether or not it counted as a fair use, whether Markie's use was transformative or parodic, whether it was going to have a negative impact on the market for the original, weighed the issues, and ruled either way. In doing so, there would have been some nice points to discuss about whether or not the breadth of fair use depends in part on the practice in the relevant artistic community, how to understand parodic reference, or the relevant markets for the work. (Biz Markie's lawyers had asked for permission to use the sample, but the Supreme Court has made clear that seeking permission does not weigh against a defense of fair use.) There were also some tricky issues about the breadth of legal rights over recordings—the right was of relatively recent creation and had some interesting limitations. Underlying it all was a more fundamental question: how do we interpret the rules of copyright so as to encourage musical creativity? After all, as this chapter has shown, borrowing and reference are a fundamental part of musical practice. We ought to think twice before concluding they are illegal. Are we to criminalize jazz? Condemn Charles Ives? And if not, what is the carefully crafted line we draw that allows some of those uses but condemns this one?

Judge Duffy, however, was uninterested in any of these subtleties.

"Thou shalt not steal" has been an admonition followed since the dawn of civilization. Unfortunately, in the modern world of business this admonition is not always followed. Indeed, the defendants in this action for copyright infringement would have this court believe that stealing is rampant in the music business and, for that reason, their conduct here should be excused. The conduct of the defendants herein, however, violates not only the Seventh Commandment, but also the copyright laws of this country.[20]

If this were a law school exam, it would get a "D." (Maybe a C given grade inflation.) Duffy makes all of the errors Jefferson warned us against. Tangible property is the same as intellectual property. Songs are the same as sheep and the same rules can apply to both. Theft is theft. The prior injunctions of the framers and the courts notwithstanding, we do not need to think carefully about the precise boundaries of intellectual property rights or worry that interpreting them too broadly is as bad as making them too narrow. So far as Judge Duffy is concerned, the tablets on Mount Sinai were inscribed with an absolute injunction against digital sampling. (The font must have been small.) But to say all this is merely to scratch the surface of how regrettable a decision it is. In the narrowest and most formalistic legal terms it is also very poor.

Judge Duffy gives not a single citation to the provisions of the Copyright Act. He ignores issues of *de minimis* copying, substantial similarity, fair use, and the differences between the right over the recording and that over the composition. In fact, he quotes the Bible more, and more accurately, than he does Title 17 of the U.S. Code—the Copyright Act. The one mention he makes of actual copyright law is at the end of the opinion, when he refers the case for criminal prosecution! When I first read this case, I seriously wondered for a moment if it were a crude parody of a legal opinion written by someone who had never been to law school.

Is the result in this case wrong? Personally, I do not think so. It is possible, even probable, that a conscientious judge who bothered to read the law could go through a careful analysis and find that Markie's use went beyond *de minimis* copying, that it was neither creative, parodic, nor short enough to count as a fair use. The judge might have presumed a negative effect on the market for Mr. O'Sullivan's song and thus could have ruled that it was a copyright infringement. In doing so, the judge would have to give some guidance to future courts about digital sampling. The most likely guidance would be "the sample here is so extensive and so unchanged, that this case says little about the wider musical practice of sampling." Judge Duffy's opinion was poor not because of the result he reached, but because he reached it in an overly broad and judicially inappropriate way that became a guideline for future cultural creation. Worse still, the industry listened to him.

In excellent books on this issue, Kembrew McLeod and Siva Vaidhyanathan each argue that *Grand Upright* was a disaster for rap music.[21] The industry's practice turned full circle almost overnight. Now every sample, no matter how tiny, had to be "cleared"—licensed from the owners of the recording. As they tell the story, this "legal" change caused an aesthetic change. The number of samples in an average song dropped precipitously. The engaging complexity of the Public Enemy "wall of sound" gave way to the simplistic thumping beat and unimaginative synthesizer lines of modern rap. I must admit to sharing McLeod's and Vaidhyanathan's musical prejudices. The causal claim is harder to substantiate, but industry lawyers and musicians both agree that changes in the industry's understanding of the law had a major role in transforming the practice of sampling.

If we disregard the Jefferson Warning and assume the recording artist has absolute property rights over his work, then we could ignore the idea that forcing people to pay for stuff they take might have a negative effect on future art and culture. Theft is theft. I might be able to make art much more easily if I did not have to pay for the paint and canvas, but that is not commonly held to excuse shoplifting from art stores. But if we take the Jefferson Warning seriously, then intellectual property's job is to balance the need to provide incentives for production and distribution with the need to leave future creators free to build upon the past. Reasonable minds will differ on where this line is to be drawn, but the process of drawing it is very different from the process Judge Duffy had in mind.

For fifteen years, critics of the decision waited for an appeals court to fix the law in this area. When the case of *Bridgeport Music, Inc. v. Dimension Films* came up, they thought they had what they wanted. The band NWA had used a tiny fragment (less than two seconds) consisting of three notes of a guitar solo from the George Clinton song "Get Off Your Ass and Jam." The fragment was an arpeggiated chord, which simply means that you strike the notes of the chord individually and in sequence. It was, in fact, a pretty standard "deedly" sound, familiar from many guitar solos. NWA then heavily distorted this fragment and looped it so that it played in the background of one part of the song—so faintly that it is almost impossible to hear and completely impossible to recognize. (With the distortion it sounds like a very faint and distant police siren.) A company called Bridgeport Music owned the sound recording copyright over the Clinton song. They sued. NWA's response was predictable—this was classic *de minimis* copying, which the law did not touch. One did not even have to get to the issue of fair use (though this surely would be one).

The appeals court did not waste any time attempting to dignify Judge Duffy's decision in *Grand Upright*.

> Although Grand Upright applied a bright-line test in a sampling case, we have not cited it as precedent for several reasons. First, it is a district court opinion and as such has no binding precedential value. Second, although it appears to have involved claims for both sound recording and musical composition copyright infringement, the trial judge does not distinguish which he is talking about in his ruling, and appears to be addressing primarily the musical composition copyright. Third, and perhaps most important, there is no analysis set forth to indicate how the judge arrived at his ruling, which has resulted in the case being criticized by commentators.[22]

They did like one thing about the decision, however: its bright-line rule, "Thou Shalt Not Steal." (Lawyers use the term "bright-line rule" to refer to a rule that is very easy to apply to the facts. A 55 mph speed limit is a bright-line rule.) The *Bridgeport* court rejected the idea that sound recording copyrights and music composition copyrights should be analyzed in the same way. They wanted to set a clear rule defining how much of a sound recording one could use without permission. How much? Nothing. To be precise, the court suggests in a footnote that taking a single note *might* be acceptable since the copyright protection only covers a "series." Anything more, however, is clearly off limits.

Though they come to a conclusion that, if anything, is more stringent than Judge Duffy's, they do so very differently. In their words, "Get a license or do not sample." Effectively, the court concludes that the sound recording copyright is different enough from the composition copyright that a court could reasonably conclude that a different analysis is required. The judges are fully aware that copyright must balance encouraging current creators and leaving raw material to future creators—the Jefferson Warning holds no novelty for them. But they conclude that a clear "one-note rule" will do, because if the costs of licenses are too high, samplers can simply recreate the riff themselves, and this will tend to keep prices reasonable.

This is an interesting idea. Why does this not happen more often? Why do samplers not simply recreate James Brown's drumbeat from "Funky Drummer," or George Clinton's solo from "Get Off Your Ass and Jam"? Musicians offer lots of different answers. They do not understand the distinction the court is drawing, so the market never develops. The samples themselves cannot be replicated, because the music has all kinds of overtones from the historical equipment used and even the methods of recording. Fundamentally, though, the answer seems to be one of authenticity, ironically enough. The original beats have a totemic significance—like the great standard chord sequences in jazz. One cannot substitute replicas for James Brown's funkiness. It just would not be the same. As Walter Benjamin pointed out long ago in "The Work of Art in the Age of Mechanical Reproduction," cheap copying actually increases the demand for authenticity.[23] The court's economic analysis—which imagines a world of fungible beats produced for music as a consumer good—deals poorly with such motivations.

When the court first released its decision, it was greeted with concern even by recording industry representatives who might have been expected to favor it, because it appeared to do away with not only the *de minimis* limitation on copyright (some portions are just too small to count as "copying") but the fair use provisions as well. The court took the very unusual step of rehearing the case and amending the opinion, changing it in a number of places and adding a paragraph that stated that when the case went back to the district court, the judge there was free to consider the fair use defense. Of course, if one takes this seriously—and, for the constitutional reasons given in Chapter 5, I agree that the court has no power to write fair use out of the statute—it undermines the supposedly clear rule. If the factors of fair use are seriously applied, how can a three-note excerpt ever fail to be fair use? And if we always have to do a conventional fair use analysis, then the apparent clarity of the one-note rule is an illusion.

The *Bridgeport* decision is a bad one, I believe. Among other things, it fails to take seriously the constitutional limitations on copyright—including the originality requirement and the First Amendment. (A three-note sample is not original enough to be protected under copyright law, in my view. There are also more speech-related issues in sampling than the court seems to realize.) The competitive licensing market the court imagines seems more like economic fantasy than reality. I think the ruling sets unnecessary barriers on musical creation and ends up with a rule that is just as blurry as the one it criticizes. I think the court's reading of the statute and legislative history is wrong—though I have not bored you with the full details of that argument. But I want to be clear that it is a very different kind of bad decision from Judge Duffy's.

The court in *Bridgeport* does see copyright as a balance. It does understand the need for future creators to build on the past, but it also shows that a simple willingness to look upon intellectual property protections in a utilitarian way does not solve all problems. It certainly does not proceed from Jefferson's presumption that intellectual property protections should be interpreted narrowly. Though it claims to have a "literal" reading of the statute, the real driving force in the analysis is an unconsummated desire for bright-line rules and a belief that the market will solve these problems by itself. The court also suggests that "[i]f this is not what Congress intended or is not what they would intend now, it is easy enough for the record industry, as they have done in the past, to go back to Congress for a clarification or change in the law." Note the assumption that "the record industry" is the most reliable guide to Congress's intentions or that it is the only entity affected by such a rule. This is truly the image of copyright law as a contract among affected industries. Of course, digital artists such as The Legendary K.O. hardly fit within such a model.

Under the rule in *Bridgeport*—"Get a license or do not sample"—Mr. Randle and Mr. Nickerson appear to be breaking the law. They did not get a license and they most definitely did sample. What about fair use?

Under fair use, copyright allows a very specific (and possibly lengthy) use of another's material when the purpose is parody of that prior work itself. The Supreme Court gave parody a unique status in the *Acuff-Rose* case. The (extremely profane) rap group 2 Live Crew had asked for permission to produce a version of Roy Orbison's "Pretty Woman." But where Orbison sang about the pretty woman walking down the street whom he would like to meet, 2 Live Crew wrote about a "big hairy woman" ("with hair that ain't legit, 'cause you look like Cousin It"). They sang about a "bald headed" woman with a "teeny weeny afro." They sang about group sex with both women. Finally, they told a "two timin' woman," "now I know the baby ain't mine." Justice Souter showed the characteristic sangfroid of a Supreme Court justice faced with raunchy rap music.

> While we might not assign a high rank to the parodic element here, we think it fair to say that 2 Live Crew's song reasonably could be perceived as commenting on the original or criticizing it, to some degree. 2 Live Crew juxtaposes the romantic musings of a man whose fantasy comes true, with degrading taunts, a bawdy demand for sex, and a sigh of relief from paternal responsibility. The later words can be taken as a comment on the naiveté of the original of an earlier day, as a rejection of its sentiment that ignores the ugliness of street life and the debasement that it signifies. *It is this joinder of reference and ridicule that marks off the author's choice of parody from the other types of comment and criticism that traditionally have had a claim to fair use protection as transformative works.*[24] [emphasis added]

Truly, the law can confront and master all cultural forms. The heart of parody as the Supreme Court described it is that one is taking aim at the original. Because 2 Live Crew could be seen as directing their song at Orbison's original, rather than using Orbison's song to make some other political or social point, the court was willing to give it the favorable consideration that parody receives as a fair use.

Does "George Bush Doesn't Care About Black People" fit that model? The Legendary K.O. were not "taking aim" at "Gold Digger." True, they quoted West's actual words from the television broadcast (also copyrighted). They even used them as their title. But they were not taking aim at his song. (Ironically, Kanye West has a better claim that he was taking aim at Ray Charles's picture of womanhood, in just the way described in the 2 Live Crew case.) Rather, The Legendary K.O. were using the sample of the song as the backing to an entirely different rap that expressed, in familiar and popular musical form, a more expansive version of his condemnation of both press and president. That does not end the inquiry. Parody is not the only form of protected criticism or commentary. But it makes it much harder for them to succeed, particularly in light of the hostility toward sampling betrayed by both *Grand Upright* and *Bridgeport*.

The videos made by The Black Lantern and Franklin Lopez present an even more complex set of questions. On top of the music copyright issues, we also have fair use claims for the extensive news footage and footage of Mr. Foxx. The Black Lantern also used some fragments of a popular video by Jib-Jab, which had a cartoon Bush and Kerry singing dueling parodied versions of Woody Guthrie's "This Land." When JibJab's video first came out, the

Guthrie estate claimed copyright infringement over the song. Assisted by a number of public interest legal groups, JibJab claimed fair use. (It eventually came out that the copyright over the song was no longer valid.) What did Jib-Jab do when The Black Lantern sampled them in their turn? In a move that both wins the prize for hypocrisy and serves to sum up the intersection of law and culture I have been describing, they sent him a cease and desist letter. The video was taken down for a week and he was eventually forced to remove the segment of their video from his work. Fair use for me, but not for thee.

CONCLUSION

The Legendary K.O. samples Kanye West, who uses a fragment from Ray Charles, who may have taken material from Will Lamartine Thompson or, more likely, from Clara Ward (who herself borrowed from a gospel standard). The chain of borrowing I describe here has one end in the hymns and spirituals of the early 1900s and the other in the twenty-first century's chaotic stew of digital sampling, remix, and mashup. Along the way, we have the synthesis of old and the invention of new musical genres—often against the wishes of those whose work is serving as the raw material. One way of viewing this story is that each of these musicians (except for some imaginary original artist, the musical source of the Nile) is a plagiarist and a pirate. If they are licensing their material or getting it from the public domain, then they may not be lawbreakers but they are still unoriginal slavish imitators. If one's image of creativity is that of the romantic, iconoclastic creator who invents the world anew with each creation, those conclusions seem entirely appropriate. The borrowing here is rampant. Far from building everything anew, these musicians seem quite deliberately to base their work on fragments taken from others.

It is important to remember that copyright does not subscribe completely to the idea of romantic creation where music is concerned. As I pointed out earlier, musical genres develop out of other genres: soul from gospel and rhythm and blues; gospel from spirituals; rhythm and blues from jazz, jump music, and Delta blues; and so on. When it comes to genres, we can play the game of musicological "six degrees of separation" all day long. Copyright is supposed to leave "holes" in its coverage so that the genre is not covered, only the specific form of creativity within the genre. I mentioned before the need to keep the lines of genre and form open, to keep them free from private property rights in order to allow musicians to develop the form by using them as common property, the "highways" of musical progress. So, for example, the twelve-bar blues uses the first, fourth, and fifth chords in a scale. That sequence cannot be owned, unless blues is to become impossible or illegal. Bebop is characterized by copious use of the flattened fifth—a sound which was jarring to audiences when it was first introduced and which marked the break with the more accessible jazz of swing and the big bands. The flattened fifth is not owned. These characteristic genre-creating sequences or sounds are supposed to be left in the public domain, though increasingly some scholars—including me—are coming to believe that we have managed to make the copyright holder's control so complete and so granular as to close those common areas and impede the development of future musical forms. The *Bridgeport* court might extend its logic and imagine that the entire musical commons could be licensed, of course. The presence of other chord sequences would keep the price down! But up to now, we have not gone that far. In theory at least, copyright is not supposed to stop the next Ray Charles, the person who wants to fuse two older forms of music to create a third.

Yet the chain of borrowing that links The Legendary K.O., Kanye West, Ray Charles, and the Bailey Gospel Singers is of a different kind. This borrowing involves taking chunks of prior musicians' melodies, their words, their lyrical patterns. This is not just copying the genre. It is copying the lines of the song within the genre. This is the kind of stuff copyright is supposed to regulate even when it is working *well*. And yet, listening to the sequence, it is hard to deny that at each stage something artistic and innovative, something remarkable, has been created. In fact, the story of this song is the striking ability of each set of artists to impose their own sound, temperament, spirituality, humor, vision of women, or, in the case of The Legendary K.O., their intense and profane political anger, onto the musical phrases they have in common.

The postmodern conclusion here is "there is nothing new under the sun"—that all creation is re-creation, that there is no such thing as originality, merely endless imitation. If this is meant to be a comment about how things get created, at least in music, I think there is some truth to it. But if it is a claim about aesthetic worth, a denial that there are more and less creative individuals in the arts, I find it as facile and unconvincing as its romantic authorial opposite.

What is fascinating about the artists I describe here is that, while they do not fit neatly into either the aesthetic ideal of independent creation or the legal model for how creative expression gets made, they each have a remarkable, palpable creativity. Each leaves us with something new, even if formed partly from the fragments of the past. One could describe Ray Charles as the merest plagiarist—making "search and replace" songs by substituting a woman for the deity in already-established hits. But if that is our conclusion, it merely proves that our theories of aesthetics are poorer than the creativity they seek to describe. So much the worse for the theories.

As Jefferson pointed out, the lines surrounding intellectual property are hard to draw—something the *Bridgeport* court got right. When we draw them, whether legally or as a matter of aesthetic morality, we do so partly with standard instances in mind. "Well, *that* can't be wrong," we think to ourselves, and reason by analogy accordingly. Yet the process of analogy fails us sometimes, because the types of borrowing change over time.

Ray Charles was frank about the way he copied the style and licks of Nat King Cole like an apprentice learning from a lawyer. But he and his estate assiduously guarded his copyrights against more modern borrowing they found to be inappropriate. Judge Duffy thunderously denounces Biz Markie. It is harder to imagine him leveling the same condemnation at Dizzy Gillespie, Charles Ives, Oscar Peterson, or, for that matter, Beethoven, though all of them made copious use of the works of others in their own. It is bizarre to imagine a *Bridgeport*-like rule being extended to composition copyrights and applied to music such as jazz. "Get a license or do not solo"? I think not. Does it make any more sense for sampling?

If there is a single reason I told the story of these songs it is this: to most of us, certainly to me, the idea that copyright encourages creativity and discourages the reuse of material created by others seems reasonable. Of course, I would want to apply the correctives implied by the Jefferson Warning—to make sure the rights were as short and as narrow as possible. But at least when it comes to copying chunks of expression still covered by copyright, our intuitions are to encourage people to create "their own work," rather than to rely on remix. What does that mean in the world of music? As the story I have told here seems to illustrate, even musicians of unquestioned "originality," even those who can make a claim to having created a new musical genre, sometimes did so by a process rather more like collage than creation out of nothing, taking chunks of existing work that were proven to work well and setting them in a new context or frame.

Imagine Ray Charles trying to create "I Got a Woman" today. Both of his possible sources would be strongly and automatically protected by copyright. The industries in which those works were produced would be much more legalistic and infinitely more litigious. The owners of those copyrights could use them to stop him from "desecrating their work"—which is literally what he is doing. We know Clara Ward objected to Charles's other borrowings from gospel. I cannot imagine Will Lamartine Thompson or his worthy neighbors in East Liverpool looking kindly on the sweet "early morning loving" outside of wedlock described in "I Got a Woman," still less the use of sacred music to glorify it. And copyright gives them the power to say no. Remember Macaulay's description of how Richardson's novels might have been censored by a moralistic heir? Even if the objections were not vetoes, but simple demands for payment, would we get "I Got a Woman" and "This Little Girl of Mine"? Given the extent of the borrowing that jump-started this particular genre-bridging effort, would we be likely to see the birth of soul music?

Congress assures us that the many increases in copyright protection have been in the name of encouraging creativity. The music industry says the same thing when its pettifogging clearance procedures and permission culture are criticized. But do we really think we are more likely to get a twenty-first-century Ray Charles, or a fusion of styles to create a new genre, in the world we have made? Do we really think that the formalist ignorance of Judge Duffy or the market optimism of the *Bridgeport* court, in which thick markets offer fungible sets of samples to be traded like commodities, are good guides for the future of music? Are we in fact killing musical creativity with the rules that are supposed to defend it?

An Internet optimist would tell us that is precisely the point. True, because of the errors described in the chapter on the Jefferson Warning, and the mistakes catalogued in the chapters on the Internet Threat and the Farmers' Tale, we have dramatically expanded the scope, length, and power of the rights that are supposed to shape our creative culture. But technology cures all. Look at The Legendary K.O., The Black Lantern, or Franklin Lopez. They are all probably breaking the law as it is currently interpreted by the courts. But their work can be created for pennies and distributed to millions. The technology allows people to circumvent the law. Admittedly, some of the copyright holders will police their rights assiduously—think of JibJab's newfound dislike of fair use and their power to alter The Black Lantern's video. But others either cannot or will not. Kanye West's representatives in particular are unlikely to be stupid enough to sue The Legendary K.O. in the first place. Internet distribution becomes a demimonde in which the rules of the rest of the society either cannot or will not be enforced. Art gets its breathing room, not from legal exceptions, but from technological enforcement difficulties. Finally, as more and more people can create and distribute digital culture, they are less likely to understand, believe in, or accept rules that are strongly at variance with their aesthetic and moral assumptions.

There is a lot to these points. The technology *does* transform the conditions of creativity, and sometimes it runs right over the law in the process. Thousands, even millions, can be reached outside of conventional distribution channels with work that is technically illegal. And attitudes toward creative propriety do not track legal rules. When I wrote to Mr. Randle and Mr. Nickerson, I found that they realized Mr. West probably had a legal right to get their work taken down, but they felt he would not use it, and they had a very commonsensical conception of what they ought to be allowed to do. They were not making any money from this. They were making a political point, drawing attention to a political and human problem. That made it okay. They would have liked more formal permission so that they could actually distribute CDs through conventional for-profit channels, perhaps with some portion of the proceeds going to disaster relief, but they understood they were unlikely to get it.

Despite all this, I am uncomfortable with the argument "do not worry, technology will allow us to evade the rules where they are stupid." A system that can only function well through repeated lawbreaking is an unstable and dangerous one. It breeds a lack of respect for the law in those who should be its greatest supporters and beneficiaries. It blurs civil disobedience and plain old lawbreaking. Sitting in on the segregated lunch counter and being willing to face the consequences is very different from parking in the disabled space and hoping you can get away with it. It also blurs our judgment of conduct. Whatever one thinks of them, The Legendary K.O. are doing something very different than a college student who just does not want to pay for music and downloads thousands of tracks for free from file sharing networks.

The problem is not simply one of blurring. Technology-based "freedoms" are not reliable (though legal ones, too, may fail). In a pinch, the technology may not save you, as thousands of those same downloaders have found out when sued by the RIAA and forced to pay thousands of dollars for an activity they thought to be private and anonymous. The Internet "solution" also leaves certain types of artistic creation dependent on the vagaries of the current technology, which may well change, eliminating some of the zone of freedom we currently rely on. But more worrisome is the fact that this "solution" actually confines certain types of art to the world of the Internet.

The video of "George Bush Doesn't Care About Black People" could be seen by many, but only if they were wired to the right technological and social network. (After all, someone has to tell you to watch.) It was a searing intervention in the national debate on Katrina. But it appeared on no television station. Like most of the mashups created online, the fact that the rights could never be cleared keeps it off mass media. Copyright acts as the barbed wire around mass media outlets. That is a shame, I think. Not because *that* video is so good—you may love it or hate it. But because this *kind* of artwork has something important to contribute to our national culture. Imagine a world in which Ray Charles could create "I Got a Woman," but could only circulate it to a narrow group of the file-trading digerati because of a flagrant violation of Clara Ward's copyright. Do we still get soul? The blues? Jazz? Or do we just get a precious and insular digital subculture, whose cultural experiments never reach the mainstream?

Throughout his life, Charles described an intimate relationship with his audience, with the public. He described their tastes as a check, as a corrective; he thought they would actually be "ahead" of the artists. He wanted to make songs that would be listened to by tens of millions of people. And he wanted to make art and lots of money. I am all for the person who wants to create as an "amateur-professional" and distribute outside the chains of commerce. I have worked with organizations that make it easier to do this. But I also believe in the power and creativity of commercial culture and political speech carried on mass media. Ironically, our current copyright system serves it poorly.

What is the solution to all of this? The music business runs on compulsory licenses, a legally granted ability to use music in certain ways without permission, though with a fee. The system seems to function pretty well. One solution is to extend that system to the world of mashups and derivative works. If you merely copy the whole of my work and circulate it on file sharing networks or on CDs, we apply the current rules and penalties. If, on the other hand, you make a "derivative" work, mixing your work with mine, then there are two alternatives. If you stay in the world of nonprofit exchange, you get a heightened presumption in favor of fair use (perhaps administered through a quicker and cheaper system of arbitration). If you move into the for-profit world, then you must pay a flat licensing fee or percentage of profits to the copyright holder.

A second solution would be to curtail the hypertrophy of protectionism that made all this happen in the first place. The copyright term could be shortened or we could require renewal every twenty-eight years. (There are international treaties that currently forbid the latter alternative.) We could cut back on excesses like the *Bridgeport* decision, create incentives to make the music industry less legalistically insistent on policing the most atomic level of creation. We could exempt samples shorter than five seconds from copyright liability, clarify the boundaries of fair use, and extend it beyond parody to other genre-smashing forms such as satire and collage.

There are enormous obstacles to all these proposals. In particular, while artists fare very poorly under the current clearance culture—paying but not receiving the benefits of payments—the middlemen who profit from transaction costs are not keen on abolishing them. Certainly if, as the *Bridgeport* court assumed, the recording industry is the party responsible for fine-tuning copyright law, we are hardly likely to see any reforms that threaten current modes of doing business. Yet there is a ray of hope. It is getting harder and harder to pretend that the rules ostensibly designed to encourage creativity are actually working. At the same time, more and more people are creating and distributing cultural objects—becoming "subjects" of intellectual property law in the process, often to their dismay and irritation. It is in that conjunction—a far cry from the industry contract envisioned by the *Bridgeport* court—that hope for the future of copyright law's treatment of culture might lie.

7

The Enclosure of Science
and Technology:
Two Case Studies

Over the last forty years, much has changed in the way that scientific research and technological development are organized, funded, and institutionally arranged. Much has also changed in the type of scientific and technical material that is covered by intellectual property rights, the ways that material is covered, the parties who hold the rights, and the state of research and development at which rights claims are made. Many academics who study both science's organizational structure and the intellectual property claims that surround it are concerned about the results. To say this is not to conjure up a tragically lost world of pure research science, untainted by property claims or profit motives. That world never existed and it is probably a good thing too. Intellectual property rights, and the profit motive more generally, have a vital and beneficial role in moving innovations from lab bench to bedside, from computer simulation to actual flight. The question is not *whether* intellectual property rights are useful as part of scientific and technological development. The question is what type of rights they should be, where in the research process those rights are best deployed, how they should coexist with state funded basic scientific and technological research, how broad they should be, how they should deal with new technologies, how long they should last, how they should treat follow-on innovations.

I cannot hope here to answer all those questions, though some fascinating research has begun the process. Instead, as with the music chapter, I will offer a case study—actually two case studies—that try to illuminate the process I am describing, to illustrate its pitfalls and its strange and unintended consequences.

The two defining technologies of the last thirty years are biotechnology and the networked computer. Each is both product and platform. Innovations themselves, they are also constitutive technologies that enable still more innovations. But at several historical moments in the development of each we came perilously close to breaking technology with law.[1] Some would say that it was not just a close shave: we actually have hampered or limited the full potential of technology, slowing down its dynamism with a host of overbroad software patents, gene patents, and materials transfer agreements. Others are more optimistic. They think that a series of rapid improvisations by courts, scientists, programmers, and businesspeople has largely mitigated any problems caused by the process of legal expansion.[2] But if mistakes were made, it is important to know what they were lest we continue or repeat them. If there were "fixes," it is important to know if they can be replicated.

So were there mistakes? If so, have they been fixed, and how? Drawing on an article I co-wrote with my brilliant colleague Arti Rai,[3] this chapter suggests some answers to those questions by sketching out some details of the legal history of those technologies, concluding with a discussion of a single promising new technology that shares aspects of both—synthetic biology. The answers are important. Behind the abstract words "innovation" or "technological development" there are lives saved or lost, communicative freedoms expanded or contracted, communities enabled or stunted, wealth generated or not. The subject would benefit from informed, sophisticated, democratic attention. It is not something you want to leave a host of lawyers and lobbyists to decide among themselves.

A MACHINE THAT CONTAINS ALL OTHER MACHINES

Imagine a person staring at an infinite roll of paper tape. On the paper are symbols in some alphabet or number system. The reader carries out simple, operable instructions on the basis of that data. "Add together the next two digits you are presented with and write down the answer. If the answer is odd, go to step 2. If the answer is even, go to step 3." Now replace the person with a mechanical head that can "read" the instructions, carry out the desired operations, and write the answer down. The British mathematician Alan Turing imagined something like this—a little more complicated, perhaps, but fairly similar. What is it? We have the reading head, the set of instructions, the data on which the instructions are to be performed, the record of the result, and some kind of "state table" that tells the machine where it is in the process. These are the component parts of Turing machines—or as we know them better, computers. More accurately, Turing machines are a method of simulating the operation of computers, a metaphor that enables us to imitate their logical processes. In the words of Wikipedia, "despite their simplicity—[they] can be adapted to simulate the logic of any computer that could possibly be constructed." And to give lawyers fits. But that is getting ahead of ourselves.

In Greek mythology, Procrustes had a bed to which he fitted its prospective occupants, whether they liked it or not. The tall were trimmed down. The short stretched on the rack. Intellectual property lawyers have many similarities to Procrustes. The technologies that are brought before them are made to fit the conceptual boxes the law provides, boxes with names such as "copyright" and "patent." Occasionally, new conceptual boxes are made, but—for very good reasons—most of the time we stick with the boxes we have. As with Procrustes, things do not always fit and the process can be distressing for its subjects.

It is important to realize that the process of trimming and stretching can be done well or badly. If it is done really badly, the technology is stunted, deformed, even destroyed. If it is done well, the law aids the development of the technology in exactly the happy way described in Chapter 1. What did our Procrustean legal system do with computers and computer science?

I will focus on software—the set of instructions the machine is to perform. How should we think of it? Software is written down by programmers. It is recorded first in a form readable to humans, or at least geeks. Then, through a series of transformations, it is turned into the machine code, the ones and zeros that will operate the computer. But at its root it can be understood through the metaphor of the simple list of instructions to be carried out in order, just as with the Turing machine and its infinite tape.

How should we fit software into the categories of intellectual property? We have "writing," fixation in some medium of symbols that can be read by others—both machine and human. Writing is normally the domain of copyright. Are computer programs copyrightable? All kinds of problems present themselves. At least in the United States, copyright covers expression. As I pointed out in a previous book, at its base is the conception of the romantic author impressing her uniqueness of spirit on the work at the moment of writing. It is that expressive choice, not the facts or ideas on which the work is based, that copyright covers. And it is *only* original expression that copyright covers. It does not cover purely functional objects, systems, processes, or methods of operation. One cannot copyright the coat hanger, the mousetrap, or long division. One cannot even copyright a "sculpture" if the main function of its design is to serve as a bicycle rack. Admittedly, one can copyright some expressive works that serve a practical purpose. A book about how to do double-entry bookkeeping is copyrightable. Yet copyright covers only the expressive choices used in selecting the words to explain the method, and the images to represent it, not the methods it describes or the facts or ideas it contains. Can copyright cover computer programs? Should we see them as copyrightable how-to books or as uncopyrightable machines made of words?

Machines and other functional innovations are normally the domain of patent rights. One can patent the mousetrap, and then one gets an exclusive right to the actual mechanically enabled method of catching mice, not just the artistic flourishes on the blueprint. Patents have more demanding criteria than copyrights. The invention needs to be novel and have utility, or usefulness; I cannot get a patent over something that would have been an obvious idea to an insider in the relevant field of technology, a "person having ordinary skill in the art," or PHOSITA, in the jargon of patent lawyers. But once I get my patent, it gives me a very strong power to exclude others from the invention—even if they came up with it independently. The right lasts for twenty years. Follow-on innovators who improve on my idea can get a patent on that improvement. They can block me from using the improvement. I can block them from using the original invention. Thus we have an incentive to negotiate if either of us wants to bring the improved innovation to market.

So where did software fit? Was it copyrightable writing or patentable invention? There are two issues here. The first is whether there should be any intellectual property rights over software at all. The basic case for that proposition is simple, a classic example of the public goods problem described in the first chapter. Software costs money to create, but is cheap to copy. When a youthful

Bill Gates wrote his 1976 letter to the wonderfully named *Dr. Dobb's Journal of Computer Calisthenics & Orthodontia*, he put the point clearly.

> Who can afford to do professional work for nothing? What hobbyist can put 3-man years into programming, finding all the bugs, documenting his product and distribute it for free? The fact is, no one besides us has invested a lot of money into hobby software. We have written 6800 BASIC, and are writing 8080 APL and 6800 APL, but there is very little incentive to make this software available to hobbyists. Most directly, the thing you do is theft.[4]

He signed the letter "Bill Gates, General Partner, Micro-Soft." The hyphen would disappear in time. The philosophy stuck around.

Though there are quibbles about the facts in Gates's letter—critics claim he himself did a lot of free riding on public domain code and government-funded computer time—his basic point is that software needs to be protected by (enforceable) property rights if we expect it to be effectively and sustainably produced. Some software developers disagree. But assuming one concedes the point for the sake of argument, there is a second question: should software be covered by copyright or patent, or some unidentified third option?

In practice, software ended up being covered by both schemes, partly because of actions by Congress, which included several references to software in the Copyright Act, and partly as a result of decisions by the Copyright Office, the Patent and Trademark Office, and judges. One could copyright one's code and also gain a patent over the "nonobvious," novel, and useful innovations inside the software.

At first, it was the use of copyright that stirred the most concern. As I explained in the last chapter, copyright seems to be built around an assumption of diverging innovation—the fountain or explosion of expressive activity. Different people in different situations who sit down to write a sonnet or a love story, it is presumed, will produce very different creations rather than being drawn to a single result. Thus strong rights over the resulting work are not supposed to inhibit future progress. I can find my own muse, my own path to immortality. Creative expression is presumed to be largely independent of the work of prior authors. Raw material is not needed. "Copyright is about sustaining the conditions of creativity that enable an individual to craft out of thin air an *Appalachian Spring*, a *Sun Also Rises*, a *Citizen Kane*."[5]

There are lots of reasons to doubt that this vision of "creation out of nothing" works very well even in the arts, the traditional domain of copyright law. The story of Ray Charles's "I Got a Woman" bears ample witness to those doubts. But whatever its merits or defects in the realm of the arts, the vision seems completely wrongheaded when it comes to software. Software solutions to practical problems do converge, and programmers definitely draw upon prior lines of code. Worse still, as I pointed out earlier, software tends to exhibit "network effects." Unlike my choice of novel, my choice of word processing program is very strongly influenced, perhaps dominated, by the question of what program other people have chosen to buy. That means that even if a programmer could find a completely different way to write a word processing program, he has to be able to make it read the dominant program's files, and mimic its features, if he is to attract any customers at all. That hardly sounds like completely divergent creation.

Seeing that software failed to fit the Procrustean bed of copyright, many scholars presumed the process of forcing it into place would be catastrophic. They believed that, lacking patent's high standards, copyright's monopolies would proliferate widely. Copyright's treatment of follow-on or "derivative" works would impede innovation, it was thought. The force of network effects would allow the copyright holder of whatever software became "the standard" to extract huge monopoly rents and prevent competing innovation for many years longer than the patent term. Users of programs would be locked in, unable to shift their documents, data, or acquired skills to a competing program. Doom and gloom abounded among copyright scholars, including many who shared Mr. Gates's basic premise—that software should be covered by property rights. They simply believed that these were the wrong property rights to use.

Copyright did indeed cause problems for software developers, though it is hard to judge whether those problems outweighed the economic benefits of encouraging software innovation, production, and distribution. But the negative effects of copyright were minimized by a remarkably prescient set of actions by courts and, to a much lesser extent, Congress, so that the worst scenarios did not come to pass. Courts interpreted the copyright over software very narrowly, so that it covered little beyond literal infringement. (Remember Jefferson's point about the importance of being careful about the scope of a right.) They developed a complicated test to work out whether one program infringed the details of another. The details give law students headaches every year, but the effects were simple. If your software was similar to mine merely because it was performing the same function, or because I had picked the most efficient way to perform some task, or even because there was market demand for doing it that way, then none of those similarities counted for the purposes of infringement. Nor did material that was taken from the public domain. The result was that while someone who made literal copies of Windows Vista was clearly infringing copyright, the person who made a competing program generally would not be.

In addition, courts interpreted the fair use doctrine to cover "decompilation"—which is basically taking apart someone else's program so that you can understand it and compete with it. As part of the process, the decompiler had to make a copy of the program. If the law were read literally, decompilation would hardly seem to be a fair use. The decompiler makes a whole copy, for a commercial purpose, of a copyrighted work, precisely in order to cause harm to its market by offering a substitute good. But the courts took a broader view. The copy was a necessary part of the process of producing a competing product, rather than a piratical attempt to sell a copy of the same product. This limitation on copyright provided by fair use was needed in order to foster the innovation that copyright is supposed to encourage. This is a nice variation of the Sony Axiom from Chapter 4.

These rulings and others like them meant that software was protected by copyright, as Mr. Gates wanted, but that the copyright did not give its owner the right to prevent functional imitation and competition. Is that enough? Clearly the network effects are real. Most of us use Windows and most of us use Microsoft Word, and one very big reason is because everyone else does. Optimists believe the lure of capturing this huge market will keep potential competitors hungry and monopolists scared. The lumbering dominant players will not become complacent about innovation or try to grab every morsel of monopoly rent, goes the argument. They still have to fear their raptor-like competitors lurking in the shadows. Perhaps. Or perhaps it also takes the consistent threat of antitrust enforcement. In any event, whether or not we hit the optimal point in protecting software with intellectual property rights, those rights certainly did not destroy the industry. It appeared that, even with convergent creativity and network effects, software could be crammed into the Procrustean bed of copyright without killing it off in the process. Indeed, to some, it seemed to fare very well. They would claim that the easy legal protection provided by copyright gave a nascent industry just enough protection to encourage the investment of time, talent, and dollars, while not prohibiting the next generation of companies from building on the innovations of the past.

In addition, the interaction between copyright and software has produced some surprising results. There is a strong argument that it is the fact that software is copyrightable that has enabled the "commons-based creativity" of free and open source software. What does commons-based creativity mean? Basically, it is creativity that builds on an open resource available to all. An additional component of some definitions is that the results of the creativity must be fed back into the commons for all to use. Think of English. You can use English without license or fee, and you can innovate by producing new words, slang, or phrases without clearance from some Academie Anglaise. After you coin your term, it is in turn available to me to build upon or to use in my own sentences, novels, or jokes. And so the cycle continues. As the last chapter showed, for the entire history of musical creativity until the last forty years or so, the same had been true of at least a low level of musical borrowing. At the basic level of musical phrases, themes, snatches of melody, even chord structures, music was commons-based creativity. Property rights did not reach down into the atomic structure of music. They stayed at a higher level— prohibiting reproduction of complete works or copying of substantial and important chunks. So in some areas of both music and language, we had commons-based creativity because there were no property rights over the relevant level. The software commons is different.

The creators of free and open source software were able to use the fact that software is copyrighted, and that the right attaches automatically upon creation and fixation, to set up new, distributed methods of innovation. For example, free and open source software under the General Public License— such as Linux—is a "commons" to which all are granted access. Anyone may use the software without any restrictions. They are guaranteed access to the human-readable "source code," rather than just the inscrutable "machine code," so that they can understand, tinker, and modify. Modifications can be distributed so long as the new creation is licensed under the open terms of the original. This creates a virtuous cycle: each addition builds on the commons and is returned to it. The copyright over the software was the "hook" that allowed software engineers to create a license that gave free access and the right to modify and required future programmers to keep offering those freedoms. Without the copyright, those features of the license would not have been enforceable. For example, someone could have modified the open program and released it without the source code—denying future users the right to understand and modify easily. To use an analogy beloved of free software enthusiasts, the hood of the car would be welded shut. Home repair, tinkering, customization, and redesign become practically impossible.

Of course, if there were no copyright over software at all, software engineers would have other freedoms—even if not legally guaranteed open access to source code. Still, it was hard to deny that the extension of the property regime had—bizarrely, at first sight—actually enabled the creation of a continuing open commons. The tempting real estate analogy would be environmentalists using strong property rights over land to guarantee conservation and open access to a green space, where, without property rights, the space could be despoiled by all. But as I have pointed out earlier, while such analogies may help us, the differences between land and intellectual property demand that they be scrutinized very carefully. It is hard to overgraze an idea.

So much for copyright. What about patents? U.S. patent law had drawn a firm line between patentable invention and unpatentable idea, formula, or algorithm. The mousetrap could be patented, but not the formula used to calculate the speed at which it would snap shut. Ideas, algorithms, and formulae were in the public domain—as were "business methods." Or so we thought.

The line between idea or algorithm on the one hand and patentable machine on the other looks nice and easy. But put that algorithm—that series of steps capable of being specified in the way described by the Turing machine—onto a computer, and things begin to look more complex. Say, for example, that algorithm was the process for converting miles into kilometers and vice versa. "Take the first number. If it is followed by the word miles, then multiply by 8/5. If it is followed by the word kilometers, multiply by 5/8 . . ." and so on. In the abstract, this is classic public domain stuff—no more patentable than $E = mc^2$ or $F = ma$. What about when those steps are put onto the tape of the Turing machine, onto a program running on the hard drive of a computer?

The Court of Appeals for the Federal Circuit (the United States's leading patent court) seems to believe that computers can turn unpatentable ideas into patentable machines. In fact, in this conception, the computer sitting on your desk becomes multiple patentable machines—a word processing machine, an e-mail machine, a machine running the program to calculate the tensile strength of steel. I want to stress that the other bars to patentability remain. My example of mile-to-kilometer conversion would be patentable subject matter but, we hope, no patent would be granted because the algorithm is not novel and is obvious. (Sadly, the Patent and Trademark Office seems determined to undermine this hope by granting patents on the most mundane and obvious applications.) But the concern here is not limited to the idea that without a subject matter bar, too many obvious patents will be granted by an overworked and badly incentivized patent office. It is that the patent was supposed to be granted at the very end of a process of investigation and scientific and engineering innovation. The formulae, algorithms, and scientific discoveries on which the patented invention was based remained in the public domain for all to use. It was only when we got to the very end of the process, with a concrete innovation ready to go to market, that the patent was to be given. Yet the ability to couple the abstract algorithm with the concept of a Turing machine undermines this conception. Suddenly the patents are available at the very beginning of the process, even to people who are merely specifying—in the abstract—the *idea* of a computer running a particular series of algorithmic activities.

The words "by means of a computer" are—in the eyes of the Federal Circuit—an incantation of magical power, able to transubstantiate the ideas and formulae of the public domain into private property. And, like the breaking of a minor taboo that presages a Victorian literary character's slide into debauchery, once that first wall protecting the public domain was breached, the court found it easier and easier to breach still others. If one could turn an algorithm into a patentable machine simply by adding "by means of a computer," then one could turn a business method into something patentable by specifying the organizational or information technology structure through which the business method is to be implemented.

If you still remember the first chapters of this book, you might wonder why we would want to patent business methods. Intellectual property rights are supposed to be handed out only when necessary to produce incentives to supply some public good, incentives that otherwise would be lacking. Yet there are already plenty of incentives to come up with new business methods. (Greed and fear are the most obvious.) There is no evidence to suggest that we need a state-backed monopoly to encourage the development of new business methods. In fact, we *want* people to copy the businesses of others, lowering prices as a result. The process of copying business methods is called "competition" and it is the basis of a free-market economy. Yet patent law would prohibit it for twenty years. So why introduce patents? Brushing aside such minor objections with ease, the Court of Appeals for the Federal Circuit declared business methods to be patentable. Was this what Jefferson had in mind when he said "I know well the difficulty of drawing a line between the things which are worth to the public the embarrassment of an exclusive patent, and those which are not"? I doubt it.

It is commonplace for courts to look at the purpose of the law they are enforcing when seeking to understand what it means. In areas of regulation which are obviously instrumental—aimed at producing some particular result in the world—that approach is ubiquitous. In applying the antitrust laws, for example, courts have given meaning to the relatively vague words of the law by turning to economic analysis of the likely effects of different rules on different market structures.

Patent law is as instrumental a structure as one could imagine. In the United States, for example, the constitutional authorization to Congress to pass patent and copyright legislation is very explicit that these rights are to be made with a purpose in view. Congress has the power "to promote the progress of science and useful arts, by securing for limited times to authors and inventors the exclusive right to their respective writings and discoveries." One might imagine that courts would try to interpret the patent and copyright laws with that purpose, and the Jefferson Warning about its constraints, firmly in mind. Yet utilitarian caution about extending monopolies is seldom to be found in the reasoning of our chief patent court.

The difference is striking. Jefferson said that the job of those who administered the patent system was to see if a patent was "worth the embarrassment to the public" before granting it. The Constitution tells Congress to make only those patent laws that "promote the progress of science and useful arts." One might imagine that this constitutional goal would guide courts in construing those same laws. Yet neither Jeffersonian ideals nor the constitutional text seem relevant to our chief patent court when interpreting statutory subject matter. Anything under the sun made by man is patentable subject matter, and there's an end to it. The case that announced the rule on business methods involved a patent on the process of keeping accounts in a "hub-and-spoke" mutual fund—which included multiplying all of the stock holdings of each fund in a family of funds by the respective current share price to get total fund value and then dividing by the number of mutual fund shares that each customer actually holds to find the balance in their accounts. As my son observed, "I couldn't do that until nearly the end of third grade!"[6]

In theory of course, if the patent is not novel or is obvious, it will still be refused. The Supreme Court recently held that the Court of Appeals for the Federal Circuit has made "nonobvious" too easy a standard to meet.[7] It is unclear, however, whether that judgment will produce concrete effects on actual practices of patent grants and litigation. The Patent and Trademark Office puts pressure on examiners to issue patents, and it is very expensive to challenge those that are granted. Better, where possible, to rule out certain subject matter in the first place. Tempted in part by its flirtation with the "idea made machine" in the context of a computer, the Court of Appeals for the Federal Circuit could not bring itself to do so. Where copyright law evolved to wall off and minimize the dangers of extending protection over software, patent law actually extended the idea behind software patents to make patentable any thought process that might produce a useful result. Once breached, the walls protecting the public domain in patent law show a disturbing tendency to erode at an increasing rate.

To sum up, the conceptual possibilities presented to copyright and patent law by the idea of a Turing machine were fascinating. Should we extend copyright or patent to cover the new technology? The answer was "we will extend both!" Yet the results of the extension were complex and unexpected in ways that we will have to understand if we want to go beyond the simple but important injunctions of Jefferson and Macaulay. Who would have predicted that software copyrights could be used to create a self-perpetuating commons as well as a monopoly over operating systems, or that judges would talk knowingly of network effects in curtailing the scope of coverage? Who would have predicted that patents would be extended not only to basic algorithms implemented by a computer, but to methods of business themselves (truly a strange return to legalized business monopolies for a country whose founders viewed them as one of the greatest evils that could be borne)?

SYNTHETIC BIOLOGY

If you are a reader of *Science, PLoS Biology,* or *Nature,* you will have noticed some attractive and bizarre photographs recently. A field of bacteria that form themselves into bull's-eyes and polka dots. A dim photograph of a woman's face "taken" by bacteria that have been programmed to be sensitive to light. You may also have read about more inspiring, if less photogenic, accomplishments—for example, the group of scientists who managed to program bacteria to produce artemesinin, a scarce natural remedy for malaria derived from wormwood. Poking deeper into these stories, you would have found the phrase "synthetic biology" repeated again and again, though a precise definition would have eluded you.

What is "synthetic biology"? For some it is simply that the product or process involves biological materials not found in nature. Good old-fashioned biotechnology would qualify. One of the first biotechnology patent cases, *Diamond v. Chakrabarty,* involved some bacteria which Dr. Chakrabarty had engineered to eat oil slicks—not their natural foodstuff.[8] The Supreme Court noted that the bacteria were not found in nature and found them to be patentable, though alive. According to the simplest definition, Dr. Chakrabarty's process would count as synthetic biology, though this example antedates the common use of the term by two decades. For other scientists, it is the *completely* synthetic quality of the biology involved that marks the edge of the discipline. The DNA we are familiar with, for example, has four "base pairs"— A, C, G, and T. Scientists have developed genetic alphabets that involve twelve base pairs. Not only is the result not found in nature, but the very language in which it is expressed is entirely new and artificial.

I want to focus on a third conception of synthetic biology: the idea of turning biotechnology from an artisanal process of one-off creations, developed with customized techniques, to a true engineering discipline, using processes and parts that are as standardized and as well understood as valves, screws, capacitors, or resistors. The electrical engineer told to build a circuit does not go out and invent her own switches or capacitors. She can build a circuit using off-the-shelf components whose performance is expressed using standard measurements. This is the dream of one group of synthetic biologists: that biological engineering truly become *engineering*, with biological black boxes that perform all of the standard functions of electrical or mechanical engineering—measuring flow, reacting to a high signal by giving out a low signal, or vice versa, starting or terminating a sequence, connecting the energy of one process to another, and so on.

Of course an engineer understands the principle behind a ratchet, or a valve, but he does not have to go through the process of thinking "as part of this design, I will have to create a thing that lets stuff flow through one way and not the other." The valve is the mechanical unit that stands for that thought, a concept reified in standardized material form which does not need to be taken apart and parsed each time it is used. By contrast, the synthetic biologists claim, much of current biotechnological experimentation operates the way a seventeenth-century artisan did. Think of the gunsmith making beautiful one-off classics for his aristocratic patrons, without standardized calibers, parts, or even standard-gauge springs or screws. The process produces the gun, but it does not use, or produce, standard parts that can also be used by the next gunsmith.

Is this portrayal of biology correct? Does it involve some hyping of the new hot field, some denigration of the older techniques? I would be shocked, shocked, to find there was hype involved in the scientific or academic enterprise. But whatever the degree to which the novelty of this process is being subtly inflated, it is hard to avoid being impressed by the projects that this group of synthetic biologists has undertaken. The MIT Registry of Standard Biological Parts, for example, has exactly the goal I have just described.

> The development of well-specified, standard, and interchangeable biological parts is a critical step towards the design and construction of integrated biological systems. The MIT Registry of Standard Biological Parts supports this goal by recording and indexing biological parts that are currently being built and offering synthesis and assembly services to construct new parts, devices, and systems. . . . In the summer of 2004, the Registry contained about 100 basic parts such as operators, protein coding regions, and transcriptional terminators, and devices such as logic gates built from these basic parts. Today the number of parts has increased to about 700 available parts and 2000 defined parts. The Registry believes in the idea that a standard biological part should be well specified and able to be paired with other parts into subassemblies and whole systems. Once the parameters of these parts are determined and standardized, simulation and design of genetic systems will become easier and more reliable. The parts in the Registry are not simply segments of DNA, they are functional units.[9]

Using the Registry, a group of MIT scientists organizes an annual contest called iGEM, the International Genetically Engineered Machine competition. Students can draw from the standard parts that the Registry contains, and perhaps contribute their own creations back to it. What kinds of "genetically engineered machines" do they build?

> A team of eight undergraduates from the University of Ljubljana in Slovenia— cheering and leaping onto MIT's Kresge Auditorium stage in green team T-shirts— won the grand prize earlier this month at the International Genetically Engineered Machine (iGEM) competition at MIT. The group—which received an engraved award in the shape of a large aluminum Lego piece—explored a way to use engineered cells to intercept the body's excessive response to infection, which can lead to a fatal condition called sepsis. The goal of the 380 students on 35 university teams from around the world was to build biological systems the way a contractor would build a house—with a toolkit of standard parts. iGEM participants spent the summer immersed in the growing field of synthetic biology, creating simple systems from interchangeable parts that operate in living cells. Biology, once thought too complicated to be engineered like a clock, computer or microwave oven, has proven to be open to manipulation at the genetic level. The new creations are engineered from snippets of DNA, the molecules that run living cells.[10]

Other iGEM entries have included *E. coli* bacteria that had been engineered to smell like wintergreen while they were growing and dividing and like bananas when they were finished, a biologically engineered detector that would change color when exposed to unhealthy levels of arsenic in drinking water, a method of programming mouse stem cells to "differentiate" into more specialized cells on command, and the mat of picture-taking bacteria I mentioned earlier.

No matter how laudable the arsenic detector or the experimental technique dealing with sepsis, or how cool the idea of banana-scented, picture-taking bacteria, this kind of enterprise will cause some of you to shudder. Professor Drew Endy, one of the pioneers in this field, believes that part of that reaction stems from simple novelty. "A lot of people who were scaring folks in 1975 now have Nobel prizes."[11] But even if inchoate, the concerns that synthetic biology arouses stem from more than novelty. There is a deep-seated fear that if we see the natural world of biology as merely another system that we can routinely engineer, we will have extended our technocratic methods into a realm that was only intermittently subject to them in a way that threatens both our structure of self-understanding and our ecosystem.

To this, the synthetic biologists respond that we are *already* engineering nature. In their view, planned, structured, and rationalized genetic engineering poses fewer dangers than poorly understood interventions to produce some specific result in comparative ignorance of the processes we are employing to do so. If the "code" is transparent, subject to review by a peer community, and based on known parts and structures, each identified by a standard genetic "barcode," then the chance of detecting problems and solving them is higher. And while the dangers are real and not to be minimized, the potential benefits—the lives saved because the scarce antimalarial drug can now be manufactured by energetic *E. coli* or because a cheap test can demonstrate arsenic contamination in a village well—are not to be minimized either.

I first became aware of synthetic biology when a number of the scientists working on the Registry of Standard Biological Parts contacted me and my colleague Arti Rai. They did not use these exact words, but their question boiled down to "how does synthetic biology fare in intellectual property's categories, and how can we keep the basics of the science open for all to use?" As you can tell from this book, I find intellectual property fascinating—lamentably so perhaps. Nevertheless, I was depressed by the idea that scientists would have to spend their valuable time trying to work out how to save their discipline from being messed up by the law. Surely it would be better to have them doing, well, science?

They have cause for concern. As I mentioned at the beginning of this chapter, synthetic biology shares characteristics of both software and biotechnology.

Remember the focus on reducing functions to black boxes. Synthetic biologists are looking for the biological equivalents of switches, valves, and inverters. The more abstractly these are described, the more they come to resemble simple algebraic expressions, replete with "if, then" statements and instructions that resolve to "if x, then y, if not x, then z."

If this sounds reminiscent of the discussion of the Turing machine, it should. When the broad rules for software and business methods were enunciated by the federal courts, software was already a developed industry. Even though the rules would have allowed the equivalent of patenting the alphabet, the very maturity of the field minimized the disruption such patents could cause. Of course "prior art" was not always written down. Even when it was recorded, it was sometimes badly handled by the examiners and the courts, partly because they set a very undemanding standard for "ordinary expertise" in the art. Nevertheless, there was still a lot of prior experience and it rendered some of the more basic claims incredible. That is not true in the synthetic biology field.

Consider a recent article in *Nature*, "A universal RNAi-based logic evaluator that operates in mammalian cells."[12] The scientists describe their task in terms that should be familiar. "A molecular automaton is an engineered molecular system coupled to a (bio)molecular environment by 'flow of incoming messages and the actions of outgoing messages,' where the incoming messages are processed by an 'intermediate set of elements,' that is, a computer." The article goes on to describe some of the key elements of so-called "Boolean algebra"— "or," "and," "not," and so on—implemented in living mammalian cells.

These inscriptions of Boolean algebra in cells and DNA sequences can be patented. The U.S. Department of Health and Human Services, for example, owns patent number 6,774,222:

> This invention relates to novel molecular constructs that act as various logic elements, i.e., gates and flip-flops. . . . The basic functional unit of the construct comprises a nucleic acid having at least two protein binding sites that cannot be simultaneously occupied by their cognate binding protein. This basic unit can be assembled in any number of formats providing molecular constructs that act like traditional digital logic elements (flips-flops, gates, inverters, etc.).

My colleagues Arti Rai and Sapna Kumar have performed a patent search and found many more patents of similar breadth.[13]

What is the concern? After all, this is cutting-edge science. These seem like novel, nonobvious inventions with considerable utility. The concern is that the change in the rules over patentable subject matter, coupled with the Patent and Trademark Office's handling of both software and biotechnology, will come together so that the patent is not over some particular biological circuit, but, rather, over Boolean algebra itself as implemented by any biotechnological means. It would be as if, right at the beginning of the computer age, we had issued patents over formal logic in software—not over a particular computer design, but over the idea of a computer or a binary circuit itself.

"By means of a computer" was the magic phrase that caused the walls around the public domain of algorithms and ideas to crumble. Will "by means of a biological circuit" do the same? And—to repeat the key point—unlike computer science, biotechnology is developing after the hypertrophy of our intellectual property system. We do not have the immune system provided by the established practices and norms, the "prior art," even the community expectations that protected software from the worst effects of patents over the building blocks of science.

Following the example of software, the founders of the MIT Registry of Standard Biological Parts had the idea of protecting their discipline from overly expansive intellectual property claims by turning those rights against themselves. Free and open source software developers have created a "commons" using the copyright over the code to impose a license on their software, one that requires subsequent developers to keep the source open and to give improvements back to the software commons—a virtuous cycle. Could the Registry of Standard Biological Parts do the same thing? The software commons rests on a license. But, as I pointed out in the last section, the license depends on an underlying property right. It is because I have automatic copyright over my code that I can tell you "use it according to these terms or you will be violating my copyright." Is there a copyright over the products of synthetic biology? To create one we would have to take the extension of copyright that was required to reach software and stretch it even further. Bill Gates might argue for intellectual property rights over software using the logic of his article in *Dr. Dobb's Journal.* Will the argument for copyrights over synthetic biological coding be "I need the property right so I can create a commons"?

In practice, I think the answer is, and should be, no. Of course, one could think of this as just another type of coding, making expressive choices in a code of A's, C's, G's, and T's, just as a programmer does in Java or C++. Yet, software was already a stretch for copyright law. Synthetic biology strikes me as a subject matter that the courts, Congress, and the Copyright Office are unlikely to want to cram into copyright's already distorted outlines—

particularly given the obvious availability of patent rights. As a matter of conceptual intuition, I think they will see biological subject matter as harder to fit into the categories of original expressive writing. On one level, yes, it is all information, but, on another level, the idea of programming with gene sequences will probably raise hackles that the idea of coding inside a programming language never would. As a normative matter, I think it would be a poor choice to apply copyright to the products of synthetic biology. Attempting to produce a particular open commons, one might enable the kind of hundred-year monopolies over functional objects that the critics of software copyright initially feared.

If one wishes to keep the basic ideas and techniques of synthetic biology open for subsequent innovators, there are alternatives to the idea of a synthetic biology open source license. The Registry of Standard Biological Parts or the BioBricks Foundation can simply put all their work into the public domain immediately. (This, indeed, is what they are currently doing.) Such a scheme lacks one key feature of open source software: the right to force subsequent innovators to release their code back into the commons. Yet it would make subsequent patents on the material impossible, because it had already been published.

Regardless of the decisions made about the future of synthetic biology, I think its story—coupled to that of software and biotechnology more generally—presents us with an important lesson. I started the chapter with the metaphor of Procrustes's bed. But in the case of software and biotechnology, both the bed—the categories of copyright and patent—and its inhabitants—the new technologies—were stretched. Cracks formed in the boundaries that were supposed to prevent copyright from being applied to functional articles, to prevent patents extending to cover ideas, algorithms, and business methods.

Until this point, though the science would have been strange to Jefferson or his contemporaries, the underlying issue would have been familiar. The free-trade, Scottish Enlightenment thinkers of the eighteenth and nineteenth centuries would have scoffed at the idea that business methods or algorithms could be patented, let alone that one could patent the "or," "if-then," and "not" functions of Boolean algebra as implemented by a biological mechanism. The response, presumably, is to fine tune our patent standards—to patent the mousetrap and the corkscrew, not the notion of catching mice or opening bottles by mechanical means. Still less should we allow the patenting of algebra. These are fine points. Later scholarship has added formulae, data, and historical analysis to back up Jefferson's concerns, while never surpassing his prose. As I said at the beginning of the book, if we were to print out the Jefferson Warning and slip it into the shirt pocket of every legislator and regulator, our policy would be remarkably improved.

But it is here that the story takes a new turn, something that neither Jefferson nor the philosophers of the Scottish Enlightenment had thought of, something that goes beyond their cautions not to confuse intellectual property with physical property, to keep its boundaries, scope, and term as small as possible while still encouraging the desired innovation.

Think of the reaction of the synthetic biologists at MIT. They feared that the basic building blocks of their new discipline could be locked up, slowing the progress of science and research by inserting intellectual property rights at the wrong point in the research cycle. To solve the problem they were led seriously to consider claiming copyright over the products of synthetic biology—to fight overly broad patent rights with a privately constructed copyright commons, to ride the process of legal expansion and turn it to their own ends. As I pointed out earlier, I think the tactic would not fare well in this particular case. But it is an example of a new move in the debate over intellectual property, a new tactic: the attempt to create a privately constructed commons where the public domain created by the state does not give you the freedom that you believe creativity needs in order to thrive. It is to that tactic, and the distributed creativity that it enables, that I will turn to now.

8

A Creative Commons

If you go to the familiar Google search page and click the intimidating link marked "advanced search," you come to a page that gives you more fine-grained control over the framing of your query. Nestled among the choices that allow you to pick your desired language, or exclude raunchy content, is an option that says "usage rights." Click "free to use or share" and then search for "physics textbook" and you can download a 1,200-page physics textbook, copy it, or even print it out and hand it to your students. Search for "Down and Out in the Magic Kingdom" and you will find Cory Doctorow's fabulous science fiction novel, online, in full, for free. His other novels are there too—with the willing connivance of his commercial publisher. Search for "David Byrne, My Fair Lady" and you will be able to download Byrne's song and make copies for your friends. You'll find songs from Gilberto Gil and the Beastie Boys on the same page. No need to pay iTunes or worry about breaking the law.

Go to the "advanced" page on Flickr, the popular photo sharing site, and you will find a similar choice marked "Creative Commons License." Check that box and then search for "Duke Chapel" and you will get a selection of beautiful photos of the lovely piece of faux Gothic architecture that sits about three hundred yards from the office where I am writing these words. You can copy those photos, and 66 million others on different subjects, share them with your friends, print them for your wall, and, in some cases, even use them commercially. The same basic tools can be found on a range of specialized search engines with names like OWL Music Search, BlipTV, SpinExpress, and OERCommons. Searching those sites, or just sticking with the advanced options on Google or Yahoo, will get you courses in music theory, moral philosophy, and C++ programming from famous universities; a full-length movie called *Teach* by Oscar-winning director Davis Guggenheim; and free architectural drawings that can be used to build low-cost housing. At the Wellcome Library, you will find two thousand years of medical images that can be shared freely. Searching for "skeleton" is particularly fun. You can even go to your favorite search engine, type in the title of this book, find a site that will allow you to download it, and send the PDF to a hundred friends, warmly anticipating their rapturous enjoyment. (Better ask them first.)

All this copying and sharing and printing sounds illegal, but it is not (at least if you went through the steps I described). And the things you can do with this content do not stop with simply reproducing it, printing it on paper, or sending it by e-mail. Much of it can be changed, customized, remixed—you could rewrite the module of the class and insert your own illustrations, animate the graphs showing calculus in action, morph the photo into something new. If you search for a musician with the unpromising name "Brad Sucks," you will find a Web site bearing the modest subtitle "A one man band with no fans." Brad, it turns out, does not suck and has many fans. What makes him particularly interesting is that he allows those fans, or anyone else for that matter, to remix his music and post their creations online. I am particularly fond of the Matterovermind remix of "Making Me Nervous," but it may not be to your taste. Go to a site called ccMixter and you will find that musicians, famous and obscure, are inviting you to sample and remix their music. Or search Google for Colin Mutchler and listen to a haunting song called "My Life Changed." Mr. Mutchler and a violinist called Cora Beth Bridges whom he had never met created that song together. He posted a song called "My Life" online, giving anyone the freedom to add to it, and she did—"My Life." Changed.

On December 15, 2002, in San Francisco, a charitable organization called Creative Commons was launched. (Full disclosure: I have been a proud board member of Creative Commons since its creation.) Creative Commons was the brainchild of Larry Lessig, Hal Abelson, and Eric Eldred. All the works I have just described—and this book itself—are under Creative Commons licenses. The authors and creators of those works have chosen to share it with the world, with you, under generous terms, while reserving certain rights for themselves. They may have allowed you to copy it, but not to alter it—to make derivative works. Or they may have allowed you to use it as you wish, so long as you do so noncommercially. Or they may have given you complete freedom, provided only that you attribute them as the owner of the work. There are a few simple choices and a limited menu of permutations.

What makes these licenses unusual is that they can be read by two groups that normal licenses exclude—human beings (rather than just lawyers) and computers. The textbooks, photos, films, and songs have a tasteful little emblem on them marked with a "cc" which, if you click on it, links to a "Commons Deed," a simple one-page explanation of the freedoms you have. There are even icons—a dollar with a slash through it, for example—that make things even clearer. Better still, the reason the search engines could find this material is that the licenses also "tell" search engines exactly what freedoms have been given. Simple "metadata" (a fancy word for tags that computers can read) mark the material with its particular level of freedoms. This is not digital rights management. The license will not try to control your computer, install itself on your hard drive, or break your TV. It is just an expression of the terms under which the author has chosen to release the work. That means that if you search Google or Flickr for "works I am free to share, even commercially," you know you can go into business selling those textbooks, or printing those photos on mugs and T-shirts, so long as you give the author attribution. If you search for "show me works I can build on," you know you are allowed to make what copyright lawyers call "derivative works."

The idea behind Creative Commons was simple. As I pointed out in the first chapter, copyright adheres automatically on "fixation." As soon as you lift the pen from the paper, click the shutter, or save the file, the work is copyrighted. No formalities. No need even to use the little symbol ©. Once copyrighted, the work is protected by the full might of the legal system. And the legal system's default setting is that "all rights are reserved" to the author, which means effectively that anyone but the author is forbidden to copy, adapt, or publicly perform the work. This might have been a fine rule for a world in which there were high barriers to publication. The material that was not published was theoretically under an "all rights reserved" regime, but who cared?

It was practically inaccessible anyway. After the development of the World Wide Web, all that had changed. Suddenly people and institutions, millions upon millions of them, were putting content online—blogs, photo sites, videologs, podcasts, course materials. It was all just up there.

But what could you do with it? You could read it, or look at it, or play it presumably—otherwise why had the author put it up? But could you copy it? Put it on your own site? Include it in a manual used by the whole school district? E-mail it to someone? Translate it into your own language? Quote beyond the boundaries of fair use? Adapt for your own purposes? Take the song and use it for your video? Of course, if you really wanted the work a lot, you could try to contact the author—not always easy. And one by one, we could all contact each other and ask for particular types of permissions for use. If the use was large enough or widespread enough, perhaps we would even think that an individual contract was necessary. Lawyers could be hired and terms hashed out.

All this would be fine if the author wished to retain all the rights that copyright gives and grant them only individually, for pay, with lawyers in the room. But what about the authors, the millions upon millions of writers, and photographers and musicians, and filmmakers and bloggers and scholars, who very much *want* to share their work? The Cora Beth Bridges of the world are never going to write individual letters to the Colin Mutchlers of the world asking for permission to make a derivative work out of "My Life." The person who translated my articles into Spanish or Mandarin, or the people who repost them on their Web sites, or include them in their anthologies might have asked permission if I had not granted it in advance. I doubt though that I would have been contacted by the very talented person who took images from a comic book about fair use that I co-wrote and mashed them up with words from a book by Larry Lessig, and some really nice music from someone none of us had ever met. Without some easy way to give permission in advance, and to do so in a way that human beings and computers, as well as lawyers, can understand, those collaborations will never happen, though all the parties would be delighted if they did. These are losses from "failed sharing"—every bit as real as losses from unauthorized copying, but much less in the public eye.

Creative Commons was conceived as a private "hack" to produce a more fine-tuned copyright structure, to replace "all rights reserved" with "some rights reserved" for those who wished to do so. It tried to do for culture what the General Public License had done for software. It made use of the same technologies that had created the issue: the technologies that made fixation of expressive content and its distribution to the world something that people, as well as large concentrations of capital, could do. As a result, it was able to attract a surprising range of support—Jack Valenti of the Motion Picture Association of America and Hillary Rosen of the Recording Industry Association of America, as well as John Perry Barlow of the Grateful Dead, whose attitude toward intellectual property was distinctly less favorable. Why could they all agree? These licenses were not a choice forced on anyone. The author was choosing what to share and under what terms. But that sharing created something different, something new. It was more than a series of isolated actions. The result was the creation of a global "commons" of material that was open to all, provided they adhered to the terms of the licenses. Suddenly it was possible to think of creating a work entirely out of Creative Commons-licensed content—text, photos, movies, music. Your coursebook on music theory, or your documentary on the New York skyline, could combine your own original material with high-quality text, illustrations, photos, video, and music created by strangers. One could imagine entire fields—of open educational content or of open music—in which creators could work without keeping one eye nervously on legal threats or permissions.

From one perspective, Creative Commons looks like a simple device for enabling exercise of authorial control, remarkable only for the extremely large number of authors making that choice and the simplicity with which they can do so. From another, it can be seen as re-creating, by private choice and automated licenses, the world of creativity before law had permeated to the finest, most atomic level of science and culture—the world of folk music or 1950s jazz, of jokes and slang and recipes, of Ray Charles's "rewording" of gospel songs, or of Isaac Newton describing himself as "standing on the shoulders of giants" (and not having to pay them royalties). Remember, that is not a world *without* intellectual property. The cookbook might be copyrighted even if the recipe was not. Folk music makes it to the popular scene and is sold as a copyrighted product. The jazz musician "freezes" a particular version of the improvisation on a communally shared set of musical motifs, records it, and sometimes even claims ownership of it. Newton himself was famously touchy about precedence and attribution, even if not about legal ownership of his ideas. But it is a world in which creativity and innovation proceed on the basis of an extremely large "commons" of material into which it was never imagined that property rights could permeate.

For many of us, Creative Commons was conceived of as a second-best solution created by private agreement because the best solution could not be obtained through public law. The best solution would be a return of the formality requirement—a requirement that one at least write the words "James Boyle copyright 2008," for example, in order to get more than 100 years of legal protection backed by "strict liability" and federal criminal law. Those who did not wish to have the legal monopoly could omit the phrase and the work would pass into the public domain, with a period of time during which the author could claim copyright retrospectively if the phrase was omitted by accident. The default position would become freedom and the dead weight losses caused by giving legal monopolies to those who had not asked for them, and did not want them, would disappear. To return to the words of Justice Brandeis that I quoted at the beginning of the book:

> The general rule of law is, that the noblest of human productions—knowledge, truths ascertained, conceptions, and ideas—become, after voluntary communication to others, free as the air to common use. Upon these incorporeal productions the attribute of property is continued after such communication only in certain classes of cases where public policy has seemed to demand it.

Brandeis echoes the Jeffersonian preference for a norm of freedom, with narrowly constrained exceptions only when necessary. That preference means that the commons of which I spoke is a relatively large one—property rights are the exception, not the norm. Of course, many of those who use Creative Commons licenses might disagree with that policy preference and with every idea in this book. They may worship the DMCA or just want a way to get their song or their article out there while retaining some measure of control. That does not matter. The licenses are agnostic. Like a land trust which has a local pro-growth industrialist and a local environmentalist on its board, they permit us to come to a restricted agreement on goals ("make sure this space is available to the public") even when underlying ideologies differ. They do this using those most conservative of tools—property rights and licenses. And yet, if our vision of property is "sole and despotic dominion," these licenses have created something very different—a commons has been made out of private and exclusive rights.

My point here is that Creative Commons licenses or the tools of free and open source software—to which I will turn in a moment—represent something more than merely a second-best solution to a poorly chosen rule. They represent a visible example of a type of creativity, of innovation, which has been around for a very long time, but which has reached new salience on the Internet—distributed creativity based around a shared commons of material.

FREE AND OPEN SOURCE SOFTWARE

In 2007, Clay Shirky, an incisive commentator on networked culture, gave a speech which anyone but a Net aficionado might have found simultaneously romantic and impenetrable. He started by telling the story of a Shinto shrine that has been painstakingly rebuilt to exactly the same plan many times over its 1,300-year life—and which was denied certification as a historic building as a result. Shirky's point? What was remarkable was not the building. It was a community that would continue to build and rebuild the thing for more than a millennium.

From there, Shirky shifted to a discussion of his attempt to get AT&T to adopt the high-level programming language Perl—which is released as free and open source software under the General Public License. From its initial creation by Larry Wall in 1987, Perl has been adapted, modified, and developed by an extraordinary range of talented programmers, becoming more powerful and flexible in the process. As Shirky recounts the story, when the AT&T representatives asked "where do you get your support?" Shirky responded, " 'we get our support from a community'—which to them sounded a bit like 'we get our Thursdays from a banana.' " Shirky concluded the speech thus:

> We have always loved one another. We're human. It's something we're good at. But up until recently, the radius and half-life of that affection has been quite limited. With love alone, you can plan a birthday party. Add coordinating tools and you can write an operating system. In the past, we would do little things for love, but big things required money. Now we can do big things for love.[1]

There are a few people out there for whom "operating systems" and "love" could plausibly coexist in a sentence not constructed by an infinite number of monkeys. For most though, the question is, what could he possibly have meant?

The arguments in this book so far have taken as a given the incentives and collective action problems to which intellectual property is a response. Think of Chapter 1 and the economic explanation of "public goods." The fact that it is expensive to do the research to find the right drug, but cheap to manufacture it once it is identified provides a reason to create a legal right of exclusion. In those realms where the innovation would not have happened anyway, the legal right of exclusion gives a power to price above cost, which in turn gives incentives to creators and distributors. So goes the theory. I have discussed the extent to which the logic of enclosure works for the commons of the mind as well as it did for the arable commons, taking into account the effects of an information society and a global Internet. What I have not done is asked whether a global network actually transforms some of our assumptions about how creation happens in a way that reshapes the debate about the need for incentives, at least in certain areas. This, however, is exactly the question that needs to be asked.

For anyone interested in the way that networks can enable new collaborative methods of production, the free software movement, and the broader but less political movement that goes under the name of open source software, provide interesting case studies.[2] Open source software is released under a series of licenses, the most important being the General Public License (GPL). The GPL specifies that anyone may copy the software, provided the license remains attached and the source code for the software always remains available.[3] Users may add to or modify the code, may build on it and incorporate it into their own work, but if they do so, then the new program created is also covered by the GPL. Some people refer to this as the "viral" nature of the license; others find the term offensive.[4] The point, however, is that the open quality of the creative enterprise spreads. It is not simply a donation of a program or a work to the public domain, but a continual accretion in which all gain the benefits of the program on pain of agreeing to give their additions and innovations back to the communal project.

For the whole structure to work without large-scale centralized coordination, the creation process has to be modular, with units of different sizes and complexities, each requiring slightly different expertise, all of which can be added together to make a grand whole. I can work on the sendmail program, you on the search algorithms. More likely, lots of people try, their efforts are judged by the community, and the best ones are adopted. Under these conditions, this curious mix of Kropotkin and Adam Smith, Richard Dawkins and Richard Stallman, we get distributed production without having to rely on the proprietary exclusion model. The whole enterprise will be much, much, much greater than the sum of the parts.

What's more, and this is a truly fascinating twist, when the production process does need more centralized coordination, some governance that guides how the sticky modular bits are put together, it is at least theoretically possible that we can come up with the control system *in exactly the same way*. In this sense, distributed production is potentially recursive. Governance processes, too, can be assembled through distributed methods on a global network, by people with widely varying motivations, skills, and reserve prices.[5]

The free and open source software movements have produced software that rivals or, some claim, exceeds the capabilities of conventional proprietary, binary-only software.[6] Its adoption on the "enterprise level" is impressive, as is the number and enthusiasm of the various technical testaments to its strengths. You have almost certainly used open source software or been its beneficiary. Your favorite Web site or search engine may run on it. If your browser is Firefox, you use it every day. It powers surprising things around you—your ATM or your TiVo. The plane you are flying in may be running it. It just works.

Governments have taken notice. The United Kingdom, for example, concluded last year that open source software "will be considered alongside proprietary software and contracts will be awarded on a value-for-money basis." The Office of Government Commerce said open source software is "a viable desktop alternative for the majority of government users" and "can generate significant savings. . . . These trials have proved that open source software is now a real contender alongside proprietary solutions. If commercial companies and other governments are taking it seriously, then so must we."[7] Sweden found open source software to be in many cases "equivalent to—or better than—commercial products" and concluded that software procurement "shall evaluate open software as well as commercial solutions, to provide better competition in the market."[8]

What is remarkable is not merely that the software works technically, but that it is an example of widespread, continued, high-quality innovation. The really remarkable thing is that it works socially, as a continuing system, sustained by a network consisting both of volunteers and of individuals employed by companies such as IBM and Google whose software "output" is nevertheless released into the commons.

Here, it seems, we have a classic public good: code that can be copied freely and sold or redistributed without paying the creator or creators. This sounds like a tragedy of the commons of the kind that I described in the first three chapters of the book. Obviously, with a nonrival, nonexcludable good like software, this method of production cannot be sustained; there are inadequate incentives to ensure continued production. *E pur si muove*, as Galileo is apocryphally supposed to have said in the face of Cardinal Bellarmine's certainties: "And yet it moves."[9] Or, as Clay Shirky put it, "we get our support from a community."

For a fair amount of time, most economists looked at open source software and threw up their hands. From their point of view, "we get our support from a community" did indeed sound like "we get our Thursdays from a banana." There is an old economics joke about the impossibility of finding a twenty-dollar bill lying on a sidewalk. In an efficient market, the money would already have been picked up. (Do not wait for a punch line.) When economists looked at open source software they saw not a single twenty-dollar bill lying implausibly on the sidewalk, but whole bushels of them. Why would anyone work on a project the fruits of which could be appropriated by anyone? Since copyright adheres on fixation—since the computer programmer already has the legal power to exclude others—why would he or she choose to take the extra step of adopting a license that undermined that exclusion? Why would anyone choose to allow others to use and modify the results of their hard work? Why would they care whether the newcomers, in turn, released their contributions back into the commons?

The puzzles went beyond the motivations of the people engaging in this particular form of "distributed creativity." How could these implausible contributions be organized? How should we understand this strange form of organization? It is not a company or a government bureaucracy. What could it be? To Richard Epstein, the answer was obvious and pointed to a reason the experiment must inevitably end in failure:

> The open source movement shares many features with a workers' commune, and is likely to fail for the same reason: it cannot scale up to meet its own successes. To see the long-term difficulty, imagine a commune entirely owned by its original workers who share pro rata in its increases in value. The system might work well in the early days when the workforce remains fixed. But what happens when a given worker wants to quit? Does that worker receive in cash or kind his share of the gain in value during the period of his employment? If not, then the run-up in value during his period of employment will be gobbled up by his successor—a recipe for immense resentment. Yet that danger can be ducked only by creating a capital structure that gives present employees separable interests in either debt or equity in exchange for their contributions to the company. But once that is done, then the worker commune is converted into a traditional company whose shareholders and creditors contain a large fraction of its present and former employers. The bottom line is that idealistic communes cannot last for the long haul.[10]

There are a number of ideas here. First, "idealistic communes cannot last for the long haul." The skepticism about the staying power of idealism sounds plausible today, though there are some relatively prominent counterexamples. The Catholic Church is also a purportedly idealistic institution. It is based on canonical texts that are subject to even more heated arguments about textual interpretation than those which surround the General Public License. It seems to be surviving the long haul quite well.

The second reason for doomsaying is provided by the word "commune." The problems Epstein describes are real where tangible property and excludable assets are involved. But is the free and open source community a "commune," holding tangible property in common and excluding the rest of us? Must it worry about how to split up the proceeds if someone leaves because of bad karma? Or is it a community creating and offering to the world the ability to use, for free, nonrival goods that all of us can have, use, and reinterpret as we wish? In that kind of commune, each of us could take all the property the community had created with us when we left and the commune would still be none the poorer. Jefferson was not thinking of software when he talked of the person who lights his taper from mine but does not darken me, but the idea is the same one. Copying software is not like fighting over who owns the scented candles or the VW bus. Does the person who wrote the "kernel" of the operating system resent the person who, much later, writes the code to manage Internet Protocol addresses on a wireless network? Why should he? Now the program does more cool stuff. Both of them can use it. What's to resent?

How about idealism? There is indeed a broad debate on the reasons that the system works: Are the motivations those of the gift economy? Is it, as Shirky says, simply the flowering of an innate love that human beings have always had for each other and for sharing, now given new strength by the geographic reach and cooperative techniques the Internet provides? "With love alone, you can plan a birthday party. Add coordinating tools and you can write an operating system." Is this actually a form of potlatch, in which one gains prestige by the extravagance of the resources one "wastes"? Is open source an implicit résumé-builder that pays off in other ways? Is it driven by the species-being, the innate human love of creation that continually drives us to create new things even when *homo economicus* would be at home in bed, mumbling about public goods problems?[11]

Yochai Benkler and I would argue that these questions are fun to debate but ultimately irrelevant.[12] Assume a random distribution of incentive structures in different people, a global network—transmission, information sharing, and copying costs that approach zero—and a modular creation process. With these assumptions, it just does not matter why they do it. In lots of cases, they *will* do it. One person works for love of the species, another in the hope of a better job, a third for the joy of solving puzzles, and a fourth because he has to solve a particular problem anyway for his own job and loses nothing by making his hack available for all. Each person has their own reserve price, the point at which they say, "Now I will turn off *Survivor* and go and create something." But on a global network, there are a lot of people, and with numbers that big and information overhead that small, even relatively hard projects will attract motivated and skilled people whose particular reserve price has been crossed.

More conventionally, many people write free software because they are paid to do so. Amazingly, IBM now earns more from what it calls "Linux-related revenues" than it does from traditional patent licensing, and IBM is the largest patent holder in the world.[13] It has decided that the availability of an open platform, to which many firms and individuals contribute, will actually allow it to sell more of its services, and, for that matter, its hardware. A large group of other companies seem to agree. They like the idea of basing their services, hardware, and added value on a widely adopted "commons." This does not seem like a community in decline.

People used to say that collaborative creation could never produce a quality product. That has been shown to be false. So now they say that collaborative creation cannot be sustained because the governance mechanisms will not survive the success of the project. Professor Epstein conjures up a "central committee" from which insiders will be unable to cash out—a nice mixture of communist and capitalist metaphors. All governance systems—including democracies and corporate boards—have problems. But so far as we can tell, those who are influential in the free software and open source governance communities (there is, alas, no "central committee") feel that they are doing very well indeed. In the last resort, when they disagree with decisions that are taken, there is always the possibility of "forking the code," introducing a change to the software that not everyone agrees with, and then letting free choice and market selection converge on the preferred iteration. The free software ecosystem also exhibits diversity. Systems based on GNU-Linux, for example, have distinct "flavors" with names like Ubuntu, Debian, and Slackware, each with passionate adherents and each optimized for a particular concern—beauty, ease of use, technical manipulability. So far, the tradition of "rough consensus and running code" seems to be proving itself empirically as a robust governance system.

Why on earth should we care? People have come up with a surprising way to create software. So what? There are at least three reasons we might care. First, it teaches us something about the limitations of conventional economics and the counterintuitive business methods that thrive on networks. Second, it might offer a new tool in our attempt to solve a variety of social problems. Third, and most speculative, it hints at the way that a global communications network can sometimes help move the line between work and play, professional and amateur, individual and community creation, rote production and compensated "hobby."

We should pay attention to open source software because it shows us something about business methods in the digital world—indeed in the entire world of "information-based" products, which is coming to include biotechnology. The scale of your network matters. The larger the number of people who use your operating system, make programs for your type of computer, create new levels for your game, or use your device, the better off you are. A single fax machine is a paperweight. Two make up a communications link. Ten million and you have a ubiquitous communications network into which your "paperweight" is now a hugely valuable doorway.

This is the strange characteristic of networked goods. The actions of strangers dramatically increase or decrease the usefulness of your good. At each stage the decision of someone else to buy a fax machine increases the value of mine. If I am eating an apple, I am indifferent about whether you are too. But if I have a fax machine then my welfare is actually improved by the decisions of strangers to buy one. The same process works in reverse. Buy a word processing program that becomes unpopular, get "locked in" to using it, and find yourself unable to exchange your work easily with others. Networks matter and increasing the size of the networks continues to add benefits to the individual members.

What's true for the users of networks is doubly so for the producers of the goods that create them. From the perspective of a producer of a good that shows strong network effects such as a word processing program or an operating system, the optimal position is to be the company that owns and controls the dominant product on the market. The ownership and control is probably by means of intellectual property rights, which are, after all, the type of property rights one finds on networks. The value of that property depends on those positive and negative network effects. This is the reason Microsoft is worth so much money. The immense investment in time, familiarity, legacy documents, and training that Windows or Word users have provides a strong incentive not to change products. The fact that other users are similarly constrained makes it difficult to manage any change. Even if I change word processor formats and go through the trouble to convert all my documents, I still need to exchange files with you, who are similarly constrained. From a monopolist's point of view, the handcuffs of network effects are indeed golden, though opinions differ about whether or not this is a cause for antitrust action.

But if the position that yields the most revenue is that of a monopolist exercising total control, the second-best position may well be that of a company contributing to a large and widely used network based on open standards and, perhaps, open software. The companies that contribute to open source do not have the ability to exercise monopoly control, the right to extract every last cent of value from it. But they do have a different advantage; they get the benefit of all the contributions to the system without having to pay for them. The person who improves an open source program may not work for IBM or Red Hat, but those companies benefit from her addition, just as she does from theirs. The system is designed to continue growing, adding more contributions back into the commons. The users get the benefit of an ever-enlarging network, while the openness of the material diminishes the lock-in effects. Lacking the ability to extract payment for the network good itself—the operating system, say—the companies that participate typically get paid for providing tied goods and services, the value of which increases as the network does.

I write a column for the *Financial Times*, but I lack the fervor of the true enthusiast in the "Great Game of Markets." By themselves, counterintuitive business methods do not make my antennae tingle. But as Larry Lessig and Yochai Benkler have argued, this is something more than just another business method. They point us to the dramatic role that openness—whether in network architecture, software, or content—has had in the success of the Internet. *What is going on here is actually a remarkable corrective to the simplistic notion of the tragedy of the commons, a corrective to the Internet Threat storyline and to the dynamics of the second enclosure movement.* This commons creates and sustains value, and allows firms and individuals to benefit from it, without depleting the value already created. To appropriate a phrase from Carol Rose, open source teaches us about the *comedy* of the commons, a way of arranging markets and production that we, with our experience rooted in physical property and its typical characteristics, at first find counterintuitive and bizarre. Which brings us to the next question for open source. Can we use its techniques to solve problems beyond the world of software production?

In the language of computer programmers, the issue here is "does it scale?" Can we generalize anything from this limited example? How many types of production, innovation, and research fit into the model I have just described? After all, for many innovations and inventions one needs hardware, capital investment, and large-scale, real-world data collection—*stuff*, in its infinite recalcitrance and facticity. Maybe the open source model provides a workaround to the individual incentives problem, but that is not the only problem. And how many types of innovation or cultural production are as modular as software? Is open source software a paradigm case of collective innovation that helps us to understand open source software and not much else?

Again, I think this is a good question, but it may be the wrong one. My own guess is that an open source method of production is far more common than we realize. "Even before the Internet" (as some of my students have taken to saying portentously), science, law, education, and musical genres all developed in ways that are markedly similar to the model I have described. The marketplace of ideas, the continuous roiling development in thought and norms that our political culture spawns, owes much more to the distributed, nonproprietary model than it does to the special case of commodified innovation that we think about in copyright and patent. Not that copyright and patent are unimportant in the process, but they may well be the exception rather than the norm. Commons-based production of ideas is hardly unfamiliar, after all.

In fact, all the mottos of free software development have their counterparts in the theory of democracy and open society; "given enough eyeballs, all bugs are shallow" is merely the most obvious example. Karl Popper would have cheered.[14] The importance of open source software is not that it introduces us to a wholly new idea. It is that it makes us see clearly a very old idea. With open source the technology was novel, the production process transparent, and the result of that process was a "product" which outcompeted other products in the marketplace. "How can this have happened? What about the tragedy of the commons?" we asked in puzzlement, coming only slowly to the realization that other examples of commons-based, nonproprietary production were all around us.

Still, this does not answer the question of whether the model can scale still further, whether it can be applied to solve problems in other spheres. To answer that question we would need to think more about the modularity of other types of inventions. How much can they be broken down into chunks suitable for distribution among a widespread community? Which forms of innovation have some irreducible need for high capital investment in distinctly nonvirtual components—a particle accelerator or a Phase III drug trial? Again, my guess is that the increasing migration of the sciences toward data- and processing-rich models makes much more of innovation and discovery a potential candidate for the distributed model. Bioinformatics and computational biology, the open source genomics project,[15] the BioBricks Foundation I mentioned in the last chapter, the possibility of distributed data scrutiny by lay volunteers[16]—all of these offer intriguing glances into the potential for the future. Finally, of course, the Internet is one big experiment in, as Benkler puts it, peer-to-peer cultural production.[17]

If these questions are good ones, why are they also the wrong ones? I have given my guesses about the future of the distributed model of innovation. My own utopia has it flourishing alongside a scaled-down, but still powerful, intellectual property regime. Equally plausible scenarios see it as a dead end or as the inevitable victor in the war of productive processes. These are all guesses, however. At the very least, there is some possibility, even hope, that we could have a world in which much more of intellectual and inventive production is free. " 'Free' as in 'free speech,' " Richard Stallman says, not "free as in 'free beer.' "[18] But we could hope that much of it would be both free of centralized control and low- or no-cost. When the marginal cost of reproduction is zero, the marginal cost of transmission and storage approaches zero, the process of creation is additive, and much of the labor doesn't charge, the world looks a little different.[19] This is at least a possible future, or part of a possible future, and one that we should not foreclose without thinking twice. Yet that is what we are doing. The Database Protection Bills and Directives, which extend intellectual property rights to the layer of facts;[20] the efflorescence of software patents;[21] the UCITA-led validation of shrinkwrap licenses that bind third parties;[22] the Digital Millennium Copyright Act's anticircumvention provisions[23]—the point of all of these developments is not merely that they make the peer-to-peer model difficult, but that in many cases they rule it out altogether. I will assert this point here, rather than argue for it, but I think it can be (and has been) demonstrated quite convincingly.[24]

The point is, then, that there is a chance that a new (or old, but underrecognized) method of production could flourish in ways that seem truly valuable—valuable to free speech, innovation, scientific discovery, the wallets of consumers, to what William Fisher calls "semiotic democracy,"[25] and, perhaps, valuable to the balance between joyful creation and drudgery for hire. True, it is only a chance. True, this theory's scope of operation and sustainability are uncertain. But why would we want to foreclose it? That is what the recent expansions of intellectual property threaten to do. And remember, these expansions were dubious even in a world where we saw little or no possibility of the distributed production model I have described, where discussion of network effects had yet to reach the pages of *The New Yorker*,[26] and where our concerns about the excesses of intellectual property were simply the ones that Jefferson, Madison, and Macaulay gave us so long ago.

LEARNING FROM THE
SHARING ECONOMY

Accept for the sake of argument that the free software community actually works, actually produces high-quality products capable of competing in the market with proprietary alternatives. Concede for a moment that the adoption of Creative Commons licenses shows there are millions of creators out there who want to share their works with others. Many of those creators even want to allow the world to build on their material. Indeed, let us concede that the whole history of the Web, from Wikipedia to the obsessive and usefully detailed sites created on everything from Vikings to shoe polishes, shows a desire to share one's knowledge, to build on the work of others one has never met. These efforts are remarkably varied. Some are ultimately aimed at profit—even if their results are free. Think of IBM's open source initiatives or musicians who release Creative Commons-licensed work in order to get more club gigs. Some are provided as a volunteer act of benevolence or civic duty, even if they "compete" with expensive proprietary alternatives. Think of Wikipedia or MIT's OpenCourseWare. When the infrastructure for this collaboration does not exist, it gets assembled—and quickly. Both the GPL and Creative Commons are examples. Accept all of this. So what?

Lesson number one comes from the nonprofit activities—everything from Wikipedia to Web sites created by enthusiasts. People like to create and wish to share. In many cases they will do so without financial reward. A surprising amount of useful, creative, or expressive activity is generated without any financial incentive at all.

Should this cause us to throw out the economic case for copyrights? No. But it should lead us to reassess it. As I explained in Chapter 1, copyright provides an incentive for two distinct activities. First, it offers an incentive to create the work in the first place. The author of *Windows for Dummies* or *Harry Potter* gets a right to exclude others from copying the work, a right that he or she can sell in the marketplace. The goal is to offer a financial reason to devote time to this particular creative activity. It is this incentive that is most often cited when attempting to persuade policy makers to expand protection. Second, it offers an incentive to distribute the work—to typeset and print large quantities of the work and to sell it to bookstores, or to broadcast it, or put it on movie screens.

Each medium is economically different, of course. The economics of the feature film are different from those of the book, the magazine, or the operating system. Thus, we have never had very good figures on the relative importance of these incentives. We can only guess at how much of the incentive from copyright goes to encouraging creation and how much to distribution. Until recently, most types of distribution demanded higher levels of capital. The industry structure that resulted often consisted of creators who worked as wage or contract labor for distributors—either never acquiring copyright in their work in the first place or immediately transferring that copyright to their employers. Because distribution was expensive, our experience with material generated for fun or out of a love of sharing was an essentially private and local one. You might have a neighbor's photocopied sheet of baking recipes that worked well at high altitudes, or of fishing techniques that worked well on a particular lake, a song that a friend created for a special occasion, or a short story you wrote for your kids—and then typed up for them to tell to theirs. Financial incentives were not needed to encourage the creation of the work, but the cost of distribution dramatically limited its dissemination.

The single most dramatic thing that the Web has done by lowering the cost of communication and distribution, at the same moment that other electronic tools lowered the cost of production, is to make this local and private activity a global and public one. Someone, somewhere, will have written the guide to fishing on that lake, baking at that altitude, washing windows, or treating stings from Portuguese man-of-war jellyfish. Someone will have taken a photo of the Duke Chapel or explained the history, economics, and chemistry of shoe polish or distilling. Someone might even have created a great class on music theory or C++ programming. Someone will have written a handy little program to manage DNS requests on a local network. Bizarrely, at least as far as the economists were concerned, these people all wanted to share what they had made. Because of the genius of search engines, and the implicit peer-review function that those engines deduce from patterns of links to pages, I can find that material when I need it.

True, much of the material on the Web is inane or insane, confused, badly written, tendentious, and inaccurate. (It should be noted that this is hardly a problem confined to the Web or volunteer-generated material. Personally, I would not want *People* magazine or Fox News in a time capsule to represent my civilization. But some of the material on the Web is clearly worse.) Yes, Wikipedia is occasionally inaccurate—though in one test in *Nature* it stacked up well against the *Encyclopedia Britannica*, and it is obviously much more encyclopedic in its coverage. But all of this misses the point.

Consider how your expectations about information retrieval have changed in the last fifteen years. We now simply assume that questions about a piece of architecture, a bit of local history, a recipe, or the true author of a song can all be answered within seconds. We have forgotten what it is like to be routinely in ignorance because of the unavailability of some piece of information. One podcaster I talked to called it being a member of "the right-click generation": "When I am walking around and I see a building, I almost feel as though I ought to be able to 'right click' it and have the architect's name pop up." Consider that it now seems normal for a gay Iraqi man in Baghdad to have a blog that offers hundreds of thousands of readers around the world a literate and touching account of the American occupation from a perspective entirely different from that provided by the mainstream press.[27] We think it normal for a person of moderate resources to be able to speak to the world from a war zone, whether or not he is affiliated with a newspaper or credentialed by a corporation.

These examples are not the end of the process. Our methods of sorting, ranking, and verifying the material generated are still evolving. They may improve even beyond this point. We are only fifteen years into this particular experiment, after all. And a huge amount of this material is produced by our fellow citizens without the profit motive.

Does this mean that we no longer need copyright or patent protection to encourage the production and distribution of creative work? No. The fishing tips are great, but I still might buy a handsomely illustrated guide to take on the lake with me or, even better, just stay at home and read *A River Runs Through It*. *The New Yorker*, and not a sheaf of printouts from the Web, still sits on my coffee table, though much of the high-quality content I read comes to me online, for free, from strangers who are generating it for pleasure, not profit, or who profit from open sharing, not closed control. The online blogosphere provides a vital counterpoint to mainstream media, but it exists in a symbiotic—some would say parasitic—relationship with that media and the network of professional news gatherers for which it pays. Some of the most interesting open source production methods actually rely on copyright. Even if they did not, open source production would not suffice to run our pharmaceutical industry (though it might help with certain stages of the drug discovery process).

Still, just as it would be silly to dismiss the importance of intellectual property based on our experience of blogs and Wikipedia and open source software, it would be equally silly to underestimate what the Web has taught us. The Web has enabled an astonishing flowering of communication and expression, an astounding democratization of creativity. We have learned just how strong, and how useful, is the human urge to express, communicate, invent, and create—provided the barriers to sharing are lowered. These are the very things that copyright and patent are supposed to encourage. For us to portray the Web—as the Internet Threat story line does—as predominantly a *threat* to creativity is simply perverse. For us to base our policies only on that notion would be a tragedy. We might end up stultifying one of the greatest explosions of human creativity the world has ever seen by treating it as an unimportant marginal case and instead designing our rules around the production processes of commercial culture in the late twentieth century.

The shape of our copyright and to a lesser extent our patent system comes from a world in which almost all large-scale distribution was an expensive, capital-intensive enterprise. The roles of gatekeeper and financier, producer and assembler, distributor and advertiser, tended naturally to coalesce into vertically integrated firms or symbiotic commercial partnerships. Those firms were presumed to be the proxy for the public interest when it came to intellectual property policy. Who would know better than they what was needed? Occasionally, device manufacturers would provide a counterweight—as in the *Sony* case—where the defense of a particular "consumer freedom" actually created a market for a complementary product. Artists and authors might be trotted out as appealing spokespersons, though the laws that were made only sporadically reflected their economic and artistic interests. Librarians and educational institutions had influence at the edges. Most of the time, though, it was the assemblers and distributors of content whose voices and assumptions about markets would be heard.

Out of this pattern of habit and influence, and out of much deeper notions about authorship and invention that I have explored elsewhere, developed an ideology, a worldview. Call it maximalism. Its proponents sincerely believed in it and pursued it even when it did not make economic sense. (Think how lucky the movie industry is that it lost the *Sony* case.) It has been the subject of this book. Its tenets are that intellectual property is just like physical property, that rights need to increase proportionately as copying costs decrease, and that, in general, increasing levels of intellectual property protection will yield increasing levels of innovation. Despite its defense of ever-increasing government-granted monopolies, this ideology cloaks itself in the rhetoric of free markets. The bumbling state, whose interventions in the economy normally spell disaster, turns into a scalpel-wielding genius when its monopolies and subsidies are provided through intellectual property rights rather than regulatory fiat. Above all, this way of seeing the world minimizes the importance of creativity, expression, and distribution that takes place outside its framework and ignores or plays down the importance of the input side of the equation—the need to focus on the material from which culture and science are made, as well as the protected expression and inventions made from that raw material.

This process was not—let me stress—was *not* a simple process of economic determinism or industry conspiracy. Anyone who claims that is the thesis of this book simply has not read it. (Reviewers beware.) Let us start with economic determinism. It was not a situation in which the law mechanistically recorded the interests of the most economically important industries in the area. This was the creation of a worldview, not the steely-eyed calculation of profit and loss. Not only did many of the rules we ended up with make no sense from the point of view of some of the largest economic players in the area—think of the device manufacturers, the search engines, and so on—they frequently made no sense from the perspective of those proposing them. Attempting to twist the law to make it illegal for technology to interfere with your old business method is frequently bad for the industry seeking the protection, as well as for the technology, the market, and the wider society. Since this worldview makes incumbents systematically blind to profit-making opportunities that could be secured by greater openness, rather than greater control, it actually disables them from pursuing some of the most promising methods by which they could have made money for their shareholders. Again, the chapter on the *Sony* decision offers a salutary example.

Economic determinism does not explain the rules we have. Neither are those rules simply a result of the manipulation of elected officials by incumbent industries through crafty campaign contributions and distorted evidence (though to be sure, there was a lot of that as well). Many of the people who put forward this worldview—both lobbyists and lobbied—sincerely believe that more rights will always lead to more innovation, that all property rights are the same, that we do not need to think about both the input and output sides of the equation, that cheaper copying techniques automatically require greater protections, and so on.

What of the modest suggestions I put forward here? We could sum them up thus: do not apply identical assumptions to physical and intellectual property. Focus on both the inputs to and the outputs of the creative process; protecting the latter may increase the cost of the former. Look both at the role of the public domain and the commons of cultural and scientific material *and* at the need to provide incentives for creativity and distribution through exclusive rights. More rights will not automatically produce more innovation. Indeed, we should confine rights as narrowly as possible while still providing the desired result. Look at the empirical evidence before and after increasing the level of protection. Pay attention to the benefits as well as the costs of the new technologies and the flowering of creativity they enable.

To me, these points seem bland, boring, obvious—verging on tautology or pablum. To many believers in the worldview I have described, they are either straightforward heresy or a smokescreen for some real, underlying agenda—which is identified as communism, anarchism, or, somewhat confusingly, both.

This account smacks of exaggeration, I know. How could things be so one-sided? The best answer I can give came from a question I was asked at a recent conference. The questioner pointed out politely that it was unlikely that the policy-making process would ignore such a fundamental and obvious set of points—points that I myself observed had been well understood for hundreds of years. I had used many examples of intellectual property rights being extended—in length, breadth, scope. Why had I not spoken, he asked, of all the times over the last fifty years when intellectual property rights had been weakened, curtailed, shortened? Since human beings were fallible, surely there were occasions when the length of a copyright or patent term had proved to be too long, or the scope of a right too large, and the rights had been narrowed appropriately by legislation. Why did I not cite any of these? The answer is simple. To the best of my knowledge, there are none. Legislatively, intellectual property rights have moved only in one direction—outward. (Court decisions present a more complex picture, as the previous chapter's discussion of software copyrights and business method patents shows.)

What are the odds that the costs of new technologies are *always* greater than their benefits as far as intellectual property rights holders are concerned? This pattern is not a matter of policies carefully crafted around the evidence. It is the fossil record of fifty years of maximalism. If I lean toward the other side of the story it is not because I am a foe of intellectual property. It is because I believe our policies have become fundamentally unbalanced—unbalanced in ways that actually blind us to what is going on in the world of creativity.

We are living through an existence-proof that there are other methods of generating innovation, expression, and creativity than the proprietary, exclusionary model of sole control. True, these methods existed before. Yet they tended to be local or invisible or both. The Internet has shown conclusively and visibly that—at least in certain sectors—we can have a global flowering of creativity, innovation, and information sharing in which intellectual property rights function in a very different way than under the standard model of proprietary control. In some cases, intellectual property rights were simply irrelevant—much of the information sharing and indexing on the Web falls within this category. In some cases they were used to *prevent* exclusivity. Think of Creative Commons or the General Public License. In some, they were actually impediments. Software patents, for example, have a negative effect on open source software development—one that policy makers are only now slowly beginning to acknowledge.

It is important not to overstate how far the sharing economy can get us. It might help to cut the costs of early-stage drug development, as the Tropical Disease Initiative attempts to do for neglected diseases. It will not generate a Phase III drug trial or bring a drug to market. Sharing methods might be used to generate cult movies such as *Star Wreck: In the Pirkinning*, which was created using techniques borrowed from open source software and is available under a Creative Commons license. They will not produce a mammoth blockbuster like *Ben Hur*, or *Waterworld* for that matter—results that will generate mixed feelings. So there are real limitations to the processes I describe.

But even acknowledging those limitations, it is fair to say that one of the most striking events to occur during our lifetimes is the transformation wrought by the Web, a transformation that is partly driven by the extraordinary explosion of nonproprietary creativity and sharing across digital networks. The cultural expectation that a web of expression and information will just *be* there—whatever subject we are discussing—is a fundamental one, the one that in some sense separates us from our children. With this as a background it is both bizarre and perverse that we choose to concentrate our policy making only on maintaining the business methods of the last century, only on the story line of the Internet Threat, only on the dangers that the technology poses to creativity (and it does pose some) and never on the benefits.

What would it mean to pay attention to the changes I have described? It would mean assessing the impact of rules on both proprietary and nonproprietary production. For example, if the introduction of a broad regime of software patents would render open source software development more difficult (because individual contributors cannot afford to do a patent search on every piece of code they contribute), then this should be reflected as a cost of software patents, to be balanced against whatever benefits the system brought. A method for encouraging innovation might, in fact, inhibit one form of it.

Paying attention to the last ten years means we need to realize that nonproprietary, distributed production is not the poor relation of traditional proprietary, hierarchically organized production. This is no hippy lovefest. It is the business method on which IBM has staked billions of dollars; the method of cultural production that generates much of the information each of us uses every day. It is just as deserving of respect and the solicitude of policy makers as the more familiar methods pursued by the film studios and proprietary software companies. Losses due to sharing that failed because of artificially erected legal barriers are every bit as real as losses that come about because of illicit copying. Yet our attention goes entirely to the latter.

The main thrust of the argument here is still firmly within the Jeffersonian, Scottish Enlightenment tradition. Jefferson does not wish to give the patent to Oliver Evans because he believes the invention will be (and has been) generated anyway without the granting of an intellectual property right and that there are sufficient information retrieval methods to have practical access to it. In this case, the information retrieval method is not Google. It is a polymath genius combing his library in Monticello for references to Persian irrigation methods. The "embarrassment" caused by the unnecessary patent is added expense and bureaucracy in agriculture and impediments to further innovators, not the undermining of open source software. But it is the same principle of cautious minimalism, the same belief that much innovation goes on without proprietary control and that intellectual property rights are the exception, not the rule. When Benjamin Franklin, a man who surely deserved patents under even the most stringent set of tests, chooses to forgo them because he has secured so much benefit from the contributions of others, he expresses Shirky's norm nicely.

Indeed, Jefferson's optimism depends partly on a view of information sharing that captures beautifully the attitudes of the generation that built the Web. The letter that I discussed in Chapter 2 was widely cited for precisely this reason. Remember these lines?

> That ideas should freely spread from one to another over the globe, for the moral and mutual instruction of man, and improvement of his condition, seems to have been peculiarly and benevolently designed by nature, when she made them, like fire, expansible over all space, without lessening their density in any point, and like the air in which we breathe, move, and have our physical being, incapable of confinement or exclusive appropriation.

What could encapsulate better the process by which information spreads on a global network? What could more elegantly state the norms of the "information wants to be free" generation? (Though those who quoted him conveniently omitted the portions of his analysis where he concedes that there are cases where intellectual property rights may be necessary and desirable.)

In some ways, then, the explosion of nonproprietary and, in many cases, noncommercial creativity and information sharing is simply the vindication of Jefferson's comparison of ideas with "fire . . . expansible over all space." The Web makes the simile a reality and puts an exclamation point at the end of the Jefferson Warning. All the more reason to pay attention to it. But the creative commons I described here goes further. It forces us to reconceptualize a form of life, a method of production, and a means of social organization that we used to relegate to the private world of informal sharing and collaboration. Denied a commons by bad intellectual property rules, we can sometimes build our own—which may in some ways do even more for us than the zone of free trade, free thought, and free action that Jefferson wished to protect.

Does all this mean that the Jefferson Warning is no longer necessary? Can we mitigate the negative effects of intellectual property expansion through a series of privately constructed commons? The answers to those questions are, respectively, "no" and "sometimes." Think of the story of retrospectively extended copyright and orphan works. In many cases the problem with our intellectual property rights is that they create barriers to sharing—without producing an incentive in return—in ways that can never be solved through private agreement. Twentieth century culture will largely remain off-limits for digitization, reproduction, adaptation, and translation. No series of private contracts or licenses can fix the problem because the relevant parties are not in the room and might not agree if they were.

Even when the parties are available and agree to share, the benefits may not flow to all equally. Beset by a multitude of vague patents of questionable worth and uncertain scope, large information technology firms routinely create patent pools. IBM tosses in thousands of patents, so does Hewlett or Dell. Each agrees not to sue the other. This is great for the established companies; they can proceed without fear of legal action from the landmine patents that litter the technological landscape. As far as the participants are concerned, the patent pool is almost like the public domain—but a privatized public domain, a park that only residents may enter. But what about the start up company that does not have the thousands of patents necessary for entry? They are not in as happy a situation. The patent pool fixes the problem of poor patent quality and unclear scope—one that Jefferson was worrying about 200 years ago. But it fixes it only for the dominant firms, hurting competition in the process.

Attempts to form a commons may also backfire. The coordination problems are legion. There are difficulties of compatibility in licenses and the process, no matter how easy, still imposes transaction costs. Nevertheless, with all of these qualifications, the idea of the privately created commons is an important addition to the world view that Jefferson provided, a new tool in our attempt to craft a working system of innovation and culture. No one who looks at the Web can doubt the power of distributed, and frequently uncompensated, creativity in constructing remarkable reference works, operating systems, cultural conversations, even libraries of images and music. Some of that innovation happens largely outside of the world of intellectual property. Some of it happens in privately created areas of sharing that use property rights and open, sometimes even machine-readable, licenses to create a commons on which others can build. The world of creativity and its methods is wider than we had thought. That is one of the vital and exciting lessons the Internet teaches us; unfortunately, the only one our policy makers seem to hear is "cheaper copying means more piracy."

9
An Evidence-Free Zone

Perhaps some of the arguments in this book have convinced you. Perhaps it is a mistake to think of intellectual property in the same way we think of physical property. Perhaps limitations and exceptions to those rights are as important as the rights themselves. Perhaps the public domain has a vital and tragically neglected role to play in innovation and culture. Perhaps relentlessly expanding property rights will not automatically bring us increased innovation in science and culture. Perhaps the second enclosure movement is more troubling than the first. Perhaps it is unwise to extend copyright again and again, and to do so retrospectively, locking up most of twentieth-century culture in order to protect the tiny fragment of it that is still commercially available. Perhaps technological improvements bring both benefits and costs to existing rights holders—both of which should be considered when setting policy. Perhaps we need a vigorous set of internal limitations and exceptions within copyright, or control over content will inevitably become control over the medium of transmission. Perhaps the Internet should make us think seriously about the power of nonproprietary and distributed production.

Saying all this gives us some guidance in how we should think. It points out certain patterns of error. But its prescriptions are not simple. Precisely because it is not a rejection of intellectual property rights, but rather a claim that they only work well through a process of consciously balancing openness and control, public domain and private right, it still leaves open the question of where that point of balance is and how to strike it.

In this chapter I want to offer a suggestion that in any other field would be stunningly obvious, boring even, but in the funhouse mirror of intellectual property appears revolutionary. We should make our policy based on empirical evidence of its likely effects and there should be a formal requirement of empirical reconsideration of those policies after they have been implemented to see if they are working. Why is this a good idea?

Imagine a process of reviewing prescription drugs that goes like this: representatives from the drug company come to the regulators and argue that their drug works well and should be approved. They have no evidence of this beyond a few anecdotes about people who want to take it and perhaps some very simple models of how the drug might affect the human body. The drug is approved. No trials, no empirical evidence of any kind, no follow-up. Or imagine a process of making environmental regulations in which there were no data, and no attempts to gather data, about the effects of the particular pollutants being studied. Even the harshest critics of regulation would admit we generally do better than this. But this is often the way we make intellectual property policy.

So how do we decide the ground rules of the information age? Representatives of interested industries come to regulators and ask for another heaping slice of monopoly rent in the form of an intellectual property right. They have doom-laden predictions, they have anecdotes, carefully selected to pluck the heartstrings of legislators, they have celebrities who testify—often incoherently, but with palpable charisma—and they have very, very simple economic models. The basic economic model here is "If you give me a larger right, I will have a larger incentive to innovate. Thus the bigger the rights, the more innovation we will get. Right?"

As I have tried to show here using the words of Jefferson and Macaulay and examples such as term extension, software copyrights, and garage door openers, this logic is fallacious. Even without data, the "more is better" idea is obviously flawed. Copyrighting the alphabet will not produce more books. Patenting $E=mc^2$ will not yield more scientific innovation. Intellectual property creates barriers to, as well as incentives toward, innovation. Jefferson agonized over the issue of when the benefits exceed the costs of a new right. "I know well the difficulty of drawing a line between the things which are worth to the public the embarrassment of an exclusive patent, and those which are not." It is not clear that contemporary policy makers approach issues with anything like the same sophistication or humility. But it would be an equal mistake to conclude, as some do, that expansions of intellectual property are never justified. Extensions of rights can help or hurt, but without economic evidence beforehand and review afterward, we will never know. This point should be obvious, banal, even deeply boring, but sadly it is not.

From Jefferson and Macaulay and Adam Smith, I derived a second point. In the absence of evidence on either side, the presumption should be against creating a new, legalized monopoly. The burden of proof should lie on those who claim, in any particular case, that the state should step in to stop competition, outlaw copying, proscribe technology, or restrict speech. They have to show us that the existing protection is not enough. But this presumption is a second-best solution and the empirical emptiness of the debates frustrating.

This makes an occasion where there *is* some evidence a time for celebration. What we need is a test case in which one country adopts the proposed new intellectual property right and another similarly situated country does not, and we can assess how they are both doing after a number of years.

There is such a case. It is the "database right."

OWNING FACTS?

Europe adopted a Database Directive in 1996 which gave a high level of copyright protection to databases and conferred a new "sui generis" database right even on unoriginal compilations of facts. In the United States, by contrast, in a 1991 case called *Feist Publications, Inc. v. Rural Telephone Service Co.*, 499 U.S. 340 (1991), the Supreme Court made it clear that unoriginal compilations of facts are not copyrightable.

What does all this mean? Take the phone directory—that was the product at issue in the *Feist* case. A white pages directory is a database of names and numbers, compiled in alphabetical order by name. Does anyone have an intellectual property right over it? Not the particular dog-eared directory lying next to your phone. Does the phone company that compiled it own the facts, the numbers inside that directory? Could they forbid me from copying them, adding others from surrounding areas, and issuing a competing directory that I believed consumers would find more valuable? This was an important issue for Feist because it went to the heart of their business. They issued regional telephone directories, combining records from multiple phone companies. In this case, all the other companies in the region agreed to license their data to Feist. Rural did not, so Feist copied the information, checked as many entries as possible, adding addresses to some of the listings, and published the combined result. Rural sued and lost. The Supreme Court declared that mere alphabetical listings and other unoriginal assemblies of data cannot be copyrighted.

> It may seem unfair that much of the fruit of the compiler's labor may be used by others without compensation. As Justice Brennan has correctly observed, however, this is not "some unforeseen byproduct of a statutory scheme." It is, rather, "the essence of copyright," and a constitutional requirement. The primary objective of copyright is not to reward the labor of authors, but "to promote the Progress of Science and useful Arts." To this end, copyright assures authors the right to their original expression, but encourages others to build freely upon the ideas and information conveyed by a work. This principle, known as the idea/expression or fact/expression dichotomy, applies to all works of authorship. As applied to a factual compilation, assuming the absence of original written expression, only the compiler's selection and arrangement may be protected; the raw facts may be copied at will. This result is neither unfair nor unfortunate. It is the means by which copyright advances the progress of science and art.[1]

Feist was not as revolutionary as some critics claimed it to be. Most of the appeals courts in the United States had long held this to be the case. As the Court pointed out in the passage above, it is a fundamental tenet of the U.S. intellectual property system that neither facts nor ideas can be owned. *Feist* merely reiterated that point clearly and stressed that it was not just a policy choice, it was a constitutional requirement—a limit imposed by the Constitution's grant of power to Congress to make copyright and patent laws.

Daily politics cares little for the limitations imposed by constitutions or for the structural principle the Court describes—that we should leave facts free for others to build upon. Since 1991, a few database companies have lobbied the Congress strenuously and continuously to create a special database right over facts. Interestingly, apart from academics, scientists, and civil libertarians, many database companies, and even those well-known property haters, the U.S. Chamber of Commerce, oppose the creation of such a right. They believe that database providers can adequately protect themselves with contracts or technical means such as passwords, can rely on providing tied services, and so on. Moreover, they argue that strong database protection may make it harder to generate databases in the first place; the facts you need may be locked up. We need to focus on the inputs as well as the outputs of the process—a point I have tried to make throughout this book. The pressure to create a new right continues, however, aided by cries that the United States must "harmonize" with Europe, where, you will remember, compilations of facts are strongly protected by intellectual property rights, even if their arrangement is unoriginal.

So here we have our natural experiment. One major economy rejects such protection and resists pressure to create a new right. A different major economic region, at a comparable level of development, institutes the right with the explicit claim that it will help to produce new databases and make that segment of the economy more competitive. Presumably government economists in the United States and the European Union have been hard at work ever since, seeing if the right actually worked? Well, not exactly.

Despite the fact that the European Commission has a legal obligation to review the Database Directive for its effects on competition, it was more than three years late issuing its report. At first, during the review process, no attention was paid to the actual evidence of whether the Directive helps or hurts the European Union, or whether the database industry in the United States has collapsed or flourished. That is a shame, because the evidence was there and it was fairly shocking. Yet finally, at the end of the process, the Commission did turn to the evidence, as I will recount, and came to a remarkable conclusion—which was promptly stifled for political reasons. But we are getting ahead of ourselves.

How do we frame the empirical inquiry? Intellectual property rights allow the creation of state-backed monopolies, and "the general tendency of monopolies," as Macaulay pointed out, is "to make articles scarce, to make them dear, and to make them bad." Monopolies are an evil, but they must sometimes be accepted when they are necessary to the production of some good, some particular social goal. In this case, the "evil" is obviously going to be an increase in the price of databases and the legal ability to exclude competitors from their use—that, after all, is the point of granting the new right. This right of exclusion may then have dynamic effects, hampering the ability of subsequent innovators to build on what went before. The "good" is that we are supposed to get lots of new databases, databases that we would not have had but for the existence of the database right.

If the database right were working, we would expect positive answers to three crucial questions. First, has the European database industry's rate of growth increased since 1996, while the U.S. database industry has languished? (The drop-off in the U.S. database industry ought to be particularly severe after 1991 if the proponents of database protection are correct; they argued the *Feist* case was a change in current law and a great surprise to the industry.)

Second, are the principal beneficiaries of the database right in Europe producing databases they would not have produced otherwise? Obviously, if a society is handing over a database right for a database that would have been created anyway, it is overpaying—needlessly increasing prices for consumers and burdens for competitors. This goes to the design of the right—has it been crafted too broadly, so that it is not being targeted to those areas where it is needed to encourage innovation?

Third, and this one is harder to judge, is the new right promoting innovation and competition rather than stifling it? For example, if the existence of the right allowed a one-time surge of newcomers to the market who then use their rights to discourage new entrants, or if we promoted some increase in databases but made scientific aggregation of large amounts of data harder overall, then the database right might actually be stifling the innovation it is designed to foment.

Those are the three questions that any review of the Database Directive must answer. But we have preliminary answers to those three questions and they are either strongly negative or extremely doubtful.

Are database rights necessary for a thriving database industry? The answer appears to be no. In the United States, the database industry has grown more than twenty-five-fold since 1979 and—contrary to those who paint the *Feist* case as a revolution—for that entire period, in most of the United States, it was clear that unoriginal databases were not covered by copyright. The figures are even more interesting in the legal database market. The two major proponents of database protection in the United States are Reed Elsevier, the owner of Lexis, and Thomson Publishing, the owner of Westlaw. Fascinatingly, both companies made their key acquisitions in the U.S. legal database market *after* the *Feist* decision, at which point no one could have thought unoriginal databases were copyrightable. This seems to be some evidence that they believed they could make money even without a database right. How? In the old-fashioned way: competing on features, accuracy, tied services, making users pay for entry to the database, and so on.

If those companies believed there were profits to be made, they were right. Jason Gelman, a former Duke student, pointed out in a recent paper that Thomson's legal regulatory division had a profit margin of over 26 percent for the first quarter of 2004. Reed Elsevier's 2003 profit margin for LexisNexis was 22.8 percent. Both profit margins were significantly higher than the company average and both were earned primarily in the $6 billion U.S. legal database market, a market which is thriving without strong intellectual property protection over databases. (First rule of thumb for regulators: when someone with a profit margin over 20 percent asks you for additional monopoly protection, pause before agreeing.)

What about Europe? There is some good news for the proponents of database protection. As Hugenholtz, Maurer, and Onsrud point out in a nice article in *Science* magazine, there was a sharp, one-time spike in the number of companies entering the European database market immediately following the implementation of the Directive in member states.[2] Yet their work, and "Across Two Worlds,"[3] a fascinating study by Maurer, suggests that the rate of entry then fell back to levels similar to those before the directive. Maurer's analysis shows that the attrition rate was also very high in some European markets in the period following the passage of the directive—even with the new right, many companies dropped out.

At the end of the day, the British database industry—the strongest performer in Europe—added about two hundred databases in the three years immediately after the implementation of the directive. In France, there was little net change in the number of databases and the number of providers fell sharply. In Germany, the industry added nearly three hundred databases immediately following the directive—a remarkable surge—about two hundred of which rapidly disappeared. During the same period, the U.S. industry added about nine hundred databases. Bottom line? Europe's industry did get a one-time boost and some of those firms have stayed in the market; that is a benefit, though a costly one. But database growth rates have gone back to pre-directive levels, while the anticompetitive costs of database protection are now a permanent fixture of the European landscape. The United States, by contrast, gets a nice steady growth rate in databases without paying the monopoly cost. (Second rule of thumb for regulators: Do no harm! Do not create rights without strong evidence that the incentive effect is worth the anticompetitive cost.)

Now the second question. Is the Database Directive encouraging the production of databases we would not have gotten otherwise? Here the evidence is clear and disturbing. Again, Hugenholtz et al. point out that the majority of cases brought under the directive have been about databases that would have been created anyway—telephone numbers, television schedules, concert times. A review of more recent cases reveals the same pattern. These databases are inevitably generated by the operation of the business in question and cannot be independently compiled by a competitor. The database right simply serves to limit competition in the provision of the information. Recently, the European Court of Justice implicitly underscored this point in a series of cases concerning football scores, horse racing results, and so on. Rejecting a protectionist and one-sided opinion from its Advocate General, the court ruled that the mere running of a business which generates data does not count as "substantial investment" sufficient to trigger the database right. It would be nice to think that this is the beginning of some skepticism about the reach of the directive. Yet the court provides little discussion of the economic reasons behind its interpretation; the analysis is merely semantic and definitional, a sharp contrast to its competition decisions.

So what kinds of creations are being generated by this bold new right? The answer is somewhere between bathos and pathos. Here are some of the wonderful "databases" that people found it worthwhile litigating over: a Web site consisting of a collection of 259 hyperlinks to "parenting resources," a collection of poems, an assortment of advertisements, headings referring to local news, and charts of popular music. The sad list goes on and on. The European Commission might ask itself whether these are really the kind of "databases" that we need a legal monopoly to encourage and that we want to tie up judicial resources protecting. The point that many more such factual resources can be found online in the United States without any legalized database protection also seems worthy of note. At the very least, the evidence indicates that the right is drawn much too broadly and triggered too easily in ways that produce litigation but little social benefit.

Now, in one sense, these lawsuits over trivial collections of hyperlinks and headlines might be seen as irrelevant. They may indicate we are handing out rights unnecessarily—did we really need a legal monopoly, and court involvement, to get someone to compile hyperlinks on a Web page? But it is hard to see social harm. As with the patents over "sealed crustless" peanut butter sandwiches or "methods of swinging on a swing," we may shake our heads at the stupidity of the system, but if the problems consist only of trivial creations, at least we are not likely to grieve because some vital piece of information was locked up. But we should not be so quick to declare such examples irrelevant. They tend to show that the system for drawing the boundaries of the right is broken—and that is of general concern, even if the issue at hand is not.

Finally, is the database right encouraging scientific innovation or hurting it? Here the evidence is merely suggestive. Scientists have claimed that the Euro-

pean database right, together with the perverse failure of European governments to take advantage of the limited scientific research exceptions allowed
by the directive, have made it much harder to aggregate data, to replicate studies, and to judge published articles. In fact, academic scientific bodies have been
among the strongest critics of database protection. But negative evidence, by
its nature, is hard to produce; "show me the science that did not get done!"
Certainly, both U.S. science and commerce have benefited extraordinarily
from the openness of U.S. data policy. I will deal with this issue in the next
part of this chapter.

If the United States does not give intellectual property protection to raw
data, to facts, how is it that the database industry has managed to thrive here
and to do better than in Europe, which has extremely strong protection? The
economists described in Chapter 1 would surely tell us that this is a potential
"public goods" problem. If it is hard to exclude others from the resource—it
is cheap and easy to copy—and if the use of the resource is not "rival"—if I
don't use up your facts by consulting them—then we ought to see the kind of
dystopia economists predict. What would that consist of? First it might result
in underproduction. Databases with a social value higher than their cost of
creation would not get made because the creator could not get an adequate
return on investment. In some cases it might even lead to the reverse—
overproduction, where each party creates the database for itself. We get a social overinvestment to produce the resource because there is no legal right to
exclude others from it. If you gave the first creator an intellectual property
right over the data, they could sell to subsequent users at a price lower than
their own cost to create the database. Everyone would win. But the United
States did not give the intellectual property right and yet its database industry
is flourishing. There are lots of commercial database providers and many different kinds of databases. How can this be? Is the economic model wrong?

The answer to that is no, the model is not wrong. It is, however, incomplete and all too often applied in sweeping ways without acknowledging that
its basic assumptions may not hold in a particular case. That sounds vague.
Let me give a concrete example. Westlaw is one of the two leading legal database providers and, as I mentioned before, one of the key proponents of creating intellectual property rights over unoriginal databases. (There is considerable
question whether such a law would be constitutional in the United States, but
I will pass over that argument for the moment.) Westlaw's "problem" is that
much of the material that it provides to its subscribers is not covered by copyright. Under Section 105 of the U.S. Copyright Act, works of the federal

government cannot be copyrighted. They pass immediately into the public domain. Thus all the federal court decisions, from district courts all the way up to the Supreme Court, all the federal statutes, the infinite complexity of the *Federal Register*, all this is free from copyright. This might seem logical for government-created work, for which the taxpayer has already paid, but as I will explain in the next section of the chapter, not every country adopts such a policy.

West, another Thomson subsidiary that owns Westlaw, publishes the standard case reporter series. When lawyers or judges refer to a particular opinion, or quote a passage within an opinion, they will almost always use the page number of the West edition. After all, if no one else can find the cases or statutes or paragraphs of an opinion that you are referring to, legal argument is all but impossible. (This might seem like a great idea to you. I beg to differ.) As electronic versions of legal materials became more prevalent, West began getting more competition. Its competitors did two things that West found unforgivable. First, they frequently copied the text of the cases from West's electronic services, or CD-ROMs, rather than retyping them themselves. Since the cases were works of the federal government, this was perfectly legal provided the competitors did not include West's own material, such as summaries of the cases written by its employees or its key number system for finding related issues. Second, the competitors would include, within their electronic editions, the page numbers to West's editions. Since lawyers need to cite the precise words or arguments they are referring to, providing the raw opinion alone would have been all but useless. Because West's page numbers were one of the standard ways to cite case opinions, competitors would indicate where the page breaks on the printed page would have been, just as West did in its own databases.

West's reaction to all of this was exactly like Apple's reaction in the story I told in Chapter 5 about the iPod or like Rural's reaction to the copying of its phone directory. This was theft! They were freeloading on West's hard work! West had mixed its sweat with these cites, and so should be able to exclude other people from them! Since it could not claim copyright over the cases, West claimed copyright over the order in which they were arranged, saying that when its competitors provided its page numbers for citation purposes, they were infringing that copyright.

In the end, West lost its legal battles to claim copyright over the arrangement of the collections of cases and the sequence in which they were presented. The Court held that, as with the phone directory, the order in which the cases were arranged lacked the minimum originality required to sustain a copyright claim.[4] At this stage, according to the standard public goods story, West's business should have collapsed. Unable to exclude competitors from much of the raw material of its databases, West would be undercut by competitors. More importantly, from the point of view of intellectual property policy, its fate would deter potential investors in other databases—databases that we would lose without even knowing they could have been possible. Except that is not the way it turned out. West has continued to thrive. Indeed, its profits have been quite remarkable. How can this be?

The West story shows us three ways in which we can leap too quickly from the abstract claim that some information goods are public goods— nonexcludable and nonrival—to the claim that this particular information good has those attributes. The reality is much more complex. Type www .westlaw.com into your Internet browser. That will take you to the home page of West's excellent legal research service. Now, I have a password to that site. You probably do not. Without a password, you cannot get access to West's site at all. To the average consumer, the password acts as a physical or technical barrier, making the good "excludable"—that is, making it possible to exclude someone from it without invoking intellectual property rights. But what about competitors? They could buy access and use that access to download vast quantities of the material that is unprotected by copyright. Or could they? Again, West can erect a variety of barriers, ranging from technical limits on how much can be downloaded to contractual restrictions on what those who purchase its service can do ("No copying every federal case," for example).

Let's say the competitor somehow manages to get around all this. Let's say it somehow avoids copying the material that West does have a copyright over—such as the headnotes and case synopses. The competitor launches their competing site at lower prices amidst much fanfare. Do I immediately and faithlessly desert West for a lower-priced competitor? Not at all. First of all, there are lots of useful things in the West database that *are* covered by copyright—law review articles and certain treatises, for example. The competitor frequently cannot copy those without coming to the same sort of agreements that West has with the copyright holders. For much legal research, that secondary material is as important as the cases. If West has both, and the competitor only one, I will stick with West. Second, West's service is very well designed. (It is only their copyright policies I dislike, not the product.) If a judge cites a law review article in a case, West will helpfully provide a hyperlink to the precise section of the article she is referring to. I can click on it and in a second see what the substance of the argument is. The reverse is true if a law review article cites a statute or a case. Cases have "flags" on them indicating whether they have been overruled or cited approvingly in subsequent decisions. In other words, faced with the competitive pressure of those who would commoditize their service and provide it at lower cost, West has done what any smart company would: added features and competed by offering a superior service. Often it has done so by "tying" its uncopyrightable data structures to its huge library of copyrighted legal material.

The company that challenged Westlaw in court was called Hyperlaw. It won triumphantly. The courts declared that federal cases and the page numbers in the West volumes were in the public domain. That decision came in 1998 and Westlaw has lobbied hard since then to reverse it by statute, to create some version of the Database Directive in the United States. To date, they have failed. The victor, Hyperlaw, has since gone out of business. Westlaw has not.

This little story contains a larger truth. It is true that innovation and information goods will, in general, tend to be less excludable and less rival than a ham sandwich, say. But, in practice, some of them will be linked or connected in their social setting to other phenomena that are highly excludable. The software can easily be copied—but access to the help lines can be restricted with ease. Audiences cannot easily be excluded from viewing television broadcasts, but advertisers can easily be excluded from placing their advertisements in those programs. The noncopyrightable court decisions are of most use when embedded within a technical system that gives easy access to other material—some of it copyrighted and all of it protected by technical measures and contractual restrictions. The music file can be downloaded; the band's T-shirt or the experience of the live concert cannot. Does this mean that we never need an intellectual property right? Not at all. But it does indicate that we need to be careful when someone claims that "without a *new* intellectual property right I am doomed."

One final story may drive home the point. When they read *Feist v. Rural,* law students often assume that the only reason Feist offered to license the white pages listings from Rural is because they (mistakenly) thought they were copyrighted. This is unlikely. Most good copyright lawyers would have told you at the time of the *Feist* case that the "sweat of the brow" decisions that gave copyright protection based on hard work were not good law. Most courts of appeals had said so. True, there was some legal uncertainty, and that is often worth paying to avoid. But switch the question around and suppose it is the day after the Supreme Court decides the *Feist* case, and Feist is heading off into another market to try to make a new regional phone directory. Do they now just take the numbers without paying for them, or do they still try to negotiate a license? The latter is overwhelmingly likely. Why? Well, for one thing, they would get a computer-readable version of the names and would not have to retype or optically scan them. More importantly, the contract could include a right to immediate updates and new listings.

The day after the *Feist* decision, the only thing that had changed in the telephone directory market was that telephone companies knew for sure, rather than merely as a probability, that if they refused to license, their competitors could laboriously copy their old listings without penalty. The nuclear option was no longer available. Maybe the price demanded would be a little lower. But there would still be lots of good reasons for Feist to buy the information, even though it was uncopyrighted. You do not always need an intellectual property right to make a deal. Of course, that is not the whole story. Perhaps the incentives provided by other methods are insufficient. But in the U.S. database industry they do not seem to have been. Quite the contrary. The studies we have on the European and the American rules on database rights indicate that the American approach simply works better.

I was not always opposed to intellectual property rights over data. Indeed, in a book written before the enactment of the Database Directive, I said that there was a respectable economic argument that such protection might be warranted and that we needed research on the issue.[5] Unfortunately, Europe got the right without the research. The facts are now in. If the European Database Directive were a drug, the government would be pulling it from the market until its efficacy and harmfulness could be reassessed. At the very least, the Commission needed a detailed empirical review of the directive's effects, and needs to adjust the directive's definitions and fine-tune its limitations. But there is a second lesson. There is more discussion of the empirical economic effects of the Database Directive in this chapter than in the six-hundred-page review of the directive that the European Commission paid a private company to conduct, and which was the first official document to consider the issue.

That seemed to me and to many other academics to be a scandal and we said so as loudly as we could, pointing out the empirical evidence suggesting that the directive was not working. Yet if it was a scandal, it was not a surprising one, because the evidence-free process is altogether typical of the way we make intellectual property policy. President Bush is not the only one to make "faith-based" decisions.

There was, however, a ray of hope. In its official report on the competitive effects of the Database Directive, the European Commission recently went beyond reliance on anecdote and industry testimony and did something amazing and admirable. It conducted an empirical evaluation of whether the directive was actually doing any good.

The report honestly described the directive as "a Community creation with no precedent in any international convention." Using a methodology similar to the one in this chapter on the subject, the Commission found that "the economic impact of the 'sui generis' right on database production is unproven. Introduced to stimulate the production of databases in Europe, the new instrument has had no proven impact on the production of databases."[6]

In fact, their study showed that the production of databases had fallen to pre-directive levels and that the U.S. database industry, which has no such intellectual property right, was growing faster than the European Union's. The gap appears to be widening. This is consistent with the data I had pointed out in newspaper articles on the subject, but the Commission's study was more recent and, if anything, more damning.

Commission insiders hinted that the study may be part of a larger—and welcome—transformation in which a more professional and empirical look is being taken at the competitive effects of intellectual property protection. Could we be moving away from faith-based policy in which the assumption is that the more new rights we create, the better off we will be? Perhaps. But unfortunately, while the report was a dramatic improvement, traces of the Commission's older predilection for faith-based policy and voodoo economics still remain.

The Commission coupled its empirical study of whether the directive had actually stimulated the production of new databases with another intriguing kind of empiricism. It sent out a questionnaire to the European database industry asking if they liked their intellectual property right—a procedure with all the rigor of setting farm policy by asking French farmers how they feel about agricultural subsidies. More bizarrely still, the report sometimes juxtaposed the two studies as if they were of equivalent worth. Perhaps this method of decision making could be expanded to other areas. We could set communications policy by conducting psychoanalytic interviews with state telephone companies—let current incumbents' opinions determine what is good for the market as a whole. "What is your emotional relationship with your monopoly?" "I really like it!" "Do you think it hurts competition?" "Not at all!"

There are also a few places where the reasoning in the report left one scratching one's head. One goal of the database right was to help close the gap between the size of the European and U.S. database markets. Even before the directive, most European countries already gave greater protection than the United States to compilations of fact. The directive raised the level still higher. The theory was that this would help build European market share. Of course, the opposite is also possible. Setting intellectual property rights too high can actually stunt innovation. In practice, as the Commission's report observes, "the ratio of European / U.S. database production, which was nearly 1:2 in 1996, has become 1:3 in 2004."[7] Europe had started with higher protection and a smaller market. Then it raised its level of protection and lost even more ground. Yet the report was oddly diffident about the possibility that the U.S. system actually works better.

In its conclusion, the report offered a number of possibilities, including repealing the directive, amending it to limit or remove the "sui generis" right while leaving the rest of the directive in place, and keeping the system as it is. The first options are easy to understand. Who would want to keep a system when it is not increasing database production, or European market share, and, indeed, might be actively harmful? Why leave things as they are? The report offers several reasons.

First, database companies want to keep the directive. (The report delicately notes that their "endorsement . . . is somewhat at odds with the continued success of U.S. publishing and database production that thrives without . . . [such] protection," but nevertheless appears to be "a political reality.") Second, repealing the directive would reopen the debate on what level of protection is needed. Third, change may be costly.

Imagine applying these arguments to a drug trial. The patients in the control group have done better than those given the drug and there is evidence that the drug might be harmful. But the drug companies like their profits and want to keep the drug on the market. Though "somewhat at odds" with the evidence, this is a "political reality." Getting rid of the drug would reopen the debate on the search for a cure. Change is costly—true. But what is the purpose of a review if the status quo is always to be preferred?

The final result? Faced with what Commission staff members tell me was a tidal wave of lobbying from publishers, the Commission quietly decided to leave the directive unchanged, despite the evidence. The result itself is not remarkable. Industry capture of a regulatory apparatus is hardly a surprise. What is remarkable is that this is one of the first times any entity engaged in making intellectual property policy on the international level has even looked seriously at the empirical evidence of that policy's effects.

To be sure, figures are thrown around in hearings. The software industry will present studies showing, for example, that it has lost billions of dollars because of illicit copying. It has indeed lost profits relative to what it could get with all the benefits of cheaper copying and transmission worldwide *and with perfect copyright enforcement as well.* (Though the methodology of some of the studies, which assumes that each copier would have paid full price—is ridiculous.) But this simply begs the question. A new technology is introduced that increases the size of your market and decreases your costs dramatically, but also increases illicit copying. Is this cause for state intervention to increase your level of rights or the funds going toward enforcement of copyright law, as opposed to any other law enforcement priority? The question for empirical analysis, both before and after a policy change, should be "Is this change necessary in order to maintain incentives for production and distribution? Will whatever benefits it brings outweigh the costs of static and dynamic losses— price increases to consumers and impediments to future innovators?" The content companies might still be able to justify the extensions of their rights. But they would be doing so in the context of a rational, evidence-based debate about the real goals of intellectual property, not on the assumption that they have a natural right to collect all the economic surplus gained by a reduction in the costs of reproduction and distribution.

DOES PUBLIC INFORMATION WANT TO BE FREE?

The United States has much to learn from Europe about information policy. The ineffectively scattered U.S. approach to data privacy, for example, produces random islands of privacy protection in a sea of potential vulnerability. Until recently, your video rental records were better protected than your medical records. Europe, by contrast, has tried to establish a holistic framework, a much more effective approach. But there are places where the lessons should flow the other way. The first one, I have suggested, is database protection. The second is a related but separate issue: the legal treatment of publicly generated data, the huge, and hugely important, flow of information produced by government-funded activities—from ordnance survey maps and weather data to state-produced texts, traffic studies, and scientific information. How is this flow of information distributed? The norm turns out to be very different in the United States and in Europe.

In one part of the world, state-produced data flows are frequently viewed as revenue sources. They are often copyrighted or protected by database rights. Many of the departments which produce them attempt to make a profit or at least to recover their entire operating costs through user fees. It is heresy to suggest that the taxpayer has already paid for the production of this data and should not have to do so twice. The other part of the world practices a benign form of information socialism. By law, any text produced by the central government is free from copyright and passes immediately into the public domain. The basic norm is that public data flows should be available at the cost of reproduction alone.

It is easy to guess which area is which. The United States is surely the profit- and property-obsessed realm, Europe the place where the state takes pride in providing data as a public service? No, actually, it is the other way around.

Take weather data. The United States makes complete weather data available to all at the cost of reproduction. If the superb government Web sites and data feeds are insufficient, for the cost of a box of blank DVDs you can have the entire history of weather records across the continental United States. European countries, by contrast, typically claim government copyright over weather data and often require the payment of substantial fees. Which approach is better? I have been studying the issue for fifteen years, and if I had to suggest a single article it would be the magisterial study by Peter Weiss called "Borders in Cyberspace," published by the National Academies of Science.[8] Weiss shows that the U.S. approach generates far more social wealth. True, the information is initially provided for free, but a thriving private weather industry has sprung up which takes the publicly funded data as its raw material and then adds value to it. The U.S. weather risk management industry, for example, is more than ten times bigger than the European one, employing more people, producing more valuable products, generating more social wealth. Another study estimates that Europe invests 9.5 billion Euros in weather data and gets approximately 68 billion back in economic value—in everything from more efficient farming and construction decisions to better holiday planning—a sevenfold multiplier. The United States, by contrast, invests twice as much—19 billion—but gets back a return of 750 billion Euros, a thirty-nine-fold multiplier.

Other studies suggest similar patterns elsewhere, in areas ranging from geospatial data to traffic patterns and agriculture. The "free" information flow is better at priming the pump of economic activity.

Some readers may not thrill to this way of looking at things because it smacks of private corporations getting a "free ride" on the public purse—social wealth be damned. But the benefits of open data policies go further. Every year the monsoon season kills hundreds and causes massive property damage in Southeast Asia. One set of monsoon rains alone killed 660 people in India and left 4.5 million homeless. Researchers seeking to predict the monsoon sought complete weather records from the United States and Europe so as to generate a model based on global weather patterns. The U.S. data was easily and cheaply available at the cost of reproduction. The researchers could not afford to pay the price asked by the European weather services, precluding the "ensemble" analysis they sought to do. Weiss asks rhetorically, "What is the economic and social harm to over 1 billion people from hampered research?" In the wake of the outpouring of sympathy for tsunami victims in the same region, this example seems somehow even more tragic. Will the pattern be repeated with seismographic, cartographic, and satellite data? One hopes not.

The European attitude may be changing. Competition policy has already been a powerful force in pushing countries to rethink their attitudes to government data. The European Directive on the Reuse of Public Sector Information takes large strides in the right direction, as do studies by the Organization for Economic Co-operation and Development (OECD) and several national initiatives.[9] Unfortunately, though, most of these follow the same pattern. An initially strong draft is watered down and the utterly crucial question of whether data should be provided at the marginal cost of reproduction is fudged or avoided. This is a shame. Again, if we really believed in evidence-based policy making, the debate would be very different.

BREAKING THE DEAL

What would the debate look like if we took some of the steps I mention here? Unfortunately there are very few examples of evidence-based policy making, but the few that do exist are striking.

In 2006, the government-convened Gowers Review of intellectual property policy in the United Kingdom considered a number of proposals on changes to copyright law, including a retrospective extension of sound recording copyright terms.[10] The copyright term for sound recordings in the United Kingdom is fifty years. (It is longer for compositions.) At the end of the fifty-year period, the recording enters the public domain. If the composition is also in the public domain—the great orchestral works of Beethoven, Brahms, and Mozart, for example, or the jazz classics of the early twentieth century—then anyone can copy the recording. This means we could make it freely available in an online repository for music students throughout Britain—perhaps preparing the next generation of performers—or republish it in a digitally cleansed and enhanced edition. If the composition is still under copyright, as with much popular music, then the composer is still entitled to a licensing fee, but now any music publisher who pays that fee can reissue the work—introducing competition and, presumably, bringing down prices of the recording.

The recording industry, along with successful artists such as Sir Cliff Richard and Ian Anderson of Jethro Tull, wished to extend the fifty-year term to ninety-five years, or perhaps even longer—the life of the performer, plus seventy years. This proposal was not just for new recordings, but for the ones that have already been made.

Think of the copyright system as offering a deal to artists and record companies. "We will enlist the force of the state to give you fifty years of monopoly over your recordings. During that time, you will have the exclusive right to distribute and reproduce your recording. After that time, it is available to all, just as you benefited from the availability of public domain works from your predecessors. Will you make records under these terms?"

Obviously, fifty years of legalized exclusivity was enough of an incentive to get them to make the music in the first place. We have the unimpeachable evidence that they actually did. Now they want to change the terms of the deal retrospectively. They say this will "harmonize" the law internationally, give recordings the same treatment as compositions, help struggling musicians, and give the recording industry some extra money that it might spend on developing new talent. (Or on Porsches, shareholder dividends, and plastic ducks. If you give me another forty-five years of monopoly rent, I can spend it as I wish.)

Change the context and think about how you would react to this if the deal was presented to you personally. You hired an artist to paint a portrait. You offered $500. He agreed. You had a deal. He painted the painting. You liked it. You gave him the money. A few years later he returned. "You owe me another $450," he said.

You both looked at the contract. "But you agreed to paint it for $500 and I paid you that amount." He admitted this was true, but pointed out that painters in other countries sometimes received higher amounts, as did sculptors in our own country. In fact, he told you, all painters in our country planned to demand another $450 for each picture they had already painted as well as for future pictures. This would "harmonize" our prices with other countries, put painting on the same footing as sculpture, and enable painters to hire more apprentices. His other argument was that painters often lost money. Only changing the terms of their deals long after they were struck could keep them in business. Paying the money was your duty. If you did not pay, it meant that you did not respect art and private property.

You would find these arguments absurd. Yet they are the same ones the record industry used, relying heavily on the confusions against which this book has warned. Is the record companies' idea as outrageous as the demands of my imaginary painter? It is actually worse.

The majority of sound recordings made more than forty years ago are commercially unavailable. After fifty years, only a tiny percentage are still being sold. It is extremely hard to find the copyright holders of the remainder. They might have died, gone out of business, or simply stopped caring. Even if the composer can be found, or paid through a collection society, without the consent of the holder of the copyright over the musical recording, the work must stay in the library. These are "orphan works"—a category that probably comprises the majority of twentieth-century cultural artifacts.

Yet as I pointed out earlier, without the copyright holder's permission, it is illegal to copy or redistribute or perform these works, even if it is done on a nonprofit basis. The goal of copyright is to encourage the production of, and public access to, cultural works. It has done its job in encouraging production. Now it operates as a fence to discourage access. As the years go by, we continue to lock up 100 percent of our recorded culture from a particular year in order to benefit an ever-dwindling percentage—the lottery winners—in a grotesquely inefficient cultural policy.

Finally, fifty years after they were made, sound recordings enter the public domain in the United Kingdom (though as I pointed out earlier, licensing fees would still be due to the composer if the work itself was still under copyright). Now anyone—individual, company, specialist in public domain material—could offer the work to the public. But not if the record companies can persuade the government otherwise. Like my imaginary painter, they want to change the terms of the deal retrospectively. But at least the painter's proposal would not make the vast majority of paintings unavailable just to benefit a tiny minority of current artists.

The recording industry's proposal for retrospective extension was effectively a tax on the British music-buying public to benefit the copyright holders of a tiny proportion of sound recordings. The public loses three times. It loses first when it is forced to continue to pay monopoly prices for older, commercially available music, rather than getting the benefit of the bargain British legislators originally offered: fifty years of exclusivity, then the public domain. The public loses a second time when, as a side effect, it is denied access to commercially unavailable music; no library or niche publisher can make the forgotten recordings available again. Finally, the public loses a third time because allowing retrospective extensions will distort the political process in the future, leading to an almost inevitable legislative capture by the tiny minority who find that their work still has commercial value at the end of the copyright term they were originally granted. As Larry Lessig has pointed out repeatedly, the time to have the debate about the length of the copyright term is before we know whose works will survive commercially.

The whole idea is very silly. But if this is the silly idea we wish to pursue, then simply increase the income tax proportionately and distribute the benefits to those record companies and musicians whose music is still commercially available after fifty years. Require them to put the money into developing new artists—something the current proposal does not do. Let all the other recordings pass into the public domain.

Of course, no government would consider such an idea for a moment. Tax the public to give a monopoly windfall to those who already hit the jackpot, because they claim their industry cannot survive without retrospectively changing the terms of its deals? It is indeed laughable. Yet it is a far better proposal than the one that was presented to the Gowers Review.

What happened next was instructive. The Review commissioned an economic study of the effects of copyright term extension—both prospective and retrospective—on recorded music from the University of Cambridge's Centre for Intellectual Property and Information Law. The resulting document was a model of its kind.[11]

With painstaking care and a real (if sometimes fruitless) attempt to make economic arguments accessible to ordinary human beings, the study laid out the costs and benefits of extending the copyright term over sound recordings. It pointed out that the time to measure the value of a prospective term extension is at the moment the copyright is granted. Only then does it produce its incentive effects. The question one must ask is how much value today does it give an artist or record company to have their copyright extended by a year at the end of the existing period of protection. Then one must look to see whether the benefits of the added incentive outweigh the social costs it imposes. To put it another way, if the state were selling today the rights to have protection from year fifty to year ninety-five, how much would a rational copyright holder pay, particularly knowing that there is only a small likelihood the work will even be commercially available to take advantage of the extension? Would that amount be greater than the losses imposed on society by extending the right?

Obviously, the value of the extension is affected by our "discount rate"—the annual amount by which we must discount a pound sterling in royalties I will not receive for fifty-one years in order to find its value now. Unsurprisingly, one finds that the value of that pound in the future is tiny at the moment when it matters—today—in the calculation of an artist or distributor making the decision whether to create. Conservative estimates yield a present value between 3 percent and 9 percent of the eventual amount. By that analysis, a pound in fifty years is worth between three and nine pence to you today, while other estimates have the value falling below one penny. This seems unlikely to spur much creativity at the margin. Or to put it in the more elegant language of Macaulay, quoted in Chapter 2:

> I will take an example. Dr. Johnson died fifty-six years ago. If the law were what my honourable and learned friend wishes to make it, somebody would now have the monopoly of Dr. Johnson's works. Who that somebody would be it is impossible to say; but we may venture to guess. I guess, then, that it would have been some bookseller, who was the assign of another bookseller, who was the grandson of a third bookseller, who had bought the copyright from Black Frank, the Doctor's servant and residuary legatee, in 1785 or 1786. Now, would the knowledge that this copyright would exist in 1841 have been a source of gratification to Johnson? Would it have stimulated his exertions? Would it have once drawn him out of his bed before noon? Would it have once cheered him under a fit of the spleen? Would it have induced him to give us one more allegory, one more life of a poet, one more imitation of Juvenal? I firmly believe not. I firmly believe that a hundred years ago, when he was writing our debates for the Gentleman's Magazine, he would very much rather have had twopence to buy a plate of shin of beef at a cook's shop underground.[12]

The art form is different, but the thought of a 1960s Cliff Richard or Ian Anderson being "cheered under a fit of the spleen" by the prospect of a copyright extension fifty years hence is truly a lovely one.

Considering all these factors, as well as the effects on investment in British versus American music and on the balance of trade, the Cambridge study found that the extension would cost consumers between 240 and 480 million pounds, far more than the benefits to performers and recording studios. (In practice, the report suggested, without changes in the law, most of the benefits would not have gone to the original recording artist in any case.) It found prospective extension led to a clear social welfare loss. What of retrospective extension?

The report considered, and found wanting, arguments that retrospective extension is necessary to encourage "media migration"—the digitization of existing works, for example. In fact, most studies have found precisely the reverse—that public domain works are more available and more frequently adapted into different media. (Look on Amazon.com for a classic work that is out of copyright—*Moby-Dick*, for example—and see how many adaptations and formats are available.) It also rejected the argument that harmonization alone was enough to justify extension—retrospective or prospective—pointing out the considerable actual variation in both term and scope of rights afforded to performers in different countries. Finally, it warned of the "hidden 'ratcheting' effect of harmonisation which results from the fact that harmonisation is almost invariably upwards." Its conclusion was simple:

> [R]etrospective term extensions **reduce** social welfare. Thus, in this case, it would seem that basic theory alone is sufficient to provide strong, and unambiguous, guidance for policy-makers. . . . We therefore see no reason to quarrel with the consensus of the profession on this issue which as summed up by Akerlof et al. . . . [states] categorically that . . . "[retrospective] extension provides essentially no incentive to create new works. Once a work is created, additional compensation to the producer is simply a windfall."[13]

The Gowers Review agreed. Its fourth recommendation read simply, "Policy makers should adopt the principle that the term and scope of protection for IP rights should not be altered retrospectively." Perhaps more important, though, was the simple paragraph at the front of the document captioned "The Approach of the Review." It begins thus: "The Review takes an evidence-based approach to its policy analysis and has supplemented internal analysis by commissioning external experts to examine the economic impact of changes. . . ."

Why specify that one was taking an "evidence-based" approach? At first, the comment seems unnecessary. What other approach would one take? Anecdotal? Astrological? But there is a framework in which empirical evidence of the effects of policy simply seems irrelevant—one based on natural right. When the Review was given to the House of Commons Select Committee on Culture, Media and Sport, that frame of mind was much in evidence:

> The Gowers Review undertook an extensive analysis of the argument for extending the term. On economic grounds, the Review concluded that there was little

evidence that extension would benefit performers, increase the number of works created or made available, or provide incentives for creativity; and it noted a potentially negative effect on the balance of trade. . . . Gowers's analysis was thorough and in economic terms may be correct. It gives the impression, however, of having been conducted *entirely* on economic grounds. We strongly believe that copyright represents a moral right of a creator to choose to retain ownership and control of their own intellectual property. We have not heard a convincing reason why a composer and his or her heirs should benefit from a term of copyright which extends for lifetime and beyond, but a performer should not. . . . Given the strength and importance of the creative industries in the U.K., it seems extraordinary that the protection of intellectual property rights should be weaker here than in many other countries whose creative industries are less successful.[14]

A couple of things are worth noting here. The first is that the Committee is quite prepared to believe that the effects of term extension would not benefit performers or provide incentives for creativity, and even to believe that it would hurt the balance of trade. The second is the curious argument in the last sentence. Other countries have stronger systems of rights and are less successful. We should change our regime to be more like them! Obviously the idea that a country's creative industries might be less successful *because* their systems of rights were stronger does not occur to the Committee for a moment. Though it proclaims itself to be unaffected by economic thought, it is in fact deeply influenced by the "more rights equals more innovation" ideology of maximalism that I have described in these pages.

Nestling between these two apparently contradictory ideas is a serious argument that needs to be confronted. Should we ignore evidence—even conclusive evidence—of negative economic effects, harm to consumers, and consequences for the availability of culture because we are dealing with an issue of moral right, almost natural right? Must we extend the rights of the artists who recorded those songs (or rather the record companies who immediately acquired their copyrights) because they are simply *theirs* as a matter of natural justice? Do performers have a natural right to recorded songs either because they have labored on them, mixing their sweat with each track, or because something of their personality is forever stamped into the song? Must we grant an additional forty-five years of commercial exclusivity, not because of economic incentive, but because of natural right?

Most of us feel the pull of this argument. I certainly do. But as I pointed out in Chapter 2, there are considerable problems with such an idea. First, it runs against the premises of actual copyright systems. In the United States, for example, the Constitution resolutely presents the opposite picture. Exclusive rights are to encourage progress in science and the useful arts. The Supreme Court has elaborated on this point many times, rejecting both labor-based "sweat of the brow" theories of copyright and more expansive visions based on a natural right to the products of one's genius—whether inventions or novels. Britain, too, has a history of looking to copyright as a utilitarian scheme—though with more reference to, and legal protection of, particular "moral rights" than one finds in the United States. But even in the most expansive "moral rights" legal systems, even in the early days of debate about the rights of authors after the French Revolution, it is accepted that there are temporal limits on these rights. If this is true of authors, it is even more true of performers, who are not granted the full suite of author's rights in moral rights jurisdictions, being exiled to a form of protection called "neighboring" rights.

In all of these schemes, there are time limits on the length of the rights (and frequently different ones for different creators—authors, inventors, performers, and so on). Once one has accepted that point, the question of how long they should be is, surely, a matter for empirical and utilitarian analysis. One cannot credibly say that natural rights or the deep deontological structure of the universe gives me a right to twenty-eight or fifty-six or seventy years of exclusivity. The argument must turn instead to a question of consequences. Which limit is better? Once one asks that question, the Gowers Review's economic assessment is overwhelming, as the Select Committee itself recognized. In the end, the government agreed—noting that a European Union study had found precisely the same thing. The sound recording right should not be extended, still less extended retrospectively. The evidence-free zone had been penetrated. But not for long. As this book went to press, the European Commission announced its support for an even longer Europe-wide extension of the sound recording right. The contrary arguments and empirical evidence were ignored, minimized, explained away. How can this pattern be broken?

In the next and final chapter, I try to answer that question. I offer a partial explanation for the cognitive and organizational blindnesses that have brought us to this point. I argue that we have much to learn from the history, theory, and organizational practices of the environmental movement. The environmental movement taught us to see "the environment" for the first time, to recognize its importance, and to change the way we thought about ecology, property, and economics in consequence. What we need is an environmentalism of mind, of culture, of information. In the words of my colleague David Lange, we need to "recognize the public domain." And to save it.

10

An Environmentalism
for Information

Over the last fifteen years, a group of scholars have finally persuaded economists to believe something noneconomists find obvious: "behavioral economics" shows that people do not act as economic theory predicts. But hold your cheers. This is not a vindication of folk wisdom over the pointy-heads. The deviations from "rational behavior" are not the wonderful cornucopia of human motivations you might imagine. There are patterns. For example, we are systematically likely to overestimate chances of loss and underestimate chances of gain, to rely on simplifying heuristics to frame problems even when those heuristics are contradicted by the facts.

Some of the patterns are endearing; the supposedly "irrational" concerns for distributive equality that persist in all but the economically trained and the extreme right, for example. But most of them simply involve the mapping of cognitive bias. We can take advantage of those biases, as those who sell us ludicrously expensive and irrational warranties on consumer goods do. Or we can correct for them, like a pilot who is trained to rely on his instruments rather than his faulty perceptions when flying in heavy cloud.

This book has introduced you to the wonders and terrors of intellectual property law—the range wars of the Internet age. There have been discussions of synthetic biology and musical sampling, digital locks and the hackers who break them, Jefferson and Macaulay, and the fight over video recorders. Now it is time to sum up.

I would argue that the chapters in this book present evidence of another kind of cognitive bias, one that the behavioral economists have not yet identified. Call it the openness aversion. Cultural agoraphobia. We are systematically likely to undervalue the importance, viability, and productive power of open systems, open networks, and nonproprietary production.

CULTURAL AGORAPHOBIA?

Test yourself on the following questions. In each case, it is 1991 and I have removed from you all knowledge of the years since then. (For some, this might be a relief.)

The first question is a thought experiment I introduced in Chapter 4. You have to design an international computer network. One group of scientists describes a system that is fundamentally open: open protocols and open systems so that anyone could connect to the system and offer information or products to the world. Another group—scholars, businesspeople, bureaucrats—points out the problems. Anyone could connect to the system! They could do anything! The system itself would not limit them to a few approved actions or approved connections. There would be porn, and piracy, and viruses, and spam. Terrorists could put up videos glorifying themselves. Your neighbor's site could compete with the *New York Times* or the U.S. government in documenting the war in Iraq. Better to have a well-managed system in which official approval is required to put up a site, where only a few selected actions are permitted by the network protocols, where most of us are merely recipients of information, where spam, viruses, and piracy (and innovation and participatory culture and anonymous speech) are impossible. Which network design would you have picked? Remember, you have no experience of blogs, or mashups, or Google; no experience of the Web. Just you and your cognitive filters.

Imagine a form of software which anyone could copy and change, created under a license which required subsequent programmers to offer their software on the same terms. Imagine legions of programmers worldwide contributing their creations back into a "commons." Is this anarchic-sounding method of production economically viable? Could it successfully compete with the hierarchically organized corporations producing proprietary, closed code, controlled by both law and technology? Be truthful.

Finally, set yourself the task of producing the greatest reference work the world has ever seen. You are told that it must cover everything from the best Thai food in Durham to the annual rice production of Thailand, from the best places to see blue whales to the history of the Blue Dog Coalition. Would you create a massive organization of paid experts, each assigned a topic, with hierarchical layers of editors above them, producing a set of encyclopedic tomes that are rigorously controlled by copyright and trademark? Or would you wait for hobbyists, governments, scientists, and volunteer encyclopedists to produce, and search engines to organize and rank, a cornucopia of information? I know which way I would have bet in 1991. But I also know that the last time I consulted an encyclopedia was in 1998. You?

It is not that openness is always right. It is not. Often we need strong intellectual property rights, privacy controls, and networks that demand authentication. Rather, it is that we need a balance between open and closed, owned and free, and we are systematically likely to get the balance wrong. (How did you do on the test?) Partly this is because we still don't understand the kind of property that lives on networks; most of our experience is with tangible property. Sandwiches that one hundred people cannot share. Fields that can be overgrazed if outsiders cannot be excluded. For that kind of property, control makes more sense. Like astronauts brought up in gravity, our reflexes are poorly suited for free fall. Jefferson's words were true even of grain elevators and hopper-boys. But in our world, the proportion of intangible to tangible property is much, much higher. The tendency to conflate intellectual and real property is even more dangerous in a networked world. We need his words more than he did.

Each of the questions I asked is related to the World Wide Web. Not the Internet, the collective name for the whole phenomenon, including the underlying methods of sending and receiving packets. Some version of the underlying network has been around for much longer, in one form or another. But it only attracted popular attention, only revolutionized the world, when on top of it was built the World Wide Web—the network of protocols and pages and hyperlinks that is so much a part of our lives and which arose only from Tim Berners-Lee's work at CERN in 1991.

My daughter will graduate from college in the year 2011. (At least, we both hope so.) She is older than the Web. It will not even have had its twentieth birthday on her graduation day. By Christmas of 2012, it will be able to drink legally in the United States. I wrote those sentences, but I find it hard to believe them myself. A life without the Web is easy to remember and yet hard to recapture fully. It seems like such a natural part of our world, too fixed to have been such a recent arrival, as if someone suggested that all the roads and buildings around you had arrived in the last fifteen years.

Some of you may find these words inexplicable because you live in a happy, Thoreau-like bliss, free of any contact with computer networks. If so, I take my hat off to you. The world of open sky and virtuous sweat, of books and sport and laughter, is no less dear to me than to you. Having an avatar in a virtual world holds the same interest as elective dental surgery. I care about the Web not because I want to live my life there, but because of what it has allowed us to achieve, what it represents for the potential of open science and culture. That, I think, is something that Thoreau (and even Emerson for that matter) might have cared about deeply. Yet, as I suggested earlier in this book, I seriously doubt that we would create the Web today—at least if policy makers and market incumbents understood what the technology might become early enough to stop it.

I am not postulating some sinister "Breakages, Limited" that stifles technological innovation. I am merely pointing out the imbalance between our intuitive perceptions of the virtues and dangers of open and closed systems, an imbalance I share, quite frankly.

In place of what we have today, I think we would try, indeed we are trying, to reinvent a tamer, more controlled Web and to change the nature of the underlying network on which it operates. (This is a fear I share with those who have written about it more eloquently than I, particularly Larry Lessig and Yochai Benkler.) We would restrict openness of access, decrease anonymity, and limit the number of actions that a network participant could perform. The benefits would be undeniable. It would cut down on spam, viruses, and illicit peer-to-peer file sharing. At the same time, it would undercut the iconoclastic technological, cultural, and political potential that the Web offers, the ability of a new technology, a new service to build on open networks and open protocols, without needing approval from regulators or entrenched market players, or even the owners of the Web pages to which you link.

Imagine, by contrast, an Internet and a World Wide Web that looked like America Online, circa 1996, or Compuserve, or the French state network Minitel. True, your exposure to penis-enhancement techniques, misspelled stock tips, and the penniless sons of Nigerian oil ministers would be reduced. That sounds pretty attractive. But the idea that the AOL search engine would be replaced by Yahoo and then Google, let alone Google Maps? That new forms of instant messaging would displace Compuserve's e-mail? That the Chinese dissident would have access to anonymized Internet services, that you might make phone calls worldwide for free from your computer, or that a blog like BoingBoing would end up having more page views than many major newspapers? Forget it. Goodbye to the radical idea that anyone can link to any page on the network without permission. A revised network could have the opposite rule and even impose it by default.

A tamer network could keep much tighter control over content, particularly copyrighted content. You might still get the video of the gentlemen doing strange things with Mentos and soda bottles, though not its viral method of distribution. But forget about "George Bush Doesn't Care About Black People" and all your favorite mashups. Its controlled network of links and its limited access would never unleash the collective fact-gathering genius the Web has shown. For a fee, you would have Microsoft Encarta and the *Encyclopedia Britannica* online. What about the "right-click universe" of knowledge about the world gathered by strangers, shared on comparatively open sites worldwide, and ordered by search engines? What about Wikipedia? I think not.

The counterfactual I offer is not merely a counterfactual. Yes, we got the Web. It spread too fast to think of taming it into the more mature, sedate "National Information Infrastructure" that the Clinton administration imagined. But as Larry Lessig pointed out years ago, the nature of a network can always be changed. The war over the control and design of the network, and the networked computer, is never-ending. As I write these words, the battles are over "trusted computing" and "Net neutrality." Trusted computing is a feature built into the operating system which makes it impossible to run processes that have not been approved by some outside body and digitally identified. It would indeed help to safeguard your computer from viruses and other threats and make it harder to copy material the content owners did not want you to copy (perhaps even if you had a right to). In the process it would help to lock in the power of those who had a dominant position in operating systems and popular programs. (Microsoft is a big supporter.) It would make open source software, which allows users to modify programs, inherently suspect. It would, in fact, as Jonathan Zittrain points out, change the nature of the general-purpose computer, which you can program to do *anything*, back toward the terminal which tells *you* what functions are allowed.[1] Think of a DVD player.

The attack on Net neutrality, by contrast, is an attempt by the companies who own the networks to be allowed to discriminate between favored and disfavored content, giving the former preferential access. (One wit analogized it to letting the phone company say, "we will delay your call to Pizza Hut for sixty seconds, but if you want to be put through to our featured pizza provider immediately, hit nine now!") Taken together, these proposals would put the control of the computer back in the hands of the owners of the content and the operating system, and control of the network users' choices in the hands of the person who sells them their bandwidth. At the same time, our intellectual property agenda is filled with proposals to create new intellectual property rights or extend old ones. That is the openness aversion in action.

Now, perhaps to you, the closed alternatives still sound better. Perhaps you do not care as much about the kind of technological dynamism, or anonymous speech, or cultural ferment that thrills the digerati. Perhaps you care more about the risks posed by the underlying freedom. That is a perfectly reasonable point of view. After all, openness does present real dangers; the same freedom given to the innovator, the artist, and the dissident is given to the predator and the criminal. At each moment in history when we have opened a communications network, or the franchise, or literacy, reasonable people have worried about the consequences that might ensue. Would expanded literacy lead to a general coarsening of the literary imagination? (Sometimes, perhaps. But it would and did lead to much more besides, to literature and culture of which we could not have dreamed.) Would an expanded franchise put the control of the state into the hands of the uneducated? (Yes, unless we had free national educational systems. "Now we must educate our masters" was the slogan of the educational reformers after the enlargement of the franchise in Britain in the nineteenth century. Openness sometimes begets openness.) Would translating the Bible from Latin into the vernacular open the door to unorthodox and heretical interpretations, to a congregation straying because they did not need to depend on a priestly intermediary with privileged access to the text? (Oh, yes indeed.) Would TV and radio play into the hands of demagogues? (Yes, and help expose their misdeeds.)

Openness is not always right. Far from it. But our prior experience seems to be that we are systematically better at seeing its dangers than its benefits. This book has been an attempt, in the sphere of intellectual property, to help us counteract that bias. Like the pilot in the cloud looking at his instruments, we might learn that we are upside down. But what do we do about it?

LEARNING FROM ENVIRONMENTALISM

I have argued that our policies are distorted not merely by industry capture or the power of incumbent firms, but by a series of cultural and economic biases or presuppositions: the equation of intellectual property to physical property; the assumption that whenever value is created, an intellectual property right should follow; the romantic idea of creativity that needs no raw material from which to build; the habit of considering the threats, but not the benefits, of new technologies; the notion that more rights will automatically bring more innovation; the failure to realize that the public domain is a vital contributor to innovation and culture; and a tendency to see the dangers of openness, but not its potential benefits.[2]

One of the most stunning pieces of evidence to our aversion to openness is that, for the last fifty years, whenever there has been a change in the law, it has almost always been to expand intellectual property rights. (Remember, this implies that every significant change in technology, society, or economy required more rights, never less, nor even the same amount.) We have done all this almost entirely in the absence of empirical evidence, and without empirical reconsideration to see if our policies were working. As I pointed out in the last chapter, intellectual property policy is an "evidence-free zone." It runs on faith alone and its faith consists of the cluster of ideas I have outlined in this book. Whether we call this cluster of ideas maximalism, cultural agoraphobia, or the openness aversion, it exercises a profound influence on our intellectual property and communications policy.

These ideas are not free-floating. They exist within, are influenced by, and in turn influence, a political economy. The political economy matters and it will shape any viable response. Even if the costs of getting the policies wrong are huge and unnecessary—think of the costs of the copyright extensions that lock up most of twentieth-century culture in order to protect the tiny fraction of it that is still commercially available—they are spread out over the entire population, while the benefits accrue to a small group of commercial entities that deeply and sincerely believe in the maximalist creed. This pattern of diffuse but large losses and concentrated gains is, as Mancur Olson taught us, a recipe for political malfunction.[3] Yet the problem is even deeper than that—in four ways.

First, though intellectual property rules will profoundly shape science, culture, and the market in the information age, they just seem obscure, wonkish, hard to get excited about. Certainly, people can get upset about individual examples—overbroad patents on human genes, copyright lawsuits against whistleblowers who leak e-mails showing corporate misdeeds that threaten the integrity of electronic voting, rules that paralyze documentary filmmakers, or require payment for sampling three notes from a prior song, extensions of rights that allow patents on auctions or business methods, make genres such as jazz seem legally problematic, create new rights over facts, or snarl up foundational technologies. But they see each of these as an isolated malfunction, not part of a larger social problem or set of attitudes.

Second, what holds true for issues, also holds true for communities. What links the person writing open source software, and trying to negotiate a sea of software patents in the process, to the film archivist trying to stir up interest in all the wonderful "orphan films"—still under copyright but with no copyright owner we can find—before they molder away into nitrate dust? When a university collaborates with Google to digitize books in their collection for the purposes of search and retrieval, even if only a tiny portion of the text will be visible for any work still under copyright, does it sense any common interest with the synthetic biologist trying to create the BioBricks Foundation, to keep open the foundational elements of a new scientific field? Both may be sued for their efforts—one connection at least.

When a developing nation tries to make use of the explicit "flexibilities" built into international trade agreements so as to make available a life-saving drug to its population through a process of compulsory licensing and compensation, it will find itself pilloried as a lawbreaker—though it is not—or punished through bilateral agreements. Will that process form any common interest with the high-technology industries in the United States who chafe at the way that current intellectual property rules enshrine older technologies and business methods and give them the protection of law? There are some links between those two situations. Will the parties see those links, or will the developing world's negotiators think that the current intellectual property rules express some monolithic "Western" set of interests? Will the high-tech companies think this is just an issue of dumb lawyers failing to understand technology? Each gap in understanding of common interest is a strike against an effective response.

Third, an effective political response would actually be easier if our current rules came merely from the relentless pursuit of corporate self-interest. (Here I part company with those who believe that self-interest is simply "there"— not shaped by socially constructed ideas, attitudes, ideologies, or biases.) In fact, the openness aversion sometimes obscures self-interest as well as the public interest. Think of the relentless insistence of the movie companies on making video recorders illegal. Nor does the framework of maximalism help if our goal is to have all the interested economic actors in the room when policy is made. For example, by framing issues of communications policy or Internet regulation as questions of intellectual property, we automatically privilege one set of interested parties—content owners—over others who also have a large economic stake in the matter.

Fourth, and finally, the biggest problem is that even if one could overcome the problems of political interest, or ideological closed-mindedness, the answers to many of these questions require balance, thought, and empirical evidence—all qualities markedly missing in the debate. If the answer were that intellectual property rights are bad, then forming good policy would be easy. But that is as silly and one-sided an idea as the maximalist one I have been criticizing here. Here are three examples:

1. Drug patents do help produce drugs. Jettisoning them is a bad idea— though experimenting with additional and alternative methods of encouraging medical innovation is a very good one.

2. I believe copyrights over literary works should be shorter, and that one should have to renew them after twenty-eight years—something that about 85 percent of authors and publishers will not do, if prior history is anything to go by. I think that would give ample incentives to write and distribute books, and give us a richer, more accessible culture and educational system to boot, a Library of Congress where you truly can "click to get the book" as my son asked me to do years ago now. But that does not mean that I wish to abolish copyright. On the contrary, I think it is an excellent system.

3. All the empirical evidence shows that protecting compilations of facts, as the European Database Directive does, has been a profound failure as a policy, imposing costs on consumers without encouraging new database production. But if the evidence said the opposite, I would support a new database right.

We need a political debate about intellectual property that recognizes these trade-offs; that does not impose simplistic, one-sided solutions; that looks to evidence. We need to understand the delicate and subtle balance between property and the opposite of property, the role of rights, but also of the public domain and the commons. Building a theory, let alone a movement, around such an issue is hard. Doing so when we lack some of the basic theoretical tools and vocabularies is daunting. We do not even have a robust conception of the public domain. If they think of it as a legal issue at all, people simply think of it as whatever is left over after an endless series of rights have been carved out. Can one build a politics to protect a *residue*?

So we have at least four problems: an issue that is perceived as obscure, affecting scattered groups with little knowledge of each other's interest, dominated by an ideology that is genuinely believed by its adherents, in the place of which we have to make careful, balanced, empirically grounded suggestions. Assume for a moment the need for a politics of intellectual property that seeks a solution to these four problems. What might such a politics look like?

I have argued that in a number of respects, the politics of intellectual property and the public domain is at the stage that the American environmental movement was at in the 1950s. In 1950, there were people who cared strongly about issues we would now identify as "environmental"—supporters of the park system and birdwatchers, but also hunters and those who disdained chemical pesticides in growing their foods. In the world of intellectual property, we have start-up software engineers, libraries, appropriationist artists, parodists, biographers, and biotech researchers. In the 50s and 60s, we had flurries of outrage over particular crises—burning rivers, oil spills, dreadful smog. In the world of intellectual property, we have the kind of stories I have tried to tell here. Lacking, however, is a general framework, a perception of common interest in apparently disparate situations.

Crudely speaking, the environmental movement was deeply influenced by two basic analytical frameworks. The first was the idea of ecology: the fragile, complex, and unpredictable interconnections between living systems. The second was the idea of welfare economics—the ways in which markets can fail to make activities internalize their full costs.[4] The combination of the two ideas yielded a powerful and disturbing conclusion. Markets would *routinely* fail to make activities internalize their own costs, particularly their own environmental costs. This failure would, routinely, disrupt or destroy fragile ecological systems, with unpredictable, ugly, dangerous, and possibly irreparable consequences. These two types of analysis pointed to a general interest in environmental protection and thus helped to build a large constituency which supported governmental efforts to that end. The duck hunter's preservation of wetlands as a species habitat turns out to have wider functions in the prevention of erosion and the maintenance of water quality. The decision to burn coal rather than natural gas for power generation may have impacts on everything from forests to fisheries. The attempt to reduce greenhouse gases and mitigate the damage from global warming cuts across every aspect of the economy.

Of course, it would be silly to think that environmental policy was fueled only by ideas rather than more immediate desires. As William Ruckelshaus put it, "With air pollution there was, for example, a desire of the people living in Denver to see the mountains again. Similarly, the people living in Los Angeles had a desire to see one another." Funnily enough, as with intellectual property, changes in communications technology also played a role. "In our living rooms in the middle sixties, black and white television went out and color television came in. We have only begun to understand some of the impacts of television on our lives, but certainly for the environmental movement it was a bonanza. A yellow outfall flowing into a blue river does not have anywhere near the impact on black and white television that it has on color television; neither does brown smog against a blue sky."[5] More importantly perhaps, the technologically fueled deluge of information, whether from weather satellites or computer models running on supercomputers, provided some of the evidence that—eventually—started to build a consensus around the seriousness of global warming.

Despite the importance of these other factors, the ideas I mentioned—ecology and welfare economics—were extremely important for the environmental movement. They helped to provide its agenda, its rhetoric, and the perception of common interest underneath its coalition politics. Even more interestingly, for my purposes, those ideas—which began as inaccessible scientific or economic concepts, far from popular discourse—were brought into the mainstream of American politics. This did not happen easily or automatically. Popularizing complicated ideas is hard work. There were popular books, television discussions, documentaries on Love Canal or the California kelp beds, op-ed pieces in newspapers, and pontificating experts on TV. Environmental groups both shocking and staid played their part, through the dramatic theater of a Greenpeace protest or the tweedy respectability of the Audubon Society. Where once the idea of "the Environment" (as opposed to "my lake," say) was seen as a mere abstraction, something that couldn't stand against the concrete benefits brought by a particular piece of development, it came to be an abstraction with both the force of law and of popular interest behind it.

To me, this suggests a strategy for the future of the politics of intellectual property, a way to save our eroding public domain. In both areas, we seem to have the same recipe for failure in the structure of the decision-making process. Democratic decisions are made badly when they are primarily made by and for the benefit of a few stakeholders, whether industrialists or content providers. This effect is only intensified when the transaction costs of identifying and resisting the change are high. Think of the costs and benefits of acid rain-producing power generation or—less serious, but surely similar in form—the costs and benefits of retrospectively increasing copyright term limits on works for which the copyright had already expired, pulling them back out of the public domain. There are obvious benefits to the heirs and assigns of authors whose copyright has expired in having Congress put the fence back up around this portion of the intellectual commons. There are clearly some costs—for example, to education and public debate—in not having multiple, competing low-cost editions of these works. But these costs are individually small and have few obvious stakeholders to represent them.

Yet, as I have tried to argue here, beyond the failures in the decision-making process, lie failures in the way we think about the issues. The environmental movement gained much of its persuasive power by pointing out that for structural reasons we were likely to make bad environmental decisions: a legal system based on a particular notion of what "private property" entailed and an engineering or scientific system that treated the world as a simple, linearly related set of causes and effects. In both of these conceptual systems, the environment actually disappeared; there was no place for it in the analysis. Small surprise, then, that we did not preserve it very well. I have argued that the same is true about the public domain. The confusions against which the Jefferson Warning cautions, the source-blindness of a model of property rights centered on an "original author," and the political blindness to the importance of the public domain as a whole (not "my lake," but "the Environment"), all come together to make the public domain disappear, first in concept and then, increasingly, as a reality. To end this process we need a cultural environmentalism, an environmentalism of the mind, and over the last ten years we have actually begun to build one.

Cultural environmentalism is an idea, an intellectual and practical movement, that is intended to be a solution to a set of political and theoretical problems—an imbalance in the way we make intellectual property policy, a legal regime that has adapted poorly to the transformation that technology has produced in the scope of law, and, perhaps most importantly, a set of mental models, economic nostrums, and property theories that each have a public domain-shaped hole at their center.

The comparison I drew between the history of environmentalism and the state of intellectual property policy had a number of facets. The environmental movement had "invented" the concept of the environment and used it to tie together a set of phenomena that would otherwise seem very separate. In doing so, it changed perceptions of self-interest and helped to form coalitions where none had existed before—just as earth science built upon research into the fragile interconnections of ecology and on the Pigouvian analysis of economic externalities. I argue that we need to make visible the invisible contributions of the public domain, the "ecosystem services" performed by the underappreciated but nevertheless vital reservoir of freedom in culture and science.[6] And, just as with environmentalism, we need not only a semantic reorganization, or a set of conceptual and analytic tools, but a movement of people devoted to bringing a goal to the attention of their fellow citizens.

I have tried hard to show that there is something larger going on under the realpolitik of land grabs by Disney and campaign contributions by the Recording Industry Association of America. But it would be an equal and opposite mistake to think that this is just about a dysfunctional discourse of intellectual property. In this part of the analysis, too, the environmental movement offers some useful practical reminders. The ideas of ecology and environmental welfare economics were important, but one cannot merely write *A Sand County Almanac* and hope the world will change. Environmentalists piggybacked on existing sources of conservationist sentiment—love of nature, the national parks movement, hikers, campers, birdwatchers. They built coalitions between those who might be affected by environmental changes. They even stretched their political base by discovering, albeit too slowly, the realities of environmental racism, on the one hand, and the benefits of market solutions to some environmental problems on the other. Some of these aspects, at least, could be replicated in the politics of intellectual property.

Ten years ago, when I first offered the environmental analogy, I claimed that intellectual property policy was seen as a contract struck between industry groups—something technical, esoteric, and largely irrelevant to individual citizens, except in that they were purchasers of the products that flowed out of the system. Whether or not that view has ever been tenable, it is not so in a digital age. Instead, I offered the basic argument laid out here—that we needed a "politics of intellectual property" modeled on the environmental movement to create a genuine and informed political debate on intellectual property policy.[7]

So far, I have concentrated on the theoretical and academic tools such a debate would need—focusing particularly on property theory and on economic analysis and its limits. But if there is to be a genuinely democratic politics of intellectual property, we would need an institutional diversity in the policy-making debate that was comparable to that of the environmental movement.

Environmentalism presents us with a remarkable diversity of organizational forms and missions. We have Greenpeace, the Environmental Legal Defense Fund, groups of concerned scientists, and the Audubon Society, each with its own methods, groups of supporters, and sets of issues. Yet we also have local and pragmatic coalitions to save a particular bit of green space, using the private tools of covenants and contracts.[8] I think we can see the beginnings of the replication of that institutional diversity in the world of intangible property.

Ten years ago, civil society had little to offer in terms of groups that represented anything other than an industry position on intellectual property, still less ones that took seriously the preservation of the public domain or the idea that intellectual property policy was a matter of balance, rather than simple maximization of rights. There were the librarians and a few academics. That was about it. This position has changed radically.

There are academic centers that concentrate on the theoretical issues discussed in this book—one of them at my university. Thanks in large part to the leadership of Pamela Samuelson, there are law student clinics that do impact litigation on issues such as fair use and that represent underserved clients such as documentarians. But beyond academic work, there are organizations that have dedicated themselves to advocacy and to litigation around the themes of preservation of the public domain, defense of limitations and exceptions in copyright, and the protection of free speech from the effects of intellectual property regulation of both content and the communications infrastructure. The Electronic Frontier Foundation did exist ten years ago, but its coverage of intellectual property issues was only episodic. Its portfolio of litigation and public education on the subject is now nothing short of remarkable. Public Knowledge's valuable lobbying and education is another obvious example. International organizations with similar aims include the Open Rights Group in the United Kingdom.[9]

Organizing has also taken place around particular cases—such as *Eldred v. Ashcroft*, the challenge to the Sonny Bono Copyright Term Extension Act.[10] Activity is not confined to the world of copyright. The Public Patent Foundation combats "patent creep" by exposing and challenging bad patents.[11]

It would be remiss not to mention the international Access to Knowledge, or A2K, movement, inspired by the work of Jamie Love.[12] While its focus is on the kinds of issues represented by the access-to-medicines movement, it has made the idea of balance in intellectual property and the protection of the public domain one of its central components. Mr. Love himself is also the central figure behind the idea of a Research and Development Treaty which would amend international trade agreements to make intellectual property merely one of a whole range of economic methods for stimulating innovation.[13] His work has touched almost every single one of the movements discussed here.

The Access to Knowledge movement has many institutional variants. The Development Agenda at the World Intellectual Property Organization (WIPO), put forward by India and Brazil, includes similar themes, as do the Geneva Declaration and the Adelphi Charter produced by the United Kingdom's Royal Society for the Encouragement of Arts, Manufactures and Commerce.[14] History is full of wordy charters and declarations, of course. By themselves they mean little. Yet the level of public and media attention paid to them indicates that intellectual property policy is now of interest beyond a narrow group of affected industries. To underscore this point, several major foundations have introduced intellectual property initiatives, something that would have been inconceivable ten years ago.[15]

Finally, to complete the analogy to the land trust, we have the organizations I mentioned earlier, such as Creative Commons and the Free Software Foundation.[16] The latter group pioneered within software the attempt to create a licensed "commons" in which freedoms are guaranteed. The licensed commons replaces the law's default rules with choices made by individuals, the effects of which are magnified by collective action. The end result is a zone of public freedom enabled by private choice.

If one looks at these institutions and actors and at the range of issues on which they focus—from software to drug patents, from reverse engineering to access to archival records—the obvious question is, how did they overcome the collective action problem? What ties together a critique of digital locks and the access-to-medicines movement? Again, I think the answer points to the usefulness of the environmental analogy. As I pointed out, the invention of the "environment" trope tied together groups whose interests, considered at a lower level of abstraction, seemed entirely different—hunters and bird-watchers, antipollution protesters and conservation biologists. The idea of the "environment" literally created the self-interest or set of preferences that ties the movement together. The same is true here. Apparently disparate interests are linked by ideas of the protection of the public domain and of the importance of a balance between protection and freedom in cultural and scientific ecology.[17]

But even a broad range of initiatives and institutions would not, in and of themselves, produce results. One must convince people that one's arguments are good, one's institutional innovations necessary, one's horror stories disturbing. Environmentalism has managed to win the battle for clarity—to make its points clearly enough that they ceased to be dismissed as "arcane" or technical, to overcome neglect by the media, to articulate a set of concerns that are those of any educated citizen. The other striking phenomenon of the last ten years is the migration of intellectual property issues off the law reviews or business pages and onto the front pages and the editorial pages. Blogs have been particularly influential. Widely read sites such as Slashdot and Boing-Boing have multiple postings on intellectual property issues each day; some are rants, but others are at a level of sophistication that once would have been confined to academic discussion.[18] Scientists passionately debate the importance of open access to scholarly journals. Geographers and climatologists fume over access to geospatial data. The movement has been pronounced enough to generate its own reaction. The popular comics site "xkcd" has strips critical of the Digital Millennium Copyright Act,[19] but also a nerdily idyllic picture of a stick figure reclining under a tree and saying, "Sometimes I just can't get outraged over copyright law."[20] That cartoon now resides on my computer desktop. (It is under a Creative Commons license, ironically enough.)

Who can blame the stick figure? Certainly not I. Is it not silly to equate the protection of the environment with the protection of the public domain? After all, one is the struggle to save a planetary ecology and the other is just some silly argument about legal rules and culture and science. I would be the first to yield primacy to the environmental challenges we are facing. Mass extinction events are to be avoided, particularly if they involve you personally. Yet my willingness to minimize the importance of the rules that determine who owns science and culture goes only so far.

A better intellectual property system will not save the planet. On the other hand, one of the most promising sets of tools for building biofuels comes from synthetic biology. Ask some of the leading scientists in that field why they devoted their precious time to trying to work out a system that would offer the valuable incentives that patents provide while leaving a commons of "biobricks" open to all for future development. I worry about these rules naturally; they were forced to do so. A better intellectual property system certainly will not end world hunger. Still it is interesting to read about the lengthy struggles to clear the multiple, overlapping patents on Golden*Rice*™—a rice grain genetically engineered to cure vitamin deficiencies that nearly perished in a thicket of blurrily overlapping rights.[21]

A better intellectual property system will not cure AIDS or rheumatoid arthritis or Huntington's disease or malaria. Certainly not by itself. Patents have already played a positive role in contributing to treatments for the first two, though they are unlikely to help much on the latter two; the affected populations are too few or too poor. But overly broad, or vague, or confusing patents could (and I believe have) hurt all of those efforts—even those being pursued out of altruism. Those problems could be mitigated. Reforms that made possible legal and facilitated distribution of patented medicines in Africa might save millions of lives. They would cost drug companies little. Africa makes up 1.6 percent of their global market. Interesting alternative methods have even been suggested for encouraging investment in treatments for neglected diseases and diseases of the world's poor. At the moment, we spend 90 percent of our research dollars on diseases that affect 10 percent of the global population. Perhaps this is the best we can do, but would it not be nice to have a vigorous public debate on the subject? Some possible innovations are much easier. A simple rule that required the eventual free publication online of all government-funded health research, under open licenses, rather than its sequestration behind the paywalls of commercial journals, could help fuel remarkable innovations in scientific synthesis and computer-aided research while giving citizens access to the research for which they have already paid.

Good intellectual property policy will not save our culture. But bad policy may lock up our cultural heritage unnecessarily, leave it to molder in libraries, forbid citizens to digitize it, even though the vast majority of it will never be available publicly and no copyright owner can be found. Would you not prefer the world in which your children could look at the Library of Congress online catalogue and click to get the book or film or song that otherwise languished as an "orphan work"? Good intellectual policy will not necessarily give us great new music. But the policy we have today would make some of the music we most cherish illegal, or at least legally questionable. Does that inspire confidence for the future? As for the World Wide Web, I offer again my thought experiment from the first part of this chapter. Would we be more likely to invent it or forbid it today? We are certainly working busily to change the openness of the general-purpose computer, the neutrality of the network, and the degree of control that content companies can exert over hardware.

I do not claim that the issues I have written about here are the most important problem the world faces. That would be ridiculous. But I do claim that they are facets of a very important problem and one to which we are paying far too little attention.

I would also be the first to admit that these issues are complicated. Even if we heeded the precepts I have outlined in this book, even if we actually started to look at intellectual property as an empirical question, even if we turned to data rather than faith for our assessments, reasonable people would disagree about much. Some of the most ludicrous recent excesses—huge retrospective copyright term extensions, database rights, proposed webcasting treaties, business method patents—do not pass the laugh test, in my view and that of most scholars. Stopping and then reversing that tide would be valuable, even transformative, but other issues are a closer call.

It is also true that we do not have all the tools we need. A lot remains to be done, both academically and practically. We need better evidence. We need property theories that give us as rich a conception of property's outside—of the public domain and the commons—as we have of property itself. We need to rethink some of our policies of international harmonization and reconsider what types of policy actually benefit the developing world. We should explore ways of compensating artists that are very different from the ones we use now, and study the use of distributed creativity and open source in new areas of science and culture.

Difficulties aside, I have tried here to show that we need a cultural environmental movement, a politics that enables us first to see and then to preserve the public domain, to understand its contributions to our art, our technology, and our culture. Where is that movement now?

There is cause for both concern and optimism. Concern, because it is still hard for courts, legislators, policy makers, and citizens to see beyond the word "property" to the reality underneath. I started this book with the question from my son about the online catalogue of the Library of Congress: "Where do you click to get the book?" In 2003 the Supreme Court heard *Eldred v. Ashcroft*, the challenge to retrospective copyright term extension. Over two strong dissents, the Court upheld the constitutionality of the act against both First Amendment and Copyright Clause challenges. The dead had their copyrights extended yet again. The widest legal restriction of speech in the history of the Republic—putting off-limits most twentieth-century books, poems, films, and songs for another twenty years without a corresponding speech benefit or incentive—can proceed without significant First Amendment review.

Does such a decision mean the task this book undertakes—to take seriously the contributions of the public domain to innovation, culture, and speech—is ultimately doomed, whatever its intellectual merits, to face a hostile or uncomprehending audience? Admittedly, *Eldred* focused specifically on two particular constitutional claims. Still, the attitude of the majority toward the importance of the public domain—whether in the textual limitations on Congress's power or the application of the First Amendment—can hardly be cause for optimism. And yet . . . The media reaction was remarkable.

The *New York Times* was sufficiently unfamiliar with the term "public domain" that it was not entirely sure whether or not to use the definite article in front of it. But unfamiliarity did not imply complacency. An editorial declared that this decision "makes it likely that we are seeing the beginning of the end of public domain and the birth of copyright perpetuity. Public domain has been a grand experiment, one that should not be allowed to die. The ability to draw freely on the entire creative output of humanity is one of the reasons we live in a time of such fruitful creative ferment."[22] The *Washington Post*, though more inclined to agree that retrospective extension might be constitutional, declared the copyright system to be "broken" in that it "effectively and perpetually protects nearly all material that anyone would want to cite or use. That's not what the framers envisioned, and it's not in the public interest."[23]

I could not agree more. But as I have tried to show here, the process is not limited to copyright, or culture, or texts, or the United States. Think of the stories about business method patents, or synthetic biology, or the regulation of musical borrowing on the atomic level. Think of the discussion of the openness aversion that began this chapter. In the middle of the most successful and exciting experiment in nonproprietary, distributed creativity in the history of the species, our policy makers can see only the threat from "piracy." They act accordingly. Our second enclosure movement is well under way. The poem with which I began Chapter 3 told us: "And geese will still a common lack / Till they go and steal it back." I cannot match the terseness or the rhyme, but if we assume that the enclosure of the commons of the mind will bring us prosperity, great science, and vibrant culture, well, we will look like very silly geese indeed.

Notes and Further Readings

NOTES TO ACKNOWLEDGMENTS

1. James Boyle, "The Second Enclosure Movement and the Construction of the Public Domain," *Law and Contemporary Problems* 66 (Winter–Spring 2003): 33–74.
2. Arti Rai and James Boyle, "Synthetic Biology: Caught between Property Rights, the Public Domain, and the Commons," *PLoS Biology* 5 (2007): 389–393, available at http://biology.plosjournals.org/perlserv/?request=get-document&doi=10.1371/journal.pbio .0050058&ct=1.
3. James Boyle, "A Politics of Intellectual Property: Environmentalism for the Net?" *Duke Law Journal* 47 (1997): 87–116, available at http://www.law.duke.edu/journals/cite.php? 47+Duke+L.+J.+87.
4. "Cultural Environmentalism @ 10," *Law and Contemporary Problems* 70 (Spring 2007): 1–210, available at http://www.law.duke.edu/ce10.

NOTES TO PREFACE

1. U.S. Patent No. 6,004,596 (filed Dec. 21, 1999), available at http://patft.uspto.gov/ netahtml/PTO/srchnum.htm (search "6,004,596"). As is required, the patent refers extensively to the "prior art"—in this case prior art in sealing sandwiches. It also refers to the classic scientific reference work "50 Great Sandwiches by Carole Handslip 81–84, 86, 95, 1994." Is this patent ridiculous? Yes, clearly so. But not so ridiculous that its eventual owner,

Smucker's, refrained from sending out cease and desist letters to competing sandwich manufacturers, and, when one of those competitors successfully requested the Patent and Trademark Office to reexamine the patent, from appealing the resulting rejection all the way through the Board of Patent Appeals and Interferences to the Court of Appeals for the Federal Circuit. The judges there were less than sympathetic at oral argument. "Judge Arthur Gajarsa noted that his wife often squeezes together the sides of their child's peanut butter and jelly sandwiches to keep the filling from oozing out. 'I'm afraid she might be infringing on your patent!' he said." The court found that the PTO got it right the second time around and agreed with the Board of Patent Appeals in rejecting the patent. Portfolio Media, "Peanut Butter and Jelly Case Reaches Federal Circuit," *IPLaw360* (April 7, 2005), available at http://www.iplawbulletin.com. For the Board of Patent Appeals's learned discussion of whether the patent was anticipated by such devices as the "Tartmaster," complete with disputes over expert testimony on the subjects of cutting, crimping, and "leaking outwardly" and painstaking inquiries about what would seem obvious to a "person having ordinary skill in the art of sandwich making," see http://des.uspto.gov/Foia/RetervePdf?system=BPAI&flNm=fd031754 and http://des.uspto.gov/Foia/RetervePdf?system=BPAI&flNm=fd031775. One could conclude from this case that the system works (eventually). Or one could ask who cares about silly patents like this—even if they are used in an attempt to undermine competition? The larger point, however, is that an initial process of examination that finds a crimped peanut butter and jelly sandwich is "novel and nonobvious" is hardly going to do better when more complex technologies are at stake. I take that point up in Chapter 2 with reference to Thomas Jefferson's discussion of patents and in Chapter 7 on synthetic biology. For a more general discussion of the flaws of the patent system see Adam B. Jaffe and Josh Lerner, *Innovation and Its Discontents: How Our Broken Patent System Is Endangering Innovation, and Progress and What To Do About It* (Princeton, N.J.: Princeton University Press, 2004).

2. These types of patents are discussed in Chapter 7.

3. *San Francisco Arts & Athletics, Inc., et al. v. United States Olympic Committee*, 483 U.S. 522 (1987). See also James Boyle, *Shamans, Software, and Spleens: Law and the Construction of the Information Society* (Cambridge, Mass.: Harvard University Press, 1996), 145–148.

4. *SunTrust Bank v. Houghton Mifflin Co.*, 268 F.3d 1257 (11th Cir. 2001).

5. See Samuel E. Trosow, "Sui Generis Database Legislation: A Critical Analysis," *Yale Journal of Law & Technology* 7 (2005): 534–642; Miriam Bitton, "Trends in Protection for Informational Works under Copyright Law during the 19th and 20th Centuries," *Michigan Telecommunications & Technology Law Review* 13 (2006): 115–176.

6. The Digital Millennium Copyright Act is discussed at length in Chapter 5. "Digital fences" include password protection, encryption, and forms of digital rights management.

7. *Dallas Cowboys Cheerleaders, Inc. v. Pussycat Cinema, Ltd.*, 604 F.2d 200 (2nd Cir. 1979).

8. "In the forests of Panama lives a Guyami Indian woman who is unusually resistant to a virus that causes leukemia. She was discovered by scientific 'gene hunters,' engaged in seeking out native peoples whose lives and cultures are threatened with extinction. Though they provided basic medical care, the hunters did not set out to preserve the people, only their genes—which can be kept in cultures of 'immortalized' cells grown in the laboratory. In 1993, the U.S. Department of Commerce tried to patent the Guyami

woman's genes—and only abandoned the attempt in the face of furious protest from representatives of indigenous peoples." Tom Wilkie, "Whose Gene Is It Anyway?" *Independent* (London, November 19, 1995), 75.

9. See Christina Rhee, "Urantia Foundation v. Maaherra," *Berkeley Technology Law Journal* 13 (1998): 69–81.

10. See James Boyle, "Intellectual Property Policy Online: A Young Person's Guide," *Harvard Journal of Law & Technology* 10 (1996): 83–94.

11. Garrett Hardin, "The Tragedy of the Commons," *Science* 162 (1968): 1243–1248.

12. *International News Service v. Associated Press*, 248 U.S. 215, 250 (1918) (Brandeis, J., dissenting); Yochai Benkler, "Free as the Air to Common Use: First Amendment Constraints on Enclosure of the Public Domain," *New York University Law Review* 74 (1999): 354–446.

CHAPTER 1:
WHY INTELLECTUAL PROPERTY?

Further Reading

This chapter argues that at least one goal we have in an intellectual property system is the attempt to solve various "public goods problems." (Subsequent chapters defend that view historically and normatively, discuss the ideas of moral right and natural right, the tradition of the *droits d'auteur*, and the similarities and dissimilarities between the arguments for tangible and intellectual property rights. Further reading on those issues can be found in the relevant chapter.)

The single best starting point for someone who wishes to understand an economic perspective on intellectual property is William M. Landes and Richard A. Posner, *The Economic Structure of Intellectual Property Law* (Cambridge, Mass.: Belknap Press, 2003). The story laid out in this chapter is one largely (but not entirely) focused on the idea of intellectual property rights offered as incentives—the carrot that induces the author to write, the inventor to research, the investor to fund that research, and the corporation to develop attractive and stable brand names that convey reliable information to consumers. This is conventionally known as the *ex ante* perspective. But as the chapter also hints, intellectual property rights, like property rights in general, have a role after the innovation has occurred—facilitating its efficient exploitation, allowing inventors to disclose their inventions to prospective licensees without thereby losing control of them, and providing a state-constructed, neatly tied bundle of entitlements that can be efficiently traded in the market. Readers interested in these perspectives will benefit from looking at these articles: Edmund Kitch, "The Nature and Function of the Patent System," *Journal of Law and Economics* 20 (1977): 265–290; Paul J. Heald, "A Transaction Costs Theory of Patent Law," *Ohio State Law Journal* 66 (2005): 473–509; and Robert Merges, "A Transactional View of Property Rights," *Berkeley Technology Law Journal* 20 (2005): 1477–1520. Of course, just as the incentives account of intellectual property has its skeptics, so these *ex post* theories attract skepticism from those who believe that, in practice, the rights will not be clear and well-delineated but vague and potentially overlapping, that the licensing markets will find themselves entangled in "patent thickets" from which the participants can escape only at great cost or by ignoring the law altogether. It is worth comparing Michael A. Heller and

Rebecca S. Eisenberg, "Can Patents Deter Innovation? The Anticommons in Biomedical Research," *Science* 280 (1998): 698–701, with John Walsh, Ashish Arora, and Wesley Cohen, "Effects of Research Tool Patents and Licensing on Biomedical Innovation," in *Patents in the Knowledge-Based Economy* (Washington D.C.: National Academies Press, 2003), 285–340. There is a nice irony to imagining that the necessary mechanism of the efficient market is "ignore the property rights when they are inconvenient."

The skeptics argue that the alternative to a deeply commodified world of invention and innovation, with hundreds of thousands of licensing markets, is a rich information and innovation commons, from which all can draw freely, supporting a thin and well-defined layer of intellectual property rights close to the ultimate commercially viable innovation. The rhetorical structure of the debate—replete with paradox and inversion—is laid out in James Boyle, "Cruel, Mean, or Lavish? Economic Analysis, Price Discrimination and Digital Intellectual Property," *Vanderbilt Law Review* 53 (2000): 2007–2039. For some of the difficulties in the attempt to arrive at a coherent economic theory of intellectual property, see James Boyle, *Shamans, Software, and Spleens: Law and the Construction of the Information Society* (Cambridge, Mass.: Harvard University Press, 1996), 35–46. Finally, while I urge that at the outset we must care about the actual effects and economic incentives provided by intellectual property rights, I am by no means asserting that we should stop there. Indeed to do so would dramatically impoverish our view of the world. James Boyle, "Enclosing the Genome: What Squabbles over Genetic Patents Could Teach Us," in *Perspectives on Properties of the Human Genome Project*, ed. F. Scott Kieff (San Diego, Calif.: Elsevier Academic Press, 2003), 97, 107–109.

In other words, as all this suggests, this chapter is only an introduction to a rich and complex debate.

Notes to Chapter 1

1. As the suggested further reading indicates, this light-hearted account of the economic basis of intellectual property conceals considerable complexity. On the other hand, the core argument is presented here—and a compelling argument it is.

2. See Jack Hirshleifer, "The Private and Social Value of Information and the Reward to Inventive Activity," *American Economic Review* 61 (1971): 561–574.

3. Unfortunately, the reality turns out to be less rosy. James Bessen, "Patents and the Diffusion of Technical Information," *Economics Letters* 86 (2005): 122: "[S]urvey evidence suggests that firms do not place much value on the disclosed information. Moreover, those firms that do read patents do not use them primarily as a source of information on technology. Instead, they use them for other purposes, such as keeping track of competitors or checking for infringement. There are, in fact, sound theoretical reasons why the disclosed information may not be very valuable. [Fritz] Machlup and [Edith] Penrose report that the argument about diffusion is an old one, popular since the mid-19th century. They also point out that, at least through the 1950s, economists have been skeptical about this argument. The problem, also recognized in the mid-19th century, is that 'only unconcealable inventions are patented,' so patents reveal little that could not be otherwise learned. On the other hand, 'concealable inventions remain concealed.'" [Citations omitted.]

4. Felix S. Cohen, "Transcendental Nonsense and the Functional Approach," *Columbia Law Review* 35 (1935): 817.

5. For contrasting views of the sequence of events, see John Feather, "Publishers and Politicians: The Remaking of the Law of Copyright in Britain 1775–1842," pt. 2, "The Rights of Authors," *Publishing History* 25 (1989): 45–72; Mark Rose, *Authors and Owners: The Invention of Copyright* (Cambridge, Mass.: Harvard University Press, 1993).

6. Tim O'Reilly points out that there are 32 million titles in the Online Computer Library Center's "WorldCat" catalogue—this is a reasonable proxy for the number of books in U.S. libraries. Nielsen's Bookscan shows that 1.2 million books sold at least one copy in 2005. This yields a ratio of books commercially available to books ever published of about 4 percent. But of those 1.2 million books, many are in the public domain—think of Shakespeare, Dickens, Austen, Melville, Kipling. Thus the percentage of books that are under copyright and commercially available may actually be considerably lower than 4 percent. See http://radar.oreilly.com/archives/2005/11/oops_only_4_of_titles_are_bein .html. For a lucid account of the statistics in the context of the Google Book Search Project, see http://lessig.org/blog/2006/01/google_book_search_the_argumen.html.

7. See Barbara Ringer, "Study Number 31: Renewal of Copyright," reprinted in U.S. Senate Committee on the Judiciary, Subcommittee on Patents, Trademarks, and Copyrights, *Copyright Law Revision*, 86th Cong., 1st Sess., Committee Print (1960), 187. See also HR Rep. 94-1476 (1976), 136; William M. Landes and Richard A. Posner, *The Economic Structure of Intellectual Property Law* (Cambridge, Mass.: Belknap Press, 2003), 210–212.

8. Details of the orphan works problem can be found in the proposals presented to the copyright office by the Center for the Study of the Public Domain; *Orphan Works: Analysis and Proposal: Submission to the Copyright Office—March 2005*, available at http:// www.law.duke.edu/cspd/pdf/cspdproposal.pdf, and *Access to Orphan Films: Submission to the Copyright Office—March 2005*, available at http://www.law.duke.edu/cspd/pdf/ cspdorphanfilm.pdf. Two recent bills, in the Senate and House, respectively, attempt to address the orphan works problems. The Shawn Bentley Orphan Works Act of 2008, S 2913, 110th Cong. (2008), would add a new section to the Copyright Act limiting remedies for infringement of orphan works and requiring the establishment of a database of pictorial, graphic, and sculptural works. The House bill, The Orphan Works Act of 2008, HR 5889, 110th Cong. (2008), is similar but not identical. While these bills are a good start, the eventual remedy will need to be more sweeping.

9. Bruce Sterling, *Heavy Weather* (New York: Bantam, 1994): 73.

CHAPTER 2:
THOMAS JEFFERSON WRITES A LETTER

Further Reading

In this chapter I offered a snapshot of the historical debate over copyright, patent and—to a lesser extent—trademark law. The argument is partly a matter of intellectual history: a claim about what various individuals and groups actually believed about intellectual property rights, and the way those beliefs shaped the policies they supported and the legal structures they created. But it is also a normative argument—a claim that this vision of intellectual property is better than the more "physicalist" and "absolutist" alternatives I described or, at the very least, that it is an important corrective to our current excesses. This dual character complicates the task of providing a guide to further reading: books could be written on either portion alone.

My own understanding of the history of "intellectual property"—itself a relatively recently invented and contentious category—has been profoundly influenced by more scholars than I can list here. Edward C. Walterscheid, *The Nature of the Intellectual Property Clause: A Study in Historical Perspective* (Buffalo, N.Y.: W. S. Hein, 2002), gives a magisterial account of the origins of the U.S. Constitution's intellectual property clause. Tyler T. Ochoa and Mark Rose, "The Anti-Monopoly Origins of the Patent and Copyright Clause," *Journal of the Patent & Trademark Office Society* 84 (2002): 909–940, offer a vision of the history that is closest to the one I put forward here. In addition, Tyler T. Ochoa, "Origins and Meanings of the Public Domain," *University of Dayton Law Review* 28 (2002): 215–267, provides the same service for the concept of the public domain. Malla Pollack provides a useful historical study of the contemporary understanding of the word "progress" at the time of the American Constitution in Malla Pollack, "The Democratic Public Domain: Reconnecting the Modern First Amendment and the Original Progress Clause (a.k.a. Copyright and Patent Clause)," *Jurimetrics* 45 (2004): 23–40. A rich and thought-provoking account of the way that ideas of intellectual property worked themselves out in the context of the corporate workplace can be found in Catherine Fisk, *Working Knowledge: Employee Innovation and the Rise of Corporate Intellectual Property, 1800–1930* (Chapel Hill: University of North Carolina Press, forthcoming 2009).

Of course, the history of copyright or of intellectual property cannot be confined to the two figures I focus on principally here—Jefferson and Macaulay—nor cannot it be confined to the Anglo-American tradition or to the debates in which Jefferson and Macaulay were participating. Carla Hesse, *Publishing and Cultural Politics in Revolutionary Paris, 1789–1810* (Berkeley: University of California Press, 1991), is vital reading to understand the parallels between the Anglo-American and *droits d'auteur* tradition. It is also fascinating reading. For studies of the broader intellectual climate, I recommend Martha Woodmansee, *The Author, Art, and the Market: Rereading the History of Aesthetics* (New York: Columbia University Press, 1994); Peter Jaszi, "Toward a Theory of Copyright: The Metamorphoses of 'Authorship,'" *Duke Law Journal* 1991, no. 2: 455–502; Mark Rose, *Authors and Owners: The Invention of Copyright* (Cambridge, Mass.: Harvard University Press, 1993); Lyman Ray Patterson, *Copyright in Historical Perspective* (Nashville, Tenn.: Vanderbilt University Press, 1968). The British debates at the time of Macaulay are beautifully captured in Catherine Seville, *Literary Copyright Reform in Early Victorian England: The Framing of the 1842 Copyright Act* (Cambridge, U.K.: Cambridge University Press, 1999). (It should be noted that, while sympathetic, she is less moved than I by Macaulay's arguments.)

Any collection of historical works this rich and complex resists summary description—nevertheless, I think it is fair to say that the vast majority of these works stress the centrality of the skeptical "antimonopolist" attitudes I use Jefferson and Macaulay to represent to the history of intellectual property. This does not mean there is unanimity or anything close to it. In particular, Adam Mossoff, "Who Cares What Thomas Jefferson Thought about Patents? Reevaluating the Patent 'Privilege' in Historical Context," *Cornell Law Review* 92 (2007): 953–1012, which came to light late in the writing of this book, offers a thoughtful historical account that criticizes the tendency to use Jefferson's views as representative of a dominant strand in American intellectual property. My agreements and disagreements with Mossoff's arguments are discussed fully later in the notes to this chapter. The central point, however, and the single strongest argument against those who would instead attempt to construct a more absolutist, physicalist or labor-based theory of intellectual property, is the problem of limits. Where does one stop? How can one put a limit on the potentially absolute claim over some intellectual creation? How can one specify the limits on prior creators that actually give me ownership over what I create, for I surely have built on the works of others? How can one circumscribe the negative effects on speech, life, and culture that the absolutist or maximalist tradition threatens to generate? My ultimate argument is that the purpose-driven, skeptical, antimonopolistic tendencies of Jefferson and Macaulay answer those questions far better than any contending theory, that they represent not merely an intellectual history sadly neglected in today's political debates, but a practical solution to the inevitable question, "where do you draw the line?"

Notes to Chapter 2

1. Letter from Thomas Jefferson to Isaac McPherson (August 13, 1813), in *The Writings of Thomas Jefferson*, ed. Albert Ellery Bergh (Washington, D.C.: The Thomas Jefferson Memorial Association of the United States, 1907), vol. XIII, 326–338 (hereinafter Letter to McPherson), available at http://memory.loc.gov/ammem/collections/jefferson_papers/mtjser1.html (follow "May 1, 1812" hyperlink, then navigate to image 1057).

2. For example, attempting to procure a former stable master a position (letter from Thomas Jefferson to Samuel H. Smith [August 15, 1813], available at http://memory.loc.gov/ammem/collections/jefferson_papers/mtjser1.html [follow "May 1, 1812" hyperlink, then navigate to image 1070]), comments on "Rudiments of English Grammar" (letter from Thomas Jefferson to John Waldo [August 16, 1813], in *Writings of Thomas Jefferson*, vol. XIII, 338–347), orthography of the plurals of nouns ending in "y" (letter from Thomas Jefferson to John Wilson [August 17, 1813], *Writings of Thomas Jefferson*, vol. XIII, 347–348), accepting the necessary delay in the publication of a study on the anatomy of mammoth bones (letter from Thomas Jefferson to Caspar Wistar [August 17, 1813], available at http://memory.loc.gov/ammem/collections/jefferson_papers/mtjser1.html [follow "May 1, 1812" hyperlink, then navigate to image 1095]), and discussing the Lewis biography (excerpt of a letter from Thomas Jefferson to Paul Allen [August 18, 1813], *Letters of the Lewis and Clark Expedition with Related Documents 1783–1854*, ed. Donald Jackson (Urbana: University of Illinois Press, 1962), 586).

It is easy, in fact, reading this prodigious outpouring of knowledge and enthusiasm, to forget the other side of Jefferson and the social system that gave him the leisure to write these letters. Just a few weeks before he wrote to McPherson, he wrote a letter to Jeremiah Goodman about a slave called Hercules who had been imprisoned as a runaway. "The folly he has committed certainly justifies further punishment, and he goes in expectation of receiving it. . . ." Letter from Thomas Jefferson to Jeremiah A. Goodman (July 26, 1813), in *Thomas Jefferson's Farm Book*, ed. Edwin Morris Betts (Charlottesville,

Va.: American Philosophical Society, 1999), 36. While leaving the matter up to Goodman, Jefferson argues for leniency and for refraining from further punishment. In that sense, it is a humane letter. But this is one of the authors of the Declaration of Independence, full of glorious principles—unalienable rights; life, liberty, and the pursuit of happiness—enunciated in the context of indignation at relatively mild colonial policies of taxation and legislation. How could a man who thought that taxing tea was tyranny, and that all men had an unalienable right to liberty, believe that it was "folly" justifying "further punishment" for a slave to run away? Reading the letter—a curiously intimate, almost voyeuristic act—one finds oneself saying "What was he *thinking?*"

3. Letter to McPherson, 333.

4. See Letter from Thomas Jefferson to Abraham Baldwin (April 14, 1802), in *Writings of Thomas Jefferson*, vol. XIX, 128–129.

5. See Paul Finkelman, *Slavery and the Founders: Race and Liberty in the Age of Jefferson*, 2nd ed. (Armonk, N.Y.: M. E. Sharpe, 2001), *ix*; Annette Gordon-Reed, *Thomas Jefferson and Sally Hemings: An American Controversy* (Charlottesville: University Press of Virginia, 1997) 1, 40–43, 60–61, 222.

6. Letter to McPherson, 336, quoted in John Perry Barlow, "Economy of Ideas," *Wired* (March 1994): 84. For a careful scholarly explanation of the antimonopolist origins of eighteenth-century ideas such as Jefferson's, see Tyler T. Ochoa and Mark Rose, "The Anti-Monopoly Origins of the Patent and Copyright Clause," *Journal of the Copyright Society of the U.S.A.* 49 (2002): 675–706. One scholar has offered a thoughtful critique that suggests Jefferson's views were not, in fact, representative either of the times or of the attitudes of the other framers toward intellectual property. See Adam Mossoff, "Who Cares What Thomas Jefferson Thought about Patents? Reevaluating the Patent 'Privilege' in Historical Context," *Cornell Law Review* 92 (2007): 953–1012.

7. Letter to McPherson, 328.

8. Letter from Thomas Jefferson to Dr. Thomas Cooper (February 10, 1814), in Thomas Jefferson, *Writings*, ed. Merrill D. Peterson (New York: Library of America, 1984), 1321.

9. Letter to McPherson, 333.

10. Ibid., 333–334.

11. Ibid.

12. Ibid., 335.

13. See ibid., 333–335.

14. Readers interested in learning more about this fascinating man could begin with George Otto Trevelyan, *The Life and Letters of Lord Macaulay*, London ed. (Longmans, 1876).

15. Thomas Babington Macaulay, speech delivered in the House of Commons (February 5, 1841), in *The Life and Works of Lord Macaulay: Complete in Ten Volumes*, Edinburgh ed. (Longmans, 1897), vol. VIII, 198 (hereinafter Macaulay Speech).

16. Ibid., 199.

17. Ibid., 198–199.

18. *Graham v. John Deere*, 383 U.S. 1, 7–11 (1966).

19. Adam Mossoff, "Who Cares What Thomas Jefferson Thought about Patents? Reevaluating the Patent 'Privilege' in Historical Context," *Cornell Law Review* 92 (2007):

953–1012. In a thoughtful, carefully reasoned, and provocative article, Professor Mossoff argues that Jefferson's views have been misused by the courts and legal historians, and that if we understand the use of the word "privilege" in historical context, we see that the "patent privilege" was influenced by a philosophy of natural rights as well as the antimonopolist utilitarianism described here. I both agree and disagree.

Professor Mossoff's central point—that the word "privilege" was not understood by eighteenth-century audiences as the antonym of "right"—is surely correct. To lay great stress on the linguistic point that the patent right is "merely" a "privilege" is to rest one's argument on a weak reed. But this is not the only argument. One could also believe that intellectual property rights have vital conceptual and practical differences with property rights over tangible objects or land, that the framers of the Constitution who were most involved in the intellectual property clause were deeply opposed to the confusion involved in conflating the two, and that they looked upon this confusion particularly harshly because of an intense concern about state monopolies. One can still disagree with this assessment, of course; one can interpret Madison's words this way or that, or interpret subsequent patent decisions as deep statements of principle or commonplace rhetorical flourishes. Still it seems to me a much stronger argument than the one based on the privilege–right distinction. I am not sure Professor Mossoff would disagree.

Professor Mossoff is also correct to point out that a "legal privilege" did sometimes mean to an eighteenth-century reader something that the state was duty-bound to grant. There was, in fact, a wide range of sources from which an eighteenth-century lawyer could derive a state obligation to grant a privilege. Eighteenth-century legal talk was a normative bouillabaisse—a rich stew of natural right, common law, utility, and progress—often thrown together without regard to their differences. Some lawyers and judges thought the common law embodied natural rights, others that it represented the dictates of "progress" and "utility," and others, more confusingly still, seemed to adopt all of those views at once.

Nevertheless, I would agree that some eighteenth-century writers saw claims of common-law right beneath the assertion of some "privileges" and that a smaller number of those assumed common-law right and natural right to be equivalent, and thus saw a strong state obligation to grant a particular privilege based on natural right, wherever that privilege had been recognized by English or U.S. common law. But here is where I part company with Professor Mossoff.

First, I do not believe that the most important architects of the intellectual property clause shared that view when it came to patents and copyrights. Jefferson, of course, was not one of those who believed the state was so bound. "Society may give an exclusive right to the profits arising from [inventions], as an encouragement to men to pursue ideas which may produce utility, but this may or may not be done, according to the will and convenience of the society, *without claim or complaint from any body*" (Letter to McPherson, 334, emphasis added). More importantly, Jefferson's thinking about patents was infused by a deeply utilitarian, antimonopolist tinge. So, I would argue, was Madison's.

The quotations from Madison which I give later show clearly, to me at least, that Madison shared Jefferson's deeply utilitarian attitude toward patent and copyright law.

I think there is very good reason to believe that this attitude was dominant among the Scottish Enlightenment thinkers whose writings were so influential to the framers. I do not think it is an exaggeration to say that the American Revolution was violently against the world of monopoly and corruption that was the supposed target of the English Statute of Monopolies (itself hardly a natural rights document). Yes, those thinkers might fall back into talking about how hard an inventor had worked or construing a patent expansively. Yes, they might think that within the boundaries of settled law, it would be unjust to deny one inventor a patent when the general scheme of patent law had already been laid down. But that did not and does not negate the antimonopolist and, for that matter, utilitarian roots of the Constitution's intellectual property clause.

Second, while I agree that there were strands of natural right thinking and a labor theory of value in the U.S. intellectual property system, and that they continue to this day—indeed, these were the very views that the *Feist* decision discussed in Chapter 9 repudiated, as late as 1991—I think it is easy to make too much of that fact. Is this signal or noise? There are conceptual reasons to think it is the latter. Later in this chapter I discuss the evolution of the *droits d'auteur* tradition in France. Here, at the supposed heart of the natural rights tradition, we find thinkers driven inexorably to consider the question of limits. How far does the supposed natural right extend—in time, in space, in subject matter? It is at that moment that the utilitarian focus and the fear of monopoly represented by Jefferson and Madison—and, for that matter, Locke and Condorcet—become so important.

Professor Mossoff is correct to criticize the focus on the word "privilege," and also correct that the ideas of natural right and the labor theory of value always color attitudes toward intellectual property claims. But it would be an equal and opposite mistake to ignore two points. First, intellectual property rights are profoundly different from physical property rights over land in ways that should definitively shape policy choices. Second, partly because of those differences, and because of the influence of free-trade Scottish Enlightenment thought on the American Revolution in particular, there was a powerful antimonopolist and free-trade sentiment behind the copyright and patent clause. Simply read the clause. Congress is given the power "to promote the Progress of Science and useful Arts, by securing for limited Times to Authors and Inventors the exclusive Right to their respective Writings and Discoveries." Does this really read like the work of a group of believers in natural right? On the contrary, it reads like a limited grant of power to achieve a particular utilitarian goal. That sentiment—nicely encapsulated in but by no means limited to the words of Jefferson—is still a good starting place for an understanding of intellectual property.

20. See, e.g., Ochoa and Rose, "Anti-Monopoly Origins," and Edward C. Walterscheid, *The Nature of the Intellectual Property Clause: A Study in Historical Perspective* (Buffalo, N.Y.: W. S. Hein, 2002). Ochoa, Rose, and Walterscheid stress the antimonopolist concerns that animated some of those who were most active in the debates about intellectual property. They also point out the influence of the English Statute of Monopolies of 1623, which attacked monopolies in general, while making an exception for periods of legal exclusivity for a limited time granted over "sole Working or Making of any Manner of new Manufacture within this Realm, to the first true Inventor or Inventors of such Manufactures which others at the time of the Making of such Letters Patents Grants did

not use, so they be not contrary to the Law, nor mischievous to the State, by Raising of the Prices of Commodities at home, or Hurt by Trade, or generally inconvenient."

21. For example, in a letter to Madison commenting on the draft of the Constitution: "I like it, as far as it goes; but I should have been for going further. For instance, the following alterations and additions would have pleased me: . . . Article 9. Monopolies may be allowed to persons for their own productions in literature, and their own inventions in the arts, for a term not exceeding . . . years, but for no longer term, and no other purpose." Letter from Thomas Jefferson to James Madison (August 28, 1789), in *Writings of Thomas Jefferson*, vol. 7, 450–451.

22. "Monopolies tho' in certain cases useful ought to be granted with caution, and guarded with strictness against abuse. The Constitution of the U.S. has limited them to two cases—the authors of Books, and of useful inventions, in both which they are considered as a compensation for a benefit actually gained to the community as a purchase of property which the owner might otherwise withhold from public use. There can be no just objection to a temporary monopoly in these cases: but it ought to be temporary because under that limitation a sufficient recompence and encouragement may be given. The limitation is particularly proper in the case of inventions, because they grow so much out of preceding ones that there is the less merit in the authors; and because, for the same reason, the discovery might be expected in a short time from other hands. . . . Monopolies have been granted in other Countries, and by some of the States in this, on another principle, that of supporting some useful undertaking, until experience and success should render the monopoly unnecessary, and lead to a salutary competition . . . But grants of this sort can be justified in very peculiar cases only, if at all; the danger being very great that the good resulting from the operation of the monopoly, will be overbalanced by the evil effect of the precedent; and it being not impossible that the monopoly itself in its original operation, may produce more evil than good. In all cases of monopoly, not excepting those in favor of authors and inventors, it would be well to reserve to the State, a right to extinguish the monopoly by paying a specified and reasonable sum. . . . Perpetual monopolies of every sort are forbidden not only by the Genius of free Governments, but by the imperfection of human foresight." James Madison, "Monopolies, Perpetuities, Corporations, Ecclesiastical Endowments" (1819), in "Aspects of Monopoly One Hundred Years Ago," *Harper's Magazine*, ed. Galliard Hunt, 128 (1914), 489–490; also in "Madison's 'Detached Memoranda,' " ed. Elizabeth Fleet, *William & Mary Quarterly*, 3rd series, 3 no. 4 (1946): 551–552, available at http://www.constitution.org/jm/18191213_monopolies.htm.

23. Adam Smith, *The Wealth of Nations*, pt. 3, *Of the Expenses of Public Works and Public Institutions*, 2nd ed. (Oxford: Oxford University Press, 1880), 2:339: "When a company of merchants undertake, at their own risk and expense, to establish a new trade with some remote and barbarous nation, it may not be unreasonable to incorporate them into a joint-stock company, and to grant them, in case of their success, a monopoly of the trade for a certain number of years. It is the easiest and most natural way in which the state can recompense them for hazarding a dangerous and expensive experiment, of which the public is afterwards to reap the benefit. A temporary monopoly of this kind may be vindicated, upon the same principles upon which a like monopoly of a new machine is

granted to its inventor, and that of a new book to its author. But upon the expiration of the term, the monopoly ought certainly to determine; the forts and garrisons, if it was found necessary to establish any, to be taken into the hands of government, their value to be paid to the company, and the trade to be laid open to all the subjects of the state. By a perpetual monopoly, all the other subjects of the state are taxed very absurdly in two different ways: first, by the high price of goods, which, in the case of a free trade, they could buy much cheaper; and, secondly, by their total exclusion from a branch of business which it might be both convenient and profitable for many of them to carry on."

24. Macaulay Speech, 200–201.

25. Ibid., 201.

26. 17 U.S.C. § 304 (1998).

27. *Eldred v. Ashcroft*, 537 U.S. 186 (2003).

28. See Brief for Hal Roach Studios and Michael Agee as Amici Curiae Supporting Petitioners, *Eldred v. Ashcroft*.

29. Sonny Bono Copyright Term Extension Act, Pub. L. No. 105-298, 112 Stat. 2827 (1998).

30. Brief of George A. Akerlof, Kenneth J. Arrow, Timothy F. Bresnahan, James M. Buchanan, Ronald H. Coase, Linda R. Cohen, Milton Friedman, Jerry R. Green, Robert W. Hahn, Thomas W. Hazlett, C. Scott Hemphill, Robert E. Litan, Roger G. Noll, Richard Schmalensee, Steven Shavell, Hal R. Varian, and Richard J. Zeckhauser as Amici Curiae In Support of Petitioners, *Eldred v. Ashcroft*, available at http://cyber.law.harvard.edu/openlaw/eldredvashcroft/supct/amici/economists.pdf.

31. U.S. Constitution, art. I, § 8, cl. 8.

32. "These are strong cases. I have shown you that, if the law had been what you are now going to make it, the finest prose work of fiction in the language, the finest biographical work in the language, would very probably have been suppressed. But I have stated my case weakly. The books which I have mentioned are singularly inoffensive books, books not touching on any of those questions which drive even wise men beyond the bounds of wisdom. There are books of a very different kind, books which are the rallying points of great political and religious parties. What is likely to happen if the copyright of one of these books should by descent or transfer come into the possession of some hostile zealot?" Macaulay Speech, 199, 206.

33. Ibid., 205.

34. Ibid., 206.

35. Margaret Mitchell, *Gone With the Wind* (New York: Macmillan, 1936).

36. *SunTrust Bank v. Houghton Mifflin Co.*, 136 F. Supp. 2d 1357 (N.D.Ga. 2001). For thoughtful commentary see Jed Rubenfeld, "The Freedom of Imagination: Copyright's Constitutionality," *Yale Law Journal* 112 (2002): 1–60. Robert S. Boynton provides a beautifully readable account of copyright's restrictions in "The Tyranny of Copyright?" *The New York Times Magazine* (January 25, 2004): 40–45, available at http://www.nytimes.com/2004/01/25/magazine/25COPYRIGHT.html?ex=1390366800&en=9eb265b1f26e8b14&ei=5007&partner=USERLAND.

37. Yochai Benkler, "Through the Looking Glass: Alice and Constitutional Foundations of the Public Domain," *Law and Contemporary Problems* 66 (Winter–Spring 2003): 173.

38. *SunTrust Bank v. Houghton Mifflin Co.* 268 F.3d 1257 (11th Cir. 2001).

39. See note 19 of this chapter for a discussion of the most recent and thoughtful challenge to this claim.

40. Lord King, *The Life of John Locke with Extracts from His Correspondence, Journals and Common-Place Books* vol. 1 (London: Henry Colburn, 1830), 379–380.

41. Archives de la Préfecture de Police de Paris, ser. AA, carton 200, feuilles 182–183, "Procès-verbal de police, section de St. Geneviève, 23–24 octobre 1791." Quoted in Carla Hesse, *Publishing and Cultural Politics in Revolutionary Paris, 1789–1810* (Berkeley: University of California Press, 1991), 91.

42. Quoted in Hesse, *Publishing and Cultural Politics*, 100.

43. Victor Hugo, speech to the Conseil d'Etat, September 30, 1849, quoted in Bernard Edelman, *Ownership of the Image: Elements for a Marxist Theory of Law* (London: Routledge & Kegan Paul, 1979), 41.

44. *Oeuvres de Condorcet*, ed. A. Condorcet O'Connor and M. F. Arago, vol. 11 (Paris: Firmin Didot Frères, 1847), 308, available at http://books.google.com/books?id—ZoGAAAAQAAJ.

45. Ibid., 308–309: "En effet, on sent qu'il ne peut y avoir aucun rapport entre la propriété d'un ouvrage et celle d'un champ, qui ne peut être cultivé que par un homme; d'un meuble qui ne peut servir qu'à un homme, et dont, par conséquent, la propriété exclusive est fondée sur la nature de la chose. Ainsi ce n'est point ici une propriété dérivée de l'ordre naturel, et défendue par la force sociale; c'est une propriété fondée par la société même. Ce n'est pas un véritable droit, c'est un privilège, comme ces jouissances exclusives de tout ce qui peut être enlevé au possesseur unique sans violence."

46. Ibid., 309: "Tout privilége est donc une gêne imposée à la liberté, une restriction mise aux droits des autres citoyens; dans ce genre il est nuisible non-seulement aux droits des autres qui veulent copier, mais aux droits de tous ceux qui veulent avoir des copies, et pour qui ce qui en augmente le prix est une injustice. L'intérêt public exige-t-il que les hommes fassent ce sacrifice? Telle est la question qu'il faut examiner; en d'autres termes, les priviléges sont-ils nécessaires, utiles ou nuisibles au progrès des lumières?"

47. James Boyle, *Shamans, Software, and Spleens: Law and the Construction of the Information Society* (Cambridge, Mass.: Harvard University Press, 1996), 55–57.

48. Hesse, *Publishing and Cultural Politics*, 121–122. As Hesse points out, this legal legerdemain also produced an interesting transformation in the status of the great authors of the French tradition. "If the Old Regime first accorded Voltaire, Rousseau, or Mirabeau the possibility of legal status as privileged authors with perpetual private lineages for their texts, the Revolution relocated these figures in the public domain, the legal parallel to the civic rituals that unearthed them from private gravesites and reposed their bodily remains in the public temple of the Pantheon." Ibid., 123. One of the central features of the debates described in this book is a starkly different set of characterizations of the public domain. Is it a communist repossession of the sacred rights of authors? The noble common store of knowledge from which all future creators can build? The worthless remainder of material that is no longer worth protecting?

49. Northrop Frye, *Anatomy of Criticism: Four Essays* (Princeton, N.J.: Princeton University Press, 1957), 96–97.

50. Mark Helprin, "A Great Idea Lives Forever. Shouldn't Its Copyright?" *New York Times* editorial (May 20, 2007), A12.
51. The two most influential and brilliant examples are Justin Hughes, "The Philosophy of Intellectual Property," *Georgetown Law Journal* 77 (1988): 287–366, and Wendy J. Gordon, "A Property Right in Self-Expression: Equality and Individualism in the Natural Law of Intellectual Property," *Yale Law Journal* 102 (1993): 1533–1610. Both of these articles attempt not to use Locke as the basis for a world of absolute right, but instead to focus on the Locke whose world of private property coexisted with a commons—albeit one much diminished after the invention of money. If one goes far enough into the Lockean conception—fine-tuning "enough and as good" so as to allow for a vigorous commons, and the claims of labor so as to take account of the importance of the embedded contributions of culture and science—then the differences between the Jeffersonian view and the Lockean view start to recede in significance. Academics have found the Lockean view attractive, noting, correctly, that Locke is commonly brandished as a rhetorical emblem for property schemes that he himself would have scorned. Yet when one looks at the actual world of intellectual property policy discourse, and the difficulty of enunciating even the simple Jeffersonian antimonopolist ideas I lay out here, it is hard to imagine the nuanced Lockean view flourishing. Consider this comment of Jeremy Waldron's and ask yourself—is this result more likely from within the Jeffersonian or the Lockean view?

> Our tendency of course is to focus on authors when we think about intellectual property. Many of us are authors ourselves: reading a case about copyright we can empathize readily with a plaintiff's feeling for the effort he has put in, his need to control his work, and his natural desire to reap the fruits of his own labor. In this Essay, however, I shall look at the way we think about actual, potential and putative infringers of copyright, those whose freedom is or might be constrained by others' ownership of songs, plays, words, images and stories. Clearly our concept of the author and this concept of the copier are two sides of the same coin. If we think of an author as having a natural right to profit from his work, then we will think of the copier as some sort of thief; whereas if we think of the author as beneficiary of a statutory monopoly, it may be easier to see the copier as an embodiment of free enterprise values. These are the connections I want to discuss, and my argument will be that we cannot begin to unravel the conundrums of moral justification in this area unless we are willing to approach the matter even-handedly from both sides of the question.

After a magisterial study of justifications for the existing world of intellectual property, Waldron concludes, "[t]he fact is, however, that whether or not we speak of a burden of proof, an institution like intellectual property is not self-justifying; we owe a justification to anyone who finds that he can move less freely than he would in the absence of the institution. So although the people whose perspective I have taken—the copiers—may be denigrated as unoriginal plagiarists or thieves of others' work, still they are the ones who feel the immediate impact of our intellectual property laws. It affects what they may do, how they may speak, and how they may earn a living. Of course nothing is settled by saying that it is their interests that are particularly at stake; if the tables were turned, we should want to highlight the perspective of the authors. But as things stand, the would-be copiers are the ones to whom a justification of intellectual property is owed." See Jeremy Waldron, "From Authors to Copiers: Individual Rights and Social Values in Intellectual Property," *Chicago-Kent Law Review* 68 (1993): 841, 842, 887. That justification seems more plausibly and practically to come from the perspective I sketch out here. See also William Fisher, "Theories of Intellectual Property," in *New Essays in the Legal and Political Theory of Property*, ed. Stephen R. Munzer (Cambridge: Cambridge University Press, 2001), 168–200.

52. Catherine Seville, *Literary Copyright Reform in Early Victorian England: The Framing of the 1842 Copyright Act* (Cambridge: Cambridge University Press, 1999), 46–48.

53. Macaulay Speech, 256.

54. This point is made today by a number of authors. See Yochai Benkler, *The Wealth of Networks: How Social Production Transforms Markets and Freedom* (New Haven, Conn.: Yale University Press, 2006), available at http://www.benkler.org/Benkler_Wealth _Of_Networks.pdf; Neil Weinstock Netanel, "Locating Copyright Within the First Amendment Skein," *Stanford Law Review* 54 (2001): 1–86; Netanel, "Copyright and a Democratic Civil Society," *Yale Law Journal* 106 (1996): 283–388; David McGowan, "First Amendment & Copyright Policy," available at http://papers.ssrn.com/sol3/ papers.cfm?abstract_id=460280; Randal Picker, "Copyright as Entry Policy: The Case of Digital Distribution," *Antitrust Bulletin* 47 (2002): 423, 424.

55. Quoted in Fritz Machlup and Edith Penrose, "The Patent Controversy in the Nineteenth Century," *Journal of Economic History* 10, no. 1 (1950): 4, n8.

56. Ironically, contemporary economists are rediscovering the attractions of patent alternatives. A paper by Steven Shavell and Tanguy Van Ypersele is particularly interesting in this regard: "Rewards versus Intellectual Property Rights," NBER Working Paper series, no. 6956, available at http://www.nber.org/papers/w6956.

57. "Governor Thomas was so pleased with the construction of this stove . . . that he offered to give me a patent for the sole vending of them for a term of years; but I declined it from a principle which has ever weighed with me on such occasions, viz.: That, as we enjoy great advantages from the inventions of others, we should be glad of an opportunity to serve others by any invention of ours; and this we should do freely and generously." Benjamin Franklin, *Autobiography*, in *The Works of Benjamin Franklin*, ed. John Bigelow, vol. 1 (New York: G. P. Putnam's Sons, 1904), 237–238.

58. Kenneth Arrow, "Economic Welfare and the Allocation of Resources for Invention," in National Bureau of Economic Research, *The Rate and Direction of Inventive Activity: Economic and Social Factors* (Princeton, N.J.: Princeton University Press, 1962), 609–626.

59. Sanford J. Grossman and Joseph E. Stiglitz, "On the Impossibility of Informationally Efficient Markets," *American Economic Review* 70 (1980), 393–408; Boyle, *Shamans*, 35–42.

CHAPTER 3:
THE SECOND ENCLOSURE MOVEMENT

Further Reading

The endnotes to this chapter supply copious particular references; this page provides the overview. Those seeking to understand the various methods by which different aspects of common land were enclosed over a 400 year history in England should start with J. A. Yelling, *Common Field and Enclosure in England, 1450–1850* (Hamden, Conn.: Archon Books, 1977). Thomas More, *Utopia* (New York: W. J. Black, 1947), provides a harsh criticism of the enclosure movement, one that is echoed hundreds of years later by Polanyi: Karl Polanyi, *The Great Transformation: The Political and Economic Origins of Our Time* (Boston: Beacon Press, 1957). Economic historians have generally believed that the enclosure movement yielded considerable efficiency gains—bringing under centralized control and management, property that had previously been inefficiently managed under a regime of common access. When efficiency gains mean higher productivity so that fewer people starve, this is no small thing. Donald N. McCloskey, "The Enclosure of Open Fields: Preface to a Study of Its Impact on the Efficiency of English Agriculture in the Eighteenth Century," *Journal of Economic History* 32 (1972): 15–35; "The Prudent Peasant: New Findings on Open Fields," *Journal of Economic History* 51 (1991): 343–355. This argument seems plausible, but it has recently received powerful challenges, for example, that by Robert C. Allen, *Enclosure and the Yeoman* (New York: Oxford University Press, 1992).

In the twentieth century, the negative effects of open access or common ownership received an environmental gloss thanks to the work of Garrett Hardin, "The Tragedy of the Commons," *Science* 162 (1968): 1243–1248. However, work by scholars such as Elinor Ostrom, *Governing the Commons: The Evolution of Institutions for Collective Action* (Cambridge: Cambridge University Press, 1990), and Carol Rose, "The Comedy of the Commons: Custom, Commerce, and Inherently Public Property," *University of Chicago Law Review* 53 (1986): 711–781, have introduced considerable nuance to this idea. Some resources may be *more* efficiently used if they are held in common. In addition, nonlegal, customary, and norm-based forms of "regulation" often act to mitigate the theoretical dangers of overuse or under-investment.

Beyond the theoretical and historical arguments about the effects of enclosure on real property lie the question of how well those arguments translate to the world of the intangible and intellectual. It is that question which this chapter raises. Christopher May, *A Global Political Economy of Intellectual Property Rights: The New Enclosures?* (London: Routledge, 2000) offers a similar analogy—as do several other articles cited in the text. The key differences obviously lie in the features of intellectual property identified in the earlier chapters—its nonrivalrousness and nonexcludability—and on the ways in which a commons of cultural, scientific, and technical information has been central to the operation of both liberal democracy and capitalist economy. I owe the latter point particularly to Richard Nelson, whose work on the economics of innovation amply repays further study: Richard Nelson, *Technology, Institutions, and Economic Growth* (Cambridge, Mass.: Harvard University Press, 2005).

Notes to Chapter 3

1. Apart from being anonymous, this poem is extremely hard to date. It probably originates in the enclosure controversies of the eighteenth century. However, the earliest reference to it that I have been able to discover is from 1821. Edward Birch was moved to compose some (fairly poor) verses in response when he reported "seeing the following *jeu d'esprit* in a Handbill posted up in Plaistow, as a 'CAUTION' to prevent persons from supporting the intended inclosure of Hainault or Waltham Forest." He then quotes a version of

the poem. Edward Birch, *Tickler Magazine* 3 (February 1821), 45. In 1860, "Exon," a staff writer for the journal *Notes and Queries*, declares that "the animosity excited against the Inclosure Acts and their authors . . . was almost without precedent: though fifty years and more have passed, the subject is still a sore one in many parishes. . . . I remember some years ago, in hunting over an old library discovering a box full of printed squibs, satires and ballads of the time against the acts and those who were supposed to favor them,—the library having belonged to a gentleman who played an active part on the opposition side." "Exon," "Ballads Against Inclosures," *Notes and Queries* 9, 2nd series (February 1860): 130–131. He reports finding the poem in that box, and quotes a verse from it. The context of the article makes it appear that the poem itself must date from the late eighteenth century. In other sources, the poem is sometimes dated at 1764, and said to be in response to Sir Charles Pratt's fencing of common land. See, e.g., Dana A. Freiburger, "John Thompson, English Philomath—A Question of Land Surveying and Astronomy," n. 15, available at http://www.nd.edu/~histast4/exhibits/papers/Freiburger/. This attribution is widespread and may well be true, but I have been able to discover no contemporary source material that sustains it. By the end of the nineteenth century, the poem was being quoted, sometimes with amusement and sometimes with agreement, on both sides of the Atlantic. See Ezra S. Carr, "Aids and Obstacles to Agriculture on the Pacific-Coast," in *The Patrons of Husbandry on the Pacific Coast* (San Francisco: A. L. Bancroft and Co., 1875), 290–291; Edward P. Cheyney, *An Introduction to the Industrial and Social History of England* (New York: Macmillan, 1901), 219.

2. Although we refer to it as *the* enclosure movement, it was actually a series of enclosures that started in the fifteenth century and went on, with differing means, ends, and varieties of state involvement, until the nineteenth. See, e.g., J. A. Yelling, *Common Field and Enclosure in England, 1450–1850* (Hamden, Conn.: Archon Books, 1977).

3. Thomas More, *Utopia* (New York: W. J. Black, 1947), 32.

4. Karl Polanyi, *The Great Transformation: The Political and Economic Origins of Our Time* (Boston: Beacon Press, 1957), 35. Polanyi continues in the same vein. "The fabric of society was being disrupted. Desolate villages and the ruins of human dwellings testified to the fierceness with which the revolution raged, endangering the defenses of the country, wasting its towns, decimating its population, turning its overburdened soil into dust, harassing its people and turning them from decent husbandmen into a mob of beggars and thieves." Ibid. See also E. P. Thompson, *The Making of the English Working Class* (London: V. Gollancz, 1963), 218.

5. See generally Lord Ernle, *English Farming Past and Present*, 6th ed. (Chicago: Quadrangle Books, 1961).

6. For an excellent summary of the views of Hobbes, Locke, and Blackstone on these points, see Hannibal Travis, "Pirates of the Information Infrastructure: Blackstonian Copyright and the First Amendment," *Berkeley Technology Law Journal* 15 (2000): 789–803.

7. More recent accounts which argue that enclosure led to productivity gains tend to be more qualified in their praise. Compare the more positive account given in Ernle, *English Farming*, with Michael Turner, "English Open Fields and Enclosures: Retardation or Productivity Improvements," *Journal of Economic History* 46 (1986): 688: "Enclosure cannot be seen as the automatic open door to this cycle of agricultural improvement, but

the foregoing estimates do suggest that perhaps it was a door which opened frequently, and with profit."

8. Most notably work by Robert C. Allen: "The Efficiency and Distributional Consequences of Eighteenth Century Enclosures," *The Economic Journal* 92 (1982): 937–953; *Enclosure and The Yeoman* (New York: Oxford University Press, 1992). Allen argues that the enclosure movement produced major distributional consequences, but little observable efficiency gain. The pie was carved up differently, to the advantage of the landlords, but made no larger. In contrast, Turner sees enclosure as one possible, though not a necessary, route to productivity gains ("English Open Fields," 688). Donald McCloskey's work also argues for efficiency gains from enclosure, largely from the evidence provided by rent increases. Donald N. McCloskey, "The Enclosure of Open Fields: Preface to a Study of Its Impact on the Efficiency of English Agriculture in the Eighteenth Century," *Journal of Economic History* 32 (1972): 15–35; "The Prudent Peasant: New Findings on Open Fields," *Journal of Economic History* 51 (1991): 343–355. In Allen's view, however, the increase in rents was largely a measure of the way that changes in legal rights altered the bargaining power of the parties and the cultural context of rent negotiations; enclosure allowed landlords to capture more of the existing surplus produced by the land, rather than dramatically expanding it. "[T]he enclosure movement itself might be regarded as the first state sponsored land reform. Like so many since, it was justified with efficiency arguments, while its main effect (according to the data analysed here) was to redistribute income to already rich landowners." Allen, "Eighteenth Century Enclosures," 950–951.

9. The possibility of producing "order without law" and thus sometimes governing the commons without tragedy has also fascinated scholars of contemporary land use. Robert C. Ellickson, *Order without Law: How Neighbors Settle Disputes* (Cambridge, Mass.: Harvard University Press, 1991); Elinor Ostrom, *Governing the Commons: The Evolution of Institutions for Collective Action* (Cambridge: Cambridge University Press, 1990).

10. The analogy to the enclosure movement has been too succulent to resist. To my knowledge, Ben Kaplan, Pamela Samuelson, Yochai Benkler, David Lange, Christopher May, David Bollier, and Keith Aoki have all employed the trope, as I myself have on previous occasions. For a particularly thoughtful and careful development of the parallel between the two enclosure movements, see Travis, "Pirates of the Information Infrastructure."

11. See, e.g., William A. Haseltine, "The Case for Gene Patents," *Technology Review* (September 2000): 59, available at http://www.technologyreview.com/articles/haseltine0900.asp; cf. Alexander K. Haas, "The Wellcome Trust's Disclosures of Gene Sequence Data into the Public Domain & the Potential for Proprietary Rights in the Human Genome," *Berkeley Technology Law Journal* 16 (2001): 145–164.

12. See, e.g., Haseltine, "The Case for Gene Patents"; Biotechnology Industry Association, "Genentech, Incyte Genomics Tell House Subcommittee Gene Patents Essential for Medical Progress," available at http://www.bio.org/news/newsitem.asp?id=2000_ 0713 _01.

13. See, e.g., Howard Markel, "Patents Could Block the Way to a Cure," *New York Times* (August 24, 2001), A19. For the general background to these arguments, see Rebecca

S. Eisenberg, "Patenting the Human Genome," *Emory Law Journal* 39 (1990): 740–744.

14. 793 P.2d 479, 488–497 (Cal. 1990).

15. Ibid., 493–494. One imagines Styrofoam coolers criss-crossing the country by FedEx in an orgy of communistic flesh-swapping.

16. Ibid., 493.

17. I might be suspected of anti-economist irony here. In truth, neither side's arguments are fully satisfying. It is easy to agree with Richard Posner that the language of economics offers a "thin and unsatisfactory epistemology" through which to understand the world. Richard Posner, *The Problems of Jurisprudence* (Cambridge, Mass.: Harvard University Press, 1990): xiv (quoting Paul Bator, "The Judicial Universe of Judge Richard Posner," *University of Chicago Law Review* 52 (1985): 1161). On the other hand, explaining what it means to "own one's own body," or specifying the noncommodifiable limits on the market, turns out to be a remarkably tricky business, as Margaret Jane Radin has shown with great elegance in *Contested Commodities* (Cambridge, Mass.: Harvard University Press, 1996).

18. Directive 96/9/EC of the European Parliament and of the Council of 11 March 1996 on the Legal Protection of Databases, 1996 *Official Journal of the European Union* (L 77) 20, available at http://europa.eu.int/ISPO/infosoc/legreg/docs/969ec.html.

19. The phrase "Washington consensus" originated in John Williamson, "What Washington Means by Policy Reform," in *Latin American Adjustment: How Much Has Happened?* ed. John Williamson (Washington, D.C.: Institute for International Economics, 1990). Over time it has come to be used as shorthand for a neoliberal view of economic policy that puts its faith in deregulation, privatization, and the creation and defense of secure property rights as the cure for all ills. (See Joseph Stiglitz, "The World Bank at the Millennium," *Economic Journal* 109 [1999]: 577–597.) It has thus become linked to the triumphalist neoliberal account of the end of history and the victory of unregulated markets: see Francis Fukuyama, *The End of History and the Last Man* (New York: Free Press, 1992). Neither of these two results are, to be fair, what its creator intended. See John Williamson, "What Should the Bank Think about the Washington Consensus?" Institute for International Economics (July 1999), available at http://www.iie.com/publications/papers/paper.cfm?ResearchID=351.

20. Garrett Hardin, "The Tragedy of the Commons," *Science* 162 (1968): 1243–1248.

21. The differences are particularly strong in the arguments over "desert"—are these property rights deserved or are they simply violations of the public trust, privatizations of the commons? For example, some would say that we never had the same traditional claims over the genetic commons that the victims of the first enclosure movement had over theirs; this is more like newly discovered frontier land, or perhaps even privately drained marshland, than it is like well-known common land that all have traditionally used. In this case, the enclosers can claim (though their claims are disputed) that they discovered or perhaps simply made usable the territory they seek to own. The opponents of gene patenting, on the other hand, turn more frequently than the farmers of the eighteenth century to religious and ethical arguments about the sanctity of life and the incompatibility of property with living systems. These arguments, or the appeals to

free speech that dominate debates over digital intellectual property, have no precise analogue in debates over hunting or pasturage, though again there are common themes. For example, we are already seeing nostalgic laments of the loss of the immemorial rights of Internet users. At the same time, the old language of property law is turned to this more evanescent subject matter; a favorite title of mine is I. Trotter Hardy, "The Ancient Doctrine of Trespass to Web Sites," 1996, art. 7, *Journal of Online Law* art. 7, available at http://www.wm.edu/law/publications/jol/95_96/hardy.html.

22. The exceptions to this statement turn out to be fascinating. In the interest of brevity, however, I will ignore them entirely.

23. Remember, I am talking here about increases in the level of rights: protecting new subject matter for longer periods of time, criminalizing certain technologies, making it illegal to cut through digital fences even if they have the effect of foreclosing previously lawful uses, and so on. Each of these has the effect of diminishing the public domain in the name of national economic policy.

24. James Boyle, *Shamans, Software, and Spleens: Law and the Construction of the Information Society* (Cambridge, Mass.: Harvard University Press, 1996), 29; William M. Landes and Richard A. Posner, "Economic Analysis of Copyright Law," *Journal of Legal Studies* 18 (1989): 325; Pamela Samuelson and Suzanne Scotchmer, "The Law & Economics of Reverse Engineering," *Yale Law Journal* 111 (2002): 1575–1664; Jessica Litman, "The Public Domain," *Emory Law Journal* 39 (1990): 1010–1011.

25. Sanford J. Grossman and Joseph E. Stiglitz, "On the Impossibility of Informationally Efficient Markets," *American Economic Review* 70 (1980): 404.

26. For a more technical account, see James Boyle, "Cruel, Mean, or Lavish? Economic Analysis, Price Discrimination and Digital Intellectual Property," *Vanderbilt Law Review* 53 (2000): 2007–2039.

27. The most recent example of this phenomenon is multiple legal roadblocks in bringing *Golden*Rice to market. For a fascinating study of the various issues involved and the strategies for working around them, see R. David Kryder, Stanley P. Kowalski, and Anatole F. Krattiger, "The Intellectual and Technical Property Components of Pro-Vitamin A Rice (*Golden*Rice™): A Preliminary Freedom-to-Operate Review," *ISAAA Briefs* No. 20 (2000), available at http://www.isaaa.org/Briefs/20/briefs.htm. In assessing the economic effects of patents, one has to balance the delays and increased costs caused by the web of property rights against the benefits to society of the incentives to innovation, the requirement of disclosure, and the eventual access to the patented subject matter. When the qualification levels for patents are set too low, the benefits are minuscule and the costs very high—the web of property rights is particularly tangled, complicating follow-on innovation, the monopoly goes to "buy" a very low level of inventiveness, and the disclosure is of little value.

28. Michael A. Heller and Rebecca S. Eisenberg, "Can Patents Deter Innovation? The Anticommons in Biomedical Research," *Science* 280 (1998): 698–701.

29. *Int'l News Serv. v. Associated Press*, 248 U.S. 215, 250 (1918) (Brandeis, J., dissenting).

30. Yochai Benkler, "Free as the Air to Common Use: First Amendment Constraints on Enclosure of the Public Domain," *New York University Law Review* 74 (1999): 354, 361, 424.

31. The so-called "business method" patents, which cover such "inventions" as auctions or accounting methods, are an obvious example. See, e.g., *State St. Bank & Trust Co. v. Signature Fin. Group, Inc.,* 149 F.3d 1368, 1373 (Fed. Cir. 1998).

32. Database Investment and Intellectual Property Antipiracy Act of 1996, HR 3531, 104th Cong. (1996); Collections of Information Antipiracy Act, S 2291, 105th Cong. (1998).

33. See, e.g., *Feist Publications v. Rural Tel. Serv. Co.,* 499 U.S. 340, 350 (1991): "Copyright treats facts and factual compilations in a wholly consistent manner. Facts, whether alone or as part of a compilation, are not original and therefore may not be copyrighted." To hold otherwise "distorts basic copyright principles in that it creates a monopoly in public domain materials without the necessary justification of protecting and encouraging the creation of 'writings' by 'authors.'" Ibid., at 354.

34. See Eisenberg, "Patenting the Human Genome"; Haas, "Wellcome Trust's Disclosures."

35. Those who prefer topographical metaphors might imagine a quilted pattern of public and private land, with legal rules specifying that certain areas, beaches say, can never be privately owned, and accompanying rules giving public rights of way through private land if there is a danger that access to the commons might otherwise be blocked.

36. See Jessica Litman, *Digital Copyright: Protecting Intellectual Property on the Internet* (Amherst, N.Y.: Prometheus Books, 2001).

37. See James Boyle, "Intellectual Property Policy Online: A Young Person's Guide," *Harvard Journal of Law & Technology* 10 (1996): 47–112.

38. *American Geophysical Union v. Texaco,* 37 F.3d 882 (2nd Cir. 1994).

39. *Los Angeles Times v. Free Republic,* 2000 U.S. Dist. LEXIS 5669, 54 U.S.P.Q.2D 1453 (C.D. Cal. 2000).

40. *eBay, Inc. v. Bidder's Edge, Inc.,* 100 F. Supp. 2d 1058 (N.D. Cal. 2000).

41. *Kelly v. Arriba Soft,* 336 F.3d 811 (9th Cir. 2003). After initially holding that while thumbnails were fair use, inline links that displayed pictures were not fair use, the court reversed itself and found fair use in both instances.

42. After a District Court issued a temporary injunction telling Static Controls that it must cease manufacturing generic toner cartridges that operated in Lexmark printers—indicating it was likely to be found to be violating the Digital Millennium Copyright Act's "anti-circumvention" provisions—the Appeals Court held that such cartridges did not in fact violate the DMCA. *Lexmark International, Inc. v. Static Control Components, Inc.,* 387 F.3d 522 (6th Cir. 2004).

43. *Madey v. Duke Univ.,* 307 F.3d 1351 (Fed. Cir. 2003), cert. denied, 539 U.S. 958 (2003).

44. "When scientists from Princeton University and Rice University tried to publish their findings [on the vulnerabilities in a copy protection scheme] in April 2001, the recording industry claimed that the 1998 Digital Millennium Copyright Act (DMCA) makes it illegal to discuss or provide technology that might be used to bypass industry controls limiting how consumers can use music they have purchased. 'Studying digital access technologies and publishing the research for our colleagues are both fundamental to the progress of science and academic freedom,' stated Princeton scientist Edward Felten. 'The recording industry's interpretation of the DMCA would make scientific progress on this important topic illegal.' . . .

"SDMI sponsored the 'SDMI Public Challenge' in September 2000, asking Netizens to try to break their favored watermark schemes, designed to control consumer access to digital music. When the scientists' paper about their successful defeat of the watermarks, including one developed by a company called Verance, was accepted for publication, Matt Oppenheim, an officer of both RIAA and SDMI, sent the Princeton professor a letter threatening legal liability if the scientist published his results." "EFF Media Release: Princeton Scientists Sue Over Squelched Research," available at http://w2.eff.org/IP/DMCA/Felten_v_RIAA/20010606_eff_felten_pr.html. After a First Amendment challenge to the relevant provisions of the DMCA, the threats were withdrawn.

45. See, e.g., Robert P. Merges, "As Many as Six Impossible Patents before Breakfast: Property Rights for Business Concepts and Patent System Reform," *Berkeley Technology Law Journal* 14 (1999): 615.

CHAPTER 4: THE INTERNET THREAT

Further Reading

The first book to read on the history of the tension between copying technologies and the law that regulates them is Paul Goldstein's effortlessly erudite *Copyright's Highway: From Gutenberg to the Celestial Jukebox*, 2nd ed. (Stanford, Calif.: Stanford University Press, 2003). Goldstein and I differ somewhat in our optimism about current regulatory developments but his work is an indispensable beginning for the inquiry and a pleasure to read. One fascinating theme in the book is that the intellectual tension between maximalists and minimalists (or optimists and pessimists as he describes them) is actually a fundamental part of copyright law's survival strategy—its dialectical method of dealing with technological change. If so, in this book I am struggling gamely to do my part by holding up my side of the dialectic. It does not seem to be winning much recently. Perhaps copyright's Hegel is asleep.

Much of this chapter concerns itself with copyright's response to the Internet. No book comes close to laying this out as well as Jessica Litman's *Digital Copyright: Protecting Intellectual Property on the Internet* (Amherst, N.Y.: Prometheus Books, 2001). Litman is a beautiful essayist and this book is both accessible and detailed. Those readers who are interested in the history of that dying technology, the VCR, will find a brilliant account in James Lardner, *Fast Forward: Hollywood, the Japanese & the VCR Wars* (New York: Norton, 1987). One needs only to scan its pages to pick up the eerie foreshadowing of the Internet Threat. Litman's article on the *Sony* case provides a detailed legal history to back up Lardner's social history. Jessica Litman, "The *Sony* Paradox," *Case Western Reserve Law Review* 55 (2005): 917–962. Pamela Samuelson has a fine article exploring the jurisprudential impact of *Sony*'s reasoning. Pamela Samuelson, "The Generativity of Sony v. Universal: The Intellectual Property Legacy of Justice Stevens," *Fordham Law Review* 74 (2006): 1831–1876.

The scholarly literature on Napster, copyright, and peer-to-peer technologies generally is both wide and deep. In addition to Litman's book, some personal favorites include: Raymond Shih Ray Ku, "The Creative Destruction of Copyright: Napster and the New Economics of Digital Technology," *University of Chicago Law Review* 69 (2002): 263–324; Mark A. Lemley and R. Anthony Reese, "Reducing Digital Copyright Infringement Without Restricting Innovation," *Stanford Law Review* 56 (2003–2004): 1345–1434; Jane C. Ginsburg, "Separating the *Sony* Sheep From the *Grokster* Goats: Reckoning the Future Business Plans of Copyright-Dependent Technology Entrepreneurs," *University of Arizona Law Review* 50 (2008): 577–609; Justin Hughes, "On the Logic of Suing One's Customers and the Dilemma of Infringement-Based Business Models," *Cardozo Arts and Entertainment Law Journal* 22 (2005): 725–766; Douglas Lichtman and William Landes, "Indirect Liability for Copyright Infringement: An Economic Perspective," *Harvard Journal of Law and Technology* 16 (2003): 395–410; and Glynn S. Lunney, Jr., "Fair Use and Market Failure: *Sony* Revisited," *Boston University Law Review* 82 (2002): 975–1030.

In addition to these articles, a number have focused specifically on alternative methods of encouraging cultural production while maximizing technological and cultural freedom. Two that have profoundly influenced my own thinking are Neil Weinstock Netanel, "Impose a Noncommercial Use Levy to Allow Free Peer-to-Peer File Sharing," *Harvard Journal of Law and Technology* 17 (2003): 1–84; and William Fisher, *Promises to Keep: Technology, Law, and the Future of Entertainment* (Palo Alto, Calif.: Stanford University Press, 2004). Fisher, whose presentations and articles reveal a cathedral-like conceptual structure that would have delighted the Encyclopedists, argues powerfully that a system of levies on broadband technology, distributed in proportion to the popularity of the music downloaded could allow us to permit "free" access to music while still compensating musicians. His responses to the problems of measurement, gaming of the system, privacy, and so on will not convince everyone but they represent by far the most systematic treatment of the subject.

Notes to Chapter 4

1. For the background to these documents see James Boyle, "Intellectual Property Policy Online: A Young Person's Guide," *Harvard Journal of Law & Technology* 10 (1996): 47–112; Jessica Litman, *Digital Copyright: Protecting Intellectual Property on the Internet* (Amherst, N.Y.: Prometheus Books, 2001).

2. Pub. L. No. 105-304, 112 Stat. 2860 (1998) (codified as amended in scattered sections of 5, 17, 28, and 35 U.S.C.).

3. *Intellectual Property and the National Information Infrastructure: The Report of the Working Group on Intellectual Property Rights* (Washington, D.C.: Information Infrastructure Task Force, 1995), 73 n. 227. Hereinafter *White Paper*.

4. *White Paper*, 84.

5. "Congress did not provide that one class in the community could combine to restrain interstate trade and another class could not. . . . It provided that 'every' contract, combination or conspiracy in restraint of trade was illegal." *Loewe v. Lawlor*, 208 U.S. 274 (1908); "Indians inhabiting this country were fierce savages, whose occupation was war, and whose subsistence was drawn chiefly from the forest. To leave them in possession of their country, was to leave the country a wilderness. . . ." *Johnson v. M'Intosh*, 21 U.S. 543, 590 (1823).

6. "As the entertainment and information markets have gotten more complicated, the copyright law has gotten longer, more specific, and harder to understand. Neither book publishers nor libraries have any interest in making the library privilege broad enough so that it would be useful to users that aren't libraries, and neither movie studios nor broadcast stations have any interest in making the broadcaster's privilege broad enough to be of some use to say, cable television or satellite TV, so that doesn't happen. Negotiated privileges tend to be very specific, and tend to pose substantial entry barriers to outsiders who can't be at the negotiating table because their industries haven't been invented yet. So negotiated copyright statutes have tended, throughout the century, to be kind to the entrenched status quo and hostile to upstart new industries." Litman, *Digital Copyright*, 25.

7. Communications Decency Act of 1996 (47 U.S.C. §§ 230, 560, 561) (1996).

8. *Reno v. ACLU*, 521 U.S. 844 (1997).

9. James Boyle, "Overregulating the Internet," *Washington Times* (November 14, 1995), A17.

10. See James Boyle, "The One Thing Government Officials Can't Do Is Threaten Their Critics," *Washington Times* (March 6, 1996), A16.

11. "The DFC was forged in 1995 in response to the release of the Clinton administration's *White Paper on Intellectual Property and the National Information Infrastructure*. The *White Paper* recommended significantly altering existing copyright law to increase the security of ownership rights for creators of motion pictures, publishers and others in the proprietary community. Members of the DFC recognized that if the policy proposals delineated in the *White Paper* were implemented, educators, businesses, libraries, consumers and others would be severely restricted in their efforts to take advantage of the benefits of digital networks." See http://www.dfc.org/dfc1/Learning_Center/about.html.

12. See the classic account in Mancur Olson, *The Logic of Collective Action: Public Goods and the Theory of Groups*, 2nd ed. (Cambridge, Mass.: Harvard University Press, 1971).

13. See note 2 above.

14. Pub. L. No. 105-147, 111 Stat. 2678 (1997) (codified as amended in scattered sections of 17 and 18 U.S.C.).

15. Pub. L. No. 105-298, 112 Stat. 2827 (1998) (codified as amended in scattered sections of 17 U.S.C.).

16. S 2291, 105th Cong. (1998).

17. *Sony Corp. of America v. Universal City Studios, Inc.*, 464 U.S. 417 (1984).

18. *See* Tina Balio, Museum of Broadcast Communications, "Betamax Case," *Encyclopedia of TV* (1997), available at http://www.museum.tv/archives/etv/B/htmlB/betamaxcase/betamaxcase.htm ("The Betamax case went all the way to the Supreme Court, which reversed the appeals court decision on 17 January 1984. By 1986, VCRs had been installed in fifty percent of American homes and annual videocassettes sales surpassed the theatrical box-office."). The year 1986 was also the peak of the video rental market: "Video's high mark, according to studies by A. C. Nielsen Media Research, was in late 1986, when an estimated 34.3 million households with VCR's took home 111.9 million cassettes a month, or an average of 3.26 movies per household." Peter M. Nichols,

"Movie Rentals Fade, Forcing an Industry to Change its Focus," *New York Times* (May 6, 1990), A1.

19. For background, see Wendy Gordon, "Fair Use as Market Failure: A Structural and Economic Analysis of the *Betamax* Case and Its Predecessors," *Columbia Law Review* 82 (1982): 1600–1657. For accounts that imagine a reduction of fair use as transaction costs fall, see Edmund W. Kitch, "Can the Internet Shrink Fair Use?," *Nebraska Law Review* 78 (1999): 880–890; Robert P. Merges, "The End of Friction? Property Rights and the Contract in the 'Newtonian' World of On-Line Commerce," *Berkeley Technology Law Journal* 12 (1997): 115–136. This argument has hardly gone unanswered with articles pointing out that it neglects both the social values of fair use and the actual economics of its operation. See Jonathan Dowell, "Bytes and Pieces: Fragmented Copies, Licensing, and Fair Use in A Digital World," *California Law Review* 86 (1998): 843–878; Ben Depoorter and Francesco Parisi, "Fair Use and Copyright Protection: A Price Theory Explanation," *International Review of Law and Economics* 21 (2002): 453–473.

20. "I believe the answer to the question of justification turns primarily on whether, and to what extent, the challenged use is *transformative*. The use must be productive and must employ the quoted matter in a different manner or for a different purpose from the original." Pierre N. Leval, "Toward a Fair Use Standard," *Harvard Law Review* 103 (1990): 1111.

21. See Neil Weinstock Netanel, "Locating Copyright Within the First Amendment Skein," *Stanford Law Review* 54 (2001): 1–86; Yochai Benkler, "Free As the Air to Common Use: First Amendment Constraints on Enclosure of the Public Domain," *New York University Law Review* 74 (1999): 354–446; Larry Lessig, Melville B. Nimmer Memorial Lecture: "Copyright's First Amendment" (March 1, 2001), in *UCLA Law Review* 48 (2001): 1057–1074; Melville B. Nimmer, "Does Copyright Abridge the First Amendment Guaranties of Free Speech and the Press?" *UCLA Law Review* 17 (1970): 1180–1204.

22. *Sega Enterprises Ltd. v. Accolade, Inc.*, 977 F.2d 1510 (9th Cir. 1992); *Atari Games Corp. v. Nintendo of America Inc.*, 975 F.2d 832 (Fed. Cir. 1992).

23. *Sony* 464 U.S. at 441 n. 21.

24. *A&M Records, Inc. v. Napster, Inc.*, 239 F.3d 1004 (9th Cir. 2001).

25. *A&M Records v. Napster.* C-SPAN Videotape 159534, Part 1 of 1 (October 2, 2000).

26. Felix Oberholzer-Gee and Koleman Strumpf, "The Effect of File Sharing on Record Sales: An Empirical Analysis," *Journal of Political Economy* 115, no. 1 (2007): 1–42.

27. Stan J. Liebowitz, "How Reliable Is the Oberholzer-Gee and Strumpf Paper on File-Sharing?" available at http://papers.ssrn.com/sol3/papers.cfm?abstract_id=1014399.

28. Rafael Rob and Joel Waldfogel, "Piracy on the High C's: Music Downloading, Sales Displacement, and Social Welfare in a Sample of College Students," available at http://www.law.upenn.edu/polk/dropbox/waldfogel.pdf.

29. M. Peitz and P. Waelbroeck, "The Effect of Internet Piracy on Music Sales: Cross-Section Evidence," *Review of Economic Research on Copyright Issues* (December 2004): 71–79, available at http://www.serci.org/docs_1_2/waelbroeck.pdf. For an excellent general discussion see Rufus Pollock's summary of the empirical evidence at http://www.rufuspollock.org/economics/p2p_summary.html.

30. *MGM Studios Inc. v. Grokster, Ltd.*, 545 U.S. 913 (2005).

31. J. H. Saltzer, D. P. Reed, and D. D. Clark, "End-to-End Arguments in System Design," *ACM Transactions on Computer Systems* (November 1984): 277.

32. Technically, this discussion fuses components of the Internet—its transfer protocols, for example—with aspects of the World Wide Web, the set of linked hypertext documents assembled on top of it.

CHAPTER 5: THE FARMERS' TALE

Further Reading

This chapter focuses primarily on the Digital Millennium Copyright Act ("DMCA"), one of the most controversial recent pieces of intellectual property legislation and the subject of extensive scholarship and commentary.

The DMCA and DRM

Once again Jessica Litman's *Digital Copyright: Protecting Intellectual Property on the Internet* (Amherst, N.Y.: Prometheus Books, 2001) is an indispensable introduction. David Nimmer offered one of the early, and prescient, analyses of the conceptual problems in the statute. David Nimmer, "A Riff on Fair Use in the Digital Millennium Copyright Act," *University of Pennsylvania Law Review* 148 (2000): 673–742. His anthology, *Copyright: Sacred Text, Technology, and the DMCA* (The Hague: Kluwer Law International, 2003), is also worthy reading for those who wish to pursue the legal issues further. Tarleton Gillespie's book *Wired Shut: Copyright and the Shape of Digital Culture* (Cambridge, Mass.: MIT Press, 2007), is an accessible but thorough introduction to the economic, political, and cultural consequences of so-called "digital rights management" or DRM. Legal scholars have been assiduous in pointing out the problems that legally backed DRM brings to science, culture, policy, and economic competition. Pamela Samuelson's "Intellectual Property and the Digital Economy: Why the Anti-Circumvention Regulations Need to be Revised," *Berkeley Technology Law Journal* 14 (1999): 519–566, is an early critique that proved to be particularly accurate in its predictions. Jerome Reichman, Graeme Dinwoodie, and Pamela Samuelson, "A Reverse Notice and Takedown Regime to Enable Public Interest Uses of Technically Protected Copyrighted Works," *Berkeley Technology Law Journal* 22 (2007): 981–1060, provides a fascinating recent proposal for a method to solve some of those problems. Dan Burk's "Anticircumvention Misuse," *UCLA Law Review* 50 (2003): 1095–1140, offers a similar piece of conceptual judo, looking at the way in which copyright's traditional concerns with anticompetitive and predatory misuse of intellectual property rights could be turned on the new legally backed digital fences of cyberspace. Julie Cohen sets the debate in the wider perspective of political theory in a way that has been influential on my own thinking. In "*Lochner* in Cyberspace: The New Economic Orthodoxy of 'Rights Management'," *Michigan Law Review* 97 (1998): 462–563, and her subsequent work, she describes the ways in which digital rights management presents fascinating echoes of the ideology of socially untrammeled property rights that dominated the first twenty years of the twentieth century in the United States and was eventually countered with the ideals of the New Deal. Finally, Jane Ginsburg, "Copyright and Control over New Technologies of Dissemination," *Columbia Law Review* 101 (2001): 1613–1647, provides a more positive account, arguing that on balance—given the dangers of illicit digital copying—the DMCA's benefits outweigh its costs.

The DMCA and Freedom of Expression

Those who are interested in the tensions between copyright law and free expression are the beneficiaries of an explosion of scholarship. I cannot begin to cite it all here. Melville Nimmer's article from 1970, "Does Copyright Abridge the First Amendment Guarantees of Free Speech and Press?" *UCLA Law Review* 17 (1970): 1180–1204, is a required starting place though its full impact was not to be felt for some time. Lawrence Lessig, "Copyright's First Amendment," *UCLA Law Review* 48 (2001): 1057–1074, provides a lovely reflection of the impact of Nimmer's arguments more than 30 years on. Neil Netanel's book *Copyright's Paradox* (Oxford: Oxford University Press, 2008), is the single most comprehensive work in the field and a fascinating read. Netanel's arguments, and those of Yochai Benkler, "Free as the Air to Common Use: First Amendment Constraints on Enclosure of the Public Domain," *New York University Law Review* 74 (1999): 354–446, and Jed Rubenfeld, "The Freedom of Imagination: Copyright's Constitutionality," *Yale Law Journal* 112 (2002): 1–60, have been influential on my own thinking in many areas. Bernt Hugenholtz has demonstrated that the concern about a tension between copyright law and freedom of expression is by no means limited to the United States. P. Bernt Hugenholtz, "Copyright and Freedom of Expression in Europe" in *Expanding the Boundaries of Intellectual Property: Innovation Policy for the Information Society*, ed. Rochelle Dreyfuss, Diane Zimmerman, and Harry First (Oxford: Oxford University Press, 2001), at 341. (This entire volume is superb, it should be noted.) L. Ray Patterson—an inspiration to the current generation of copyright scholars—summed up the intellectual current well when he compared the DMCA to the methods of censorship imposed by the seventeenth century Licensing Act. L. Ray Patterson, "The DMCA: A Modern Version of the Licensing Act of 1662," *Journal of Intellectual Property Law* 10 (2002): 33–58.

Last, but by no means least, is the new book by my brilliant colleagues, David Lange and H. Jefferson Powell: *No Law: Intellectual Property in the Image of an Absolute First Amendment* (Stanford, Calif.: Stanford University Press, forthcoming 2008). *No Law* offers a fascinating thought experiment: what would a First Amendment jurisprudence look like that took seriously the premise that "no law" is allowed to restrict 'the freedom of speech' protected by the First Amendment and then turned its eyes on copyright? It is the answer to the question "and what exactly does 'the freedom of speech' permit?" that is most intriguing. Interestingly, though Lange and Powell find many copyright doctrines problematic, they are inclined to view the DMCA more charitably. I disagree for the reasons given in this chapter.

Notes to Chapter 5

1. Pub. L. No. 105-304, 112 Stat. 2860 (1998) (codified as amended in scattered sections of 5, 17, 28, and 35 U.S.C.).
2. See Electronic Frontiers Foundation, "Unintended Consequences," available at http://www.eff.org/wp/unintended-consequences- seven-years-under-dmca.

3. See DVD Copy Control Association, "Frequently Asked Questions," available at http://www.dvdcca.org/faq.html.

4. Thomas Mennecke, "Slyck.com Interviews Jon Lech Johansen" (April 4, 2005), available at http://www.slyck.com/news.php?story=733.

5. As is often the way, these pages have now been modified on Wikipedia. At the time of writing, this excerpt can still be found at http://www.indopedia.org/Eric_Corley.html.

6. Abraham Lincoln, Lecture on Discoveries and Inventions (April 6, 1858), available at http://showcase.netins.net/web/creative/lincoln/speeches/discoveries.htm.

7. See Neil Weinstock Netanel, "Locating Copyright Within the First Amendment Skein," *Stanford Law Review* 54 (2001): 15 (citing *Houghton Mifflin Co. v. Noram Publ'g Co.*, 28 F. Supp. 676 (S.D.N.Y. 1939); *Houghton Mifflin Co. v. Stackpole Sons, Inc.*, 104 F.2d 306 (2nd Cir. 1939) (upholding the validity of the U.S. copyright in *Mein Kampf*); Anthony O. Miller, "Court Halted Dime Edition of 'Mein Kampf': Cranston Tells How Hitler Sued Him and Won," *Los Angeles Times*, February 14, 1988, § 1, 4 (giving Cranston's version of the case's underlying facts)).

8. The *Corley* court was uncertain about this point. ("Preliminarily, we note that the Supreme Court has never held that fair use is constitutionally required, although some isolated statements in its opinions might arguably be enlisted for such a requirement."). *Universal City Studios v. Corley*, 273 F.3d 429, 458 (2d Cir. 2001). In my view, both logic and those "isolated statements" suggest that fair use is required. As I point out later, when the Supreme Court revisited the matter in the case of *Eldred v. Ashcroft*, 537 U.S. 186 (2003), it stressed that it was precisely the internal limitations such as fair use that made copyright law normally immune to First Amendment scrutiny. The Court added "when . . . Congress has not altered the traditional contours of copyright protection, further First Amendment scrutiny is unnecessary." Ibid. at 221 (citing *Harper & Row*, 471 U.S. at 560). Yet that is exactly what the DMCA does: alters "the traditional contours of copyright protection" by handing out the exclusive right at the same time as it confers a legal power to remove the privilege of fair use.

9. See *Universal City Studios, Inc. v. Reimerdes*, 111 F. Supp. 2d 294, 304–5 (S.D.N.Y. 2000).

10. Ibid., 329–30 (quoting *Turner Broadcasting System, Inc. v. FCC*, 512 U.S. 622, 662 (1997) (quoting *U.S. v. O'Brien*, 391 U.S. 367, 377 (internal quotations omitted))).

11. Ibid., 331–332.

12. One empirical study seems to challenge this assumption, though at modest levels. Rafael Rob and Joel Waldfogel, "Piracy on the Silver Screen," *Journal of Industrial Economics* 55 (2007): 379–395. Rob and Waldfogel surveyed college students—traditionally a population that engages in high levels of downloading since they have "free" and extremely high speed Internet connections, lots of leisure time, and low disposable income. Even among this group, the authors found that total levels of downloading were low—2.1 percent of paid consumption. The authors also assumed that all unpaid downloading or DVD burning was equal to piracy—an assumption that is clearly false. The *Sony* case makes that clear. In fact, Rob and Waldfogel found a *positive* relationship between second time unpaid viewings and future paid viewings; watching the movie a second time on a downloaded or privately made copy burned from the airwaves actually was associated with more paid purchases. The authors were skeptical of any causal link, however. Ibid., 389.

13. Admittedly, section 1201 only affects works protected under the copyright act, so arguably the legal protection of the digital fence would expire with the copyright term. But even if the courts interpreted the statute this way, two problems would remain. First, since the DMCA prohibited the trafficking in tools which allowed the breaking of the encryption, the law would have effectively forbidden the production of wire cutters for gaining access to identically encrypted public domain works—remember Judge Kaplan's discussion of the irrelevance of Mr. Johansen's motives. Second, it would be trivially easy to add a trivial amount of new copyrighted material to the work that had fallen into the public domain. Access to the public domain work would then be prohibited for another period of life plus seventy years. And so on. The Copyright Office holds hearings on the question of whether there are any "classes of work" that need exemption from the DMCA's provisions. So far, those exemptions have been highly restrictive in application.

14. *Eldred v. Ashcroft*, 537 U.S. 186 (2003) at 221 (citing *Harper & Row*, 471 U.S. at 560).

15. Rob Pegoraro, "RealPlayer's iPod-Compatible Update 'Stunned' Apple," *Washington Post* (August 8, 2004), F6.

16. *Lexmark, Int'l v. Static Control Companies, Inc.*, 387 F.3d 522 (6th Cir. 2004).

17. *Chamberlain Group, Inc. v. Skylink Tech., Inc.*, 381 F.3d 1178 (Fed. Cir. 2004). This of course was exactly the claim that Mr. Corley's lawyers made, to no avail.

CHAPTER 6: I GOT A MASHUP

Further Reading

Musical borrowing is the subject of the next "graphic novel"—which is to say comic book—produced by me, Keith Aoki, and Jennifer Jenkins: *Theft!: A History of Music* (Durham, N.C.: Center for the Study of the Public Domain, forthcoming 2009). Our earlier effort to make intellectual property accessible to film makers and mashup artists can be found in *Bound By Law* (Durham, N.C.: Center for the Study of the Public Domain, 2006), available in full at http://www.law.duke.edu/cspd/comics. An expanded edition of *Bound By Law* will be published in the Fall of 2008 by Duke University Press. However, neither graphic novel can provide a sense of the scholarly literature in music, musicology, law, and biography that enabled me to write this chapter.

Musical History

The indispensable guide to music history is J. Peter Burkholder, Donald Jay Grout, and Claude V. Palisca, *A History of Western Music*, 7th ed. (New York: W. W. Norton, 2006). For those who have access through a university or library the Grove Music database is the single most comprehensive computer-aided source: Grove Music Online, http://www .grovemusic.com/index.html. A fascinating book by Frederic Scherer, *Quarter Notes and Bank Notes: The Economics of Music Composition in the Eighteenth and Nineteenth Centuries* (Princeton, N.J.: Princeton University Press, 2004), explores different incentive systems—such as patronage or markets enabled by intellectual property rights—and their respective effect on musical aesthetics and musical production. Scherer is one of the foremost contemporary economists of innovation. To have him writing about the practices of court composers and manuscript publishers is completely fascinating. At the end of the day, he diplomatically refuses to say whether patronage or market mechanisms produced "better" music but the careful reader will pick up indications of which way he leans.

Musical Borrowing

There is a vast scholarly literature on musical borrowing—indeed the discipline of musicology takes the study of borrowing, in its largest sense, as one of its main organizing themes. Beyond a personal tour provided by Professor Anthony Kelley of Duke University, I found a number of books particularly useful. Burkholder's *History* (J. Peter Burkholder, Donald J. Grout, and Claude V. Palisca, *A History of Western Music*, 7th ed. (New York: W. W. Norton, 2006)) is full of examples of borrowing and influence—whether of style, notation, musical conventions, or melody itself. But it is Burkholder's book on Charles Ives—that fertile early-twentieth-century borrower—that was most influential: J. Peter Burkholder, *All Made of Tunes: Charles Ives and the Uses of Musical Borrowing* (New Haven, Conn.: Yale University Press, 1995). Ives's own thoughts on his mashup of prior American musical forms can be found in Charles Ives, *Memos*, ed. John Kirkpatrick (New York: W. W. Norton, 1991), 10–25. David Metzer's *Quotation and Cultural Meaning in Twentieth-Century Music* (Cambridge: Cambridge University Press, 2003), throws light on the way that quotations or borrowings came to have a particular cultural meaning in different musical traditions. Honey Meconi's collection *Early Musical Borrowing*, ed. Honey Meconi (New York: Routledge, 2004), discusses—among many other things—the issue of borrowing between the secular and religious musical traditions, something that helped me work through that issue in this chapter. Finally, "Musical Borrowing: An Annotated Bibliography" (http://www.chmtl.indiana.edu/borrowing/) provides a searchable database of articles about musical borrowing.

Music and Copyright Law

I was particularly influenced by two books and two articles. The books are Kembrew McLeod, *Owning Culture: Authorship, Ownership and Intellectual Property Law* (New York: Peter Lang, 2001), and Siva Vaidhyanathan, *Copyrights and Copywrongs: The Rise of Intellectual Property and How It Threatens Creativity* (New York: New York University Press, 2001). McLeod and Vaidhyanathan are the authors who sounded the alarm about the cultural and aesthetic effects of the heavy-handed legal regulation of musical borrowing. Together with the work of Larry Lessig (particularly his writing on the "permissions culture") Lawrence Lessig, *The Future of Ideas: The Fate of the Commons in a Connected World* (New York: Random House, 2001), their scholarship has defined the field.

The two articles that influenced me the most focus more specifically on the details of the evolution of music on the one hand and music copyright on the other. Both of them are by Michael Carroll: "The Struggle for Music Copyright," *Florida Law Review* 57 (2005): 907–961, and "Whose Music Is It Anyway?: How We Came to View Musical Expression as a Form of Property," *University of Cincinnati Law Review* 72 (2004): 1405–1496. But these two pieces by no means exhaust the literature. Olufunmilayo Arewa has written memorably on copyright and musical borrowing in "Copyright on Catfish Row: Musical Borrowing, *Porgy & Bess* and Unfair Use," *Rutgers Law Journal* 37 (2006): 277–353, and "From J. C. Bach to Hip Hop: Musical Borrowing, Copyright and Cultural Context,"

North Carolina Law Review 84 (2006): 547–645. I also recommend K. J. Greene, "Copyright, Culture & Black Music: A Legacy of Unequal Protection," *Hastings Communications & Entertainment Law Journal* 21 (1999): 339–392. There is much, much more. Finally, Joanna Demers's recent book *Steal This Music: How Intellectual Property Law Affects Musical Creativity* (Athens: University of Georgia Press, 2006), provides a more comprehensive coverage than I can hope to in a single chapter.

Beyond the scholarly literature, two websites allow you to experiment with these issues online. The History of Sampling created by Jesse Kriss, http://jessekriss.com/projects/samplinghistory/, allows you to explore visually exactly which hip-hop samplers borrowed from which older songs and to trace the process backwards or forwards. Extremely cool. The Copyright Infringement Project, sponsored by the UCLA Intellectual Property Project and Columbia Law School, http://ccnmtl.columbia.edu/projects/law/library/caselist.html, is an extremely useful educational site that gives examples of cases alleging musical copyright infringement, including the relevant sound files. The older version of this project confusingly referred to these cases as "plagiarism" cases—something that judges themselves also frequently do. Plagiarism is the moral, academic, or professional sin of taking ideas, facts or expression and passing them off as your own. If I take the central arguments from your book and completely reword them, or if I present a series of facts you uncovered as an historian and include them in my own book without attribution, you may accuse me of plagiarism, though not of copyright infringement. If I take the words of Shakespeare or Dickens and pass them off as my own, I am committing plagiarism but certainly not copyright infringement, for even under today's rules those works have long since entered the public domain. If I credit T. S. Eliot but then proceed to reprint the entire of "The Love Song of J. Alfred Prufrock" without the permission of the copyright holders, I am committing copyright infringement, but certainly not plagiarism. At best, plagiarism and copyright infringement overlap to some extent, but each regulates large areas about which the other is indifferent. We sap the strength of both norm systems by confusing them. The new incarnation of the project, at UCLA, has removed the word "plagiarism" from its title.

The People and the Music

A brief biography of Will Lamartine Thompson can be found in C. B. Galbreath, "Song Writers of Ohio (Will Lamartine Thompson)," *Ohio Archaeological and Historical Quarterly* 14 (January, 1905): 291–312. Since the copyright has expired you can read it in full, and see the picture of Thompson, at http://books.google.com/books?id=3N-WqdvA6T4C&printsec=titlepage#PRA1-PA291,M1.

The best book on Clara Ward is Willa Ward-Royster, Toni Rose, and Horace Clarance Boyer, *How I Got Over: Clara Ward and the World Famous Ward Singers* (Philadelphia, Penn.: Temple University Press, 1997).

The best biography of Ray Charles is Michael Lydon, *Ray Charles: Man and Music* (New York: Routledge, 2004). Charles's autobiography is also a fascinating read. Ray Charles and David Ritz, *Brother Ray: Ray Charles' Own Story* (Cambridge, Mass.: Da Capo Press, 1992). Charles's website, which contains useful biographical and discographical information, is at www.raycharles.com. There is much more, of course, but these resources provide a good starting place.

There are several hagiographic biographies of Mr. West, but none worth reading. Those who have not already been inundated with information through the popular press could do worse than to start with his rather breathless Wikipedia entry http://en.wikipedia.org/wiki/Kanye_West.

The main source of information on The Legendary K.O.—a name they now use intermittently—is their website is www.k-otix.com. (I am grateful to Mr. Nickerson and Mr. Randle for confirming additional portions of the story by e-mail.) The song "George Bush Doesn't Like Black People" is no longer available on their website, however an audio version of it is currently available at http://www.ourmedia.org/node/53964. The Black Lantern's video can be found at http://www.theblacklantern.com/george.html. Franklin Lopez's video can currently be found at http://www.youtube.com/watch?v=UGRcEXtLpTo. Whether any of those sites will be available in a year's time is hard to tell. Those who plan to listen or view are reminded that the lyrics are 'explicit.'

The songs by Clara Ward, Ray Charles, and Kanye West are widely available through a variety of commercial outlets, as are several commercial versions of "Jesus is All the World to Me" by Mr. Thompson.

I would recommend The Clara Ward Singers, *Meetin' Tonight* (Vanguard Records, 1994), compact disc. It includes a version of "Meetin' Tonight: This Little Light of Mine" in which the human limits on the ability to sustain a note are broken repeatedly. Any Ray Charles compilation will feature some of the songs discussed here. The most economical is probably Ray Charles, *I've Got a Woman & Other Hits* by Ray Charles (Rhino Flashback Records, 1997), compact disc. It includes "I Got a Woman" and "This Little Girl of Mine." Kanye West, *Late Registration* (Roc-a-Fella Records, 2005), compact disc, contains the full version of "Gold Digger."

Finally, I would love to be able to play you the full version of the Bailey Gospel Singers "I Got a Savior" (B-Side: "Jesus is the Searchlight") (Columbia Records, 1951), 78 rpm phonograph record. Unfortunately, given the legal uncertainties I am forbidden from doing so, and I know of no licit way—for free or for pay—that you can listen to it, short of traveling to the Rodgers and Hammerstein Archives of Recorded Sound at the New York Public Library for the Performing Arts yourself and asking to hear the original 78. Perhaps that simple fact is the most elegant encapsulation of my argument here.

Notes to Chapter 6

1. Lisa de Moraes, "Kanye West's Torrent of Criticism, Live on NBC," *Washington Post* (September 3, 2005), C1, available at http://www.washingtonpost.com/wp-dyn/content/article/2005/09/03/AR2005090300165.html.
2. John Leland, "Art Born of Outrage in the Internet Age," *New York Times* (September 25, 2005), D3.
3. Ray Charles and David Ritz, *Brother Ray: Ray Charles' Own Story* (Cambridge, Mass.: Da Capo Press, 1978), 86.
4. Robert W. Stephens, "Soul: A Historical Reconstruction of Continuity and Change in Black Popular Music," *The Black Perspective in Music* 12, no. 1 (Spring 1984): 32.
5. *Forever Ray,* available at http://www.raycharles.com/the_man_biography.html.
6. Michael Lydon, *Ray Charles* (New York: Routledge, 2004), 419: "Arnold Shaw, in *The*

Rockin' 50's says that 'I Got a Woman' is based on Jesus is All the World to Me. Because Renald Richard left Ray's band before the song was recorded, he was not at first properly credited: some record labels list [Ray Charles] alone as the songwriter. Richard, however, straightened that out with Atlantic, and he has for many years earned a substantial income from his royalties."

7. See Stephens, "Soul," 32. The standard biographical literature also repeats the same story:

> In 1954 an historic recording session with Atlantic records fused gospel with rhythm-and-blues and established Charles' "sweet new style" in American music. One number recorded at that session was destined to become his first great success. Secularizing the gospel hymn "My Jesus Is All the World to Me," Charles employed the 8- and 16-measure forms of gospel music, in conjunction with the 12-measure form of standard blues. Charles contended that his invention of soul music resulted from the heightening of the intensity of the emotion expressed by jazz through the charging of feeling in the unbridled way of gospel.

"Ray Charles," *Encyclopedia of World Biography*, 2nd ed., vol. 3 (Detroit, Mich.: Gale Research, 1998), 469. Popular accounts offer the same story:

> This young, blind, black, gravelly-voiced singer brought together the most engaging aspects of black music into one form and began the process of synthesis that led to soul and, ultimately, funk a decade later. He would turn around gospel standards like "My Jesus Is All the World to Me," recreating it as "I Got a Woman[.]"

Ricky Vincent, *Funk: The Music, The People, and the Rhythm of the One* (New York: St. Martin's Griffin, 1996), 121. See also Joel Hirschhorn, *The Complete Idiot's Guide to Songwriting* (New York: Alpha Books, 2004), 108: "*I Got a Woman* was Ray's rewrite of 'My Jesus Is All the World to Me.'"

Charles himself was more equivocal about the origins of the song:

> So I was lucky. Lucky to have my own band at this point in my career. Lucky to be able to construct my musical building to my exact specifications. And lucky in another way: While I was stomping around New Orleans, I had met a trumpeter named Renolds [sic] Richard who by thus time was in my band. One day he brought me some words to a song. I dressed them up a little and put them to music. The tune was called "I Got a Woman," and it was another of those spirituals which I refashioned in my own way. I Got a Woman was my first real smash, much bigger than ["]Baby Let Me Hold Your Hand[.]" This spiritual-and-blues combination of mine was starting to hit.

Charles and Ritz, *Brother Ray*, 150.

8. See Lydon, *Ray Charles*, 419.
9. James Boyle, *Shamans, Software, and Spleens: Law and the Construction of the Information Society* (Cambridge, Mass.: Harvard University Press, 1996).
10. James Henke, Holly George-Warren, Anthony Decurtis, and Jim Miller, *The Rolling Stone Illustrated History of Rock and Roll: The Definitive History of the Most Important Artists and Their Music* (New York: Random House, 1992), 130.

11. Great American Country, "Ray Charles Biography," available at http://www.gactv .com/gac/ar_artists_a-z/article/0,,GAC_26071_4888297,00.html.

12. "His 1955 smash 'I've Got a Woman,' for example, was adapted from a gospel number he'd liked called 'I've Got a Savior.' " Chip Deffaa, *Blue Rhythms: Six Lives in Rhythm and Blues* (Urbana: University of Illinois Press, 1996), 161.

13. Columbia Catalog Number CO45097, available at http://settlet.fateback.com/ COL30000.htm.

14. J. C. Marion, "Ray Charles: The Atlantic Years," JammUpp 2 no. 32 (2004): 32, http:// home.earthlink.net/~vitiger/jammuppvol2.html.

15. "If one can pinpoint a moment when gospel and blues began to merge into a secular version of gospel song, it was in 1954 when Ray Charles recorded 'My Jesus Is All the World to Me,' changing its text to 'I Got A Woman.' The following year, he changed Clara Ward's 'This Little Light of Mine' to 'This Little Girl of Mine.' " Stephens, "Soul," 32.

16. Robert Lashley, "Why Ray Charles Matters," Blogcritics Magazine, December 17, 2005, http://blogcritics.org/archives/2005/12/17/032826.php:

> But it was the staggering, nearly byzantine ambition that encompassed Charles' musical mind which is the foundation for his art. You can hear it in his first imprint on the pop music world, 1955's I Got A Woman. The shuffling big beat borrows from Louis Jordan's big band fusion, the backbeat is 2/4 gospel. The arrangement is lucid, not quite jazz, not quite blues, definitely not rock and roll but something sophisticated altogether. The emotions are feral, but not quite the primitiveness of rock and roll. It is the sound of life, a place where there is an ever flowing river of cool. It, you might ask? Rhythm and Blues, Ray Charles' invention.
>
> A volcano bubbling under the surface, Ray spent the mid 50's crafting timeless songs as if there were cars on an assembly[.] Start with the blasphemous fusion of Hallelujah I [L]ove Her So and This Little Girl of Mine, where Ray changes the words from loving god to loving a woman, yet, in the intensity of his performance, raises the question if he's still loving the same thing.

The anonymous encyclopedists at Wikipedia agree:

> Many of the most prominent soul artists, such as Aretha Franklin, Marvin Gaye, Wilson Pickett and Al Green, had roots in the church and gospel music and brought with them much of the vocal styles of artists such as Clara Ward and Julius Cheeks. Secular songwriters often appropriated gospel songs, such as the Pilgrim Travelers' song "I've Got A New Home," which Ray Charles turned into "Lonely Avenue," or "Stand By Me," which Ben E. King and Lieber and Stoller adapted from a well-known gospel song, or Marvin Gaye's "Can I Get A Witness," which reworks traditional gospel catchphrases. In other cases secular musicians did the opposite, attaching phrases and titles from the gospel tradition to secular songs to create soul hits such as "Come See About Me" for the Supremes and "99½ Won't Do" for Wilson Pickett.

"Urban Contemporary Gospel," *Wikipedia*, http://en.wikipedia.org/wiki/urban_ contemporary_gospel.

17. Northrop Frye, *Anatomy of Criticism: Four Essays* (Princeton, N.J.: Princeton University Press, 1957), 96–97.

18. John Leland, "Art Born of Outrage in the Internet Age," *New York Times* (September 25, 2005), D3.

19. *Grand Upright Music, Ltd. v. Warner Bros. Records, Inc.*, 780 F. Supp. 182 (S.D.N.Y. 1991).

20. Ibid., 183.

21. Kembrew McLeod, *Owning Culture: Authorship, Ownership and Intellectual Property Law* (New York: Peter Lang, 2001), and Siva Vaidhyanathan, *Copyrights and Copywrongs: The Rise of Intellectual Property and How It Threatens Creativity* (New York: New York University Press, 2001).

22. *Bridgeport Music, Inc. v. Dimension Films*, 410 F.3d 792, 804n16 (6th Cir. 2005).

23. Walter Benjamin, "The Work of Art in the Age of Mechanical Reproduction," in *Illuminations: Essays and Reflections*, ed. Hannah Arendt, trans. Harry Zohn (New York: Harcourt, Brace & World, 1968), 217–42.

24. *Campbell v. Acuff-Rose Music, Inc.*, 510 U.S. 569, 583 (1994).

CHAPTER 7:
THE ENCLOSURE OF SCIENCE AND TECHNOLOGY

Further Reading

As the introduction to this chapter suggests, the intersection of intellectual property law and science and technology has been attracting considerable attention from scholars recently, some of it dismayed. The difficulty—and this is why I chose the case-study method for this chapter—is that there are multiple sets of concerns and they resist easy summary.

The first set of concerns is that the granting of intellectual property rights far "upstream"—that is very close to basic science—is impeding the process of science and technology. In addition, scholars have argued that the sheer volume of intellectual property claims will produce an anti-commons effect or patent thicket. Michael A. Heller and Rebecca S. Eisenberg, "Can Patents Deter Innovation? The Anticommons in Biomedical Research," *Science* 280 (1998): 698–701. The argument here is that the closer one is to basic research the stronger the case is for leaving the information untouched by property rights—allowing all to draw on it and develop "downstream" innovations, which can then be covered by intellectual property rights. In practice, two concerns are often alluded to: the fact that much of the basic research is state funded and conducted in nonprofit universities and the belief that the transaction costs of licensing will inhibit research or concentrate it in a few hands. Research on genes indicating a propensity to breast cancer is a frequently cited example of the latter problem. Fabienne Orsi and Benjamin Coriat, "Are 'Strong Patents' Beneficial to Innovative Activities? Lessons from the Genetic Testing for Breast Cancer Controversies," *Industrial and Corporate Change* 14 (2005): 1205–1221. But here, too, anecdote outweighs evidence. Timothy Caulfield, Robert M. Cook-Deegan, F. Scott Kieff, and John P. Walsh, "Evidence and Anecdotes: An Analysis of Human Gene Patenting Controversies," *Nature Biotechnology* 24 (2006): 1091–1094. On the other side of this debate is the argument that having intellectual property rights, even on state-funded university research, will facilitate commercialization—allowing the commercial investor to know that it will acquire sufficient rights to exclude others from the innovation. This is the premise behind "Bayh-Dole," the act (P.L. 96-517, Patent and Trademark Act Amendments of 1980; codified in 35 U.S.C. § 200–212 and implemented by 37 C.F.R. 401) that sets up the framework for technology transfer from state funded university research.

To date, the evidence for the anti-commons effect inside academia has been equivocal, at best. Walsh, Cohen, and Arora found no such effect—but one main reason for the absence of problems appeared to be that scientists were simply flouting the law (or were ignorant of it). John P. Walsh, Ashish Arora, and Wesley M. Cohen, "Effects of Research Tool Patents and Licensing on Biomedical Innovation," in *Patents in the Knowledge-Based Economy*, ed. Wesley M. Cohen and Stephen A. Merrill (Washington D.C.: National Academies Press, 2003), 285–340. I would question whether a research system based on massive law-breaking is sustainable, particularly after the U.S. Court of Appeals for the Federal Circuit clarified for us that there effectively is no academic research exemption in U.S. patent law. *Madey v. Duke University*, 307 F.3d 1351 (Fed. Cir. 2002). The National Research Council's committee on the subject found few problems now but possible cause for concern in the future. Committee on Intellectual Property Rights in Genomic and Protein Research and Innovation, National Research Council, *Reaping the Benefits of Genomic and Proteomic Research: Intellectual Property Rights, Innovation, and Public Health* (Washington D.C.: National Academy Press, 2005). A study by the American Academy for the Advancement of Science also reported few problems, though a closer reading revealed that licensing produced delays in research—some of them considerable—but did not cause it to be abandoned. The effects were greatest on industry scientists. American Association for the Advancement of Science, Directorate for Science and Policy Programs, *International Intellectual Property Experiences: A Report of Four Countries* (Washington, D.C.: AAAS, 2007), available at http://sippi.aaas .org/Pubs/SIPPI_Four_Country_Report.pdf. Fiona Murray and Scott Stern, "Do Formal Intellectual Property Rights Hinder the Free Flow of Scientific Knowledge? An Empirical Test of the Anti-Commons Hypothesis," *Journal of Economic Behavior & Organization* 63 (2007): 648–687, found a definite but modest anti-commons effect, restricting further research and publication on patented materials. Similar concerns have been raised about access to scientific data. J. H. Reichman and Paul Uhlir, "A Contractually Reconstructed Research Commons for Scientific Data in a Highly Protectionist Intellectual Property Environment," *Law and Contemporary Problems* 66 (2003): 315–462.

What about the opposite question? Are we getting benefits from the process of increasing the use of intellectual property rights in basic university research? The best study of the effects of the current university technology transfer process found little definitive evidence of net benefits and some cause for concern that the traditional role of universities in freely supplying knowledge is being undermined. David Mowery, Richard Nelson, Bhaven Sampat, and Arvids Ziedonis, *Ivory Tower and Industrial Innovation: University-Industry Technology Transfer Before and After the Bayh-Dole Act* (Palo Alto, Calif.: Stanford Business Press, 2004).

Beyond the questions about the effects of upstream intellectual property rights on basic research lay the much harder questions about the effects of intellectual property rights on the development of technologies. Here there is much evidence that decisions about patent scope are vital and, as Robert Merges and Richard Nelson reveal, that poor decisions can hamper or cripple the development of disruptive technologies. Robert Merges and Richard

R. Nelson, "On the Complex Economics of Patent Scope," *Columbia Law Review* 90 (1990): 839–916; Suzanne Scotchmer, "Standing on the Shoulders of Giants: Cumulative Research and the Patent Law," *Journal of Economic Perspectives* 5 (1991): 29–41. The fear, highlighted in this chapter, is that poor decisions about patent scope and subject matter can inhibit technological change. On the subject of that fear, there is much more evidence. James Bessen and Michael J. Meurer, *Patent Failure: How Judges, Bureaucrats, and Lawyers Put Innovators at Risk* (Princeton: N.J.: Princeton University Press, 2008); and Adam Jaffe and Josh Lerner, *Innovation and Its Discontents: How Our Broken Patent System is Endangering Innovation and Progress, and What To Do About It* (Princeton, N.J.: Princeton University Press, 2004).

Notes to Chapter 7

1. See, e.g., Pamela Samuelson, Randall Davis, Mitchell D. Kapor, and J. H. Reichman, "A Manifesto Concerning the Legal Protection of Computer Programs," *Columbia Law Review* 94 (1994): 2308–2431; Michael A. Heller and Rebecca S. Eisenberg, "Can Patents Deter Innovation? The Anticommons in Biomedical Research," *Science* 280 (1998): 698–701.

2. Wes Cohen's empirical studies, for example, suggest that some of the potential dangers from overbroad gene patents have been offset by widespread lawbreaking among academic research scientists, who simply ignore patents that get in their way, and by more flexible licensing practices than the anticommons theorists had predicted. John P. Walsh, Ashish Arora, and Wesley Cohen, "Effects of Research Tool Patents and Licensing on Biomedical Innovation," in *Patents in the Knowledge-Based Economy*, ed. W. Cohen and S. A. Merrill (National Research Council, 2003), 285–340.

3. Arti Rai and James Boyle, "Synthetic Biology: Caught between Property Rights, the Public Domain, and the Commons," *PLoS Biology* 5 (2007): 389–393, available at http://biology.plosjournals.org/perlserv/?request=get-document&doi=10.1371/journal.pbio.0050058&ct=1.

4. William Gates III, *An Open Letter to Hobbyists*, February 3, 1976, quoted in Wallace Wang, *Steal This Computer Book 4.0: What They Won't Tell You About the Internet* (San Francisco: No Starch Press, 2006), 73.

5. Paul Goldstein, "Copyright," *Journal of the Copyright Society of the U.S.A.* 38 (1991): 109–110.

6. *State St. Bank & Trust Co. v. Signature Fin. Group, Inc.,* 149 F.3d 1368, 1373 (Fed. Cir. 1998).

7. *KSR Int'l Co. v. Teleflex Inc.,* 550 U.S. ___ (2007), 127 S. Ct. 1727 (2007).

8. *Diamond v. Chakrabarty,* 447 U.S. 303 (1980).

9. http://parts.mit.edu/registry/index.php/Help:About_the_Registry.

10. "Gene Machine: Cells Engineered to Prevent Sepsis Win Synthetic Biology Competition," *Science Daily* (November 15, 2006), available at http://www.sciencedaily.com/releases/2006/11/061114193826.htm.

11. http://web.mit.edu/newsoffice/2006/igem.html.

12. Keller Rinaudo et al., "A universal RNAi-based logic evaluator that operates in mammalian cells," *Nature Biotechnology* 25 (2007): 795–801.

13. Sapna Kumar and Arti Rai, "Synthetic Biology: The Intellectual Property Puzzle," *Texas Law Review* 85 (2007): 1745–1768.

CHAPTER 8: A CREATIVE COMMONS

Further Reading

Distributed Creativity

The most remarkable and important book on "distributed creativity" and the sharing economy is Yochai Benkler, *The Wealth of Networks: How Social Production Transforms Markets and Freedom* (New Haven, Conn.: Yale University Press, 2006). Benkler sets the idea of "peer production" alongside other mechanisms of market and political governance and offers a series of powerful normative arguments about why we should prefer that future. Comprehensive though this book may seem, it is incomplete unless it is read in conjunction with one of Benkler's essays: Yochai Benkler, "Coase's Penguin, or, Linux and the Nature of the Firm," *Yale Law Journal* 112 (2002): 369–446. In that essay, Benkler puts forward the vital argument—described in this chapter—about what collaborative production does to Coase's theory of the firm.

Benkler's work is hardly the only resource however. Other fine works covering some of the same themes include: Cass R. Sunstein, *Infotopia: How Many Minds Produce Knowledge* (New York: Oxford University Press, 2006), and Rishab Aiyer Ghosh, ed., *CODE: Collaborative Ownership and the Digital Economy* (Cambridge, Mass.: MIT Press, 2005), which includes an essay by me presenting an earlier version of the "second enclosure movement" argument. Clay Shirky's recent book, *Here Comes Everybody: The Power of Organizing without Organizations* (New York: Penguin Press, 2008), is an extremely readable and thoughtful addition to this body of work—it includes a more developed version of the speech I discuss. Eric Von Hippel's *Democratizing Innovation* (Cambridge, Mass.: MIT Press, 2005), is a fascinating account of the way that innovation happens in more places than we have traditionally imagined—particularly in end-user communities. In one sense, this reinforces a theme of this chapter: that the "peer production" and "distributed creativity" described here is not something new, merely something that is given dramatically more salience and reach by the Web. Dan Hunter and F. Gregory Lastowka's article, "Amateur-to-Amateur," *William & Mary Law Review* 46 (2004): 951–1030, describes some of the difficulties in adapting copyright law to fit "peer production." Finally, Jonathan Zittrain's *The Future of the Internet—And How to Stop It* (New Haven, Conn.: Yale University Press, 2008)—also relevant to Chapter 10— argues that if the democratically attractive aspects of the Internet are to be saved, it can only be done through enlisting the collective energy and insight of the Internet's users.

Free and Open Source Software

Free and open source software has been a subject of considerable interest to commentators. Glyn Moody's *Rebel Code: Linux and the Open Source Revolution* (Cambridge, Mass.: Perseus Pub., 2001), and Peter Wayner's *Free for All: How Linux and the Free Software Movement Undercut the High-Tech Titans* (New York: HarperBusiness, 2000), both offer readable and accessible histories of the phenomenon. Eric S. Raymond, *The Cathedral* and the Bazaar: Musings on Linux and Open Source by an Accidental Revolutionary, revised edition (Sebastapol, Calif.: O'Reilly, 2001), is a classic philosophy of the movement, written by a key participant—author of the phrase, famous among geeks, "given enough eyeballs, all bugs are shallow." Steve Weber, in The Success of Open Source (Cambridge, Mass.: Harvard University Press, 2004), offers a scholarly argument that the success of free and open source software is not an exception to economic principles but a vindication of them. I agree, though the emphasis that Benkler and I put forward is rather different. To get a sense of the argument that free software (open source software's normatively charged cousin) is desirable for its political and moral implications, not just because of its efficiency or commercial success, one should read the essays of Richard Stallman, the true father of free software and a fine polemical, but rigorous, essayist. Richard Stallman, Free Software, Free Society: Selected Essays of Richard M. Stallman, ed. Joshua Gay (Boston: GNU Press, 2002). Another strong collection of essays can be found in Joseph Feller, Brian Fitzgerald, Scott A. Hissam, and Karim R. Lakhani, eds., Perspectives on Free and Open Source Software (Cambridge, Mass.: MIT Press, 2005). If you only have time to read a single essay on the subject it should be Eben Moglen's "Anarchism Triumphant: Free Software and the Death of Copyright," First Monday 4 (1999), available at http://www .firstmonday.dk/issues/issue4_8/moglen/.

Creative Commons

Creative Commons has only just begun to attract its own chroniclers. Larry Lessig, its founder, provides a characteristically eloquent account in "The Creative Commons," Montana Law Review 65 (2004): 1–14. Michael W. Carroll, a founding board member, has produced a thought-provoking essay discussing the more general implications of organizations such as Creative Commons. Michael W. Carroll, "Creative Commons and the New Intermediaries," Michigan State Law Review, 2006, n.1 (Spring): 45–65. Minjeong Kim offers an empirical study of Creative Commons licenses in "The Creative Commons and Copyright Protection in the Digital Era: Uses of Creative Commons Licenses," Journal of Computer-Mediated Communication 13 (2007): Article 10, available at http://jcmc.indiana.edu/vol13/ issue1/kim.html. However, simply because of the rapidity of adoption of Creative Commons licenses, the work is already dramatically out of date. My colleague Jerome Reichman and Paul Uhlir of the National Academy of Sciences have written a magisterial study of the way in which tools similar to Creative Commons licenses could be used to lower transaction costs in the flow of scientific and technical data. J. H. Reichman and Paul Uhlir, "A Contractually Reconstructed Research Commons for Scientific Data in a Highly Protectionist Intellectual Property Environment," Law and Contemporary Problems 66 (2003): 315–462. Finally, the gifted author, David Bollier, is reportedly writing a book on Creative Commons entitled Viral Spiral: How the Commoners Built a Digital Republic of Their Own (New York: New Press, forthcoming 2009).

Niva Elkin-Koren offers a more critical view of Creative Commons in "Exploring Creative Commons: A Skeptical View of a Worthy Pursuit," in The Future of the Public Domain—Identifying the Commons in Information Law, ed. P. Bernt Hugenholtz and Lucie Guibault (The Hague: Kluwer Law International, 2006). Elkin-Koren's argument is that Creative Commons has an unintended negative effect by leading individuals to think of themselves through the reified categories of legal subjects and property owners—forcing into a legalized realm something that should simply be experienced as culture. Elkin-Koren is a perceptive and influential scholar; some of her early work on bulletin boards for example, was extremely important in explaining the stakes of regulating the Internet to a group of judges and policy makers. I also acknowledge the truth of her theoretical point; in many ways Creative Commons is offered as a second best solution. But I am unconvinced by the conclusion. Partly, this is because I think Elkin-Koren's account of the actual perceptions of license users is insufficiently grounded in actual evidence. Partly, it is because I think the legalization—undesirable though it may be in places—has already happened. Now we must deal with it. Partly, it is because I believe that many of the activities that the licenses enable—a global commons of free educational materials, for example—simply cannot be produced any other way in the political reality we face, and I have a preference for lighting candles rather than lamenting the darkness.

Notes to Chapter 8

1. Clay Shirky, "Supernova Talk: The Internet Runs on Love," available at http://www .shirky.com/herecomeseverybody/2008/02/supernova-talk-the-internet-runs-on-love.html; see also Clay Shirky, *Here Comes Everybody: The Power of Organizing Without Organizations* (New York: Penguin Press, 2008).

2. See Glyn Moody, *Rebel Code: Linux and the Open Source Revolution* (Cambridge, Mass.: Perseus Pub., 2001); Peter Wayner, *Free for All: How Linux and the Free Software Movement Undercut the High-Tech Titans* (New York: HarperBusiness, 2000); Eben Moglen, "Anarchism Triumphant: Free Software and the Death of Copyright," *First Monday* 4 (1999), http://firstmonday.org/issues/issue4_8/index.html.

3. Proprietary, or "binary only," software is generally released only after the source code has been compiled into machine-readable object code, a form that is impenetrable to the user. Even if you were a master programmer, and the provisions of the Copyright Act, the appropriate licenses, and the DMCA did not forbid you from doing so, you would be unable to modify commercial proprietary software to customize it for your needs, remove a bug, or add a feature. Open source programmers say, disdainfully, that it is like buying a car with the hood welded shut. See, e.g., Wayner, *Free for All*, 264.

4. See Brian Behlendorf, "Open Source as a Business Strategy," in *Open Sources: Voices from the Open Source Revolution*, ed. Chris DiBona et al. (Sebastapol, Calif.: O'Reilly, 1999), 149, 163.

5. One organization theorist to whom I mentioned the idea said, "Ugh, governance by food fight." Anyone who has ever been on an organizational listserv, a global production process run by people who are long on brains and short on social skills, knows how accurate that description is. *E pur si muove*.

6. See Bruce Brown, "Enterprise-Level Security Made Easy," *PC Magazine* (January 15, 2002), 28; Jim Rapoza, "Open-Source Fever Spreads," *PC Week* (December 13, 1999), 1.

7. "UK Government Report Gives Nod to Open Source," *Desktop Linux* (October 28, 2004), available at http://www.desktoplinux.com/news/NS5013620917.html.

8. "Cases of Official Recognition of Free and Open Source Software," available at http:// ec.europa.eu/information_society/activities/opensource/cases/index_en.htm.

9. E. Cobham Brewer, *The Dictionary of Phrase and Fable* (London: John Cassell, 1894), 1111–1112.

10. Richard Epstein, "Why Open Source Is Unsustainable," FT.com (October 21, 2004), available at http://www.ft.com/cms/s/2/78d9812a-2386-11d9-aee5-00000e2511c8 .html.

11. For a seminal statement, see Moglen, "Anarchism Triumphant," 45: " '[I]ncentives' is merely a metaphor, and as a metaphor to describe human creative activity it's pretty crummy. I have said this before, but the better metaphor arose on the day Michael Faraday first noticed what happened when he wrapped a coil of wire around a magnet and spun the magnet. Current flows in such a wire, but we don't ask what the incentive is for the electrons to leave home. We say that the current results from an emergent property of the system, which we call induction. The question we ask is 'what's the resistance of the wire?' So Moglen's Metaphorical Corollary to Faraday's Law says that if you wrap the Internet around every person on the planet and spin the planet, software flows in the network. It's an emergent property of connected human minds that they create things for one another's pleasure and to conquer their uneasy sense of being too alone. The only question to ask is, what's the resistance of the network? Moglen's Metaphorical Corollary to Ohm's Law states that the resistance of the network is directly proportional to the field strength of the 'intellectual property' system. So the right answer to the econodwarf is, resist the resistance."

12. Benkler's reasoning is characteristically elegant, even formal in its precision, while mine is clunkier. See Yochai Benkler, "Coase's Penguin, or, Linux and the Nature of the Firm," *Yale Law Journal* 112 (2002): 369–446.

13. Yochai Benkler, *The Wealth of Networks: How Social Production Transforms Markets and Freedom* (New Haven, Conn.: Yale University Press, 2006), 46–47.

14. See Karl Popper, *The Open Society and Its Enemies* (London: Routledge, 1945).

15. See http://www.ensembl.org.

16. See, e.g., NASA's "Clickworkers" experiment, which used public volunteers to analyze Mars landing data, available at http://clickworkers.arc.nasa.gov/top.

17. Benkler, "Coase's Penguin," 11.

18. Free Software Foundation, http://www.gnu.ai.mit.edu/philosophy/free-sw.html.

19. Exhibit A: the Internet—from the software and protocols on which it runs to the multiple volunteer sources of content and information.

20. See, e.g., the Database Investment and Intellectual Property Antipiracy Act of 1996, HR 3531, 104th Cong. (1996); The Consumer Access Bill, HR 1858, 106th Cong. § 101(1) (1999); see also Council Directive 96/9/EC of the European Parliament and the Council of 11 March 1996 on the Legal Protection of Databases, 1996 *Official Journal of the European Union*, L77 (27.03.1996): 20–28.

21. See generally Julie E. Cohen and Mark A. Lemley, "Patent Scope and Innovation in the Software Industry," *California Law Review* 89 (2001): 1–58; see also Pamela Samuelson et al., "A Manifesto Concerning the Legal Protection of Computer Programs," *Columbia Law Review* 94 (1994): 2308–2431.

22. Uniform Computer Information Transactions Act, available at http://www.law.upenn .edu/bll/archives/ulc/ucita/2002final.htm.

23. 17 U.S.C. § 1201 (2002).

24. This point has been ably made by Pamela Samuelson, Jessica Litman, Jerry Reichman, Larry Lessig, and Yochai Benkler, among others. See Pamela Samuelson, "Intellectual Property and the Digital Economy: Why the Anti-Circumvention Regulations Need to Be Revised," *Berkeley Technology Law Journal* 14 (1999): 519–566; Jessica Litman, *Digital Copyright: Protecting Intellectual Property on the Internet* (Amherst, N.Y.: Prometheus Books, 2001); J. H. Reichman and Paul F. Uhlir, "Database Protection at the Crossroads: Recent Developments and Their Impact on Science and Technology," *Berkeley Technology Law Journal* 14 (1999): 793–838; Lawrence Lessig, "Jail Time in the Digital Age," *New York Times* (July 30, 2001), A17; and Yochai Benkler, "Free as the Air to Common Use: First Amendment Constraints on Enclosure of the Public Domain," *New York University Law Review* 74 (1999): 354–446. Each has a slightly different focus and emphasis on the problem, but each has pointed out the impediments now being erected to distributed, nonproprietary solutions. See also James Boyle, "Cruel, Mean, or Lavish? Economic Analysis, Price Discrimination and Digital Intellectual Property," *Vanderbilt Law Review* 53 (2000): 2007–2039.

25. William W. Fisher III, "Property and Contract on the Internet," *Chicago-Kent Law Review* 73 (1998): 1217–1218.

26. See James Boyle, "Missing the Point on Microsoft," Salon.com (April 7, 2000), http://www.salon.com/tech/feature/2000/04/07/greenspan/index.html.

27. See "Salam Pax," *Wikipedia*, available at http://en.wikipedia.org/wiki/Salam_Pax.

CHAPTER 9: AN EVIDENCE-FREE ZONE

Further Reading

Database Rights

Mark J. Davison, *The Legal Protection of Databases* (Cambridge: Cambridge University Press, 2003), provides a fine introduction to the legal, and legalistic, issues surrounding the legal protection of databases. Precisely because of the need to focus on those issues, and that audience, the discussion is internal to the conceptual categories of the various legal systems he discusses, rather than focusing on the external questions I discuss here. Insiders will find the discussion indispensable. Outsiders may find it hermetic. For those readers, an article by Davison and Hugenholtz may be more accessible. It points out the ways in which the European Court of Justice has tried to rein in the database right. Mark J. Davison and P. Bernt Hugenholtz, "Football Fixtures, Horseraces and Spinoffs: The ECJ Domesticates the Database Right," *European Intellectual Property Review* 27, no. 3 (2005): 113–118.

When it comes to the general intellectual framework for thinking about database rights, Jerome Reichman and Pamela Samuelson provide the germinal point of view: J. H. Reichman and Pamela Samuelson, "Intellectual Property Rights in Data?" *Vanderbilt Law Review* 50 (1997): 51–166. Frequent readers of Reichman will be unsurprised that "take and pay" liability rules make an appearance as a possible solution. Yochai Benkler's article, "Constitutional Bounds of Database Protection: The Role of Judicial Review in the Creation and Definition of Private Rights in Information," *Berkeley Technology Law Journal* 15 (2000): 535–604, indicates the free expression and self-determination problems presented by intellectual property rights over facts. By contrast, J. H. Reichman and Paul F. Uhlir, "Database Protection at the Crossroads: Recent Developments and Their Impact on Science and Technology," *Berkeley Technology Law Journal* 14 (1999): 793–838, point out their negative effects on science and technological development. Increasingly, science will depend on the recombination of multiple databases to solve problems. At first, this will be done for huge and important projects. But increasingly, it will be done to solve smaller problems—scientists will seek to mix and mash a variety of data sources into an interoperable whole in order to solve the scientific problem *du jour*. Unfortunately, there are many obstacles to this promising tendency to harness digital technology to scientific research. Some of them are technical, some social, some semantic, some legal. One of the legal problems is posed by the expansion of database rights: the tendency to have intellectual property rights penetrate down to the most basic, unoriginal, or atomic level of data—a move that, as I point out in this chapter, is empirically shown to be counterproductive. Stephen M. Maurer, P. Bernt Hugenholtz, and Harlan J. Onsrud, "Europe's Database Experiment," *Science* 294 (2001): 789–780. Further information on the various barriers to data aggregation can be gleaned from the website of Science Commons (http://www.sciencecommons.org), an organization with which I am associated.

Evidence-based Policy

The move toward evidence-based policy has garnered considerable support in academia, but, as yet, only a little traction among policy makers. Readers interested in exploring the issue further can find a series of my *Financial Times* articles on the subject at http://www.ft.com/techforum. James Bessen and Michael J. Meurer, *Patent Failure: How Judges, Bureaucrats, and Lawyers Put Innovators at Risk* (Princeton, N.J.: Princeton University Press, 2008), is a sterling example of the way in which we could and should be looking at policy proposals. That book's list of references provides a nice overview of recent work in the field. As the title indicates, Bessen and Meurer do not grade our current system highly. Adam Jaffe and Josh Lerner, *Innovation and Its Discontents: How Our Broken Patent System is Endangering Innovation and Progress, and What To Do About It* (Princeton, N.J.: Princeton University Press, 2004), offers an earlier, and similar, assessment backed by data rather than faith. For us to have evidence-based policy, we need actual evidence. Here the work of empiricists such as my colleague Wes Cohen has proven vital. Much of this work is comparative in nature—relying on the kind of "natural experiment" I describe in this chapter. A fine example is provided by Wesley M. Cohen, Akira Goto, Akiya Nagata, Richard R. Nelson, and John P. Walsh, "R&D Spillovers, Patents and the Incentives to Innovate in Japan and the United States," *Research Policy* 31 (2002): 1349–67.

All of this may seem obvious. Where else would intellectual property academics turn in order to assess the effect of various policy alternatives than to empirical and comparative data? Yet as the chapter points out, that simple conclusion has yet to become a standard assumption in the making of policy. The Gowers Review mentioned in the chapter is a nice example of how things might be otherwise. *Gowers Review of Intellectual Property* (London: HMSO, 2006), available at http://www.hm-treasury.gov.uk/media/6/E/pbr06_gowers_report_755.pdf. Of course, a turn to evidence is only the beginning. It hardly means that the evidence will be clear, the points of view harmonious, or the normative assessments shared. But at least the conversation is beginning from a rooting in facts rather than faith.

Publicly Generated Information

Access to public, or state generated, data is not simply a matter of economic efficiency. Wouter Hins and Dirk Voorhoof, "Access to State-Held Information as a Fundamental Right under the European Convention on Human Rights," *European Constitutional Law Review* 3 (2007): 114–126. But in efficiency terms, it does seem to present some clear benefits. Peter Weiss, "Borders in Cyberspace: Conflicting Government Information Policies and their Economic Impacts," in *Open Access and the Public Domain in Digital Data and Information for Science: Proceedings of an International Symposium* (Washington, D.C.: National Academies Press, 2004), 69–73. The issues of publicly generated information are particularly pressing in geospatial data—which can be vital for academic research and economic development. Bastiaan van Loenen and Harlan Onsrud, "Geographic Data for Academic Research: Assessing Access Policies," *Cartography and Geographic Information Science* 31 (2004): 3–17. It is an issue that is gaining attention in Europe: "Directive 2003/98/EC of the European Parliament and of the Council of 17 November 2003 on the Re-use of Public Sector Information," *Official Journal of the European Union* 46 (31.12.2003) 90–96 (L 345). However, there is a long way to go.

Sound Recording Rights

A good place to start is the Gowers Review, cited above, and the report generated by the Centre for Intellectual Property and Information Law, University of Cambridge, *Review of the Economic Evidence Relating to an Extension of the Term of Copyright in Sound Recordings* (2006), available at http://www.hm-treasury.gov.uk/media/B/4/gowers_cipilreport.pdf. My own views are close to those put forward by this excellent article: Natali Helberger, Nicole Dufft, Stef van Gompel, and Bernt Hugenholtz, "Never Forever: Why Extending the Term of Protection for Sound Recordings is a Bad Idea," *European Intellectual Property Review* 30 (2008): 174–181.

Notes to Chapter 9

1. *Feist Publications, Inc. v. Rural Telephone Service Co.*, 499 U.S. 340 (1991).
2. Stephen M. Maurer, P. Bernt Hugenholtz, and Harlan J. Onsrud, "Europe's Database Experiment," *Science* 294 (2001): 789–790.
3. Stephen M. Maurer, "Across Two Worlds: US and European Models of Database Protection," paper commissioned by Industry Canada (2001).
4. *Matthew Bender & Co. v. West Publishing Co.*, 158 F.3d 674 (2nd Cir. 1998).
5. James Boyle, *Shamans, Software, and Spleens: Law and the Construction of the Information Society* (Cambridge, Mass.: Harvard University Press, 1996).
6. *First evaluation of Directive 96/9/EC on the legal protection of databases*, DG Internal Market and Services Working Paper (Brussels, Belgium: Commission of the European Communities, 2005), 5.
7. Ibid., 22.
8. In *Open Access and the Public Domain in Digital Data and Information for Science: Proceedings of an International Symposium* (Washington, D.C.: National Academies Press, 2004), 69–73, available at http://books.nap.edu/openbook.php?record_id=11030&page=69.

9. Directive 2003/98/EC of the European Parliament and of the Council of 17 November 2003 on the Re-use of Public Sector Information, *Official Journal of the European Union*, L 345 (31.12.2003): 90–96; *Public Sector Modernisation: Open Government*, Organization for Economic Co-operation and Development (2005), available at http://www .oecd.org/dataoecd/1/35/34455306.pdf; The Socioeconomic Effects of Public Sector Information on Digital Networks: Toward a Better Understanding of Different Access and Reuse Policies (February 2008 OECD conference), more information at http:// www.oecd.org/document/48/0,3343,en_2649_201185_40046832_1_1_1_1,00.html;   and the government sites of individual countries in the European Union such as Ireland (-http://www.psi.gov.ie/).

10. Andrew Gowers, *Gowers Review of Intellectual Property* (London: HMSO, 2006), available at http://www.hm-treasury.gov.uk/media/6/E/pbr06_gowers_report_755.pdf.

11. University of Cambridge Centre for Intellectual Property and Information Law, *Review of the Economic Evidence Relating to an Extension of Copyright in Sound Recordings* (2006), available at http://www.hm-treasury.gov.uk/media/B/4/gowers_ cipilreport.pdf.

12. Ibid., 21–22.

13. Ibid.

14. House of Commons Select Committee on Culture, Media and Sport, Fifth Report (2007), available at http://www.publications.parliament.uk/pa/cm200607/cmselect/ cmcumeds/ 509/50910.htm.

CHAPTER 10:
AN ENVIRONMENTALISM FOR INFORMATION

Further Reading

Those who are interested in the evolution of the analogy between environmentalism and the movement to recognize and safeguard the public domain can start with the editors' introductions to the Symposium *Cultural Environmentalism @ 10*, James Boyle and Lawrence Lessig, eds., *Law and Contemporary Problems* 70 (2007) 1–21, available at http://www.law .duke.edu/ce10.

The single best chronicle of the Access to Knowledge ("A2K") movement is Amy Kapczynski, "The Access to Knowledge Mobilization and the New Politics of Intellectual Property," *Yale Law Journal* 117 (2008): 804–885. Lawrence Lessig's work has been a common point of reference: Lawrence Lessig, *The Future of Ideas: The Fate of the Commons in a Connected World* (New York: Random House, 2001), and Lawrence Lessig, *Free Culture* (New York: Penguin, 2004). Many of the key political initiatives have come from James Love and the Consumer Project on Technology. A wealth of material can be found at http://www.cptech.org/a2k/ and at Knowledge Ecology International, http://www.keionline.org/index.php. The inaugural edition of the journal *Knowledge Ecology Studies* presents an informal discussion of the origins of the idea at http://www .kestudies.org/ojs/index.php/kes/article/view/29/53.

For the ways in which the A2K movement has involved both criticism of and attempts to reform international bodies such as the World Intellectual Property Organization

("WIPO") see James Boyle, "A Manifesto on WIPO and the Future of Intellectual Property," *Duke Law and Technology Review* 0009 (2004): 1–12, available at http://www.law.duke.edu/journals/dltr/articles/PDF/2004DLTR0009.pdf, and Christopher May, *The World Intellectual Property Organization: Resurgence and the Development Agenda* (London: Routledge, 2006).

The minimalist or antimonopolistic attitude toward intellectual property has a long history, as this book has tried to show. The specific concern with the public domain is of more recent origin. The foundational essay was published by my colleague David Lange, "Recognizing the Public Domain," *Law and Contemporary Problems* 44, no. 4 (1981): 147–178. I would also recommend *Collected Papers, Duke Conference on the Public Domain*, ed. James Boyle (Durham, N.C.: Center for the Study of the Public Domain, 2003), which contains scholarly articles on the history, constitutional status, scientific importance, musical significance, property theory, and economic effects of the public domain. The entire volume can be read online at http://www.law.duke.edu/journals/lcp/indexpd.htm.

Finally, Duke's Center for the Study of the Public Domain, which has generously supported the writing of this book has a wide variety of resources—ranging from scholarly texts to films and comic books—on the subjects of intellectual property, the public domain and idea of an environmentalism for information. Those resources can be found at http://www.law.duke.edu/cspd.

Notes to Chapter 10

1. Jonathan Zittrain, *The Future of the Internet—And How to Stop It* (New Haven, Conn.: Yale University Press, 2008).

2. Of course, these are not the only assumptions, arguments, and metaphors around. Powerful counterweights exist: the ideas of Jefferson and Macaulay, which I described here, but also others, more loosely related—the Scottish Enlightenment's stress on the political and moral benefits of competition, free commerce, and free labor; deep economic and political skepticism about monopolies; the strong traditions of open science; and even liberalism's abiding focus on free speech and access to information. If you hear the slogan "information wants to be free," you may agree or disagree with the personification. You may find the idea simplistic. But you do not find it incomprehensible, as you might if someone said "housing wants to be free" or "food wants to be free." We view access to information and culture as vital to successful versions of both capitalism and liberal democracy. We apply to blockages in information flow or disparities in access to information a skepticism that does not always apply to other social goods. Our attitudes toward informational resources are simply different from our attitudes toward other forms of power, wealth, or advantage. It is one of the reasons that the Jefferson Warning is so immediately attractive. It is this attitudinal difference that makes the political terrain on these issues so fascinating.

3. Mancur Olson, *The Logic of Collective Action: Public Goods and the Theory of Groups* (Cambridge, Mass.: Harvard University Press, 1965) and Mancur Olson, *The Rise and Decline of Nations: Economic Growth, Stagflation, and Social Rigidities* (New Haven, Conn.: Yale University Press, 1982).

4. "The source of the general divergences between the values of marginal social and marginal private net product that occur under simple competition is the fact that, in some occupations, a part of the product of a unit of resources consists of something, which, instead of coming in the first instance to the person who invests the unit, comes instead, in the first instance (i.e., prior to sale if sale takes place), as a positive or negative item, to other people." Arthur C. Pigou, "Divergences between Marginal Social Net Product and Marginal Private Net Product," in *The Economics of Welfare* (London: Macmillan, 1932), available at http://www.econlib.org/Library/NPDBooks/Pigou/pgEW1.html. Ironically, so far as I can find, Pigou does not use the word "externality."

5. William D. Ruckelshaus, "Environmental Protection: A Brief History of the Environmental Movement in America and the Implications Abroad," *Environmental Law* 15 (1985): 457.

6. As always, Jessica Litman provides the clearest and most down-to-earth example. Commenting on Rebecca Tushnet's engrossing paper on fan fiction (Rebecca Tushnet, "Payment in Credit: Copyright Law and Subcultural Creativity," *Law and Contemporary Problems* 70 (Spring 2007): 135–174), Litman describes copyright's "balance between uses copyright owners are entitled to control and other uses that they simply are not entitled to control." Jessica Litman, "Creative Reading," *Law and Contemporary Problems* 70 (Spring 2007), 175. That balance, she suggests, is not bug but feature. The spaces of freedom that exist in the analog world because widespread use is possible without copying are neither oversights, nor temporarily abandoned mines of monopoly rent just waiting for a better technological retrieval method. They are integral parts of the copyright system.

7. James Boyle, "A Politics of Intellectual Property: Environmentalism for the Net?" *Duke Law Journal* 47 (1997): 87–116.

8. Molly Shaffer Van Houweling, "Cultural Environmentalism and the Constructed Commons," *Law and Contemporary Problems* 70 (Spring 2007): 23–50.

9. See http://www.eff.org/IP/, http://www.openrightsgroup.org/, http://www.public knowledge.org/.

10. *Eldred v. Ashcroft*, 537 U.S. 186 (2003). Once again, Professor Lessig had the central role as counsel for petitioners.

11. See http://www.pubpat.org/.

12. See Access to Knowledge, http://www.cptech.org/a2k/. Some of Mr. Love's initiatives are discussed at http://www.cptech.org/jamie/.

13. Tim Hubbard and James Love, "A New Trade Framework for Global Healthcare R&D," *PLoS Biology* 2 (2004): e52.

14. WIPO Development Agenda, available at http://www.cptech.org/ip/wipo/da.html. The Geneva Declaration on the Future of the World Intellectual Property Organization, available at http://www.cptech.org/ip/wipo/futureofwipodeclaration.pdf. In the interest of full disclosure, I should note that I wrote one of the first manifestos that formed the basis for earlier drafts of the Declaration. James Boyle, "A Manifesto on WIPO and the Future of Intellectual Property," *Duke Law & Technology Review* 0009 (2004): 1–12, available at http://www.law.duke.edu/journals/dltr/articles/PDF/2004DLTR0009.pdf. The Adelphi Charter on Creativity, Innovation, and Intellectual

Property, available at http://www.adelphicharter.org/. The Charter was issued by the British Royal Society for the Encouragement of Arts, Manufactures and Commerce (RSA). For discussion of the Charter see James Boyle, "Protecting the Public Domain," Guardian.co.uk (October 14, 2005), available at http://education.guardian.co.uk/ higher/comment/story/0,9828,1591467,00.html; "Free Ideas," *The Economist* (October 15, 2005), 68. Again, in the interest of full disclosure, I should note that I advised the RSA on these issues and was on the steering committee of the group that produced the Charter.

15. An example is the MacArthur Foundation Program on Intellectual Property and the Public Domain: "The General Program . . . was begun in 2002 as a short-term project to support new models, policy analysis, and public education designed to bring about balance between public and private interests concerning intellectual property rights in a digital era." See http://www.macfound.org/site/c.lkLXJ8MQKrH/b.943331/k.DA6/ General_Grantmaking__Intellectual_Property.htm. The Ford Foundation has a similar initiative. Frédéric Sultan, "International Intellectual Property Initiative: Ford Foundation I-Jumelage Resources," available at http://www.vecam.org/ijumelage/spip .php?article609.

16. See http://www.creativecommons.org and http://www.fsf.org.

17. This process runs counter to the assumptions of theorists of collective action problems in a way remarkable enough to have attracted its own chroniclers. See Amy Kapczynski, "The Access to Knowledge Mobilization and the New Politics of Intellectual Property," *Yale Law Journal* 117 (2008): 804–885. Economists generally assume preferences are simply given, individuals just have them and they are "exogenous" to the legal system in the sense that they are unaffected by the allocation of legal rights. The emergence of the movements and institutions I am describing here paints a different picture. The "preferences" are socially constructed, created through a collective process of debate and decision which shifts the level of abstraction upwards; and, as Kapczynski perceptively notes, they are highly influenced by the legal categories and rights against which the groups involved initially defined themselves.

18. See "News for Nerds: Stuff That Matters," http://www.slashdot.org, and "A Directory of Wonderful Things," http://www.boingboing.net.

19. Pub. L. No. 105-304, 112 Stat. 2860 (1998) (codified as amended in scattered sections of 5, 17, 28, and 35 U.S.C.).

20. For the former see "Content Protection," http://xkcd.com/c129.html, and "Digital Rights Management," http://xkcd.com/c86.html. For the latter, see "Copyright," http://xkcd.com/c14.html.

21. R. David Kryder, Stanley P. Kowalski, and Anatole F. Krattiger, "The Intellectual and Technical Property Components of Pro-Vitamin A Rice (*Golden*Rice™): A Preliminary Freedom-to-Operate Review," *ISAAA Briefs* No. 20 (2000), available at http:// www.isaaa.org/Briefs/20/briefs.htm.

22. "The Supreme Court Docket: The Coming of Copyright Perpetuity," *New York Times* editorial (January 16, 2003), A28.

23. "Free Mickey Mouse," *Washington Post* editorial (January 21, 2003), A16.

INDEX

2 Live Crew, 151–152.

2600: The Hacker Quarterly, 92–93, 96–97

A&M Records v. Napster, 239 F.3d 1004 (9th Cir. 2001). See *Napster* case.

Abelson, Hal, ix, 181.

Access to Knowledge (A2K) movement, 243–244, 293–294, 296n17; Adelphi Charter, 244, 295n14; Geneva Declaration, 244, 295n14; WIPO Development Agenda, 244, 294, 295n14.

Acuff-Rose case (*Campbell v. Acuff-Rose Music, Inc.*, 510 U.S. 569 (1994)), 151–152, 283n23.

Adelphi Charter on Creativity, Innovation, and Intellectual Property. See Access to Knowledge movement, Adelphi Charter.

"Ain't That Good News" (*song*), 133.

Allen, Robert C., 45, 264, 266n8.

"Alone Again (Naturally)" (*song*, Sullivan)

and "Alone Again" (*song*, Biz Markie), 146. See also *Grand Upright* case.

Amazon.com, 58, 81, 227.

America Online, 233.

American Association for the Advancement of Science (AAAS), study on effects of intellectual property, 284.

American Geophysical Union v. Texaco, 27 F.3d 882 (2d Cir. 1994), 52, 269n38.

anticircumvention provisions of DMCA. See DMCA.

anti-dilution. See trademark, antidilution.

antimonopolistic attitudes toward intellectual property. See intellectual property.

Anton, Jim, viii.

Aoki, Keith, 45, 266n10, 277.

Apple Computer, controversy with RealNetworks, 110–114.

Arewa, Olufunmilayo, 278–279.